BATS
A NATURAL HISTORY

John E. Hill

BRITISH MUSEUM (NATURAL HISTORY)

AND

James D. Smith

CALIFORNIA STATE UNIVERSITY,
FULLERTON

Published in co-operation with the
British Museum (Natural History)

UNIVERSITY OF TEXAS PRESS
AUSTIN

To Glover Merrill Allen

We have great pleasure in dedicating this work to the memory of the late Glover Merrill Allen, whose book Bats, *published in 1939, first brought the story of these unique animals to the notice of the reading public, and today remains an indispensable source of information.*

International Standard Book Number 0-292-70752-5
Library of Congress Catalog Card Number 83-51654
Copyright © 1984 by John E. Hill and James D. Smith
All rights reserved

First Edition, 1984

Printed in England by Heffers Printers Ltd., Cambridge

Contents

Acknowledgements

Any book such as this must depend heavily on the work of many naturalists past and present and we gratefully acknowledge the debt that we owe to our predecessors and colleagues upon whose published studies we have drawn so freely in its preparation. Without their contributions the book would not have been possible. We have to acknowledge also the help given by those of our colleagues with whom various aspects of this book have been discussed especially M. J. O'Farrell and family, and Dr D. L. Harrison.

Our thanks are due to Ms Judy Astone for providing original Chinese antiques for illustration, and we have especially to acknowledge the contribution made by our artists, Ms Susan E. Smith in the United States and Ms Pat Butterworth in Great Britain, who have given extensively of their time and talent. We have also to thank the staff of the Publications Section of the British Museum (Natural History), particularly Mr Robert Cross and Mr Christopher Owen, who have piloted this book through the many vicissitudes leading to publication.

JOHN EDWARDS HILL
JAMES DALE SMITH
March, 1983

Bats constitute one of the largest and most widely distributed groups of mammals, with a total of some 950 living species. In these respects they are second only to the ubiquitous rodents, and apart from the cold regions north of the Arctic Circle, the Antarctic, and a few isolated islands, there is no part of the world where bats are not to be found. They are unique among mammals in their mastery of true flight–a fundamental evolutionary step that opened the way to an entirely new and largely unoccupied part of the environment at least 55 million years ago. The opportunities presented by this vacant niche–nocturnal life, flight, insects and tropical fruits and flowers–allowed the bats to undergo a marked degree of adaptive radiation, evolving into an astonishing diversity in a relatively short period of time.

Initially, the early zoologists were concerned chiefly with recognizing and describing this multitude of species as they were discovered by advancing exploration, a process reaching a peak in the latter half of the nineteenth century and in the early part of the present century. In the past fifty years, however, scientists have turned their attention increasingly to the biology and physiology of bats. Although much remains to be studied, it is probably true to say that the basic biology of bats is at least as well known and in some ways better understood than that of most other groups of mammals.

Our objective in this book has been to present the general reader or serious student with a review of the fundamental aspects of bat biology. We have tried to demonstrate how bats conform to the biological principles common to all mammals, or have adapted and modified these to suit their own requirements. To accomplish this we have included relevant anatomical and physiological information set in an environmental and behavioural background, with some indication of the taxonomic and systematic foundation of the classification of bats as a whole. The study of bats and their natural history has been and to some extent remains esoteric, and a large part of this basic information is scattered through a wide diversity of original sources to which the general reader has no ready access. Throughout this book we have attempted to draw together the many threads that this vast mass of research contains, and to provide within

a reasonable compass a comprehensive account of the natural history of these unique animals.

THE NAMES OF BATS

Vernacular names

Most peoples, even the most primitive, have names in their own languages for the many different plants and animals in their environment. In New Guinea, for example, local tribes often discriminate accurately between many different kinds of birds and mammals. Moreover, the majority of well known animals such as fish, lizard, frog, bird, rat or bat also have names in all of the major European languages. Usually these are modified by a descriptive word or words to define the animal concerned more accurately. Flying fish or Goldfish, Frilled lizard, Horned frog, Hummingbird, Black rat or fruit bat define more fully the animals to which they refer. Sometimes such multiple names may provide even more information, as for example Long-tailed Giant rat, or Spotted-winged fruit bat. These are known as vernacular or common names.

Although many animals, including bats, have English vernacular names, many others do not. Also, a vernacular name can be applied to more than one kind of animal and this can easily lead to confusion, while such names do not necessarily have the same meaning in different languages. In this book English vernacular names have been used whenever possible, but are followed (in parentheses) by the appropriate scientific name to avoid these difficulties. Where no commonly accepted vernacular name is available we have used the scientific name, and in a few cases for clarity and brevity scientific names have been employed rather than the vernacular.

Scientific names

The scientific names of plants and animals are always written in Latin, partly because this was the common language of early naturalists who began the process of formal description, and also because although now archaic, Latin is internationally accepted for this purpose to overcome the problems of translation.

Scientific names (usually printed in italic typescript) have two important elements, the first or generic name that indicates the relationship of the species concerned to other species, and a second or specific name that signifies the particular species in question. Sometimes a third or subspecific name may be used to indicate small variants within the species, as for example slightly differing populations of the same species on different islands. Latinized scientific names are frequently but not necessarily derived from roots in classical Greek and often suggest the nature of the organism to which they refer, or draw attention to some significant feature or habit. Sometimes a name indicates the geographical region whence the organism came, or may commemorate a person, possibly the naturalist who discovered it. Scientific names do not have to be constructed in this way, however, and can be quite arbitrary.

Among bats, scientific names often involve *Nycteris*, the Greek word for bat, perhaps an obvious choice. Not only is it used unornamented as the generic name for the Slit-faced or Hollow-faced bats of Africa but it has also been used as a root for numerous other generic names such as *Nanonycteris* or 'Dwarf bat', *Eonycteris* or 'Dawn bat' and *Hylonycteris*, a 'Wood bat' or 'Forest bat'. The allusion in a name may be oblique as in *Chironax*, from the Greek word meaning 'one who is master of his hands', a reference to bat flight. Scientific names can be very descriptive, *Saccopteryx bilineata* for instance referring to the wing sacs and to the two stripes on the back of the bat to which it applies. *Laephotis wintoni* is the Large-eared (literally 'sail-ear') bat named after the naturalist W. E. de Winton, *Laephotis angolensis* its relative described from Angola. Bats boast the shortest scientific name among mammals - *Ia io*, proposed by the mammalogist Oldfield Thomas reputedly for its brevity, in response to a challenge to produce the shortest possible name. *Io* was a young woman of classical times and Thomas apparently considered many women of that age to be essentially flighty, like bats.

Species, genera, families, suborders and orders

The species is the lowest major category in classification and the many different species of bats are recognized by such features as differences in body or skull size, in colour, in such structures as their noseleaves or ears, or by small differences in cranial or dental morphology. Such features are used by the taxonomist to determine to which species any given bat belongs and to indicate relationships to other species. Often the differences between species are very small and quite subtle, and careful study is required to distinguish them, particularly when closely related species occur together. Occasionally a clue is provided by some apparently quite unrelated circumstance, as for example by the small mites that infest the dental membranes of *Leptonycteris nivalis*, a species of American Long-nosed bat. These cause small pits to appear in the bony palate near the teeth, the like of which are not found even in the closely related species *Leptonycteris sanborni*.

Genera as a rule bring together species with common similarities but occasionally have only a single, prominently characterized species. They are customarily recognized by more far reaching external, cranial and dental characters, different workers placing a greater or lesser emphasis on different features. The wide range of variation found in bats has led to a large number of recognized genera, although sometimes these are based on relatively small differences. The family usually unites a number of related genera but again some bat families contain only one especially distinctive and isolated genus. Genera are sometimes divided into two or more subgenera, and families similarly into subfamilies. Family names always have the termination *idae* i.e. Phyllostomidae, while subfamily names have the suffix *inae* as their ending i.e. Glossophaginae. At this level, skeletal structure, with special emphasis on the skull and on the bony structures associated with the shoulder and wing, provides much of the basis of classification. Currently some 950 species of Recent bats are recognized, grouped into perhaps 190 genera, but these numbers vary slightly from one authority to another since the limits of the species and especially of the genus are subjective. Depending on the emphasis given to the features adopted for further classification, the modern genera are grouped variously in 17, 18 or 19 families, which themselves constitute the two major groups or suborders of bats, one the Megachiroptera or Old World fruit bats, including but one family, and the other the Microchiroptera, basically insect-eating bats, including all of the remaining families. Together, the two suborders form the order Chiroptera, itself a major division of the class Mammalia.

A resurgence of interest in the study of bats and in their relationships with each other at all levels of classification has led to the application of new and modern techniques, such as the study of bat chromosome patterns, comparison of the composition of the blood in different groups of bats, or detailed studies of bat parasites. This research is suggesting ways in which the traditional classification might be changed, especially at the familial and generic levels. A particularly good example concerns the true vampire bats of the New World, so much modified for an exclusive diet of blood obtained by biting other animals that they have long been considered to represent a family of their own, the Desmodontidae. Studies of their chromosomes, the properties of their blood, the morphology of their sperm, their echolocation system and parasites have indicated a close affinity with certain members of another New World family, the Phyllostomidae. As a result, most authorities now consider that the vampire bats should be more correctly classified as a subfamily of the Phyllostomidae, rather than as an independent family. The traditional classification is also being challenged by new ways of assessing taxonomic characters and indeed by widening their range to include a greater variety of the morphological features of the hard and soft anatomy. The relatively recent recognition of familial status as the Mormoopidae for the Naked-backed, Moustached and Ghost-faced bats of the New World is an example of this kind of study and similar research is widening our understanding of the relationships and classification of the nectar-feeding bats of the New World family Phyllostomidae. Such studies often employ computer techniques and the increasing use of these and of computer-based statistical analysis is broadening and extending our knowledge of geographical variation within the species and of interspecific differences in bats, as well as helping to illuminate and unravel their relationships at higher levels of classification.

Sources

In attempting this factual survey of many facets of the biology of bats we have relied upon many sources ranging from the abundant literature on this subject to discussions with colleagues and personal experience. Published information about many aspects of the biology of these fascinating animals has increased annually very rapidly over the past two or three decades and it is probably correct to say that more papers and books about bats have appeared in the past 25 years than in the century preceding this period. This increase is basically the result of a greater awareness of bats as research subjects, of the development of more effective techniques and equipment for studying them and of improved opportunities for field and laboratory work, together with a wider recognition of the need to understand and conserve the unique natural resource that bats represent. We have been fortunate, however, that as a principal reference for a number of chapters of this book we have been able to rely upon the excellent volumes *Biology of bats* edited by W. A. Wimsatt and published in 1970 and 1977 by Academic Press, New York. The numerous articles by specialist authors that these books bring together provide not only an unrivalled source of biological information but also a detailed and comprehensive bibliography of each topic.

Clearly, to detail every published study that we have consulted in the preparation of a book of this nature would greatly complicate and lengthen the text. Instead, we have provided, in a terminal bibliography, a list of the major works that are concerned with bats in the broadest sense. Faunal studies giving general accounts of bats of various parts of the world are also included. To these we have added a chapter by chapter bibliography that details the major reference or references that we have used, together with any later studies that have been relevant or seemed pertinent. We have tried to ensure that as major sources we have included one or more papers with an extensive bibliography that will provide the reader with a further overview of the topic concerned.

Chapter 2 Form and structure

Bats are mammals and, as such, possess all of the features characteristic of this vertebrate class. These features include most notably: possession of a body covering of hair (pelage or fur) as opposed to scales (reptiles) or feathers (birds); mammary glands for the production of milk which is used to suckle and nourish the newborn young prior to the development of its own ability to acquire food; a single bone (dentary or mandible) constituting the lower jaw as opposed to the complex of bones found in the lower jaws of other terrestrial vertebrates such as reptiles and birds; three ear bones or ossicles (named for their shape, malleus–hammer; incus–anvil; stapes–stirrup) in the middle ear region; the single replacement of at least a portion of the dentition (milk teeth); and the ability to maintain a constant body temperature (warm-blooded). In addition, bats belong to the large and progressive infraclass Eutheria (placental mammals that give birth to young after a substantial period *in utero* where they are maintained and nourished by means of a specialized embryo-maternal structure called the placenta). This general scheme of reproduction is in marked contrast to the relatively more primitive modes of egg-laying found in the monotremes (Duck-billed platypus and Spiny anteater) or that found among marsupials (Kangaroos

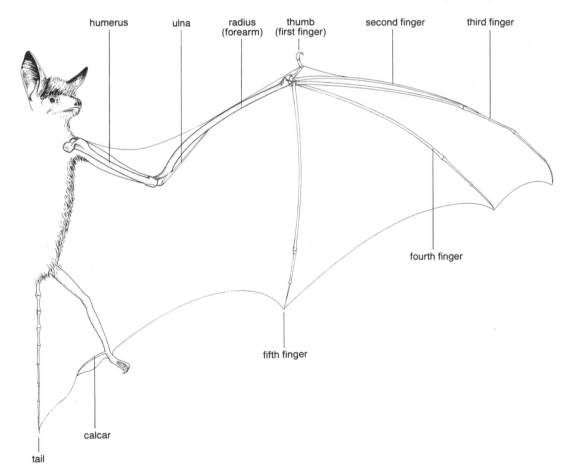

Fig. 2.1 Structure of bat wing.

and Opossums) in which the developing young passes a brief gestation period *in utero*, is born, and then spends a substantial period of its postnatal life attached to a teat in its mother's specialized pouch.

Since bats are mammals, it is true that their form (anatomy, both external and internal) is basically like that of other mammals. However, their adaptation to true flight (especially in darkness) has resulted in their unique form and appearance. They are easily recognized as the only winged or flying mammals. In this chapter we shall examine the unique form of bats. In subsequent chapters we shall explore in more detail some of their particular adaptations including such things as flight, echolocation, feeding, and thermoregulation (hibernation).

EXTERNAL FORM

The wing and associated flight membranes

The wing of a bat is perhaps the singlemost diagnostic feature of this unique group of mammals. It supersedes nearly all of their other less obvious, but perhaps more interesting, special adaptations. We shall discuss the functional aspects of bat wings in Chapter 4; here we describe the general structure of the wing and other associated flight membranes.

Unlike birds and the extinct flying reptiles (Pterosaurs) in which the bony (skeletal) structure of the wing comprises greatly modified forelimb bones, the wing skeleton of bats is not much different from that of the forelimb of most normal mammals (Fig. 2.1). By comparison, a bat's wing is not as drastically modified (skeletally, at least) as the forelimb of a horse, deer, elephant, or whale. As the Greek name for the order Chiroptera (hand wing) implies, the wing is simply a modified hand. The skeletal elements, and indeed much of the soft anatomy in the wing of a bat, may be directly compared to the arm and hand of a human.

The upper arm bone (humerus) is essentially the same as that found in all mammals. This bone articulates at the shoulder joint with the shoulder blade (scapula). The muscles that bind and move this bone are essentially the same, although proportionately larger, than those found in man. Of all the wing bones, the humerus is less elongated, relatively, than any of the others.

The forearm of bats illustrates the first in a series of specialized modifications. In typical mammals and other four-footed terrestrial vertebrates the forearm comprises two bones, the radius and ulna (Fig. 2.1). These two bones articulate with the humerus in the elbow region and, in humans, are constructed in such

a way as to allow the turning of the hand from a palm down position (pronation) to a palm up position (supination). In bats, the ulna is greatly reduced in size and it appears as a thin thread-like bone fused to the much larger and elongated radius. The articulation of the forearm and humerus at the elbow is dominated by the greatly expanded radius (Fig. 2.2). The olecranon portion of the ulna is the largest vestige of this bone and is usually fused to the radius. Its primary function is to lock or otherwise stiffen the elbow joint when the wing is extended and being used in the power generating portion of the wing beat. Overall, the forearm of bats is greatly elongated compared to other mammals. In some bats, especially those with very long wings, the length of the forearm may be nearly equal to the combined length of the head and body. Because of the structural requirements of rigidity and strength to withstand the enormous air pressures developed during flight, the radius has lost its ability to rotate (pronate and supinate).

The wrist region of bats is essentially the same as in other mammals. However, it is less flexible because the ulna is reduced and the radius has lost its rotational ability. The many carpal bones in the wrist are shaped and articulate in such a fashion as to allow restricted movement in the forward and backward

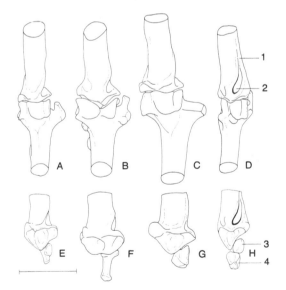

Fig. 2.2 Anterior view of elbow regions of four bats. A, Pteronotus parnellii (Mormoopidae); B, Mormoops megaphylla (Mormoopidae); C, Artibeus toltecus (Phyllostomidae); D, Molossus molossus (Molossidae). Below each (E–H) the articular facets of the radius are shown. 1, radius; 2, flexor fossa for the attachment of the biceps brachii and brachialis muscles; 3, reduced ulna; 4, sesamoid (extra) bone. Line below E is 4 mm in length.

plane (extension and flexion, respectively). This is another apparent adaptation to withstand the tremendous buckling forces that are placed on all wing joints during flight.

Except for the great elongation of the bony elements (phalanges), the hand portion of a bat's wing is not markedly different from the structure of the human hand (Fig. 2.3). The thumb is perhaps the least modified of all of the digits. It is directed more forward than in the human hand and bears a strong terminal claw in nearly all bats: in one family (Furipteridae) the claw is minute and apparently functionless and in another (Myzopodidae) there is only a rudimentary claw. The length of the thumb varies considerably among bats, being very short in some microchiropteran families (Natalidae, Furipteridae, Myzopodidae and some Vespertilionidae) to relatively long in the Old World fruit bats or flying foxes (Megachiroptera). In the latter, the thumb is extremely mobile and is regularly used in locomotion, food handling, and fighting. Vampire bats (Phyllostomidae) crawl, hop or jump quite readily. Like Old World fruit bats they also have relatively long and strong thumbs which are used to help lift the bat and pull it forward when crawling and which play an

important part in helping to provide thrust when these bats hop or jump. The second digit or index finger in bats is composed primarily of a long metacarpal element (main bone of the human palm). One or two short phalanges (finger bones) may be found in this digit. In most Old World fruit bats (Megachiroptera), this digit terminates with a strong claw but in some the claw is reduced in size or absent. The terminal claw on the second finger is absent in all microchiropterans except the fossil species *Icaronycteris index* and, perhaps, *Archaeonycteris trigonodon*. The third, fourth, and fifth fingers are essentially the same in overall structure, the largest element in each being the elongated metacarpal. The number of phalanges in the third finger varies from two to three and there are only two bony phalanges in the fourth and fifth fingers. None of these three fingers has a claw. The length of the finger bones varies from one family to another and this variation produces wings of different shapes and apparent flight potentials.

The flight surface of the wing of bats consists of a flexible membrane stretched around and between the skeletal framework just outlined (Fig. 2.3). This membrane is anchored at the point of the shoulder and extends along the upper arm and forearm to an

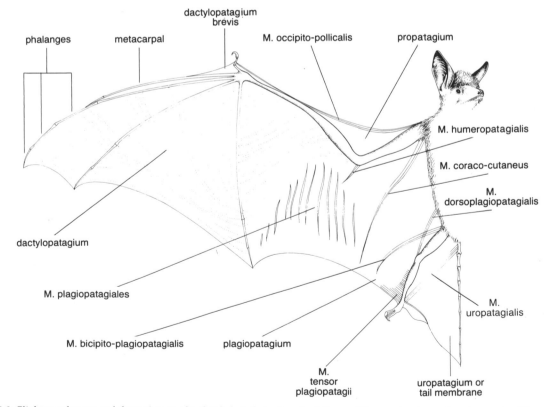

Fig. 2.3 Flight membranes and the major muscles that help to keep them taut. Some of the muscles shown do not occur in all bats.

attachment at the base of the thumb. The leading edge of this portion of the wing membrane incorporates a special muscle (M. occipito-pollicalis) which, when it contracts, causes a general down-turning and increase in the surface area of this portion of the wing. This flight surface–the propatagium–is used to increase or decrease the aerodynamic curvature (camber) of the wing. The portion of the wing membrane forming an elastic webbing between the fingers of the hand is called the dactylopatagium or chiropatagium and a small segment of this membrane extending from the thumb to the second finger is sometimes called the dactylopatagium brevis. It and the propatagium form the leading edge of the wing. The flight membrane that extends from the sides of the body, hindlimb, and foot, along the rear portion of the upper arm, forearm, and fifth finger is called the plagiopatagium. The camber or curvature of the dactylopatagium and plagiopatagium is controlled by the degree of flexion of the fingers and body axis.

As a general rule, the wing membrane attaches to the body along the side. Occasionally, the attachment of the wing membrane may be located rather high on the flank or, in several species, the wing membranes unite and attach on or near the centre of the back to give the back a naked appearance. This condition is found in several megachiropterans (*Pteralopex*, *Dobsonia* and one species of *Rousettus*) and in several species of microchiropterans of the mormoopid genus *Pteronotus*. The function of this peculiar wing attachment is not known, but it may allow an increase in effective flight surface without adding to the total span of the wing.

The effective area of the wing membrane may be augmented by an associated flight membrane that is not directly involved in the structure of the wing proper. This consists of a membrane–the uropatagium or interfemoral membrane–stretched between the hindlimbs and tail (Fig. 2.3). In many bat species, the uropatagium may be further supported by a long cartilaginous spur (calcar) that articulates with the heel of the foot (Fig. 2.1) and which may enable an increase in its area. The form and extent of the uropatagium and the presence or absence of a calcar varies among bat species (Fig. 2.10).

The membranes of the wing and uropatagium are simply extensions of the general body integument (skin) and, as such, have an outer epidermis (cornified layer) and an inner dermis (vascular layer). The flight membranes are especially thin (Table 2.1) and translucent to light in most cases. The dermal layer has a higher than usual concentration of elastic fibres and intrinsic, striated (voluntary) muscle bundles. These anatomical features provide the necessary elasticity and flexibility of the flight membranes which must be held taut during flight and be easily collapsible when the wing is not in use.

Although the flight membranes are delicate in appearance, they are comparatively tough and resilient as they must be able to resist tearing and puncture by sharp objects such as thorns and twigs often encountered in the bat's feeding or roosting environs. Table 2.1 shows the tensile strength of the flight membranes of several bat species compared to those of rubber surgical gloves and commercial plastic sandwich bags. Whereas the rubber gloves are thicker and considerably more elastic than wing membranes, they are more prone to puncture than are

TABLE 2.1 Some physical properties of bat wings compared to other materials.

Subject	N	Thickness (mm)	Puncture strength (kg mm)	Elasticity (mm/kg)
Rubber glove	10	0.234	2.80	35.1
Sandwich bag	10	0.020	8.63	18.7
Myotis lucifugus	10	0.030	5.81	14.0
Myotis thysanodes	10	0.243	9.37	12.9
Myotis yumanensis	3	0.023	7.28	15.5
Eptesicus fuscus (adult)	7	0.038	9.72	9.5
Eptesicus fuscus (young)	8	0.034	5.62	14.0
Plecotus townsendii	1	0.032	7.19	12.3
Antrozous pallidus	2	0.033	7.72	11.9
Tadarida brasiliensis	1	0.063	3.00	15.4

Numbers are mean values; N - number examined. Puncture strength determined as the weight (kg) required to puncture membrane per mm of membrane thickness. Elasticity determined as mm of depression per kg of weight added. (After Studier, 1972).

bat wings. On the other hand, plastic sandwich bags are about equal to wing membranes in thickness, only slightly more elastic, and have nearly the same puncture strength. This table also illustrates the relative high elasticity and low puncture strength of the flight membranes of young Big Brown bats (*Eptesicus fuscus*); adults of this vespertilionid species have tougher, less elastic membranes. The wing membranes are generally stronger and less elastic in bats that feed on the ground or in and around thorny vegetation such as the Pallid bat (*Antrozous pallidus*), Fringed myotis (*Myotis thysanodes*), or Big Brown bat.

One might wonder about the extent and frequency of damage to bat wing membranes. Although there is little quantitative information on the matter, a number of bat biologists have noted a rather high incidence of healed scars from tears or punctures in the wings of captured bats. Some individuals have been captured with as much as 10-20 per cent of the wing-tip missing. Wound healing in these delicate membranes is apparently quite rapid.

The flight membranes are generally naked in appearance, although microscopic examination reveals many short, transparent hairs on both the upper and lower surfaces. Specialized bands of bristles may be found on the underside of the uropatagium of some species and these are thought to form an 'insect trap' used during in-flight foraging. Other specialized bands and fringes may be found on the upper surfaces of the wing. These may facilitate the airflow over the wing during flight. The body fur may extend onto the upper surface of the wing along the upper arm and forearm, or out onto the plagiopatagium adjacent to the attachment of the wing on the sides of the body. In a similar manner, the uropatagium may be partially furred. In the North American tree-dwelling bats of the genus *Lasiurus* and the Asian Tube-nosed bats (*Murina*), the proximal portion of the plagiopatagium and the uropatagium is densely clothed with hair.

The wing and associated flight membranes are usually black or greyish brown in colour, but in some African vespertilionids such as the Light-winged Lesser House bat (*Scotoecus albofuscus*) and White-winged bats (*Eptesicus tenuipinnis* and *E. rendalli*), the wing membranes are white or greyish white. Whitish wings also occur in the African molossid *Tadarida pumila* and the Neotropical emballonurid *Diclidurus virgo*. White wing-tips are commonly found among members of the New World leaf-nosed bats (Phyllostomidae). Yellow and white spots are found on the wings of the Tube-nosed fruit bats *Nyctimene* and *Paranyctimene* which live in the Indo-Australian region. The wings of some species of the vespertilionid genus *Glauconycteris* are ornately variegated with cream white, light browns, and shades of black. In the African vespertilionid, *Myotis welwitschii*, and the Papuan Black-bellied fruit bat, *Melonycteris melanops*, the wings are rich reddish-orange. And, the wings of the Painted bat (*Kerivoula picta*) have highly contrasting orange and black markings (Fig. 2.4). The function of such beautifully coloured wings and ornate body colour patterns is not well understood. These animals are colour-blind and active at night. Presumably, these markings may serve a protective or camouflage function in those species that roost in trees or other exposed sites. Perhaps, in the case of white wings or wing-tips, the contrast may serve a disruptive function to confuse nocturnal and/or crepuscular avian predators such as owls and hawks.

While it is true that the primary purpose of the wing and associated membranes is flight, these specialized features also serve a number of non-flight functions. Several species of vespertilionids (*Myotis*) have been observed (with the use of high speed

Fig. 2.4 Wing coloration of painted bat (Kerivoula picta – *Vespertilionidae*).

motion pictures) using the wings to capture insects in flight. In these film sequences, the wing is used much like a tennis racket is used as an extension of the human arm, to deflect insect prey toward the mouth or into the basket-like pocket formed by the hind-limbs, tail and uropatagium. In the course of this 'fielding' behaviour, the bat may collapse both wings around the body, tuck the head into the uropatagium, and perform an aerobatic somersault.

The wings possess a rich supply of blood vessels that serve to transport oxygen and nutrients to the flight muscles. In addition, this expansive vascular network may also radiate excess heat and thereby function as a cooling device. Some flying foxes, such as *Pteropus*, roost in trees and are exposed to the high temperatures of the noonday sun. These bats have adopted a behavioural use of the cooling ability of their expansive wing surfaces. Under high heat stress they urinate on their wings which are tightly folded around their bodies and use the effect of evaporation to cool themselves. This blade, however, has two edges. Certainly, the dissipation of excess heat is to the bat's advantage. On the other hand, the un-controlled loss of heat would be a marked disadvantage, especially during flight on cool nights. The Western Pipistrelle (*Pipistrellus hesperus*) of the south-western regions of the United States regularly flies on winter nights in air temperatures as low as −5°C. Such heat loss problems will be discussed in Chapter 6.

Another function of the wings, also associated with the rich vascular network, is one of gas exchange. During flight a great deal of carbon dioxide is generated as a by-product of the high metabolic activity of the flight muscles. Normally, in mammals, this excess excretory product is exchanged in the lungs through normal respiration. Bats also do this. However, it has been shown that individual Big Brown bats (*Eptesicus fuscus*), at rest and at 18°C, exchange 0.4 per cent of their total carbon dioxide production through the wing membranes. Active individuals of this species, at 27.5°C, dissipate 11.5 per cent of their carbon dioxide production via these membranes. This is a direct result of the thinness of the membranes and their rich blood supply. One might wonder if oxygen might also be taken in across the wing membranes; that is, do the wings serve a true respiratory function? The answer is no. In order for oxygen to be efficiently exchanged, it must first be dissolved in water as in the case of a fish's gill or in the moist environment of the lungs. As wing membranes are dry, oxygen exchange is insignificant. Although the wings are the most immediately obvi-ous features of bats, they are by no means the only interesting characteristic of these unique mammals.

The head

Perhaps more than any other group of mammals, bats display a wide range of variation in the shape of the head. Consider for a moment the general lack of variation in head shape among wild or domestic hoofed mammals–horses, deer, and antelope. Also note the generally stereotypic shape of the heads of dogs and cats (non-domestic) and rabbits. Birds also possess a generally recognizable head shape. True, they do vary in the shape and size of such features as beaks and eyes. The lack of variation among some groups of mammals and the beak variation observed in birds all reflect adaptations to particular diets or food-getting behaviour. Hoofed mammals all utilize food items that require a fair amount of chewing, and so tend to have long muzzles that reflect their long jaws which support long and massive batteries of grinding teeth. Similarly, hummingbirds, hawks, and ducks exhibit a range of beak variation geared to specific food capture and utilization mechanisms. The wide range of variation in the shape of bat heads also reflects a wide variation in diet and food capture.

The ancestors of bats, or at least of microchropte-rans, are thought to have been insectivorous (catch-ing and feeding on insects). Insectivory is wides-pread among bats and is perhaps the most common food habit (approximately 70 per cent of the living species of bats are insectivores). Generally speaking, bats with this kind of diet have moderately long, pointed noses. The eyes are small and the back part of the head is round in appearance. Variations on this general theme appear to correlate with the kinds of insects utilized in the diet. Those bats that eat soft-bodied insects such as moths, mosquitoes, and other small flies may have slightly longer, shallow muzzles or their faces may be short and broad. Bats that eat hard-bodied insects (such as beetles) may have somewhat shorter and deeper muzzles, and the back of the head may be wide and highly domed. The width and domed appearance of the back of the head is usually associated with moderate to high crests and ridges or a greatly expanded braincase surface. All of the modifications relate directly to increasing the size of the temporalis muscle used to operate the massive jaws in the chewing of these hard-bodied insects.

Some bats, approximately 0.7 per cent of the living species, are carnivorous (eat flesh) and this is reflec-ted in the shape of their heads. For example, the head of the American False Vampire (*Vampyrum spectrum*–Phyllostomidae) is dog-like in appearance. While less dog-like in overall appearance, other carnivorous bats such as *Macroderma gigas* (Megadermatidae) and *Phyllostomus hastatus* (Phyllostomidae) have long, stout muzzles and long, rounded heads. Fish-eating or piscivorous bats (approximately 0.6 per cent of all living species) such as *Noctilio leporinus* tend to have short, deep faces and high-domed heads like bulldogs. Indeed, the common name for this particular species is the Bulldog bat. On the other hand, the head of the fish-eating vespertilionid *Pizonyx vivesi* is not markedly dissimilar from its insectivorous relatives.

Frugivory (fruit-eating), the second most common chiropteran diet (approximately 23 per cent of the living species), also results in a wide range of head shapes. Among the Old World fruit bats (Megachiroptera), the snout may be long, deep, and pointed, with the rear portion of the head widely rounded. This is the case in *Pteropus*, *Rousettus*, and *Dobsonia*. Among the New World leaf-nosed bats (Phyllostomidae), this general head shape is exemplified by *Phyllostomus discolor*, *Carollia perspicillata*, and *Brachyphylla cavernarum*. This head shape may be generally primitive and, like that of hoofed mammals, provide room for the massive grinding teeth (molars). On the other hand, another expression of frugivory in the shaping of the head is a trend toward the extreme shortening of the face and high doming of the braincase. A full spectrum of variation occurs between these extremes. In such bats as the phyllostomids *Centurio senex* and *Ametrida centurio*, the face is very broad, nearly flat (monkey-like), and the back of the head rises sharply above the level of the eyes (Fig. 2.8).

Among the most curious of head shapes in bats are those found in the nectar and pollen eaters (nectarivory, approximately 5 per cent of the living species). In these, the muzzle is long and tubular and the back of the head is low and rounded. As in hummingbirds (which are the avian and diurnal equivalent of these bats), there is a wide range of variation in snout length. The phyllostomid *Musonycteris harrisoni* is perhaps the most extreme in this regard, with a snout that is nearly two and a half times the length of the braincase.

Whereas the shape of the head generally reflects the dietary habits of bats, other considerations also may influence the shape of the head. One particular roosting habit, that of occupying tight spaces such as narrow rock crevices or the hollow internodes of bamboo, is associated with a trend to flattened heads. Extremes in flat-headedness are seen in the vespertilionid Bamboo bats (*Tylonycteris pachypus* and *T. robustula*), and the rock-dwelling molossid Flat-headed bats (*Sauromys petrophilus* and *Platymops setiger*). Aerodynamic considerations (especially among the swifter flying bat species) may influence the shape of the head. In these, the shape of the head is fusiform (bullet-shaped, or at least conical), while slow-flying bats display a wider range of head shapes that are presumably less restricted by aerodynamic forces.

Associated with the head are a number of other features that add to the wide range of appearances of bats. These include the ears, eyes, nostrils, and various facial excrescences which are collectively referred to as noseleaves.

The ears

In most mammals, and other vertebrates as well, hearing is an important sense for determining various aspects of the surrounding environment. In the lighted diurnal world, hearing acuity may be superseded by visual perception. For bats, the majority of which hunt or otherwise orient in their environment by means of acoustic perception (echolocation), hearing is of paramount importance. We will discuss acoustic orientation in Chapter 8. Here we will examine the variation in size and shape of the external ears (pinnae) and associated structures.

Ear shape among the megachiropterans is not especially variable nor very spectacular. The ears of these bats are usually short and generally rounded. Some species, such as those of the genera *Pteropus* and *Dobsonia* may have long, somewhat pointed ears. For the most part, the ears of these bats are not strikingly disproportionate in size compared to the head and body. At their base, where they join the head, the ears of megachiropterans form a complete ring; that is, they are tubular. The external pinnae of these bats are never connected and a wide array of voluntary integumental (skin) muscles allow a considerable range of independent movement of the ears. While hanging in the roost or being held in a captor's hand, the ears are constantly twitching and moving about. Megachiropterans are thought to orient primarily by vision and this may account for the lack of specially adapted ears. Even the ears of *Rousettus*, which is known to have a crude form of echolocation, are not noticeably different from those of other megachiropterans.

In contrast to the Megachiroptera, the Microchiroptera display a wide range of variation in ear shape and size. Some are quite bizarre. Before discussing these variations, it is necessary to describe the components of microchiropteran ears. The bulk of the ear is composed of the large flap-like external pinna (Fig. 2.5). Unlike the megachiropterans, the base of the pinna of microchiropteran ears is generally open at the front; that is, not forming a complete ring or tube. The inside surface of the ear conch frequently has several transverse ridges or a series of longitudinal ridges. The function of these is not known, but they

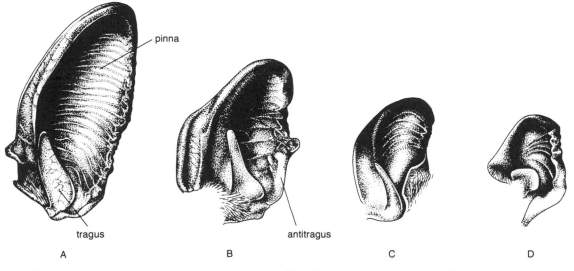

Fig. 2.5 Variation of ear and associated structures. A, Long-eared bat (Plecotus auritus); *B, Barbastelle* (Barbastella barbastellus); *C, Daubenton's bat* (Myotis daubentonii); *D, European noctule* (Nyctalus noctula) *(all Vespertilionidae).*

are presumed to provide structural support for the pinna. They may also be involved in collecting certain kinds or frequencies of sound. In addition, bands of hair in particular, and diagnostic patterns, may be found inside the ears of some microchiropterans. The function of these is not known.

Two other ear components are found in the Microchiroptera. The first of these is the tragus. Its presence or absence and size and shape are used in the taxonomic identification and recognition of many species (Fig. 2.6). The tragus, sometimes called the 'earlet', corresponds to the small cartilaginous knob located just above the ear notch of the human ear. The tragus is absent in all megachiropterans. Among microchiropterans, it is absent in the Rhinolophidae and Hipposideridae and is quite small in the Molossidae. In other microchiropterans the tragus is moderately to well developed. The tragus of Tomes' Long-

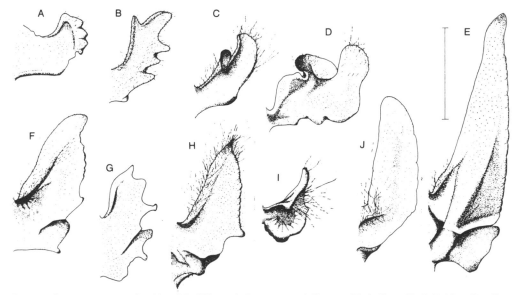

Fig. 2.6 Tragus of some representative New World bats. A, Saccopteryx bilineata (Emballonuridae); B, Noctilio albiventris (Noctilionidae); C, Pteronotus macleayii (Mormoopidae); D, Mormoops megalophylla (Mormoopidae); E, Lonchorhina aurita (Phyllostomidae); F, Carollia perspicillata (Phyllostomidae); G, Ametrida centurio (Phyllostomidae); H, Desmodus rotundus (Phyllostomidae); I, Natalus stramineus (Natalidae); J, Eptesicus fuscus (Vespertilionidae). Line adjacent to E is 5 mm in length.

eared bat (*Lonchorhina aurita*) is almost as long as the ear conch (Fig. 2.6E). The second ear component is the antitragus (Fig. 2.5) and its presence and shape are occasionally used for taxonomic purposes. There is no easily explained equivalent in the human ear, although it would be situated below the notch and just above the ear lobe. When present, the antitragus is a broad process or flap that is continuous with the outer margin of the pinna (Fig. 2.7). It is well developed in rhinolophids, hipposiderids, and molossids.

The range of variation in the size and shape of microchiropteran ears is almost as large as the number of species in this group. Relatively simple ears are found among the vespertilionids and some of the New World leaf-nosed bats (Phyllostomidae). The three small families of New World bats (Natalidae, Thyropteridae, and Furipteridae) have funnel-shaped ears with a short, generally blunt tragus. Craseonycterids, rhinopomatids, and emballonurids have simple but broadly rounded and cup-shaped ears; the tragus may be long and slender or short and broad. The ears of these bats are never connected, but there may be a short flap extending onto the forehead above the eyes.

The ears of horseshoe bats (Rhinolophidae) and Old World leaf-nosed bats (Hipposideridae) (Fig. 2.7) are similar in general appearance. The range of variation is great, with short (round or pointed) ears to large, broadly rounded, nearly funnel-shaped ears. The size of the ear conch may proportionately exceed the size of the head. The tragus is always small (scarcely more than a small knob deep inside the ear) or absent and the complexity of the ear may be augmented by a large, flap-like antitragus.

A number of microchiropterans have exceptionally long ears. Long ears are characteristic of three families: Nycteridae, Megadermatidae and Myzopodidae. Long-eared species also occur among the Phyllostomidae (*Lonchorhina, Tonatia, Chrotopterus, Macrotus,* and *Mimon*); Vespertilionidae (*Plecotus, Idionycteris, Euderma, Histiotus, Otonycteris, Antrozous,* and *Nyctophilus*); and Molossidae (several species of *Eumops*). The long ears of megadermatids are always united for at least a third of their length from the base. The ears of most molossids, whether long or short, are usually connected by a strong band above the eyes. The ears of the Sucker-footed bat (*Myzopoda aurita*), from Madagascar, are exceptionally long and slender and not connected. In addition, the tragus is long and fused to the inner margin of the pinna. The antitragus is a peculiar mushroom-like pad that fills most of the space at the base of the ear conch.

The long ears of megadermatids, nycterids, myzo-podids, and phyllostomids are structurally rigid and under normal circumstances stand erect above the head. Those of most of the long-eared vespertilionids are the same, but the long ears of the vespertilionid genera *Plecotus, Idionycteris,* and *Euderma* are peculiar in the following respect. While resting in the day roost or in temporary night roosts, these bats fold their long ears into tightly curled bundles on either side of the head. Actually, they deflate their ears by closing special valves in blood vessels that enter the ear conch, thereby allowing the ears to collapse. When these bats become active, the vascular valves leading into the conch are opened and in-rushing blood slowly unfurls the collapsed ear. In a few seconds, the ears are pumped up to their fully erect posture. The functional significance of this behaviour is not fully understood, but it is thought to be a means of reducing heat (and perhaps water) loss while the bat is at rest or in hibernation.

Unlike other bats with long ears that stand more or less perpendicular to the long axis of the head, the ears of molossid bats (both long and short) lie forward, nearly parallel to the long axis of the head and body. As we noted above, the inner margins of the ears are usually connected by a band of skin. The reason for this ear posture seems to be correlated with the swift flight of these bats and functional aerodynamic requirements operating on the shape of the head. These ears are structurally rigid and have thick cartilaginous margins that maintain their streamlined aerodynamic shape.

The eyes

Most bats (Microchiroptera) rely almost exclusively on acoustic orientation and, therefore, usually have rather small to minute eyes. The small size of most bats' eyes and the fact that they are often hidden in the fur of the face has led many people to the common notion that bats either have no eyes or they are necessarily blind. This misconception is far from true, although the degree to which visual orientation is utilized by bats is not well understood. Studies on the Pallid bat (*Antrozous pallidus*) clearly indicate that it has an exceptional ability to discriminate patterns, even in extremely low light situations. Experiments with point sources of light also suggest that the Big Brown bat (*Eptesicus fuscus*) should be able to see bright stars. Individuals of some cave-dwelling species become restless before it is dark outside and hover or mill about the cave entrance as though checking the level of light. Visual acuity may be important in recognizing landmarks among species that forage over long distances or for those species that migrate long distances seasonally. Among the

Microchiroptera, only the members of the Phyllostomidae have large eyes and it is thought that they may rely more on visual acuity in their nightly activities. Two phyllostomid species, Seba's Short-tailed bat (*Carollia perspicillata*) and Geoffroy's Tail-less bat (*Anoura geoffroyi*), have been observed (experimentally) to recognize and discriminate patterns.

In sharp contrast to the Microchiroptera, the eyes of megachiropterans are exceptionally large. These bats unquestionably utilize visual orientation more than audition. The light-sensitive part of the eye, the retina, is uniquely constructed with an outer layer (choroid) with numerous papillae that project back into the retinal surface. This may increase the available retinal surface area and thereby enhance the visual acuity in low light conditions. Many (perhaps all) megachiropterans have a tapetum lucidum that causes the eyes to shine bright red in a spotlight. The use of vision is discussed in relationship to migration and homing in Chapter 9.

The nostrils

The external nares (nostrils) of bats are usually located at the apex of the muzzle or nose. Typically these are round and open to the side of the muzzle. In many species the nostrils may be incorporated into discrete narial pads as in the Hog-nosed bat (*Craseonycteris thonglongyai*) or the Mouse-tailed bats of the genus *Rhinopoma*. The latter inhabit arid regions of the Old World and the nostrils are slit-like rather than rounded or crescentic in shape and they are valvular. This may allow them to close the narial passage and thereby exclude the dust from their dry and sandy surroundings. In bats that have noseleaves, the nostrils are intricately incorporated into these integumental ornamentations and they usually open upward. Several bat species, notably the Tube-nosed fruit bats (*Nyctimene* and *Paranyctimene*–Pteropodidae) and the Tube-nosed bats (*Murina*–Vespertilionidae), have nostrils opening laterally at the ends of short tubes–hence the common name 'tube-nosed'. The Bulldog bat (*Noctilio leporinus*–Noctilionidae) and the New Zealand Short-tailed bat (*Mystacina tuberculata*–Mystacinidae) have nostrils opening from a short tubercle at the end of the muzzle.

Facial foliations

While the faces of many bats possess no other distinctive features than those described above, several families of bats have curious and prominent fleshy excrescences of skin ornamenting the face. These usually take the form of leaf-like appendages associated with the nose region and are generally referred to as noseleaves. Noseleaves are characteristic features of the Rhinolophidae, Hipposideridae, Megadermatidae, and Phyllostomidae. Although not closely related in terms of genealogy, the noseleaves of the families Megadermatidae and Phyllostomidae are similar in appearance. In these families, the single blade-like noseleaf arises from a fleshy plate that surrounds the nasal apertures and stands erect behind these openings. The noseleaves of these bats may be long or short, slender or broad. In the phyllostomid Long-eared bat (*Lonchorhina aurita*), the length of the noseleaf nearly equals the length of its extremely elongated ears. This is also the case in its close relative, the Long-legged bat (*Macrophyllum macrophyllum*). It is interesting to note that the scientific (generic) names of these two bats refer to the shape and size of the noseleaf, *Lonchorhina* meaning literally 'spear nose' and *Macrophyllum* 'large leaf.' In another phyllostomid (*Sphaeronycteris toxophyllum*) the species name reflects a falsely attributed poisonous quality of the noseleaf that may portray the supposedly sinister nature of this bat. In reality, this bat is a quite docile and contented fruit-eating species. In the true vampire bats (Phyllostomidae) the noseleaf has been greatly reduced and modified into a complex series of folds and bumps around the ornamented narial plate.

The noseleaves of the Rhinolophidae and Hipposideridae are much more complex than those described above (Fig. 2.7). In both of these families the nasal apertures are surrounded by a broad, U-shaped plate. The resemblance of this plate to a horseshoe has led to the common name 'Horseshoe bats' for the family Rhinolophidae. The hipposiderids are simply called the Old World leaf-nosed bats.

In the rhinolophids, there is a vertical projection (sella) from the centre of the horseshoe behind the nostrils (Fig. 2.7). Occasionally the sella may incorporate secondary flaps of skin at its base to form a cup-shaped structure overlying the nasal openings. Behind the sella is a large, usually pointed, leaf called the lancet, that bears a number of complex folds and pockets along its edges. The sella and lancet are joined by a connecting process that also may have a curious shape. In addition, the noseleaf of rhinolophids may have a distinctly arranged pattern of sensory hairs.

The noseleaf of hipposiderids, while similar in some respects to those of rhinolophids, is often more complex. In its simplest form, there are two leaves or flaps behind the narial openings (Fig. 2.7). The hindmost (posterior leaf) may have several deep, forward facing pockets. The intermediate leaf is located just behind the nostrils and may have swollen areas or finger-like projections on its dorsal border.

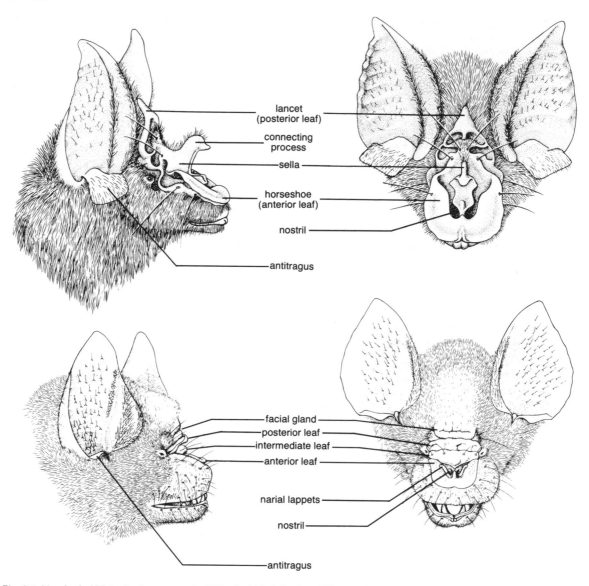

Fig. 2.7 Noseleaf of Rhinolophus euryotis *(Rhinolophidae) (top) and* Hipposideros maggietaylorae *(Hipposideridae) (bottom).*

Additional complexity of the hipposiderid noseleaf may involve ornamental flaps around the nostrils, plate-like structures between the nostrils, and spikes, bumps, and complex folds on the dorsal margin of the posterior leaf. Several secondary leaflets occasionally occur under the antero-lateral edges of the horseshoe.

In some species of rhinolophids and hipposiderids, the structure of the noseleaf is truly bizarre. It is often used to characterize species or groups of species. The function of all noseleaves is not known, but they are thought to contribute to directing the acoustic orientation sounds that these bats produce.

Other facial foliations involve flaps and plates of skin not directly associated with the nose region. Notable examples are the bats of the family Mormoopidae (Moustached bats and Ghost-faced bats), in which the lips and chin regions are ornamented with complex foliations. These may function in directing the acoustic orientation sounds like a megaphone or they may augment the funnel shape of the mouth and thus facilitate the capture of insects as the bat flies through the air.

The bats of the family Nycteridae (Slit-faced bats) have a peculiar facial ornamentation. There is a longitudinal furrow or slit on the upper surface of the muzzle. In front of and on either side of this slit are noseleaf-like structures that may be extremely complex.

The Wrinkle-faced bat (*Centurio senex*) has, perhaps, the most bizarre and grotesque face of all bats (Fig. 2.8). It is a New World leaf-nosed bat adapted to feeding on fruit and has a much flattened, naked face. Being a phyllostomid, it has a noseleaf, but, in addition, its face is covered with a complex array of wart-like outgrowths, folds, and flaps. Even more peculiar is a deep chin fold which can be drawn over the face when the bat is at rest.

Fig. 2.8 Facial ornamentation of the Wrinkle-faced bat (Centurio senex–Phyllostomidae).

Finally, many bats have large fleshy lips that may contribute to facial ornamentation. In the Free-tailed bats (Molossidae) the lips are highly wrinkled, whereas in the Bulldog bats (*Noctilio*), the upper lips are large and covered with many small bumps.

Body size

While it is generally true that the bats of the suborder Megachiroptera are large and those of the Microchiroptera are small, there is considerable overlap in size. The largest bats (*Pteropus giganteus* and *Acerodon jubatus*) are megachiropterans and have a wing span of nearly two metres. The smallest bat, *Craseonycteris thonglongyai*, is a microchiropteran and has a wing span of 130-145 mm. However, between these extremes we find *Macroglossus minimus* (Megachiroptera) with a wing span of 210-240 mm and *Vampyrum*

spectrum (Microchiroptera) with a wing span of almost a metre. Weights also reflect these differences in size. *Pteropus* weigh 500-1200 g and *Craseonycteris* tips the scales at about 2 g.

Body size of bats appears to be closely related to food habits and modes of flight. Physiological factors also play a part. Fruit-eating species are generally large in size as are carnivorous bats such as *Vampyrum spectrum* (Phyllostomidae) and *Macroderma gigas* (Megadermatidae). These large-sized species usually have long, broad wings and are capable of lifting heavy weights; flight speeds are relatively slow in these species. Large-sized species have an extra advantage over smaller species in that they have a relatively lower surface to volume ratio and do not lose body heat so rapidly.

Insect-eating bats are generally smaller than fruit-eating bats. Insects are highly dispersed in the environment and may be somewhat elusive; more than a few are required for a sufficiently energy-rich meal. Capturing insects on the wing requires fast and highly manoeuverable flight styles which themselves require high energy input. Thus, insectivorous bats must eat large quantities of insects on a regular basis; some experts estimate anywhere from one quarter to one half of their body weight nightly.

Body shape

Aerodynamic forces that occur during flight are a major factor determining body shape in bats as well as in other organisms that fly or glide. The bodies of bats are somewhat flattened and tapered from the shoulders to the hip region. The bulk of the weight is distributed in the upper chest region (centre of gravity) and is composed primarily of the heavy flight muscles. Bats utilize muscles located on the chest and back to operate their wings. In contrast, birds are deep-chested because all of their flight musculature is located in this ventral position. The breast bone of birds is strongly keeled to accommodate this mass of muscles. This bone is not markedly keeled in bats.

The hindlimb and foot

Much attention has been directed toward the modification of the forelimb (wing) of bats. However, the hindlimb has also undergone a number of changes associated with the flying ability of bats. For the most part, the hindlimbs have lost their function as locomotory appendages. This is not to say that bats are incapable of moving about on the ground; some are quite agile. Nonetheless, the hindlimb of bats is no longer a weight-bearing appendage such as that of a human leg. The most striking feature of the hindlimb is that the upper leg bone (femur) has been rotated 180° from its normal position in other terrestrial mammals. Whereas the knee is directed forward in most other mammals, it is directed rearward (actually upward) in bats. Thus, the posture of the hindlimb of a bat at rest, on a flat surface, is rather spider-like. This curious limb posture has to do with the attachment of the wing membranes to the hindlimb as well as the attachment of the interfemoral membrane (uropatagium) and the co-ordinated control of these flight membranes. The bones of the leg, like those of the wing, are long and slender. Indeed they are longer and more slender than would be expected in a normal four-footed mammal of equal size and weight. They would, no doubt, break or bend if subjected to the weight-bearing stresses (compression) of a normal leg. However, bats do not walk, in the strict sense, on their legs; they hang suspended by them from a foothold in the roost. The weight-bearing forces of suspension (tension) are very different from those of compression. Imagine balancing a kilogram block on top of a dried strand of spaghetti; it would shatter under the compressive force. On the other hand, imagine suspending the same block from the strand of spaghetti; it would probably hold the weight. The same dynamic principles apply to a bat's leg. Indeed, the spider-like posture of the hindlimbs cradles (suspends) the body and is geared to reducing compressive stresses when bats move around on the ground. Species such as the Pallid bat (*Antrozous pallidus*) and the Common vampire (*Desmodus rotundus*) that frequently move about on the ground have slightly stouter leg bones than those species that do not.

The feet of bats are usually small. The toes are rather long and terminate with strong, sharp claws. In fish-eating species such as the Bulldog bat (*Noctilio leporinus*), Fishing bat (*Pizonyx vivesi*), and Kei myotis (*Myotis stalkeri*), the foot is unusually large and the toes are compressed laterally and terminate with a large sharp claw. These are adaptations for seizing and holding the prey.

The tendons in the legs and feet of bats are organized in such a way that the suspended weight of the hanging bat causes the toes and claws to grip the foothold in the roost firmly, even while the bat is sleeping (Fig. 2.9). A foot structure that allows an automatic grasping ability while at rest is also found in passerine (perching) birds. However, in these animals the anatomical arrangement is designed for an upright roosting posture.

Another structure that is associated with the foot and is unique to bats is the calcar (Fig. 2.1). This usually long cartilaginous structure articulates with the heel bone (calcaneum) and is bound in the

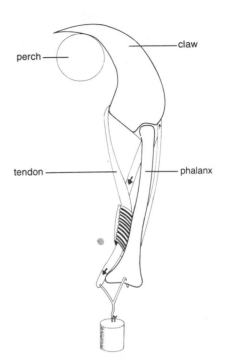

Fig. 2.9 A tendon in the foot helps to keep the claws firmly hooked to the perch by utilizing the weight of the hanging bat (After Schaffer, 1905).

uropatagium. Its function is to support the trailing edge of this interfemoral flight membrane and by muscular control it can be used to make camber changes in the uropatagium during flight. In the fishing species, it is usually very long and blade-like and serves to hold the posterior portion of the uropatagium out of the water as the bat is grasping its prey. The degree to which the calcar is developed in other species is variable and in many it may have a fleshy keel. These features are often used in the identification of particular species or groups of species. The Hog-nosed bat (*Craseonycteris thonglongyai*) and Mouse-tailed bats (Rhinopomatidae) do not have a calcar (Fig. 2.10E-F); it is knob-like in the vampires (Desmodontinae).

In a few species, there are peculiar sucker-like pads or discs attached to the side of the foot as well as the wrist region. These structures facilitate the curious roosting behaviour of these species which usually involves seeking shelter inside the rolled leaves of bananas and other similar plants. In the African Banana bat (*Pipistrellus nanus*–Vespertilionidae) there is a slightly developed pad on the palmar surface of the wrist; they lack a sucker on the foot. There is a moderately well-developed adhesive pad on the wrists and feet of the Club-footed bats (*Tylonycteris*) and Thick-thumbed pipistrelles (*Glischropus*). Similar

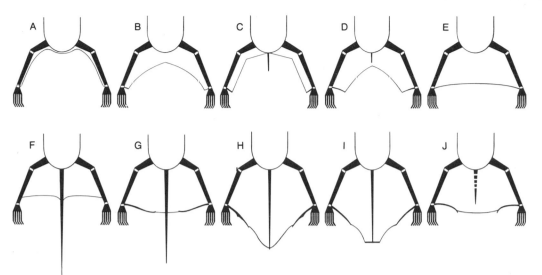

Fig. 2.10 *Tail and uropatagium of bats. See text for discussion.*

adaptations are found in the Disc-footed bat (*Eudisco-pus denticulus*) and in *Myotis rosseti*. All four of the aforementioned species are members of the Vesperti-lionidae and live in southeastern Asia. The most highly developed sucker-discs are found in the Sucker-footed bat (*Myzopoda aurita*–Myzopodidae) of Madagascar and the New World Disc-winged bats (*Thyroptera*–Thyropteridae).

The tail and interfemoral membrane

Nearly all bats have a tail, although like many of the structures discussed above, there is considerable variation. The Mouse-tailed bats (*Rhinopoma*) are so named for their long, free tail (Fig. 2.10F). By 'free-tailed' we mean that the tail or some substantial portion of it is not bound in the interfemoral membrane and trails freely behind the bat. In rhinopomatids the tail is very long and thread-like and not as thick as a mouse's tail. The bats of the family Molossidae are all characterized by having at least half of the tail protruding from the rear margin of the uropatagium (Fig. 2.10G). Indeed, they are called Free-tailed bats. A long, free tail is found in the Long-tailed fruit bat (*Notopteris macdonaldi*– Pteropodidae) which is found in the New Hebrides (Vanuatu), New Caledonia, and Fiji. This pteropodid, as well as members of the family Rhinopomatidae are thought by some bat biologists to be very primitive because of their long tails since it is supposed that the ancestors of bats had long, free tails. While this may or may not be true, these long-tailed species do not appear to be as primitive or as ancestral as many

would desire. Long tails are a general characteristic of the Evening bats (Vespertilionidae). Their tails, however, are completely (or nearly so) bound within the uropatagium (Fig. 2.10H). Similar conditions are found in the Rhinolophidae, Hipposideridae, and Megadermatidae (tail may be absent in some). The tail of nycterids is also long and enclosed in the uropatagium. In addition, there is usually a T- or Y-shaped cartilage at the tip of the tail (Fig. 2.10I). In three families (Emballonuridae, Noctilionidae, and Mormoopidae), the tail protrudes for about 10-15 mm from the top surface of the interfemoral membrane at about the level of the knee (Fig. 2.10J). These bats have moderately well-developed calcars and these help fold the posterior, tail-less portion of the uropatagium forward under the anterior portion of the uropatagium. In this posture, these bats appear to have a 'free tail.'

The tail may be short or absent in some species. *Craseonycteris thonglongyai* is peculiar because it has an extensive uropatagium but lacks any remnant of a tail or calcars (Fig. 2.10E). This is odd because a reduction in the length of the tail is usually accompanied by a similar reduction in the expanse of the uropatagium.

Most pteropodids do not have tails or much of an interfemoral membrane. Short, free tails are found in the rousettes (*Rousettus*) and the Tube-nosed fruit bats (*Nyctimene* and *Paranyctimene*–Fig. 2.10C). Within the New World leaf-nosed bats (Phyllostomi-dae) there is considerable variation relative to the length of the tail and the form of the uropatagium (Fig. 2.10A-B, D).

Hair

Hair is a unique characteristic of mammals and the bodies of nearly all bats are covered with a coat of hair or fur. Hair consists of dead epidermal cells that contain keratin, a tough, flexible substance made of proteins. Keratin is also found in nails and claws. The hair filament, although dead, grows from living cells located in special bulb-shaped structures called hair follicles at the root of each hair in the epidermis of the skin.

Each hair consists of three distinct, microscopic regions. The centre of a hair is called the medulla and, in most mammals it contains air spaces and colour pigments. The hairs of vespertilionids lack a medulla. In addition, the medulla is absent in some species of the Emballonuridae, Nycteridae, Rhinolophidae, Hipposideridae, Noctilionidae, Phyllostomidae, Natalidae, Thyropteridae, Myzopodidae, Mystacinidae, and Molossidae. Nearly all megachiropterans (Pteropodidae) have a medulla as do megadermatids. When present, the medulla is usually fragmented; that is, it appears as a string of beads running through the core of the hair. The bulk of the hair is made up of the cortex. This region may also contain colour pigments and in most bats the cortex accounts for the overall coloration of the fur. The outside of the hair filament is covered with many flat scale-like cells called cuticular or coronal scales. These scales often have distinctive shapes and features that may be seen only under very high magnification such as provided by the scanning electron microscope (Fig. 2.11). These scales may be closely appressed to the hair shaft (Fig. 2.11A, F) or they may be divergent (Fig. 2.11B-E, G). In addition, their margins may be smooth or entire (Fig. 2.11A-B, F), mildly crenulate (saw-toothed as in Fig. 2.11G), or strongly denticulate (Fig. 2.11C, E). The characteristics of coronal scales have been used by some to identify species or groups of species. However, the effort and expense required to see them often makes them difficult to study. There is no apparent correlation between the structure of the coronal scales and the habits of bats.

The coat of hair is called fur or pelage and it functions primarily as insulation. The pelage of most mammals may be divided into several different kinds of hairs. The most prominent of these are the underfur (fine and very dense) and the overfur or guard hairs (usually long and coarse). In most bats, there is little or no distinction between these two kinds of hairs. In fact, the pelage of most bats is rather uniform in length and overall density. Some vespertilionids may have distinct guard hairs with the outer third of the hair filament somewhat expanded.

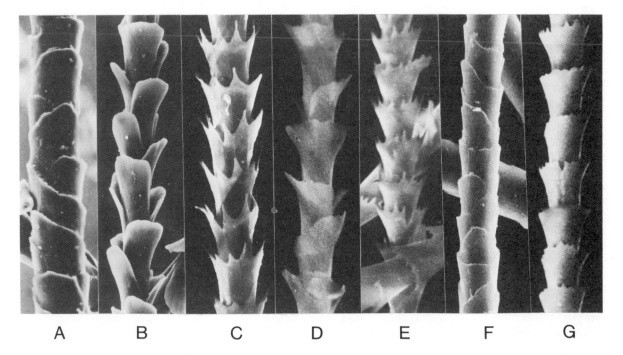

A   B   C   D   E   F   G

Fig. 2.11 Scanning electro-micrographs of cuticular (coronal) scales of bat hair. A, Macroglossus sobrinus *(Pteropodidae);* B, Epomophorus anurus *(Pteropodidae); C,* Rhinopoma hardwickei *(Rhinopomatidae); D,* Emballonura nigrescens *(Emballonuridae); E,* Mormoops megalophylla *(Mormoopidae); F,* Natalus stramineus *(Natalidae); G,* Eumops perotis *(Molossidae). Scale approx.* × *1000.*

The length of the pelage of bats varies from 3-4 mm in some vespertilionids and molossids to 40 mm in *Acerodon* (Pteropodidae). Species that roost in outdoor situations such as trees often have very dense and moderately long fur. Short but frequently dense fur is found on most cave-dwelling species. The pelage may be sparse and coarse in tropical species or those that inhabit arid or semi-arid regions. The greatest variation in the nature of the pelage may be found in the Megachiroptera. Among microchiropterans, extremely woolly (underfur) pelages are found in such species as the Woolly False vampire (*Chrotopterus auritus*–Phyllostomidae), Commerson's leaf-nosed bat (*Hipposideros commersoni*–Hipposideridae), Lesser Woolly Horseshoe bat (*Rhinolophus sedulus*–Rhinolophidae), and Woolly bats of the genus *Kerivoula* (Vespertilionidae). These long, woolly coats are exceptional, perhaps because they are difficult to dry. The pelage of some vespertilionids and most molossids is very short and silky. In the latter, fresh pelage may have a glossy sheen or lustre.

There is only one naked bat, the Hairless bat (*Cheiromeles torquatus*–Molossidae). The Bare-backed fruit bats (*Dobsonia*–Pteropodidae) and the Naked-backed bats (*Pteronotus davyi* and *P. gymnonotus*–Mormoopidae) have backs that appear to be nude. However, these bats are not truly naked-backed. The naked skin is the fused wing membranes that meet on the midline of the back; beneath them is the normally furred back.

The length and texture of the pelage may play an important role in aerodynamically contouring or smoothing the body surface of bats. Many of the swift-flying species tend to have moderately short to close-cropped fur and the individual hairs are often very fine. In the genus *Pteropus*, the fur on different parts of the body may differ in length and texture. Often these bats have a collar (mantle) of woolly fur on the neck and shoulder region and short sparse fur on the back. The rump area may be clothed with fur similar to that on the back or it may be somewhat longer and more woolly.

Specialized patches or bands of hair are found in some species of bats. These patches are often more highly developed in males of the species. Males of the pteropodid genera *Rousettus*, *Myonycteris*, and *Megaloglossus* often have a collar or 'ruff' of coarse specialized hairs extending across the upper chest between the shoulders. White tufts of specialized hairs are found on the shoulders of the Epauletted bats (*Epomops* and *Epomophorus*–Pteropodidae). These specialized patches of hair are usually associated with skin glands and together they may function in male territorial behaviour and/or sex recognition. Brush-like clumps of stiff hairs are sometimes found

protruding from the centre of the facial gland (Fig. 2.7) in males of the genus *Hipposideros* or from the gular sac of the molossid genus *Platymops*. Other molossids have an erectile crest of hairs on top of the head that develops during the reproductive season.

Specialized hairs also include those with a sensory or tactile function. These are whisker-like hairs found on the muzzle or other facial regions. The noseleaves of the rhinolophids and hipposiderids often have a distinct pattern of tactile hairs (Fig. 2.7). Sensory hairs are also found on the tip of the tail or on the uropatagium. In the Molossidae, there are special spoon-shaped tactile hairs on the outer and inner toes of the foot.

Since hair is non-living, it is susceptible to wear and bleaching. Thus, it is replaced periodically by a process called moulting. Whereas other mammals may have two moults in a year, bats appear to moult only once a year. This is usually accomplished in late spring by males and non-reproducing females. Reproductive females delay moulting until after the young are weaned and lactation ceases. Brown and reddish-orange colour phases have been reported in some species of bats. However, in most cases, the brown individuals are males and/or non-reproductive females with fresh new pelage and the reddish individuals are lactating females with old bleached pelage.

In adult bats the annual moult usually follows a specific pattern (Fig. 2.12). On the back, moult centres first appear on top of the head, shoulder region, and on the rump. On the venter, moult usually starts as a band on the throat. From these initial centres, the moult spreads and progresses to all parts of the body. At first, this involves vascularization of the skin, but soon new hair growth begins. In other mammals, the new coat of hair is usually well developed before the old hair starts to fall out or is sloughed off in patches. In the few bats that have been studied, the old hairs apparently drop out as new hairs grow into place. Thus, there is usually no outward sign that the bat is moulting. This, too, has contributed to the confusion concerning colour phases in bats. In a population there may appear to be a brown phase and a red phase, with no apparent moult. However, in most of the species with reported colour phases, individuals have been discovered with old red hairs and new brown ones.

Coloration

Unlike ornately coloured birds and insects that rely on visual perception of colour and nuances of colour patterns in their social behaviour, bats do not appear

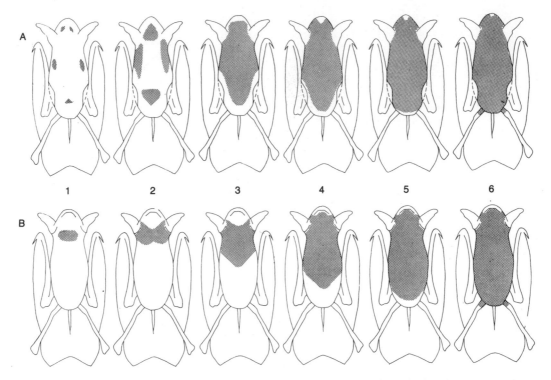

Fig. 2.12 Generalized diagram of moult progression in Pteronotus parnellii *(Mormoopidae). The dorsal views (A) and ventral views (B) depict moult progression (shaded area—stages 1–6) from left to right.*

to use these features in their social organization or individual discrimination. Striking colours and colour patterns are uncommon among bats and they are mostly varying shades of brown and grey. Although uncommon, some bats do have very striking and attractive colours and colour patterns. Many of these bat species roost outdoors in trees or other exposed shelters. Bats that inhabit arid to semi-arid regions tend to be pale in colour, whereas species from humid tropical and subtropical regions tend to be darker in colour. We have already commented on the colourful pigmentation that may be found in the flight membranes.

The overall colour or hue of the fur is determined by the genetically controlled distribution of colour pigments in the medulla or cortex of the hair. These pigments are usually distributed in bands of colour along the strand and there may be as many as three, perhaps more, such bands on any one hair. The individual hair filaments of drably coloured bats are usually monocoloured or bicoloured with light or dark bases and black or brownish tips. The coloration of some species may be enhanced by a lighter coloured band(s) either at the base of the hair filament or somewhere along the hair shaft. Depending on the intensity and extent of dark and light bands on such hairs, the overall colour of the fur may be pale or

appear mottled or multicoloured. Some species such as the vespertilionid Hoary bat (*Lasiurus cinereus*) and the Silver-haired bat (*Lasionycteris noctivagans*) have a white frosting on the fur that gives it an attractive grizzled or hoary appearance. This frosted effect occurs when monocoloured white or white-tipped hairs are scattered among the other coloured hairs of the fur. Whereas most mammals have pale coloured bellies, often in sharp contrast to the colour of the back, bats usually are uniformly coloured. Their bellies may be somewhat paler than the dorsal coloration.

In contrast to the norm among bats, there are several entirely white bats. These are the Ghost bat (*Diclidurus virgo*–Emballonuridae) and the White bat (*Ectophylla alba*–Phyllostomidae); both inhabit the tropics of the New World. In addition, both of these bats combine yellowish pigmentation on the ears or other membranes for a distinctive general appearance. Neither species is albinistic and true albinism has been reported only rarely in bats. Likewise, all black or melanistic individuals are rare among bats.

Some species of New World leaf-nosed bats such as *Uroderma bilobatum*, *Vampyrops helleri*, and *Chiroderma salvini*, have a single white stripe extending from the back of the head, down the centre of the back, to the rump. The White-lined bats of the New

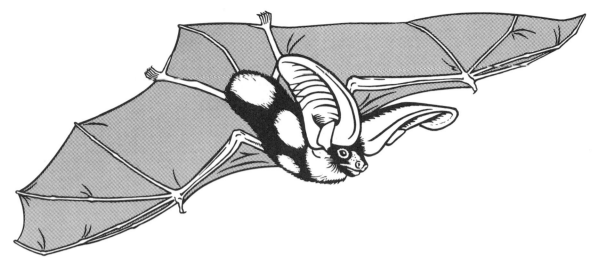

Fig. 2.13 North American Spotted bat (Euderma maculatum–Vespertilionidae). Also note large ears.

World emballonurid genus *Saccopteryx* have a pair of white stripes on the back. A light to dark black stripe is found on some species of Tube-nosed fruit bats (*Nyctimene*). In the Broad-striped Tube-nosed bat (*Nyctimene aello*), that lives in Papua New Guinea, this stripe has been expanded into a 15-20 mm wide black band. In contrast, the Big-eared Free-tailed bat (*Tadarida lobata*), a molossid from Kenya and Zimbabwe, has a small white interscapular spot, and white shoulder spots or patches of specialized hair (epaulettes) are found in some phyllostomids and among epomophorine pteropodids.

Among the most attractively coloured bats are those that have pure white spots, stripes, and/or a combination of these on jet black fur. The North American Spotted bat (*Euderma maculatum*) is one such species (Fig. 2.13). It has three large white spots arranged in a triangular pattern on the back. Its long, pale pink-coloured ears and pale flight membranes add to the contrasting colour pattern of this desert bat. The African Pied bat (*Glauconycteris superba*) has a similar colour pattern of white spots and bars on a black background. Indeed, nearly all species of the vespertilionid genera *Glauconycteris* and *Chalinolobus* have extraordinarily attractive colour patterns.

INTERNAL FORM

Skeletal system

The development of flight is undoubtedly the most important evolutionary innovation acquired by bats. Not unexpectedly, many of the adaptive features related to this unique mode of locomotion are reflected in the structure and organization of the skeletal system (Fig. 2.14). We have previously discussed many of these adaptations as they relate to the structure of the appendicular skeleton (wing and hindlimb). The axial skeleton (cranium, vertebral column, ribs, sternum, and pelvis) also reflects flight adaptations as well as other specializations unique to bats. Overall, the major modification to the chiropteran skeletal system involves the reduction in size and thickness of skeletal elements and the promotion of a sturdy yet lightweight support system.

The size and shape of the cranium varies widely among the many species of bats (Fig. 2.15). Its form is more directly related to food habits and feeding styles than to specific modifications for flight.

Perhaps the most obvious feature of the cranium is the dentition. Bats, like most other mammals, have a fully differentiated set of teeth. These include: incisors (front teeth), canines, premolars, and molars. All except the molars are deciduous; that is, they are replaced once in the life span of the individual. The deciduous teeth are often called milk teeth because these are the first teeth that suckling young acquire. In most mammals, the milk teeth are more or less similar in appearance to the permanent teeth which replace them sometime at or near adulthood. In bats, these teeth are highly specialized and unique in form. They are tiny, sharp-pointed, and hooked spicules that erupt in the mouth of young bats either prior to birth or very shortly thereafter. These specialized teeth enable the young bat to cling more effectively to the teat of its mother while she is carrying her offspring in flight. The claws on the feet and thumbs are also well-developed at this time. As the young bat

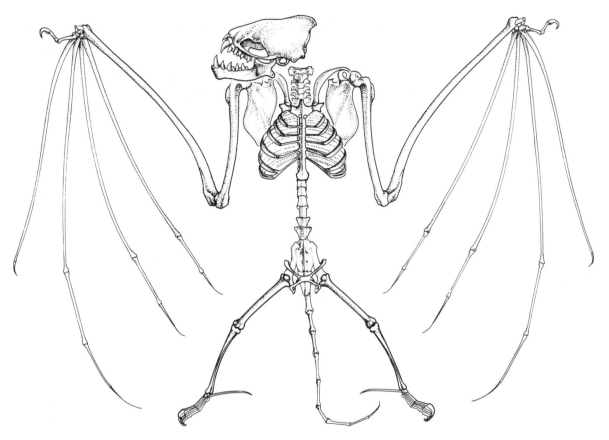

Fig. 2.14 Bat skeleton.

matures and is able to survive on its own, the milk teeth are replaced by the permanent dentition.

The basic or primitive number of teeth for placental (eutherian) mammals is 44. These are: three upper and lower incisors (I), one upper and lower canine (C), four upper and lower premolars (P), and three upper and lower molars (M). This representation includes a count of only one side (one-half) of the dentition and, thus, must be doubled to account for all teeth in both upper and lower jaws. The number of teeth found in a particular species or group of species is usually written as an abbreviated notation called the dental formula. The dental formula for the primitive eutherian mentioned above would be: I 3/3, C 1/1, P 4/4, M 3/3 = 44. The largest number of teeth found in bats is 38. This means that bats are specialized compared to primitive mammals by having lost six teeth. This reduced dental formula is illustrated by the vespertilionid genus *Myotis* with: I 2/3, C 1/1, P 3/3, M 3/3 = 38. Note that one upper incisor and one upper and lower premolar are absent. The fewest number of teeth found in any bat is 20. This occurs in the Common vampire (*Desmodus*

rotundus) with: I 1/2, C 1/1, P 1/2, M 1/1 = 20. Again, notice that two upper and one lower incisors, three upper and two lower premolars, and two upper and lower molars are lost. Another interesting variation in dental reduction is shown by the Tube-nosed fruit bats (*Nyctimene*) with: I 1/0, C 1/1, P 3/3, M 1/2 = 24. Notice the complete loss of lower incisors and nearly complete loss of upper molars. There are over 50 dental formulae for bats, which highlights their wide diversity of dental adaptation. These modifications always involve incisors, premolars, and/or molars; all bats have a full complement of canines. As might be expected, there are many intermediate dental formulae and there are also many possible ways to acquire the same number, but different complements of teeth. For example, 30 teeth is a common number, but it is accomplished in 13 different ways. Related genera and families of bats tend to have similar patterns of tooth loss. The amount of dental variation in bats far exceeds that of all other groups of mammals. On occasion there is also some individual variation in the number of teeth. Among Old World fruit bats, for example, the Blossom bat (*Syconycteris australis*) may

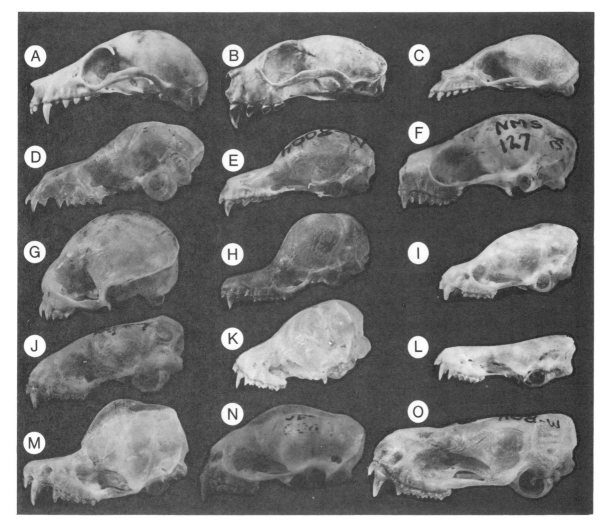

Fig. 2.15 Variation in the shape of the cranium. A, Melonycteris melanops *(Pteropodidae);* B, Nyctimene major
(Pteropodidae); C, Phyllostomus discolor *(Phyllostomidae);* D, Macrotus californicus *(Phyllostomidae);* E, Erophylla
sezekorni *(Phyllostomidae);* F, Uroderma bilobatum *(Phyllostomidae);* G, Centurio senex *(Phyllostomidae);* H, Natalus
stramineus *(Natalidae);* I, Pipistrellus angulatus *(Vespertilionidae);* J, Antrozous pallidus *(Vespertilionidae);*
K, Nyctophilus microtis *(Vespertilionidae);* L, Tylonycteris pachypus *(Vespertilionidae);* M, Miniopterus tristis
(Vespertilionidae); N, Molossus ater *(Molossidae);* O, Eumops perotis *(Molossidae).*

have four or five cheek teeth (premolars and molars) in the upper jaw and five, six or seven lower cheek teeth, while Anchieta's fruit bat *(Plerotes anchietai)* has similarly four or five upper cheek teeth but five or six in the lower jaw. Additionally, one pair of the usual four lower incisors of this species may be missing. In microchiropterans the tiny anterior upper premolar normally found in the vespertilionid genus *Pipistrellus* may be absent, while in the closely related genus *Eptesicus* the reverse may occur. In another vespertilionid genus, *Myotis*, the absence of the small second premolars may vary among individuals or in some cases is apparently characteristic of the species.

As in *Pipistrellus* there may be rarely a small supernumerary premolar crowded into the toothrow. Other aspects of the dentition will be discussed in Chapter 4.

Another variable aspect of the cranium is the size and shape of the braincase which directly reflects the size and shape of the brain (Fig. 2.15). Studies on mammals have shown that brain size is generally a direct function of body size. Thus, the size of the braincase, and the head in general, reflects the overall size of the body of the bat. The primary function of the braincase is to protect the brain from possible injury. Since it is also the site of attachment for the temporal muscles which are involved in closing the jaws and chewing of food, its relative surface area is also an important consideration. Frequently, a prominent flange-like sagittal crest may be present on the dorsal midline of the cranium (Figs. 2.15M-N and 2.16A-C). Such a crest is present as a low to moderately well developed blade in many species. It is especially well developed in carnivorous or fish-eating bats or other large-sized bats that eat large beetles. A similar, but transverse lambdoid crest may be present on the rear portion of the braincase. Both of these crests provide an increase in surface area for the attachment of the temporal muscles. Occasionally, both sagittal and lambdoid crests may be drawn posteriorly past the rear margin of the braincase. This causes some fibres of the temporal muscles to be longer which consequently lengthens the effective lever arm of the jaw and provides a more forceful bite. The Hairless bat (*Cheiromeles torquatus*), the American False vampire (*Vampyrum spectrum*), and some large-sized species of Tomb bats (*Taphozous*) have such an arrangement in addition to heavy jaws. These are both features of a powerful biting mechanism (Fig. 2.16A-B, E). It is interesting to note in passing that similar crests are found in lions and tigers as well as many other large, powerful carnivores. In the vampire bats, the cranium is smooth and lacks any crests (Fig. 2.16D) but it is inflated and highly arched giving it the same general appearance as the carnivorous species just mentioned. This provides for the attachment and lengthening of the temporal muscles whose biting force is thereby focused on the blade-like canines and incisors.

Another departure from the normal shape of the braincase occurs among some species of Old World fruit bats (Pteropodidae) and, to a lesser extent, in some New World leaf-nosed bats (Phyllostomidae). In these, the braincase is deflected (bent) downward, often at a marked angle from the longitudinal axis of the skull (Fig. 2.15A). The most extreme cases of this deflection are found in the Pteropodidae. This has the same effect of lengthening some of the fibres of the temporal muscle. In this case, however, the force of the bite is not focused near the front of the mouth (at or near the canines), but is concentrated on the grinding teeth (molars).

The zygomatic arches are another component of the chiropteran cranium which may also reflect feeding adaptations. Typically, these are thin bars of bone that form an arc from just above the last upper molar tooth to a point just in front of and above the ear region (Figs. 2.15 and 2.16). In humans, this is called the cheek bone. The zygomatic arches serve as the attachment sites for the masseteric (chewing) muscles. These arches may be extremely fine and filamen-tous or even partially absent in some of the small delicate insectivorous species (Fig. 2.15D-E, L). In large bats that capture and chew hard-bodied insects such as beetles, or in some fruit-eating species, these bones are stout and well developed. They may be arched upward or widely flared, in either case lengthening the effective lever arm of the muscles they support. Occasionally they may have large flanges that provide additional surface area for the attachment of the masseteric muscles (Fig. 2.16C-D, G).

The lower jaws of bats also express a variety of forms depending on the food habits of a particular species. The length of the lower jaw may reflect the degree to which the dentition has been reduced. Long jaws generally have more teeth, whereas shorter jaws have fewer teeth. This is not entirely true, however, as pteropodids have generally long jaws but the teeth are often widely spaced along the length (Figs. 2.15A and 2.16G). In the nectar-eating phyllostomids (Glossophaginae) the jaws are quite elongated and the teeth are reduced both in size and number. This is also true in the nectar-eating pteropodids (Macroglossinae). The depth of the jaw ramus varies widely depending on the hardness or coarseness of food items. Thin and long-jawed species usually eat soft-bodied insects (flies and moths) or they may eat nectar or pollen (Fig. 2.16F-G). Short and thick-jawed species usually eat hard-bodied insects or vertebrate prey or they may eat tough-skinned or coarse, pulpy fruits (Fig. 2.16A-C, E). The jaw of the vampire (Fig. 2.16D) is also quite stout as it must bear the force of inflicting a substantial wound.

The rostral portion of the cranium is usually moderately long and pointed in most bats (Fig. 2.17A-B). In these the toothrows usually are attenuated (pointed) anteriorly. This is thought to be the primitive condition for bats. In the Old World fruit bats (Pteropodidae) there appears to be a trend toward shortening the rostrum. Short 'pugged' noses are found in the Dog-faced fruit bats (*Cynopterus*), Short-nosed fruit bats (*Penthetor lucasi*), and the Tube-nosed fruit bats (*Nyctimene* and *Paranyctimene*). In the microchiropteran family Emballonuridae, the rostral region is usually short and broad. In addition, sinuses in the rostral portion of the maxillary bone may be greatly inflated, thus further contributing to the broadening of the nose region. In the genus *Cheiromeles* (Molossidae), the nose is short (Figs. 2.16A and 2.17C) and straight-sided; the toothrows are only slightly attenuated anteriorly. The highest degree of facial shortening occurs among the fruit-eating leaf-nosed bats (Phyllostomidae) of the subfamily Stenodermatinae. Of these, the Wrinkle-faced bat (*Centurio senex*) is the most extreme (Figs. 2.15G

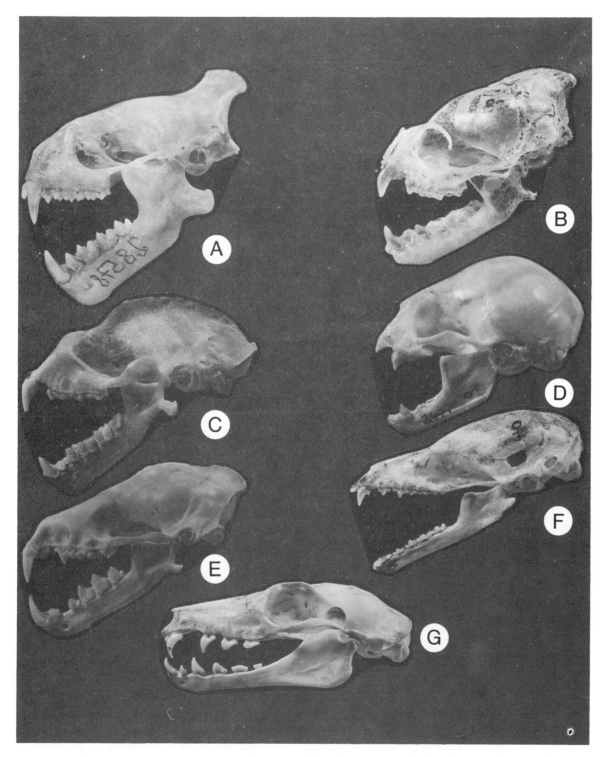

Fig. 2.16 Lateral views of cranium and lower jaw showing variation in cranial shape and sagittal crests. A, Cheiromeles torquatus *(Molossidae); B,* Taphozous saccolaimus *(Emballonuridae); C,* Hipposideros diadema *(Hipposideridae); D,* Diaemus youngi *(Phyllostomidae); E,* Vampyrum spectrum *(Phyllostomidae); F,* Leptonycteris curasoae *(Phyllostomidae); G,* Epomophorus anurus *(Pteropodidae).*

and 2.17D). In these bats, the nose is almost flat and the toothrows are curved into a flattened arch. A similar but less extreme tendency to shorten the rostrum is also found among genera of the microchiropteran family Vespertilionidae. The molossid *Tadarida gallagheri* from Zaire has greatly inflated rostral swellings similar to those of emballonurids, while in the Mouse-tailed bats (Rhinopomatidae) and the Old World leaf-nosed bats (Hipposideridae) the rostrum is swollen, or broadened and sometimes slightly raised by the inflation of its interior compartments. In the Horseshoe bats (Rhinolophidae) the anterior part of the rostrum is inflated dorsally by paired swellings that merge to form a distinctly dome-like structure. Rostral swellings such as these may be connected with the emission of the high frequency sounds used by these bats in acoustic orientation (echolocation).

The form and structure of the premaxillary bones varies more in bats than in any other group of vertebrates except, perhaps, some bony fishes and snakes. The reasons for this variation are not fully understood. The paired premaxillary bones carry the upper incisors and typically they are fused to the maxillary and palatal bones by vertical nasomaxillary and horizontal palatal branches, respectively. In addition, the two members of the pair may be fused together at the midline. The typical condition is found among noctilionid, mormoopid, phyllostomid, and molossid bats. In three families (Rhinopomati-

dae, Craseonycteridae, and Emballonuridae), the palatal branches of the premaxillary bones are greatly reduced. The denticulous nasomaxillary branches of the premaxillaries articulate (not fused) in a groove on the front of the maxillary bone. The members of the pair may be independent and unfused (Emballonuridae), fused on the midline below the nasal aperture (Rhinopomatidae), or fused above and below the nasal aperture (Craseonycteridae). A condition similar to that found in the Emballonuridae exists in the Megadermatidae, but the nasomaxillary branch of the premaxillary is extremely reduced (thread-like) and all incisors are absent. These tiny bones are frequently lost when the cranium is prepared for study and this has led some bat biologists to conclude wrongly that they are absent in this family. In the Rhinolophidae and Hipposideridae, the nasomaxillary branches are absent and all that remains of the premaxillary bones are the paired palatal branches that jut forward between the large canine teeth. These bones are fused together but their fusion to the palatal bone is rather weak and they may be flexed upward. A similar arrangement is encountered in the Nycteridae, although these bones are somewhat larger in size in this family. In the remaining vespertilionoid families, the palatal branches are lost and the nasomaxillary portions of the premaxillary bones are solidly fused with the maxillary bones. In addition, the two members of the pair of premaxillaries are widely separated (unfused) at the midline. This

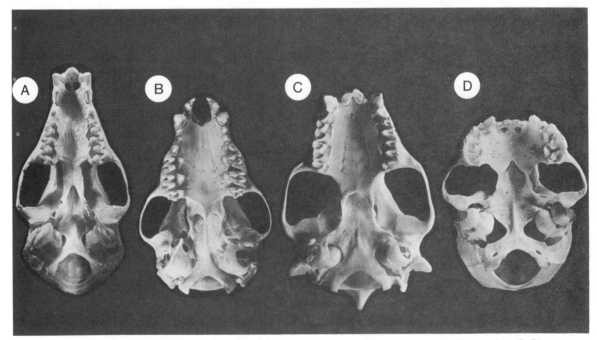

Fig. 2.17 Palatal view showing modification of nose and toothrows. A, Micronycteris hirsuta *(Phyllostomidae); B,* Pizonyx vivesi *(Vespertilionidae); C,* Cheiromeles torquatus *(Molossidae); D,* Centurio senex *(Phyllostomidae).*

results in a deep U-shaped cleft at the front of the cranium (Fig. 2.17B).

The post-cranial axial skeleton of bats reflects modifications more typically associated with flight. The bodies of bats are relatively short (Fig. 2.14). This is expressed in the antero-posterior compression of the individual vertebrae of the vertebral column. Not only are the vertebrae compressed, but their articular surfaces fit snugly together thereby greatly restricting their individual movement. In some families (Nycteridae, Rhinolophidae, Hipposideridae, Megadermatidae, Molossidae, and some species of the Vespertilionidae), the last cervical (neck) vertebra is fused solidly to the first thoracic vertebra. In the Hipposideridae, this fusion incorporates the second thoracic vertebra as well. The first and second thoracic vertebrae are fused in the Thyropteridae. In several other families there is extensive fusion of the lumbar (lower back) vertebrae. These include the Craseonycteridae, Hipposideridae (part), Mormoopidae (part), Natalidae, and Furipteridae. The sacral (hip) vertebrae are also fused for the most part. These fusions in the axial skeleton promote the rigidity and limited movement of the main body axis which facilitates flight.

The rib cage and sternum are other portions of the axial skeleton. The rib cages of bats are proportionately larger than those of other mammals of comparable size. In addition, they are considerably broader and deeper than those of other mammals (Fig. 2.14). The ribs themselves are markedly broadened and those in the anterior portion of the rib cage nearly touch. In hipposiderids, there is considerable fusion in this region.

The sternum (breastbone) is T-shaped in most bats (Fig. 2.14). The manubrium (anterior element of the sternum) is greatly enlarged. In hipposiderids the manubrium is fused with a number of the ribs and the entire complex is shield-shaped or plate-like. Often there is a short keel-like flange on the manubrium. The remaining sternal elements are usually fused into a single flat bar. The expanse and degree of fusion of the rib cage and the sternum all contribute to providing a solid surface on which the enlarged flight muscles attach.

The scapula (shoulder blade) is an important component in the wing skeleton of bats. In birds, this bone is long and narrow. In most mammals, the scapula is triangular or subtriangular in shape. It is roughly rectangular in bats, presumably to accommodate the attachment of the flight muscles (Fig. 2.14). The scapula is anchored to the massive sternal complex by the long and slightly bowed clavicle (collar bone).

Above we commented on the unusual modifications of the hindlimb. The rotation of the femur is also reflected in the shape of the pelvic bone. The ilium or innominate bone is rotated so that the gluteal surfaces (attachment sites for the gluteus muscles) are directed upward rather than to the side as in terrestrial mammals. The acetabulum (articular socket for the femur) also faces dorso-laterally.

Muscular system

Of all the internal systems of vertebrates, the muscular system is perhaps the most adaptable. Thus, while bats have a mammalian muscular system, there are many marked differences between the muscle arrangements found in bats and those of terrestrial mammals. These differences involve the relative sizes of muscles as well as their attachments and functions. In terrestrial mammals, the limbs are postured beneath the body and are nearly vertical to the ground. The modes of locomotion used by terrestrial mammals are varied, but most rely on an antero-posterior movement of the limb. This movement requires the interaction of muscles that move the limb back and forth. In bats, the wings stretch out to the sides of the body and move in an up-and-down manner. This requires the interaction of a somewhat different set of muscles than are used by terrestrial mammals. In addition, bats possess five muscles that do not occur in any other mammals. These all extend into and are involved with controlling the flight membranes. They are: M. occipito-pollicalis, M. coraco-cutaneus, M. humeropatagialis, M. plagiopatagii, and M. depressor ossis styliformis. The latter muscle is rigged between the calcar and the ankle and facilitates the spreading of the uropatagium. These and other flight muscles will be considered in more detail in Chapter 4.

The muscles that are not involved in flight are essentially similar to those of other terrestrial mammals. These include the jaw and head musculature which as noted above is influenced by the dietary habits of bats.

Nervous system

The nervous system of bats has not been studied extensively. Nonetheless, the structure and organization of this system seem to reflect modifications relating to flight adaptations and those involved with orientation in the environment. The apparent differences between the two suborders of bats (Mega- and Microchiroptera) have been the focus of most of the studies to date. As is the case with many other aspects of chiropteran form and structure, the nervous system exhibits both primitive and specialized features.

The nervous system of bats and other vertebrates may be divided into two functional units. These are the central nervous system (brain and spinal cord) and the peripheral nervous system (ganglia and nerves). Very little is known about the peripheral nervous system.

The brain of bats is variable in size and this seems to be closely associated with body size. Other variations in the brain relate to differences in diet, locomotion, and mode of orientation. The brain may be divided into two basic parts: the forebrain (cerebrum or neocortex); and the hindbrain (cerebellum and medulla oblongata or brain stem). Generally speaking, the forebrain is much enlarged in the Megachiroptera, whereas the hindbrain is well developed in the Microchiroptera (Fig 2.18). The phyllostomids (Microchiroptera) have a rather large forebrain and are, therefore, somewhat exceptional in this regard. The forebrain consists of the olfactory lobes and the neocortex. Mammals, as a group, are distinguished from all other vertebrates by having a well-developed neocortical region. The neocortex is enlarged to accommodate the location of many nerve centres that are either absent or were formerly located in the hindbrain of other vertebrates. One of the nerve centres that is found in the neocortex is that associated with vision. This seems to account for the large neocortical regions found in megachiropterans which rely heavily on visual orientation rather than acoustic orientation (echolocation) as used by microchiropterans. Phyllostomids also have large eyes as well as a well-developed sense of smell (olfaction) the nerve centres of which are also located in the neocortex. The enlargement of the neocortex is generally regarded as a specialized condition and, indeed, higher Primates (including man) also have large cerebral hemispheres. Microchiropterans have a neocortical region, but it is less well developed and in these bats the hindbrain is rather large. The nerve centres associated with acoustic orientation are found in this region of the brain. Also, most of the motor control centres for flight are housed here. In many

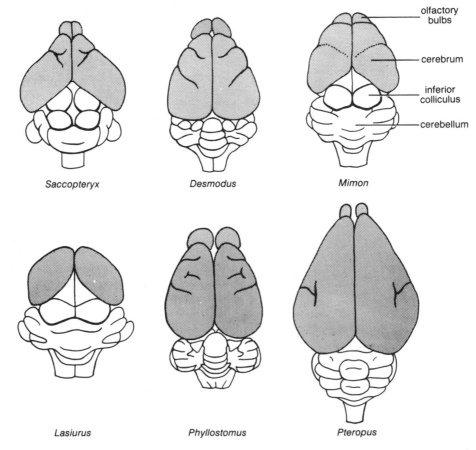

Saccopteryx   Desmodus   Mimon

olfactory bulbs

cerebrum

inferior colliculus

cerebellum

Lasiurus   Phyllostomus   Pteropus

Fig. 2.18 Diagrammatic view of the brain in Saccopteryx *(Emballonuridae),* Desmodus, Mimon *(both Phyllostomidae),* Lasiurus *(Vespertilionidae),* Phyllostomus *(Phyllostomidae) and* Pteropus *(Pteropodidae).*

microchiropterans (except phyllostomids), the olfactory lobes are very small. We shall discuss additional aspects of the brain in Chapter 8.

The spinal cord of bats is greatly shortened; that of microchiropterans is perhaps the shortest known among mammals. In *Pteronotus parnellii* (Mormoopidae), the spinal cord ends at the level of the twelfth thoracic vertebra and in *Artibeus jamaicensis* (Phyllostomidae) at the eighth or ninth thoracic vertebra. This is roughly equal to approximately half the length of the human spinal cord. The general reduction of the locomotory function of the hindlimbs seems to account for this marked truncation in the spinal cord of bats. In humans and other mammals there is an enlarged swelling in the upper portion of the spinal cord called the cervical enlargement. Many ganglia and nerves associated with the movement and control of the arm enter and leave the spinal cord at this swelling. In bats, the cervical enlargement begins just behind the brain and extends for nearly half the length of the shortened spinal cord. This, of course, reflects the influence of having wings and flight. There are also some interesting differences in the spinal cords of mega- and microchiropterans. Lying along each side of the spinal cord are a series of ganglia that receive peripheral nerves and shunt these by way of the dorsal root into the spinal cord. Nerve impulses travelling along these nerves enter the grey matter of the spinal cord where their information is transmitted to the brain and back out to the peripheral regions as an action response via the ventral root. The entry and exit of dorsal and ventral roots, respectively, differs between the two suborders. A large mass of white matter (dorsal funiculus) wedges into the top portion of the spinal cord in megachiropterans and other mammals. As a result the dorsal root enters the spinal cord in a dorso-lateral location (Fig. 2.19). The dorsal funiculus is deeply embedded in the spinal cord of microchiropterans and the dorsal root enters at the dorsal midline of the cord (Fig. 2.19). This latter condition is unique among mammals and therefore appears to be a specialized adaptation of microchiropterans. The functional ramifications of these two distinctive types of spinal cord are not known.

Circulatory system

Compared to the extremely diverse evolutionary radiation in the chiropteran body form, the known modifications in the circulatory system seem to have been rather conservative. Most of the changes relate to functional requirements associated with flight or concern thermoregulatory adaptations reflecting the development of daily torpor and hibernation in some

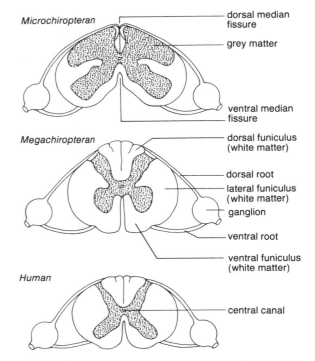

Fig. 2.19 Diagrammatic cross-sectional views of the spinal cord of bats compared to that of a human. See text for discussion.

species. These specializations will be discussed in Chapters 4 and 6.

The most prominent organ of the circulatory system is the heart. Bat hearts are extremely large relative to their body size. The heart of the European mouse-eared bat (*Myotis myotis*–20 g) is nearly three times larger than that of a laboratory mouse of equal weight. As a direct result of body shortening, the position of the heart in bats has been modified. In the generally long-bodied megachiropterans the heart is located near the centre of the chest and only slightly tilted to the left. However, in the short-bodied microchiropterans, the heart is rotated and assumes a nearly transverse (sideways) position. Overall, the hearts of bats tend to be more elongated than in other mammals.

Heart rates (beats per minute) are strikingly higher in bats than in most other mammals. However, there is considerable variation depending on the environmental temperature and the state of activity of the individual. The heart rate of active (flying) pteropodids at a thermoneutral temperature (approx. 30°C) ranges between approximately 100-400 beats min^{-1}. In microchiropterans, heart rates as high as 900-1000 beats min^{-1} (*Eptesicus fuscus*) are frequently recorded. During daily torpor, heart rates in microchiropterans drop to 40-80 beats min^{-1}, whereas in hibernating individuals, heart rates as low as 20 beats min⁻¹ have been reported.

In addition to large hearts and high heart rates, bats have correspondingly impressive stroke volumes (the amount of blood pumped by the heart in one beat cycle). The right ventricle is large in size and this appears to be directly related to the large quantities of blood pumped during any single stroke. Furthermore, the internal structure of the heart, primarily the arrangement and muscularity of anti-backflow valves, correlates with these increased stroke volumes.

The coronary circulation (the heart's blood supply) is much larger and more expansive in bats than in other mammals. Likewise, the pulmonary (lung) circulation is greatly enhanced compared with that of other mammals. These features of bats make them good medical research models for understanding human pulmonary and cardiovascular problems.

Other than special modifications of the arteries, veins, and capillaries in the flight membranes, the peripheral circulation of bats does not appear to be much different from that found in other mammals. There are fewer, but larger, vessels in the shoulder region of bats than are found in other mammals.

Bats have the unique ability to control (regulate) the quantity of blood circulating in the wing at any particular time. This control of blood dispersal and movement in the extensive capillary network of the wings is accomplished with special shunts or valves. Depending on the circumstances, the circulation of blood in whole segments of the wing may be cut off or greatly reduced. This ability is especially important since the wing membranes are excellent heat exchangers and the controlled reduction or increase of heat loss provides an efficient means of regulating the internal body temperature of these warm-blooded animals. For example, during flight, a considerable amount of excess heat is generated and this is dissipated (radiated) across the flight membranes by opening the capillary shunts. On the other hand, these are closed to conserve heat while the bat is at rest.

Digestive system

In general organization, the digestive system of bats is essentially like that of other mammals. However, the wide variety of food habits found among bats is reflected in the anatomy of some components of this system, especially the stomach and intestine. The digestive system of bats has not been well-studied, but a fair amount of information exists for the New World leaf-nosed bats (Phyllostomidae). This micro-

chiropteran family also exhibits the widest range of food habits, including nearly all of those found in bats. A more detailed discussion of the digestive system will be presented in Chapter 5.

Urinary system

Relatively little is known with regard to the urinary system of bats. This system includes the kidneys, ureters, urinary bladder, and urethra. Its primary function is to maintain a physiological balance (homeostasis) between water and salt (various electrolytes) concentrations in the body. In other mammals, the urinary system (primarily the kidneys) responds (is adapted) to different diets (watery or salty) and/or differences in habitat, especially arid or semi-arid regions where free-standing, fresh drinking water is at a premium. The mammalian kidney is highly specialized for water conservation compared to those of other vertebrates and it produces a high concentration of urea in the urine.

There is little to indicate that the kidneys of bats are markedly different from the generalized mammalian kidney. As noted above, the bodies of bats are generally shortened and we noted that the position of the heart was altered by this modification in body proportion. The kidneys are located somewhat lower in the abdomen of bats than in other mammals and the right kidney may be positioned slightly higher than the left. The right kidney may even be embedded in a dimple in the right lateral lobe of the liver.

Bats occupy a number of different and diverse habitats (see Chapter 9) and, as a result, face a variety of water/salt balance situations. For example, after a blood meal, vampire bats face three important water problems. The first two are physiological and, initially, concern excretion of the excess water in the blood meal which would overly dilute the concentration of body fluids. Later, the digestion of the high protein content of the meal requires the conservation of water. The third concern is aerodynamic and also requires the excretion of excess water in order to lighten the overall weight of the bat so that it can fly. Fruit-eating species also need to dispose of excess water. The protein content of their foods is not as high as that of blood and, since most inhabit tropical regions of the world where free-standing drinking water is usually available, water conservation is not so much of a problem.

Another interesting physiological problem is found in the Fishing bat (*Pizonyx vivesi*) that lives in the arid regions of Baja California. These bats often forage over marine lagoons and eat marine fish that are generally high in salt content. In addition to this, these bats also face the normal problems of desert environments; that is, water conservation. Like many other desert-dwelling mammals, the kidneys of *Pizonyx* are specially adapted to conserve water and excrete a highly concentrated urine. These bats may even drink seawater which would fatally tax the kidneys of normal mammals.

Bats that hibernate also face a water conservation problem. This is alleviated somewhat by selecting hibernation sites that have a high relative humidity, thus reducing loss of water by evaporation. Also, metabolic water is released into the system as the fat stores are broken down during this period of lower metabolic activity (see Chapter 6). The kidneys of these bats are adapted to conserve and use metabolic water during this period of inactivity. Some hibernating bats such as the Western pipistrelle (*Pipistrellus hesperus*), which inhabits the southwestern deserts of the United States, frequently awaken during intermittent warm spells and drink water to replenish their depleted reserves. During these periods of arousal, they may also feed on any insects that happen to be out.

Reproductive system

The wide diversity of reproductive patterns found among bats (see Chapter 7) contrasts with the anatomical aspects of their reproductive systems that are basically the same as those in other eutherian mammals. There are, however, a few noteworthy specializations that might be mentioned here.

The ovaries and ovulatory processes in bats are essentially like those of other mammals. The ovaries of hibernating bats with delayed ovulation develop special glandular tissue around the mature ovum and maintain it through the hibernation period. Ovulation and fertilization in these bats occur early in the spring at the time of emergence or shortly before. In others, ovulation and fertilization occur prior to entering hibernation and the unimplanted embryo is maintained in a quiescent state through hibernation. In still others, copulation occurs prior to or during hibernation and the uterine mucosa is specially adapted to maintaining the live sperm throughout the hibernation period.

Like most mammals, nearly all bats ovulate from either ovary; that is, ovulation is symmetrical. In some bat species, ovulation is restricted to either the right or left ovary. Right-sided ovulators include members of the Vespertilionidae, Natalidae, Rhinolophidae, Hipposideridae, and Mormoopidae. Left-sided ovulators include members of the Molossidae and Megadermatidae.

In all mammals, the ovaries produce specific hormones (estrogens and progesterones) that travel in the blood to the uterus where they cause specific physiological and morphological responses. In the few bats that have been examined, there is a special set of blood vessels that runs between the ovaries and uterus and facilitates the transport of these hormones.

The uterus of bats is generally bicornuate; that is, there is a single and distinct uterine body which divides into two uterine horns. In all of the New World leaf-nosed bats (Phyllostomidae), except *Macrotus*, *Micronycteris*, and the vampires (Desmodontinae), the uterine horns are completely fused to form a single or simplex uterine body. A similar uterus is found in higher Primates such as man. The asymmetry mentioned with regard to the ovaries is also found in the functional development of right and left uterine horns. Typically, in eutherian mammals, fertilization occurs in the oviduct and the blastocyst (zygote or embryo) migrates to the uterus where it implants and undergoes its gestational development. There are generally no specializations in the oviducts. In bats, the walls of the oviduct, in which fertilization occurs, become highly glandular and the blastocyst may pass some time therein before moving to the uterus and subsequent implantation. Implantation sites are variable among bats, but are usually near the oviduct/uterine junction.

The mammary glands of bats are paired and located in the pectoral region as in Primates. However, their position is more axial (nearer the armpit) than in Primates. The location of the mammae in this region may relate to aerodynamic considerations involving placement of the centre of gravity when the female is carrying nursing young. Several families (Rhinopomatidae, Craseonycteridae, Nycteridae, Megadermatidae, Rhinolophidae, Hipposideridae, and some species of the Vespertilionidae) have an additional pair of teats located in the inguinal region (near the groin) just above the external genitalia. These do not secrete milk, but serve as a holdfast for the young bat while the mother is in flight.

The male reproductive tract of bats is less specialized than that of the female. The testes may be seasonally active or active year-round. They may descend into a discrete scrotum or they may be maintained in an abdominal pouch. In vespertilionids, the testes descend into a scrotal sac that has been incorporated into the uropatagium on either side of the tail. The penis, which becomes erect through vascular engorgement is pendulous in most bats and similar in appearance to that of Primates. It varies considerably in size and structure, reaching an extreme in *Scotoecus* where its length may approach that of the upper leg bone. Among other vespertilionids the penis of Hemprich's Long-eared bat

(*Otonycteris hemprichi*) has a curious appearance, the glans (head) expanded vertically to project between two lateral swellings, with a third dorsal swelling above and behind it, while in the New Guinea Brown bat (*Philetor brachypterus*), the penis is similarly complex, the glans emerging from a swollen preputial structure that dorsally bears a small cushion-like pad covered with short, stiff bristles and projects ventrally as a preputial flap or fold. In some species, again especially in the Vespertilionidae, the prepuce may contain erectile tissue that facilitates copulation in these bats. Many bat species have a reduced os penis or baculum (penile bone); its form may be simple or complex.

The origin and evolution of bats is poorly understood. A meagre representation in the fossil record is often cited as the prime reason for the lack of evolutionary knowledge concerning bats. The first fossil bats were recognized in the early part of this century. Since then approximately 30 fossil genera (representing eleven families) have been described. In addition, 37 living genera have been discovered in the fossil record, many of these occurring in bat faunas of the Ice Age. These 67 genera contain 40 fossil bat species and another 92 species that are still living; again, many of the latter lived in the Ice Age. The fossil record of bats extends back to the early Eocene (approx. 60 million years ago), and has been documented (earliest record in parentheses) on five continents: Europe (Eocene), Africa (Oligocene), Asia (Miocene), North America (Eocene) and South America (Miocene). Thus, we see that representation is not the problem as bats are relatively well represented as fossils. The problem concerns two difficulties: firstly, the majority of the fossils are highly fragmentary (isolated jaws and teeth in most cases) and secondly, all fossil bats, even the oldest, are clearly fully developed bats and so they shed little light on the transition from their terrestrial ancestor.

It is perhaps fortunate that the best preserved bats are the oldest known. These include: *Palaeochiropteryx*, *Archaeonycteris*, and *Hassianycteris* from the early Eocene of West Germany and *Icaronycteris index* from the early Eocene of North America. Although primitive in some features, these bats possessed some characteristics that are as advanced as some of the modern living species of Microchiroptera, the suborder to which they are assigned. *Icaronycteris index* was thought to be intermediate between the two chiropteran suborders Megachiroptera and Microchiroptera. This notion was based largely on the fact that the index finger of the wing has a strongly developed claw, a feature found in most living megachiropterans, but absent in all living microchiropterans. *Icaronycteris*, as well as the other Eocene fossil bats, was an insectivore as judged by the presence of a set of distinctively insectivorous teeth.

The Megachiroptera are first represented in the fossil record in the Oligocene (35 million years ago) of Italy by *Archaeopteropus transiens*. It has all of the post-cranial features of a pteropodid including a clawed index finger. The latter feature has led many bat biologists to the mistaken conclusion that Eocene bats like *Icaronycteris* were ancestral to the pteropodids. All of the known Eocene fossil bats are well-differentiated microchiropterans and undoubtedly were *not* the ancestors of the Megachiroptera. All existing evidence suggests that bats evolved very early and have changed relatively little compared to other mammals as a group. For example, bats were flying at about the time when the ancestors of horses were no larger than a dog and had many toes. Bats were catching insects in the prehistoric evening when the ancestors of man himself were but early primates no larger than the lemurs that occur today on Madagascar. It is suspected that bats originated much earlier, perhaps in the early Paleocene or mid- to late Cretaceous (70-100 million years ago).

Any scenario concerning the origin and early evolution of bats as well as other organisms is clearly speculation. The evolutionary events leading to these modern animals and plants are so remote that the truth of their nature is unknowable. What, then, can we reasonably conjecture about the origin and evolution of bats? We know that species evolve through the process of descent with modification. Descendants with special features may have a selective advantage over descendants that do not have such features. These features are produced by mutations that may cause only subtle changes and thus evolution would be expected to proceed slowly (microevolution). Recent studies are showing that mutations may involve larger portions of an organism's genetic make-up and evolution may thereby proceed by fast leaps and bounds (macroevolution).

The origin and evolution of bats revolves primarily around the origin of the wing and the development of its use in sustained flight. Wings have evolved independently at least three times among terrestrial vertebrates: pterosaurs (Reptiles); birds (Aves); and bats (Mammalia). These wings all vary in their structure and it is safe to say that they probably evolved under different circumstances. The pterosaur wing is perhaps most similar to that of a bat. Both are membranous and both rely upon modified fingers to

Fig. 3.1 Palaeochiropteryx tupaiodon *from Grube Messel, near Darmstadt, West Germany (Middle Eocene). Dark mass in abdomen is fossilized stomach contents containing moths.*

support the flight membrane. There are a number of other parallels between pterosaurs and bats such as marked body shortening; involvement of the hind-limb in the flight membrane; use of dorsal and ventral thoracic muscles to operate the wing; and various modifications of the tail. Pterosaurs apparently were a moderately successful group for many millions of years and were moderately diversified as they ranged in size from about equal to a medium-sized bat with a wing span of 500-800 mm to the incredibly large *Quetzalcoatlus northropi* with a wingspan of 11-12 metres. Little is known regarding the habits of pterosaurs and there is some question as to whether they were capable of sustained flight (see Chapter 4); the larger species must surely have been gliders. Some pterosaurs are found in association with ancient seashores and it is thought that they may have launched from high sea cliffs, or at least heights above the ground, much like some modern sea birds. Launching from the ground would seem to be

aerodynamically impossible for pterosaurs. Pterosaurs died out with the dinosaurs and many other groups at the end of the Mesozoic era.

The circumstances under which birds developed their wings were clearly different from those that governed the origin and evolution of the wing in bats and presumably pterosaurs. There is no doubt that birds are the descendants of bipedal dinosaurs. Unlike either bats or pterosaurs, birds retained a well-developed terrestrial hindlimb. The forelimb of birds was already freed from its role in terrestrial (quadrupedal) locomotion prior to the evolution of the wing. The impetus to develop wings and flight in birds may have been to pursue a predaceous mode of life, to escape predators, for dispersal, or a combination of these factors. Certainly, aerial insectivory has been important in the adaptation and diversification of birds, but this particular feeding strategy has not been the central focus in their speciation.

The evolutionary impetus for the origin and adaptation of all of these winged vertebrates, especially bats, must be viewed in the overall context of developing global ecological complexity. Reasonable conjecture places the origin of bats in the early Paleocene or perhaps late Cretaceous. At this time, flowering plants (angiosperms) were at their initial stages of diversification. Also, by the close of the Cretaceous, the anthophilous (pollen-eating) insect orders Coleoptera (beetles), Diptera (flies), and quite probably the Lepidoptera (moths and butterflies), all potential prey of insectivorous bats, were well established in an evolutionary and ecological sense. At this prehistoric time, eutherian and metatherian mammals were well differentiated and both were expanding into numerous terrestrial niches. If tooth structure is any indication, most of the terrestrial niches available to early mammals were geared to some form of insectivory or carnivory. Generalized herbivory or omnivory would certainly have been within the functional potential of these small warm-blooded vertebrates.

Bats (at least the Microchiroptera) are thought to be the descendants of small quadrupedal and arboreal insectivores that may have possessed gliding membranes. The living mammalian Order Insectivora (shrews, moles, hedgehogs, etc.) is often cited as the definitive ancestor of bats. This is unlikely inasmuch as these living insectivores are highly specialized and bear little resemblance to bats. However, it is possible that bats (at least the Microchiroptera) and Insectivora share a remote common ancestor and are therefore closely related.

The argument for an arboreal ancestor of bats as opposed to a strictly terrestrial ancestor seems reasonable in light of the fact that all volant mammals launch from trees or heights above the ground. There are no known mammals that normally run along the ground and then leap into the air to glide and/or fly. Some bats such as the Pallid bat (*Antrozous pallidus*) and the Common vampire (*Desmodus rotundus*) are capable of taking off from the ground, but normally launch from heights. All gliding mammals, such as 'flying' squirrels, marsupial sugar gliders, and the Colugo (Order Dermoptera) have flexible membranes that extend from the sides of the body and stretch between the appendages to some extent. Only in the case of the Colugo does this gliding membrane also include a webbing between the fingers and toes; also, the uropatagium is well developed. It is not hard to imagine a patagial arrangement, similar to that of the Colugo, in the early ancestor of bats. Indeed, the hypothetical ancestors portrayed in Figure 3.2 and the supposed scheme of bat wing development shown in Figure 3.3 are derived from a Colugo-like model. Up-and-down movement of the hand portion of the

gliding surfaces allow the Colugo to make changes in direction and possibly increase its lift potential during any one gliding sortie. Lengthening of the digits would allow for an increase in this portion of the patagium. Ultimately, however, digital elongation would have reached a point of diminishing returns in that further progression would have produced an ungainly and clumsy structure that necessitated movement as a wing rather than use as a fixed gliding device. Evolution at this transitional stage of chiropteran development may have proceeded rapidly. Having successfully traversed this critical point in wing development, further refinements probably related to such parameters as manoeuverability and speed. Claws were probably lost very early from the tips of the third, fourth, and fifth fingers. However, the claw on the index finger may have been retained for grasping or climbing; it was ultimately lost in all microchiropterans and in a few mostly small-sized megachiropterans.

The movement of the modified forelimb as a wing would not have required any great modification. The mammalian chest and back musculature are 'preadapted' for such a use. The hand wing of bats also is a much more efficient way of controlling and shaping the flight membranes than that of pterosaurs.

Whereas the notion of an arboreal, gliding ancestor of bats seems to be a reasonable conjecture, the supposed insectivory of this ancestor may be open to question. This notion is founded on the fact that the primitive dentition of Mesozoic mammals was modified in the earliest bats to a dilambdodont condition with a marked W-shaped ectoloph (see Chapter 5). Such a tooth allows an increase in the number of shearing facets that are usually associated with insect-eating. Certainly, all Eocene fossil bats and the majority of the Microchiroptera (except some phyllostomids) have such teeth.

The dentition of the Megachiroptera is bizarre and highly specialized for crushing pulpy fruit. It is difficult, if not impossible to derive the dentition of these fruit-eating bats from the insectivorous teeth with W-shaped ectolophs. Indeed, no megachiropteran has teeth that even remotely resemble the teeth of insectivorous mammals. Even among the phyllostomids (microchiropterans that have also incorporated frugivory in their wide diversification of food habits) some species retain recognizable features of the insectivorous dentition.

If the Megachiroptera and Microchiroptera shared a common ancestor, and they must in order to be considered closely related, then that ancestor must have had somewhat less insectivorous teeth and presumably a broader range of food preference. The alternative to this notion has far reaching evolution-

Fig. 3.2 Hypothetical arboreal, insectivorous ancestor of bats (Microchiroptera) showing patagial development.
Opposite. *Hypothetical intermediate ancestor of bats (Microchiroptera) showing further development of the wing. (Smith, 1977).*

ary ramifications that are not widely accepted among bat biologists. That is, the Megachiroptera and Microchiroptera are not closely related and that wings and flight have developed twice, independently, in these two groups of flying mammals. While this idea may seem far-fetched at first, there is some evidence in its support. The Megachiroptera share a number of special features with the Primates; these features are not also shared with the Microchiroptera. These shared features include various aspects of the brain and central nervous system; musculature; skeletal system (including portions of the wing); circulatory system; and reproductive system. In addition, the curious frugivorous dentition of megachiropterans is more readily derived from that of early Primates that were also arboreal. The Colugo appears to be more closely related, in an evolutionary sense, to the

Primates and Megachiroptera than it is to the Microchiroptera. Regardless of the relationships between the two suborders, adaptively each has pursued markedly different life styles–the microchiropterans having exploited the vast potential of night-flying insects.

Another aspect associated with the origin and evolution of bats is the development of acoustic orientation (echolocation). The origin of this complex navigational system is not well understood. Some insectivores (shrews) appear to possess the ability to produce these high frequency sounds. High frequency sounds are also produced by young mice in which they are thought to be used to establish mother-infant identity, and by cetaceans (whales and dolphins). In bats, this type of echolocation is highly complex and found exclusively among the Microchir-

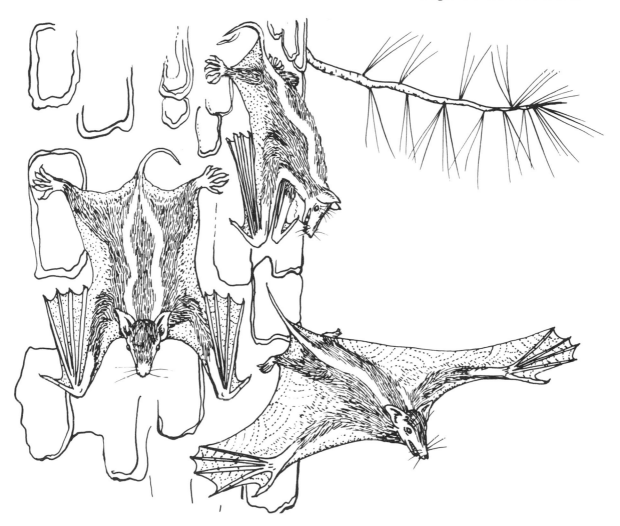

optera. These sounds are produced in the larynx and are very sophisticated, varying in length and intensity as well as through many frequencies (10-120 kHz) and harmonics (see Chapter 8).

Among the Megachiroptera, none but *Rousettus* (and perhaps *Epomophorus*) has developed echolocation. These fruit bats use a crude system of clicks made by the rear portion of the tongue rather than in the larynx. Those who ascribe to the view that mega- and microchiropterans share a common ancestor propose that echolocation was lost very early in the evolution of megachiropterans. Given the benefits that such an orientation system would have in the nocturnal niche and the degree to which this system has developed in the Microchiroptera, it seems highly unlikely that megachiropterans would have lost such an adaptation only to redevelop it in another form.

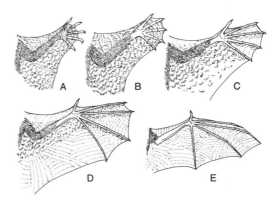

Fig. 3.3 Hypothetical progressive stages in the development of the wing of bats. A–C, early stages in which emphasis was on gliding. D, an intermediate stage in wing development. E, a fully developed bat wing. (Smith, 1977).

There can be little doubt that the ancestor of mega-chiropterans (whether shared with microchiropterans or not) did not possess echolocation and that its occurrence in *Rousettus* is an independently-derived feature.

It is supposed that the arboreal ancestor of the Microchiroptera had the ability to produce high frequency sounds and receive and interpret, perhaps crudely, the information contained in the echo. Although it is highly speculative and beyond proof, echolocation sounds may have evolved as a prey-distracting attack cry emitted as these small arboreal insectivores leaped off branches in pursuit of passing prey. Another notion is that these sounds were first used in mother-infant recognition. Whatever the case may have been, these early ancestors of microchiropterans may have laid in ambush, tracking and plotting intercepts of flying insect prey; some living megadermatids and species of *Hipposideros* employ this mode of hunting. With the development of a fully functional wing, taking this sophisticated tracking and pursuit system into the air would not have required major modifications. It is true that a fruit does not employ evasive action to avoid capture and one might not expect echolocation to be particularly useful to a fruit-eating bat. Nonetheless, such a system would be of extreme benefit in navigating in darkness through the tangle of branches and limbs in search of ripe fruit. Indeed, the fruit-eating micro-chiropterans (Phyllostomidae) retain a sophisticated echolocation system.

Evolution within the Microchiroptera and the relationships among the various families remains poorly understood. Since the late 1800s, the living microchiropteran families have been grouped together into four superfamilies. These are as follows: Emballonuroidea (Emballonuridae, Rhinopomatidae and Craseonycteridae); Rhinolophoidea (Rhinolophidae, Hipposideridae, Nycteridae, and Megadermatidae); Phyllostomoidea (Phyllostomidae, Mormoopidae, and Noctilionidae); and Vespertilionoidea (Vespertilionidae, Natalidae, Furipteridae, Thyropteridae, Mystacinidae, Myzopodidae, and Molossidae). These superfamilies are thought to be natural groups; that is, including all of the descendant species of a common ancestral species. This may be the case, although there are serious doubts that the Vespertilionoidea is indeed a natural group as currently understood. For instance, recent work suggests that the Thyropteridae would be better aligned with the Phyllostomoidea. Much of the concern regarding the relationships of the Microchiroptera, and the Chiroptera in general, has focused on defining the 'most primitive' family or group of families. The Rhinopomatidae and Emballonuridae, both members of the Emballonuroidea, have been implicated as 1) the 'most primitive' bats, and 2) the ancestors of all other microchiropterans. On the other hand, the Vespertilionoidea are generally considered to be the 'most advanced' bats. This opinion also seems flawed.

Unlike any other group of mammals, bats present the student of evolution with a tremendously complicated adaptive mosaic. This results from three major adaptive regimes that interact on bat morphology. These are: 1) adaptations for flight and styles of flight involving mostly skeletal and muscular features; 2) adaptation for food capture and feeding styles involving dental, skeletal (cranial), muscular, and alimentary features; 3) adaptations for orientation (visual vs. acoustic) involving mostly neural features. Most certainly, there are other important adaptive considerations (physiological, reproductive, behavioural, etc.), but these three regimes pretty well determine what a bat will look like.

These adaptive regimes may interact dependently or they may evolve independently. The outcome is very much akin to the situation involving taxi cabs in Peru in the early sixties. Peru imported a number of different kinds of old scrapyard cars (Fords, Chryslers, Plymouths, etc.), all non-functional and of 1930-40 vintage, from the United States. The industrious Peruvian cab drivers set about assembling a functional taxi cab. They took engines out of Fords, fenders and bumpers from other makes, and bonnets and boots, doors, windscreens, etc. from still other models. The result was a functional taxi cab, but one that was unrecognizable, from any viewpoint, as a particular make of car.

In bats, this adaptive mosaic has produced species with primitive wings and flight styles, highly advanced food capture and feeding styles, and intermediate orientation devices. On the other hand, there are others with highly advanced wings and flight styles, primitive food capture and feeding styles, and sophisticated orientation systems. If one were to focus on any one of these adaptations or related features, one could without much doubt judge any family to be 'most primitive.' Such a practice would produce a notion of relationship, but one hinged on the particular primitive adaptive feature selected as most important. There is a better than even chance that such a scheme would not portray the true genealogical relationships of the bats in question. The unravelling of this chiropteran mosaic rests in determining the special (advanced) features shared by various groups of bats. Unfortunately, the breadth of knowledge concerning such features is not yet sufficient to provide such an answer.

For the moment, there appear to be two basic

lineages of microchiropterans. One includes the Emballonuroidea and Rhinolophoidea. The other includes the Phyllostomoidea and Vespertilionoidea; all but one (*Hassianycteris*) of the early Eocene bats seem to be related to the last two groups. The Emballonuroidea are differentiated, for the most part, in the Old World; a group of emballonurids has been isolated for some time and diversified in the New World tropics. The Rhinolophoidea are found exclusively in the Old World. The Phyllostomoidea are restricted, at least in so far as currently understood, to the New World tropics. The Vespertilionoidea are generally worldwide in distribution with some families and/or groups of species isolated in particular regions. For example, the families Natalidae, Thyropteridae, and Furipteridae are restricted to the New World tropics, and the family Myzopodidae is restricted to Madagascar (with an Ice Age occurrence in East Africa). The megachiropteran family Pteropodidae is restricted to the Old World tropics.

Bats are unique among mammals in their possession of wings and their ability to move about under true sustained flight. Unlike birds, which can simply fold their wings when not in use and walk about on relatively unspecialized hindlimbs, bats are essentially incapable of alternative forms of locomotion when not in flight. Of course, all bats can scurry about to some extent and vampires (Desmodontinae) are quite agile, walking on their elbows and wrists. However, by virtue of their anatomical adaptations for flight, bats have largely abandoned their terrestrial (i.e., quadrupedal) locomotory abilities. No other volant animal, except the reptilian pterosaur, has made such a drastic and complete modification in its locomotory style.

Among vertebrates, the ability to achieve true sustained flight must be considered a rare event having occurred only in birds and bats. Pterosaurs (prehistoric reptiles that became extinct at the end of the Mesozoic Era, about eighty million years ago), possessed wings that in some respects resembled those of bats. Indeed, some of the smaller species of pterosaurs may have been capable of flapping flight, although most probably used their wings to soar. Insects (invertebrates) are the only other group of animals to possess the capability of sustained flight.

The rarity of adaptations for true flight, among vertebrates at least, appears to be associated with a wide array of morphological, physiological, and aerodynamic factors that preclude aerial locomotion by most vertebrates. However, once developed, flight confers a distinct evolutionary advantage to those organisms that possess it. The capture and exploitation of flying insects as a food source (aerial insectivory) is absolutely restricted to flying birds and bats. In microchiropteran bats, the development of acoustic orientation (echolocation) has allowed them to carry this unique foraging strategy into the nocturnal realm. Other benefits accrued from flight include: escape from predators; expanded daily foraging ability; potential for dispersal across barriers that are otherwise insurmountable, or nearly so, by non-flying, terrestrial animals; long-distance, seasonal migration; and occupation of roosting and nesting sites not readily available to non-flying animals. To say that flight was the sole factor accounting for the diversification and radiation of birds and bats would be much too simplistic. Nonetheless, flight apparently has been a primary contributing factor in the evolution and success of these groups.

Regarding pterosaurs, the evolutionary innovation of wings in this group of reptiles certainly must have conveyed some of the benefits noted above. However, the known diversity of this group (20 genera) does not approach that of either birds or bats and, indeed, the lack of further refinements of the wing for sustained flight may have contributed to the demise (extinction) of these 'flying' reptiles. Competition with birds is often cited as the cause for the extinction of pterosaurs. This seems unlikely and we suspect that the failure of pterosaurs concerns more the inadequate design and structure of their wing and its limited use as an efficient flying device.

There can be little doubt that the possession of wings and flight were important in the evolution and adaptations of insects. But, the loss or absence of wings in many species and/or life stages of species (larvae, pupae, etc.) as well as an array of other modes of locomotion, would seem to suggest a role of lesser importance for flight in insects than in flying vertebrates.

The importance of aerial locomotory adaptations is further illustrated by the number of vertebrates that have acquired the ability to glide. Gliding usually results in the loss of altitude over a given distance, is never sustained, and, therefore, cannot be categorized as true flight. On the other hand, adaptations for gliding are much less drastic, in terms of anatomical modifications, and less rigorous, in terms of aerodynamic constraints. Gliding, among non-mammalian vertebrates, occurs in 'flying' fish, several 'flying' frogs (*Rhacophorus* and some hylids), several 'flying' lizards (*Draco*–Agamidae and *Ptychozoon*–Gekkonidae), and a 'flying' snake (*Chrysopelea*–Colubridae). In flying fish, the pectoral fins are enlarged, and various sorts of webbing between the toes and lateral abdominal flaps of skin are utilized by flying frogs and the flying gekko. *Draco* and the flying snake utilize special, extendible ribs and associated membranes in their gliding adaptations.

Gliding adaptations occur in several groups of mammals and include: Sugar gliders (Order Marsupialia); the 'Flying' lemur or Colugo (Order Dermoptera); and several different groups of 'Flying' squirrels (Order Rodentia). All have an elastic membrane along the sides of the body joining the legs. The fingers and toes of the Sugar gliders and all Flying squirrels are not webbed and there is little or no membrane in front of the forelimb or between the hindlimbs. The tail remains free, for the most part, and it is usually quite bushy, except in Scaly-tailed flying squirrels. Colugos have more extensive membranes including: webbing between the digits of both the hand and foot; between the forelimb and neck (propatagium); and between the hindlimbs including the tail (uropatagium). Like most bats, Colugos have difficulty locomoting when on the ground, but, in the air, they are quite graceful and capable of gliding flights of several hundred metres. The general resemblance of the rigging of the flight membranes of Colugos to that of bats has prompted the notion that bats evolved through a 'colugo-stage' in their evolution. Unlike Colugos, the toes of the foot are not webbed in bats and the thumb is largely free. During gliding sorties, Colugos move their hands in an up-and-down fashion, not flapping as in bats, but they are able to effect various turns and other altitudinal manoeuvers. While Colugos are not the ancestors of bats, they do appear to be closely related to bats, especially to the Megachiroptera.

ANATOMICAL REQUIREMENTS FOR FLIGHT

True sustained flight requires three basic anatomical modifications for versatility and efficiency. First and foremost is the development of a wing of sufficient length and with specific aerodynamic characteristics that will allow it to lift and support the body and associated payloads (e.g., food or prey items; reproductive products such as developing embryos or suckling young, etc.) during flight activity. Secondly, sustained flight requires a source or means of propulsion, and thirdly, the body must be sufficiently streamlined to permit efficient flight that is both aerodynamically feasible and metabolically economical.

The events leading to an historic winter morning (December 17, 1903) at Kill Devil Hills, near Kitty Hawk, North Carolina, when man first achieved true sustained flight, are an interesting history of the human experience and the development of powered flight. A wealth of mythological writings and drawings portray man's early dreams of flight. Most of our first experiments with flight involved attempts to emulate the flapping flight of birds with various

bird-like wings and contraptions. Some early, would-be aviators even covered their bodies with feathers in the hope that these would provide the essence of flight. The successful pathfinders settled on fixed-wing devices and experimented with gliding and soaring. The next task was to find a sufficient, non-flapping means of powering their winged aircraft. This, of course, led to various propeller-like contraptions and eventually to the successes at Kitty Hawk. Man's breakthrough with flight is no less an evolutionary event than the development of flight by animals. Note the rapid radiation and diversification of aircraft in the past eighty years and the marked influence of these on the social and technological aspects of human culture.

Although man took many cues from flying animals, especially birds, in his development of powered flight, he has not been able to equal the dynamics and manoeuverability of flapping flight. In all truly flying animals, including insects, the wing serves a dual function. It provides the aerodynamic lifting qualities required for flight as well as the driving, propulsive force for sustained, powered flight. The wings and general appearance of pterosaurs, bats, and birds are similar. However, each of these animals has developed these structures in drastically different anatomical ways and the flight characteristics of these respective groups are markedly different.

Pterosaur wing

Like birds and bats, the wing of pterosaurs evolved through the modification of the forelimb. Proceeding outward from the shoulder joint, the proximal portion of the pterosaur wing consisted of the humerus and the fused radio-ulna (Fig. 4.1A). Next came the compacted carpals of the wrist, and then the elongated metacarpals of four digits (2-5), closely bound together. At this level of the wing, three fingers (2-4) were more or less normal in appearance, free of the wing proper, and directed forward, these presumably were used to grasp and climb about. Beyond this level of the wing were four elongated phalanges of the fifth finger. [There is some confusion regarding the loss of the thumb (digit 1) or the fifth finger. Some authors identify the long finger of the pterosaur as the fourth digit thereby implying the loss of the fifth finger. Others identify the four existing fingers as we have (2-5) and imply the loss of the thumb. On the anterior portion of the wrist region, there is an elongated and recurved bone (pteroid) that supports a propatagial flight membrane. It is difficult to determine, with certainty, whether or not this is a modified thumb or an osteological innovation. Without evidence to the contrary, we regard it as the thumb.] Like the bones of

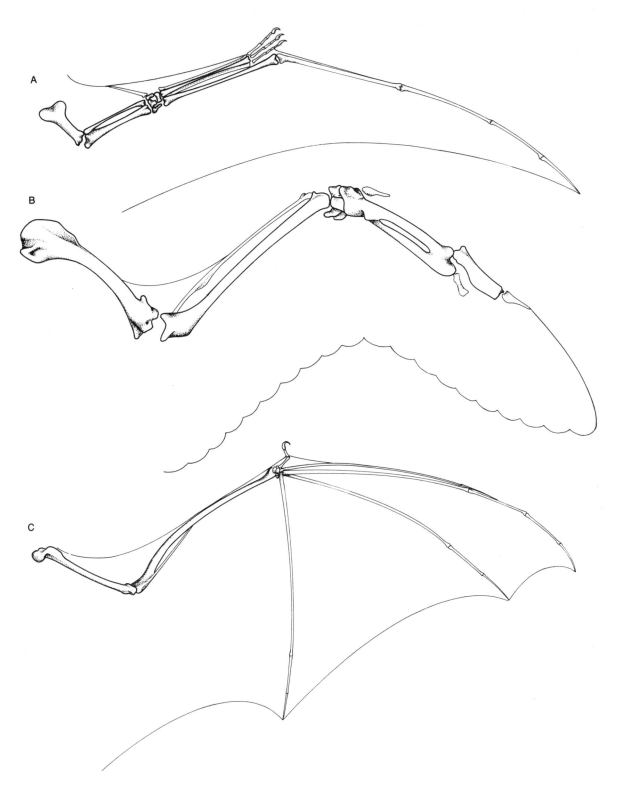

Fig. 4.1 A, Wing of pterosaur; B, wing of bird; C, wing of bat.

birds, the bones of pterosaurs were extremely light-weight and hollow or pneumatic (air-filled). The bones of bats are not pneumatic but those of the wing skeleton are very slender which contributes to low weight.

The main flight membrane was attached on the rear margin of the long wing spar that consisted of the arm and elongated fifth finger as described above. This membrane attached along the sides of the body and the elongated hindlimb. Such an arrangement surely would have hampered the mobility of pterosaurs on the ground. As noted above there was a propatagium attached to the pteroid (thumb?) bone. The control of this flight membrane was accomplished by a pteroid muscle that attached to the anterior margin of the humerus.

The wing of pterosaurs was similar to that of bats in that it was an elastic, membranous wing as opposed to a feathered wing as found in birds. The control of wing camber (see below) would have been extremely limited in the pterosaur wing. Flexion of the body axis could have produced varying degrees of curvature. Presumably, there was a muscle, an elastic tendon, or a combination of these that extended from the tip of the fifth digit, along the rear edge of the wing, to the leg region. Such a device would have permitted the control, by tension, of the trailing edge of the flight membrane thereby causing different degrees of cross-sectional curvature of the wing. The wing of pterosaurs had reduced adaptive potential, mostly relating to the limited control of camber. Other aspects of pterosaur anatomy leave considerable room to doubt that their wings were capable of vigorous flapping movement as characterized by birds and bats. Gliding or dynamic soaring was probably the extent of their flight ability. As we noted earlier, this inadequate aerodynamic design may have been an important factor in their extinction.

Bird wing

The wing of birds is perhaps the most radical and novel structure ever to develop in the evolutionary history of vertebrates. Whereas the wings of pterosaurs and bats may also appear to be rather bizarre structures, they are rather simplistic in their modification of pre-existing structures. The proximal portion of the wing of birds consists of an elongated humerus, followed by separate, well-developed ulna and radius. Beyond these relatively unmodified bony elements, there is a drastic reduction and fusion of bony structures (Fig. 4.1B). Articulating with the radius and ulna is a large carpo-metacarpal bone (composed of fused carpals and metacarpals). The reduced first digit (thumb) articulates on the anterior,

proximal margin of this fused bone. Distally, the much shortened phalanges of the second digit and the vestigial remains of the third digit attach to the carpo-metacarpal.

The main portions of the wing (flight surfaces) are made up of several different kinds of feathers (themselves unique and complex structures) that attach to the rear portion of the main spar of the wing described above. Long, stiff primary feathers attach to the carpometacarpal and phalanges of the second digit. Specialized, primary-like feathers attach to the thumb or first digit; it is usually referred to as the alula. Somewhat shorter, but stiff secondary feathers attach to the ulna. The contour of the upper side of the wing is provided by a series of specialized feathers known as lesser, medial, and secondary coverts. The contour of the underside of the wing is provided by lesser under and greater under coverts. As should be apparent, the cross-sectional shape of the wings of birds is fixed much like that of wings of airplanes. Certainly, man has devised ways of changing the cross-sectional shape of his wings. The point to be made here is that unlike bats, and perhaps pterosaurs to a lesser extent, birds cannot greatly modify the curvature (camber) of their wings. Like pterosaurs and bats, birds also have a propatagial fold of skin in front of the wing, between the shoulder and wrist. A muscle (tensor patagii longus) similar to that found in bats (occipito-pollicalis) and pterosaurs (pteroideus) controls the curvature of this membrane. Changing the shape of this membrane is virtually the only means of wing camber modification in the wing of birds.

The evolution of wings and flight in birds is a much debated topic. Whereas pterosaurs and bats are presumed to have passed through a gliding stage that required a launch site from trees or heights above the ground, the development of bird flight is not so tied to such a progression. An outstanding feature of birds is that virtually all possess a dual locomotory system with wings for flight (some for swimming such as penguins) and hindlegs for normal bipedal walking and running. Indeed, birds are thought to have evolved from already bipedal, reptilian ancestors. Thus, birds could have evolved flight from either the ground or from arboreal situations; the former seems likely.

Bat wing

We have already described the general anatomical aspects of bat wings in Chapter 2. To summarize briefly, almost no part of the forelimb of bats has been reduced or lost. On the contrary, all elements, except those of the thumb, are greatly elongated and very slender; the ulna has been reduced and in most species is restricted to the elbow region (Fig. 4.1C). The pelvis and hindlimbs are much less developed than in birds, and the legs are so totally involved in the support and control of the wing membranes that they have lost the normal quadrupedal ability of other terrestrial vertebrates. As noted earlier, many bats have a membrane (uropatagium) between the legs that often includes the tail or a portion thereof. This permits an increase in the total flight surface area.

PRINCIPLES OF AERODYNAMICS

In simple terms, flight depends on the overall effect of four forces–lift (upward force), drag (resistant rearward force), thrust (forward force), and gravity (downward force)–as air moves over and under the surface of the wing. As we have noted above, wings always have some degree of cross-sectional curvature; that is, they are not flat. Thus, a wing or airfoil may be characterized as being convexly curved on the upper side; the underside may be flattened or somewhat concave (Fig. 4.2). The degree of curvature

or convexity is referred to as camber and the extent to which this curvature can be modified is referred to as 'camberability.' Such cambered flight surfaces have a particular characteristic that permits flight to occur. As a stream of air strikes the leading edge of a horizontal airfoil, it is divided into two layers (Fig. 4.3A). One of these layers flows over the top surface of the airfoil while the other layer passes along the bottom surface of the airfoil; these two layers are reunited when they meet behind the trailing edge of the airfoil. Because of the convex curvature (camber) of the upper surfaces of airfoils, the air that flows over the top side of wings must move faster than the air passing under the relatively flat lower surface. As a result of the faster movement of air on the top side of airfoils, a negative pressure occurs (following Bernoulli's theorem). This negative pressure on the top side of the airfoil causes the wing to rise. The force resulting in this levitation is called lift. Two factors that effect lift in a positive way are: 1) the speed of the air as it flows over and under the airfoil or the speed that the airfoil moves through the air (this is called relative wind); and 2) the degree of convexity or camber of an airfoil. To a point, as these two factors

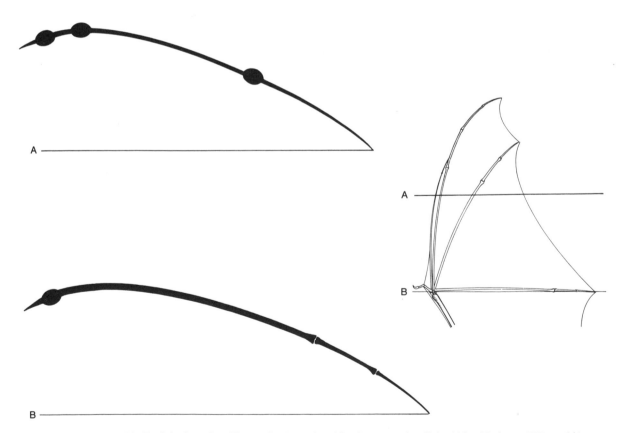

Fig. 4.2 *Cross-sections (A, B) of the bat wing. The camber is produced by the supporting digits (After Norberg, 1972a and b).*

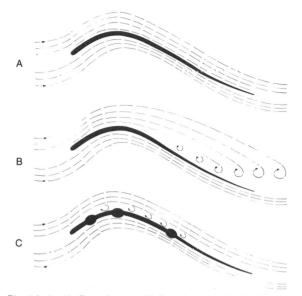

Fig. 4.3 A, Air flow above and below the wing; B, air flow with turbulence above rear of wing; C, the rounded projection of the digits helps to reduce turbulence and drag.

are increased, lift also increases. In fact, there is an inverse relationship (trade off) between these two factors; greater camber permits a particular amount of lift at lower speeds of the air stream.

Another way to effect lift positively without changing the camber or air speed is to change the angle of attack. For example, if we tilt upward, slightly, the previously horizontal airfoil, we have changed the angle of attack. This change, like an increase in camber, causes the air flowing over the top of the airfoil to move faster, thereby causing a greater negative pressure, and so, an increase in lift. However, as we continue to tilt the airfoil upwards (increase the angle of attack), the smooth, laminar flow of air over the wing begins to pull away from the rear portion of the airfoil, thus creating an area of disruptive turbulence. This turbulence erodes the force of lift and it is referred to as drag. Increasing the camber of a horizontal airfoil has the same effect.

Drag counteracts the forces of lift and thrust. Drag force on a wing at a particular angle of attack can be countered by an increase in the speed of the air over the wing or by reducing the wing camber or the angle of attack. If the force of drag is allowed to increase (either by continually increasing the angle of attack, slowing the air stream, increasing the camber of the airfoil, or some combination of these), the turbulence on the upper side of the wing will eventually erode the lifting force to a point where the airfoil will cease to rise. At this point, the wing stalls, the force of gravity takes over and the flying object will fall. Stalling depends on the angle of attack and airspeed.

Birds, bats, presumably pterosaurs, and man all utilize controlled stalling when they land.

The upper surfaces of animal wings are rarely smooth; even the apparently smoothly contoured wings of birds have small irregularities that cause some minor turbulence in the layer of air nearest the wing (boundary layer). The bones and knobbly joints of membranous wings, such as those of bats, also cause minor turbulence. This minor turbulence is beneficial in that it causes the boundary layer of air to be held firmly on the wing surface (Fig. 4.3B-C).

Thus far, we have considered the aerodynamic characteristics of airfoils with regard to camber, angle of attack, and air speed. In addition, the aerodynamic performance and load-carrying capacity of a wing are also determined by its effective area and shape. Wing shapes vary along a continuum from short and broad to long and narrow. These dimensions are expressed in terms of aspect ratio. Aspect ratio is derived by dividing the wing span by its average width or chord. Since the average chord may be impossible to determine, aspect ratios (A) are usually determined by the formula, $A = \text{span}^2/\text{area}$. Long, narrow wings have high aspect ratios, while short, broad wings are low in aspect ratio. Wing loading (WL) is the weight of the flyer distributed over the area of the flight surfaces or WL = total weight/wing area. Since small animals have more surface area in relation to their volume than do larger animals of identical proportions, small birds and bats have relatively low wing loading without having especially large wings. Wings that have a high aspect ratio tend to have high wing loading values, although this is not always the case. High aspect wings generally have high performance characteristics–fast flight, hovering ability, or dynamic soaring ability. Low aspect wings generally have lower loading and are capable of lifting greater weight, are efficient at low speeds, and are more versatile (manoeuverable) than high aspect wings. On the average, bats achieve slightly higher aspect ratios than do birds and wing loading in bats tends to be lower, overall, than in birds.

BAT FLIGHT

The wing of bats may be divided into three discrete areas; each has a particular aerodynamic function. The propatagium is that portion of the flight membrane in front of the wing between the shoulder and the wrist. Its leading edge is controlled (stiffened) by the occipito-pollicalis muscle. When this muscle contracts, the leading edge of the propatagium is stiffened and pulled downward, thereby increasing the convexity (camber) of the leading edge. The plagiopatagium is the large portion of the wing that attaches behind the humerus and elongated radius and stretches between the body and hindlimb to the fifth finger. This portion of the wing is the lift-generating section and its camber is controlled by flexing the body axis and/or the fifth digit. The length of the respective elements of this finger (metacarpal, first and second phalanges) will determine the amount and degree to which the surface area may be cambered. The uropatagium serves to increase the effective lifting area of the wing and operates in conjunction with the plagiopatagium. Also, it may act as an airbrake or, as we noted earlier, a receptacle for catching insects.

The propelling or power-generating portion of the wing is the dactylopatagium. This is the distal section of the wing and it stretches between the second and fifth fingers. The camber of this section of the wing may be changed by flexing the digits. And again, the amount and degree to which this area may be cambered depends on the respective lengths of the metacarpals and phalangeal elements. The membranous areas of the wing are reinforced by many elastic fibres and muscular strands.

These same lift and propulsive areas are present in the wing of birds but as we noted above, the avian wing is less dynamic; that is, incapable of marked changes in camber. However, birds may vary their wing area, aspect ratio, and wing loading by drawing the wings closer to the body. Bats are less able to do this because the elastic and membranous nature of their wings necessitates the full extension of the flight surfaces.

Wing beat cycle of bats

In flight the downstroke (or powerstroke) begins with the wings raised well above the horizontal over the back and extended slightly back and behind the centre of gravity. From this position, the wings are fully extended, having just unfurled from their folded posture in the upstroke (or recovery stroke). As the downstroke proceeds, the wings sweep forward and sharply downward at a high angle of attack. The body axis is convexly curved upward thereby causing the hindlimbs, tail, and uropatagium (in those species that have one) to be bent downward. Midway through the downstroke the plagiopatagium is strongly curved convexly by the air pressure under the wing pushing up on the taut, elastic membrane and by the flexure of the fifth digit. Thus, at this point in the powerstroke, the large plagiopatagial portions of the wings and the strongly cambered body and uropatagium are generating maximum lift. These

lift-generating surfaces retain this posture throughout the remainder of the powerstroke.

During the powerstroke, the dactylopatagium goes through a number of dynamic changes. Since this region of the wings generates the propelling force, these surfaces must generate forward movement. The spinning propeller of an airplane is no less an airfoil than the fixed wings of the airplane that it carries forward. The notable difference is that a propeller blade is oriented vertically in the airstream, whereas the wing is horizontal. Lift produced on the upper surface of the wing causes upward movement, whereas the lift produced on the front surfaces of the vertically oriented propeller causes forward movement. The blades of some propellers are mechanically arranged so that they can rotate at their root (near the hub). This allows the pilot to change the 'pitch' or the angle of attack of the spinning propeller to suit whatever the particular thrust requirements might be. The dynamic changes in the thrust-generating portion of a bat's wing are similar to the pitch modifications of a propeller. Although the dactylopatagium is not a spinning device like an airplane's propeller, its lifting surfaces behave like one, and indeed, these surfaces rotate, not in a vertical plane, but in the horizontal.

An analogy, using the human hand, will help explain the posture (pitch) changes of a bat's 'hand' (dactylopatagium) during the powerstroke. We should note here that thrust is produced during both the powerstroke and the recovery stroke. Note first that the human hand may be rotated (in the horizontal plane) from a 'palm down' posture (pronated) to a 'palm up' posture (supinated). While a bat's hand is not as mobile as the human hand, it is capable of limited pronation and supination. At the start of the powerstroke, the hand, in the pronated position with the top surface tilted forward, is brought forward and down at a sharp angle. Lift generated in this posture will not cause the hand to rise, but instead, to be pulled forward and slightly upward. As the powerstroke continues, the air pressure under the hand (or dactylopatagium) will cause the membrane to billow upwards (enhancing its camber) and also will cause the tip and rear margin to be bent upward, thereby further increasing the angle of attack. To this point, forward lift (thrust) has to be generated on the top surface of the hand (or dactylopatagium).

At the bottom of the powerstroke, the hand is quickly supinated, turned so that the palm faces forward and is tilted slightly rearward. This quick rotation (supination) in a bat's wing is called the 'flick' phase because of its 'snappy', rapid occurrence. The flick phase initiates the beginning of the recovery stroke. Several things happen in the recovery stroke, the most important being the return of the wing to the top of the powerstroke. This must be accomplished with the generation of minimal drag. To do this, large portions of the wing (plagiopatagium) are collapsed or furled and the wings are raised (partially folded) over the back.

At the instant that the hand (dactylopatagium) is flicked forward, two things occur. First, the plagiopatagium is collapsed. During the powerstroke, air has been compressed beneath the entire wing and especially under the plagiopatagium. The supination of the dactylopatagium (to initiate the flick) affects the entire wing and causes the plagiopatagium to supinate slightly. This changes the orientation of the compressed air under the wing from an upward pressure to a rearward pressure. When the plagiopatagium is collapsed, this air pressure is released and it jets rearward causing the bat to be thrust forward. In effect the release of this air pressure acts like a mini-jet engine. Second, as the wing-tip is flicked, it pushes against the compressed air mass that it has generated during the powerstroke. This changes the inertia of the wing-tip and starts it on its way through the recovery stroke. The dactylopatagium does not fully collapse in the recovery stroke; instead it slices at an angle, upward and rearward. Because the wing has been supinated, the palm becomes the top surface. As it is drawn upward and rearward a small amount of forward lift is generated on the palmar surface. In the wing beat cycle, the wing-tip tracks through a figure 8. Thus, as a result of the pronation of the dactylopatagium through the powerstroke and supination through the recovery stroke, the wing-tip is rotated horizontally. Using first the camber of the top side then the camber of the underside, thrust (forward lift) is generated. At the same time, the cambered plagiopatagium, body, and uropatagium are capturing upward lift.

Flight is rarely conducted as a straight and level activity into a uniform, head-on airstream. Thus, manoeuvers such as climbing, diving, and turning are needed and corrections are required to compensate for irregularities or changes in the direction of the airstream. Thus, flying objects must be able to control pitch (up and down rotation), roll (rotation around the longitudinal axis), and yaw (side to side rotation). Airplanes are equipped with various control surfaces (movable or winged airfoils): ailerons in the wings control roll or assist turning; horizontal stabilizers in the tail control pitch and assist climbing and diving; a vertical stabilizer in the tail controls yaw and assists in turning. Co-ordinated (lift efficient or drag-minimizing) manoeuvers are accomplished by the careful manipulation of these mechanical control surfaces by the trained pilot.

Most flying animals do not have the benefit of separate control surfaces to conduct their manoeuvers. These are accomplished by subtle changes in the wing beat cycle or by differentially moving the wings during the wing beat. Birds and bats do have horizontal stabilizers of sorts; the tail or uropatagium. Up and down movement of the tail or uropatagium permits control of pitch. The usually long tail of birds can be moved freely from side to side and thereby control yaw. To a lesser extent, bats can rotate the uropatagium and compensate for changes in yaw.

Take-off

All airplanes require a certain distance or runway length to take off. During the take-off roll, the forward lift from the engine-driven propellers or the thrust of jet or rocket engines pull or push, respectively, the wing(s) through the air until sufficient lift is generated to lift the weight of the aircraft into the air. Most airplanes are equipped with extendible flaps that cause either increased wing chord and area (low aspect ratio), increased camber, or both. This permits greater lift and weight bearing at lower speeds. Were it not for these devices, the lengths of runways at international and military airports would be considerably longer. Helicopters, of course, can take off straight upward and do not require a take-off roll. This is accomplished essentially by attaching the engine to a rotating wing or horizontal propeller.

On the other hand, animal flyers must take off, fly, and land solely by using the lift and thrust generating capabilities of their wings. As we have noted several times, birds have the separate and independent use of the hindlimbs, a luxury not present in bats or pterosaurs. Many birds, such as ducks, albatrosses, and the like, run (or swim) for a distance while flapping their wings, until their wings are able to lift them into the air. Other birds are capable of taking flight directly from the perch or ground.

All bats launch by releasing their hold from the roost or resting site. Some open their wings and accomplish several wing beats before releasing their grip. Free-tailed bats (Molossidae), as a group, have wings of moderate to very high aspect ratios that require faster than normal air speeds to become airborne. Species such as the Greater Mastiff bat (*Eumops perotis*) select roosting sites that are 10 to 15 metres above the ground. When these bats launch, they free fall five to six metres to gain airspeed before they unfurl their wings to take flight. Another rather spectacular instance of free falling, not associated with launching, is used by the Mexican Free-tailed bat (*Tadarida brasiliensis*–Molossidae) upon returning to their roost at Carlsbad Caverns, New Mexico.

These bats approach the cave entrance at about 300 to 400 metres altitude. When they are directly over the entrance, they fold their wings and free fall to about two to three metres above the ground, then snap open their wings and shoot into the cave.

Many bat species are able to take off from the ground (or water surface) by beating their wings until they are airborne. Some ground-foraging species such as the Pallid bat (*Antrozous pallidus*–Vespertilionidae) and the Common vampire bat (*Desmodus rotundus*–Phyllostomidae) regularly take flight by launching from the ground. Vampires do this by moving the folded wing through a typical powerstroke. When the forearms contact the ground, the bat is catapulted into the air. Some forward thrust is gained in the recovery stroke, and with the next powerstroke they are fully airborne.

Landing

The termination of flight is another critical manoeuver for flyers. Whereas take-off occurs under ever increasing airspeeds, landing occurs at ever decreasing airspeeds to a point of stall when the wing will no longer support the weight of the flyer. Normally the wing stops flying at the desired landing point. Airplanes and some birds approach the landing point at a low glide angle, but high angle of attack and low airspeed. Airplanes, again, utilize mechanical structures such as flaps to increase the chord (camber) of the wing to enhance lift at these low speeds. Birds utilize the alula (feathered thumb, see discussion above) as a movable appendage in front of and slightly above the leading edge of the wing. With this structure, they are able to hold or channel the boundary layer of air on top of the wing at higher angles of attack than would be possible without such a structure. Recall that at high angles of attack the boundary layer starts to peel away from the rear portion of the airfoil until the stall occurs. The alula permits higher, stall-free, angles of attack and consequently greater lift at low airspeeds. Large jetliners have similar devices along the leading edges of their wings.

Bats do not normally alight on the ground. Instead, they must land on the ceiling of caves or on branches of trees. Large, tree-dwelling flying foxes (Pteropodidae) land by ungracefully crashing onto the branches or clumps of their companions near the roost site. Once they have landed, they simply crawl to their roosting space and hang upside down. Most bats either hover at the desired landing spot, grab hold, and swing into the typical upside down posture, or some species perform an aerobatic somersault in mid-air in order to gain a holdfast.

FLIGHT MUSCULATURE

The power required for bat flight, like any other mode of animal locomotion, is generated by pairs of muscles or muscle groups arranged in such a way that their actions are antagonistic. This antagonism is required because all muscles are only capable of contracting. These muscles are anchored to relatively immobile attachment sites (origin) and attach (insert) somewhere along a lever arm, usually across a pivotal joint or fulcrum. One pair of muscles or muscle group moves the lever arm in one direction, whereas the antagonistic muscles move it in the opposite direction.

Power and recovery muscles

The flight muscles that pull the wing of the bat through the powerstroke are located on the chest and upper part of the humerus (Fig. 4.4A). The muscles that lift the wing through the recovery stroke are located on the upper part of the back (Fig. 4.4B). The mass of these muscles is located on the body and thereby contributes to the stability of the centre of gravity and does not add to the kinetic weight of the wing proper.

Four large muscles act on the humerus during the powerstroke (Fig. 4.4). These are: M. pectoralis (origin: clavicle and sternum, insertion: proximal humerus); M. clavodeltoideus (origin: clavicle, insertion: proximal humerus); M. serratus anterior (origin: broad band from mid-section ribs one to four, insertion: antero-medial portion of scapula); and M. subscapularis (origin: ventral surface of scapula, insertion: proximal humerus). Most of these muscles act directly on the humerus to drive it downward during the powerstroke. The pectoralis is by far the largest of these, weighing approximately 65 per cent of the combined weight of the other three. However, in relation to the total body weight the pectoralis muscle of bats consistently comprises less than ten per cent of the total weight, regardless of the overall size of the bat. In birds, pectoralis weight/total weight varies considerably and is generally higher than in bats; 12 to 22 per cent among flycatchers, 14 per cent in the Black vulture, and 21 per cent in the Bobwhite quail.

Five muscles or muscle groups are involved in the recovery of the wing (Fig. 4.4B). These are: [trapezius group] M. acromiotrapezius, and M. spinotrapezius (origin: cervical and thoracic vertebrae, insertion: medial surface and vertebral border of scapula); M. rhomboideus (origin: thoracic vertebrae one through seven, insertion: medial border of scapula); [supra-

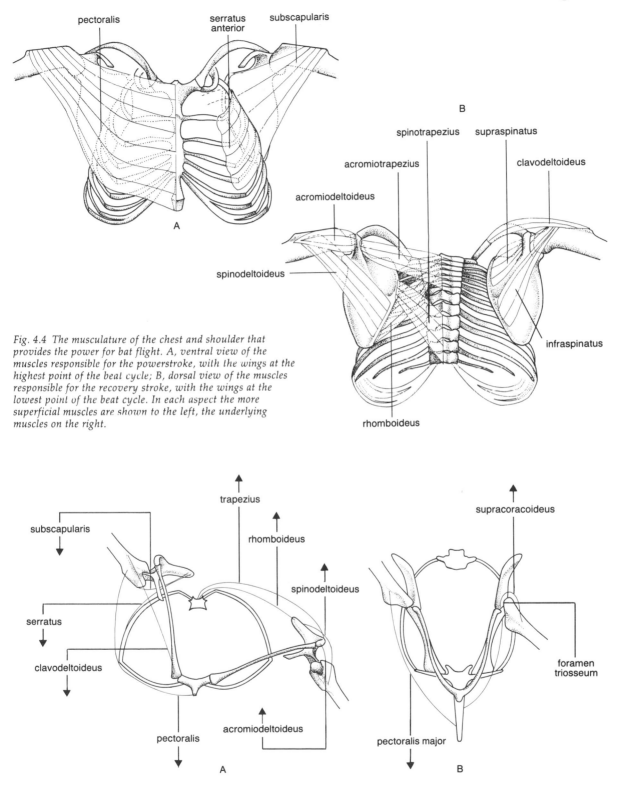

Fig. 4.4 *The musculature of the chest and shoulder that provides the power for bat flight. A, ventral view of the muscles responsible for the powerstroke, with the wings at the highest point of the beat cycle; B, dorsal view of the muscles responsible for the recovery stroke, with the wings at the lowest point of the beat cycle. In each aspect the more superficial muscles are shown to the left, the underlying muscles on the right.*

Fig. 4.5 *The action of the major flight muscles in A, bat, B, bird in anterior view. The muscles responsible for the powerstroke (↓) are indicated to the left, those for the recovery stroke (↑) to the right.*

scapular group] M. infraspinatus (origin: lateral surface scapula, insertion: proximal humerus) and M. supraspinatus (origin: medial surface of scapula, insertion: proximal humerus); [deltoideus group] M. acromiodeltoideus (origin: spine of scapula, insertion: proximal humerus) and M. spinodeltoideus (origin: vertebral border of scapula, insertion: proximal humerus). These muscles are smaller, in overall size, than those which act during the powerstroke. Most act directly on the scapula and indirectly on the humerus.

To illustrate how these muscles function during the wing beat cycle, we begin as the wing is being recovered (Fig. 4.5A). The recovery muscles on the back have been stretched, and the scapula has been tilted outward and downward. The muscles anchored to the thoracic vertebrae and inserted on the scapula contract to rock the scapula back. At the same time, the muscles anchored to the scapula and inserted on the proximal humerus contract to raise the humerus which carries the wing upward. The upward inertia of the wing being raised eventually rocks the scapula upward. At this point, the serratus anterior (a powerstroke muscle) is stretched. In some bats, there is a special process on the proximal humerus that contacts and locks onto the scapula (Fig. 4.6). The stretching of the serratus anterior along with the humerus/scapula contact act as a shock absorber.

The serratus anterior is the first of the powerstroke muscles to contract; its contraction stops the upward inertia of the wing in the recovery stroke and starts the powerstroke (Fig. 4.5). Soon after the serratus anterior contracts, the other powerstroke muscles contract and drive the wing downward.

Although the flapping flight of bats generally resembles that of birds, the arrangement of the flight muscles in birds further illustrates the marked evolutionary differences between these two groups of flyers (Fig. 4.5B). Whereas bats, and presumably pterosaurs, utilize antagonistic groups of muscles located on the chest (power) and back (recovery), respectively, birds have both power and recovery muscles (still antagonistic) located on the chest. In addition, birds utilize fewer muscles to accomplish the wing beat cycle. These muscular differences are also reflected in the skeletal systems of birds. The sternum is massive and strongly keeled in birds; also, the clavicles (wishbone) and coracoid bones are large (Fig. 4.7B). On the other hand, the scapula is rather reduced and does not play an important role in the wing beat cycle. The position and function of the large pectoralis muscle is similar to that described for bats. The recovery of the wing of birds is accomplished by the M. supracoracoideus (origin: keel of sternum, insertion: top of proximal humerus). It is the rigging of this latter muscle that is peculiar. From the sternum, the muscle passes through a hole (foramen triosseum) in the shoulder girdle, formed by the clavicle, coracoid, and scapula, to an attachment on the upper surface of the humerus.

The basic differences in the anatomical aspects of birds and bats no doubt reflect their different evolutionary histories. Both groups originated from reptiles. However, bats (mammals) are the descendants of the therapsid reptiles that departed early from the stem reptiles. On the other hand, birds and pterosaurs evolved from diapsid reptiles (including dinosaurs and crocodiles) that were a later, relatively more specialized group. Although different ancestry may account for some of the anatomical differences, it is

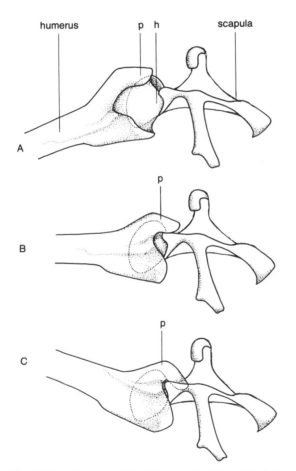

Fig. 4.6 *Anterior view of the right shoulder joint of the bat* Cheiromeles torquatus *(Molossidae). The projection (p) locks the humerus and scapula during the upper part of the wing beat cycle. A, Wing lowered, the humerus folded back towards the body so that its head (h) can be seen articulating with the scapula; B, wing horizontal, the humerus extended slightly away from the body; C, wing raised and fully extended, the projection (p) articulating fully with the upper surface of the scapula.*

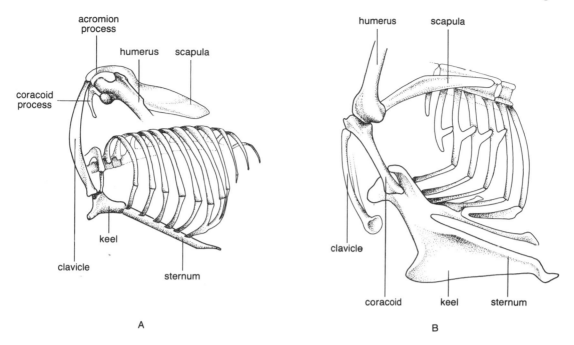

Fig. 4.7 Lateral view of the pectoral skeleton of A, bat, B, bird. Birds have a strong coracoid, a slender clavicle and a massive sternum; in bats the clavicle rather than the coracoid supports the scapula and the sternum is much less substantial.

more likely that the retention or further development of bipedalism by birds has had a marked impact on the nature of their flight morphology. Launching from trees or other high places would seem to require the modification of a quadrupedal morphology; that is, limbs operated by both chest and back musculature. Presumably, flight developed in these animals (bats and pterosaurs) by way of a gliding stage. The fact that birds and pterosaurs, with their markedly different flight morphologies, are more closely related to each other than either is to bats would seem to corroborate this notion that flight morphology is associated with bipedal versus quadrupedal launching.

Control of the wing

In order to overcome the inertial forces at the end of the powerstroke and recovery stroke, the wings of flying animals must be lightweight. The thin, pneumatic bones of birds and pterosaurs and the long, slender bones of bats are adaptations for this purpose. In addition to being lightweight, the structural (skeletal) components of the wing must be able to withstand the buckling forces generated by air pressure under the wing during the powerstroke. These buckling forces are focused at the elbow and wrist in all flying vertebrates and at the finger joints of bats and pterosaurs. In most vertebrates, flexible

joints are supported by heavy bindings of tough fibrous ligaments and muscles. However, in the case of flying vertebrates with critical weight constraints, heavy muscular and tendinous bulk must be minimized. Thus, joint strength in the wings of vertebrates is accomplished by articular modifications of the joints themselves so that movement is restricted (locked) to those planes (horizontal in most cases) that are perpendicular to the buckling forces.

In bats, the elbow joint is designed in such a way, with deep grooves and bony flanges, that the joint opens and closes in the horizontal plane. Some bats have refined this arrangement by angling the grooves and flanges so that as the joint opens (extends) it tightens or locks in much the same fashion that a screw tightens as it is turned down. The wrist joint is a complex articulation with many carpals interposed between the distal portion of the forearm and the digits. Normally, this joint permits a wide range of movements. In bats, the wrist joint is especially complex in that it must resist buckling as well as allow the co-ordinated movement of the digits. Thus, the carpals are broadened, reduced in size, and articulated in such a manner to permit movement in a horizontal plane similar to that of a folding fan. Although bats have reduced the role of muscles in bolstering joints, the wing still must be controlled by muscular actions. Bats and birds have overcome some of the problems associated with muscle mass and

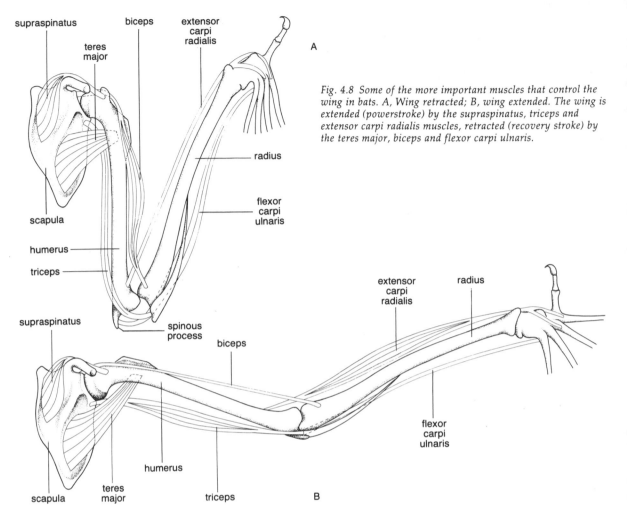

Fig. 4.8 *Some of the more important muscles that control the wing in bats. A, Wing retracted; B, wing extended. The wing is extended (powerstroke) by the supraspinatus, triceps and extensor carpi radialis muscles, retracted (recovery stroke) by the teres major, biceps and flexor carpi ulnaris.*

weight by reducing the size of muscles and restricting the heavy belly portions of muscles to regions close to the centre of gravity. These muscles operate by way of long, thread-like tendons that attach to and control movement in various wing components (Fig. 4.8). In addition, these muscles are arranged in such a way that the action of one or several muscles causes a series of automatic actions in the outer portions of the wing.

The automatic nature of wing control in bats can be illustrated by examining the action between the antagonistic biceps and triceps muscle groups. These two muscle groups attach in much the same manner as in the human arm: M. biceps brachii (origin: two heads attached to coracoid process of scapula, insertion: flexor fossa on proximal radius) and M. triceps brachii (origin: lateral and medial heads attached to posterior surface of proximal humerus and long head attached to lateral border of scapula, insertion:

olecranon process, rear of proximal radius). During the powerstroke, the triceps contracts and opens the elbow joint (extends the radius). At the same time, the biceps pulls and rotates the humerus forward; the contraction of the triceps also enhances the tension of the biceps. When the triceps relaxes at the bottom of the powerstroke, the elasticity of the tendon of the biceps allows the humerus and radius to be flexed (elbow joint closed) passively. The respective actions of these two muscle groups on the humerus and radius cause other automatic actions in the outer wing. The extension of the radius by the triceps triggers the action of two highly inelastic and tendinous muscles. These are: M. extensor carpi radialis longus (origin: lateral epicondyle of distal humerus, insertion: proximal portion of first and second metacarpals) and M. extensor carpi radialis brevis (origin: lateral epicondyle of distal humerus, insertion: proximal portion of third metacarpal). As the elbow joint opens, the origin of these two muscles on the distal humerus moves away from the wrist. This action causes the tendons of these muscles to pull (extend) on the first, second, and third fingers and thereby open (extend) the dactylopatagium. Thus, the triceps effects the full opening of the wing during the powerstroke.

The action of the biceps has a similar automatic but reverse, effect on muscles in the outer portion of the wing during the recovery stroke. This involves the M. flexor carpi ulnaris (origin: spinous process of medial epicondyle of distal humerus, insertion: pisiform carpal that articulates with fifth metacarpal). As the radius and humerus are flexed (elbow joint closed) during the recovery stroke, the origin of the M. flexor carpi ulnaris is moved away from the wrist. This action causes the tendon of this muscle to pull on the fifth metacarpal and thereby partially collapse the dactylopatagium. In some bats, such as molossids, mormoopids, and other assorted species, a spinous process on the distal humerus may be greatly elongated causing the origin of the M. flexor carpi ulnaris to rotate through a wider arc and thereby enhancing the automatic nature of wing flexion during recovery. Bats with this adaptation have high performance wings and are mostly swift flyers. Other, less automatic muscles, assist in the dextrous control of the wing during the wing beat cycle.

As we have noted throughout, the anatomical structure of the avian wing is quite different from that of bats. Nonetheless, birds utilize various automatic devices to control the outer portion of their wings. Recall that the radius and ulna are large bones in the wing of birds. These two bones and their associated articulations with the humerus (proximally) and the fused carpometacarpal (distally) act as a flexible parallelogram. The extension and flexion of this skeletal complex automatically extends and flexes the outer wing.

FLIGHT STYLE AND WING SHAPE

Much speculation has been advanced concerning wing shape and flight style of bats, yet only a handful of species has been studied critically in this regard. Part of the reason for this is the secretive nocturnal habits of bats that makes their direct observation difficult. Other reasons concern the high cost of high-speed motion picture cameras, film, wind tunnels, and other laboratory-based equipment. In addition, bats must be captured, brought into, maintained, and trained to fly in the laboratory under controllable light and airspeeds.

Morphometric studies of many species, preserved in museum collections throughout the world, have shown that bats possess a wide variety of wing sizes and shapes. Wing size appears to be directly correlated with body size. However, wing shape appears to be independent of overall body size. The shape of the wing is controlled by the lengths of the various skeletal components of the wing. Most past studies concerned with the shape of bat wings have overly relied upon the silhouette or aspect ratio of the wing. These studies portray bat wings as low, intermediate, or high in aspect ratio. Certainly, the overall shape or silhouette may be important from the standpoint of such aerodynamic factors as wetted surface area or wing loading. However, the internal composition of the wing (length of various skeletal components) determines the camberability and ultimately the dynamics of lifting potential and manoeuverability.

Generally speaking, bats with relatively short, broad wings (low aspect) are slow flyers. The breadth of the wing chord permits high lift and high weight-bearing potential. Nearly all frugivorous bats (pteropodids and phyllostomids) and many insectivorous species have low aspect wings. In addition, wings with low aspect apparently permit highly manoeuverable flight styles in and around a tangled environment. On the other hand, bats with long, narrow wings (high aspect) are generally swift flyers. Wings of this sort require fast airspeeds and have low weight-bearing potential. Also, these high aspect wings are less capable of manoeuverability in confined spaces. Molossid bats have the highest aspect wings, and they are often cited as the epitome of high performance flight. However, other bats such as noctilionids, mormoopids, and some emballonurids also possess wings of high aspect; not all of these are noted for swift flight.

In reality, every bat family has a distinctive wing shape. The shape of the wing is better understood by examining its functional areas; that is, plagiopatagium and dactylopatagium. The wings of pteropodids (Megachiroptera) are unique among bats by having a broad plagiopatagium and dactylopatagium. In particular, the lengths of the metacarpals of digits three to five are nearly equal or subequal. Also, all of the phalangeal elements are nearly equal in length. This degree of isometry does not occur in any other family of bats. The functional results of such a wing should be a high degree of camberability and consequently high lifting potential. As noted earlier, the Megachiroptera include the largest bats and most are heavy bodied. None is thought to be capable of hovering, but *Pteropus*, and perhaps others, frequently glide for long distances.

The wing shape of rhinopomatids is rather curious.

These bats have an extremely high aspect plagiopatagium and a rather short, broad, (low aspect) dactylopatagium. Overall, the wing is below the average aspect ratio of all bats. The flight style of Mouse-tailed bats (*Rhinopoma*) has been described as a series of alternating flutters and glides as well as swift in open country. This versatility would seem to agree with the flight potential such a wing should possess.

The aspect ratio of the plagiopatagium in emballonurids is only slightly lower than that of rhinopomatids. However, the dactylopatagium of this family is extremely long and narrow. Some species, such as those of the genus *Taphozous*, are fast flyers, whereas most of the other species are capable of rather slow, highly manoeuverable flight.

Wing shape in the Rhinolophidae, Hipposideridae, Nycteridae, and Megadermatidae is quite similar and varies only in the relative proportions of the digital elements. In these families, the plagiopatagium is very short and broad. The dactylopatagium is also low in aspect ratio. The terminal (second) phalanx of the third digit is peculiar in these families. In proportion to the other elements of this finger, this element is very long. In addition, it is permanently bowed and the wing membrane, captured in this bow, is always taut, even in preserved specimens. The articulation of this phalanx with the first phalanx is extremely mobile and may somehow enhance the thrust potential of the wing-tip.

Noctilionids, mormoopids, and phyllostomids have wings in which the plagiopatagium is rather low in aspect. The third finger of these families is very long; the wing chord (length of the fifth finger) also is rather long. In noctilionids and mormoopids, the overall silhouette is high in aspect. In the phyllostomids, the overall shape is just below the average aspect ratio of all bats. In two phyllostomid subfamilies (Glossophaginae and Carolliinae), the plagiopatagium is quite short and broad and the bulk of the wing is composed of the long wing-tip. These bats, especially the glossophagines, are nectarivorous (nectar-eating) and are capable of sustained hovering flight. Other phyllostomids also are capable of varying degrees of hovering. The wings of phyllostomids are capable of bearing considerable weight. Some of the frugivorous species of *Artibeus* and *Phyllostomus* are frequently observed carrying fruits that weigh one-half to two-thirds their body weight. The large carnivorous species such as *Vampyrum spectrum* are capable of capturing and carrying away adult parrots. In addition, the females of all phyllostomids carry large full-term embryos, and large newborn are frequently carried by the foraging mother for several days after birth.

The Vespertilionidae, as a group, fall near the average of all bats with regard to wing shape. The plagiopatagium and dactylopatagium are generally short and broad. However, there is a wide array of wing shapes and, presumably, flight styles. Some species, such as *Otonycteris*, *Kerivoula*, *Miniopterus*, *Lasiurus*, and *Eudiscopus*, have wing-tips with relatively high aspect ratios. The metacarpals of digits three through five are usually very long comprising 50 to 80 per cent of the length of the respective digit.

The wings of molossid bats are extremely long and narrow (high aspect). The majority of this wing shape is contributed by the long, narrow dactylopatagium. The terminal phalanges of digits three to five are very short, and the fifth metacarpal is extremely short compared to those of digits three and four. As we noted above, molossids are generally swift flyers. Their wing beat cycle is very rapid, shallow, and highly stereotypic; that is, without much variation. The humerus of these bats has a secondary articulation with the scapula which serves to restrict the vertical movement of the wing, and the automatic flexing and extending devices in the outer wing are highly developed (Figs. 4.6 and 4.8). Molossids usually forage in open areas that are unencumbered by obstacles. On the ground these bats are virtually helpless and must crawl up a vertical surface in order to launch into the air.

PHYSIOLOGY OF FLIGHT

Thus far, we have discussed the various anatomical and aerodynamic aspects of bat flight. Closely associated with these parameters are the physiological and energetic prerequisites of this highly specialized mode of locomotion. Just as there are parallels and contrasts between birds and bats with respect to anatomical and aerodynamic adaptations for flight, there are similarities and differences between these two groups of flying vertebrates with regard to their physiological adaptations for aerial locomotion.

There is considerably more information concerning the energetics of bird flight than there is for bat flight. Although there is a wealth of information regarding other aspects of chiropteran physiology, the flight physiology of only three bat species (*Phyllostomus hastatus*, *Pteropus alecto*, and *Pteropus poliocephalus*) has been studied in any detail. Again, a large part of the problem of investigating chiropteran flight physiology involves getting the experimental subjects to fly naturally under controlled circumstances (in laboratory-based wind tunnels) with an array of physiological probes, encumbering leads, and other gadgetry. For example, monitoring ventilation and oxygen consumption requires placing a mask over the face of the animal during flight activity. Birds accept these masks rather easily. However, with bats, difficulties arise because, in addition to breathing through the mouth and/or nose, they also emit their acoustic orientation sounds through the mouth and/or nose. Facial masks interfere with these orientation sounds and cause either abnormal flight or the animals refuse to fly altogether. Also, the weight of monitoring equipment that must be borne by the animal in flight limits the size of species that can be studied. Thus, it should be no surprise to find that the three species that have been studied are large species with low aspect (high weight-bearing) wings that either rely little on acoustic orientation (*Phyllostomus*) or do not use it (*Pteropus*).

Basic energetics

The energy to do the mechanical work accomplished by the muscles of any animal is derived from the oxidation of some fuel (food), either carbohydrate or fat. These contain chemical energy in varying quantities and qualities. During the oxidation process (in muscle cells), about 20-25 per cent of the stored chemical energy is released to accomplish mechanical work; the remaining 75-80 per cent is released as excess heat. Compared to other modes of locomotion, flight activity is extremely expensive in terms of its energetic requirements.

Flight muscles of birds and bats may be specialized to operate on either carbohydrates or fats; in some cases, a muscle may be mixed. Carbohydrates must be stored in a hydrated (dissolved in water) form. Therefore, for a given amount of energy, the mass (weight) of carbohydrate fuel that must be lifted, in flight, is approximately eight times that of an equivalent unit of fat. On the other hand, oxidation of a unit of fat produces about twice the energy yield of an equivalent unit of carbohydrate. In addition, fat does not require hydration. In terms of mass per unit of energy, fat contains 0.11 milligrams per calorie (mg/cal). By comparison, honey contains about 20 per cent water and about 0.33 mg/cal; nectar contains about 60 per cent water and about 0.67 mg/cal; and glycogen contains 73 per cent water and 0.88 mg/cal. Thus, fat is a more compact, energy economical fuel.

In addition to the mechanical apparatus (skeletal and muscular) required for flight, the complete animal must have supporting systems (respiratory and circulatory) capable of delivering fuel and oxygen to the cells of flight muscles as required and able to remove and dispose of various chemical by-products, such as lactic acid and carbon dioxide, and excess heat produced in the metabolic (oxidative) process.

Flight exertion

Two general types of flight exertion, 'cruise' and 'sprint,' may be distinguished. Under prolonged cruising flight, oxygen must be absorbed in the respiratory organs and delivered to the flight muscles at the same rate as the muscles are using it. Similarly, in the steady state demand, fuel must be removed from storage and delivered to the flight muscles at the rate of use, and metabolic wastes (including excess heat) must be removed at the rate at which they are produced. These equalities determine the minimum capacities of the respiratory, circulatory, and heat disposal systems required to permit continuous, prolonged flight. Fats are consumed in cruising flight and cellular metabolism (oxidation) is aerobic (steady state oxygen utilization).

In sprinting flight, the power output and demand of the flight muscles temporarily exceeds the capacity of the supporting systems to deliver oxygen and fuel, and remove chemical wastes and excess heat. Under these circumstances, which can prevail for only short periods of time, the burst of activity of the flight muscles quickly depletes the small fuel reserves in the muscle cells. Carbohydrates are consumed during these short bursts and cellular metabolism (oxidation) is conducted under anaerobic (without oxygen) conditions. Since this activity exceeds the supply and demand of the flight muscles, they accumulate waste by-products (including excess heat) and develop an oxygen debt. This deficit must be cleared by a subsequent increase in oxygen consumption; excess heat is absorbed by a temporary rise in body temperature.

Ventilation rate

The high metabolic requirements of flight place heavy demands on the ventilatory apparatus of bats. *Phyllostomus hastatus* (Phyllostomidae) and *Pteropus alecto* (Pteropodidae) maintain a rigid 1:1 synchronization between ventilation and the wing beat cycle; *P. hastatus* with ten cycles per second. The phase relationship is such that inspiration is always associated with the powerstroke; expiration occurs during the recovery stroke. [It is of interest to note here that *Phyllostomus hastatus* emits its ultrasonic vocalizations during the expiratory phase of ventilation.] As a result of the 1:1 synchronization of ventilation and the wing beat cycle, there is an abrupt increase in the breathing rate at the initiation of flight and a similarly abrupt decline as soon as the bat lands (Fig. 4.9). In *Phyllostomus hastatus*, this amounts to approximately 7 cm³ of oxygen per gram body weight per

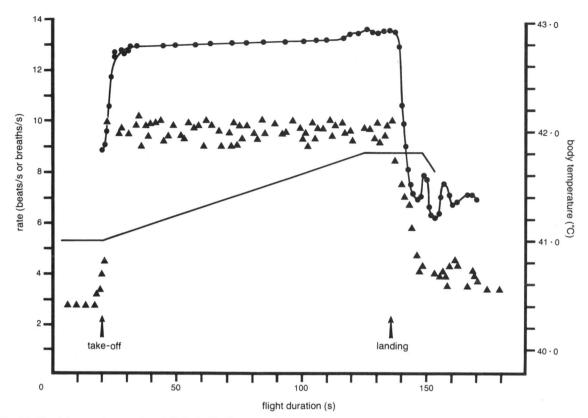

Fig. 4.9 Physiology and energetics of flight in Phyllostomus hastatus *(Phyllostomidae). Top line with dots is cardiac response (heart beats/s) showing sudden increase in heart rate at the start of flight, constant rate during flight, and rapid return to pre-flight levels upon landing. Triangles show respiratory rate (breaths/s) during the same flight. Straight line in middle of graph shows the increase in core body temperature before, during, and after the flight. Ambient temperature during flight trial was 25° to 26° C. (Thomas & Suthers, 1972).*

hour ($cm^3g^{-1}h^{-1}$) before flight to about 27 $cm^3g^{-1}h^{-1}$ during flight.

The correlation of ventilation with wing beat has been examined in many bird species. Whereas some such as the pigeon seem to maintain a 1:1 synchrony, most others show considerable variability. The budgerigar (*Melopsittacus undulatus*) has a constant wing beat cycle (840 beats min⁻¹) at all flight speeds; its ventilatory rate varies continuously with changes in flight speed. In other species, several wing beats occur in one ventilation cycle.

In both *Phyllostomus hastatus* and *Pteropus alecto*, the ventilatory frequency and inspired tidal volume (amount of air entering and leaving the lungs) are dependent on airspeed and flight angle. Ventilatory frequency (and wing beat frequency) are inversely related to airspeed; both decline at higher airspeeds. On the other hand, inspired tidal volume increases with airspeed mostly as the result of the fact that more air is forced (rammed) into the lungs at higher speeds. The relationship is not surprising since the oxygen requirements and rate of gas exchange in the lung are

higher at faster flight speeds. These two bat species are slightly below and above, respectively, the expected ventilation rates of birds of equivalent body size. Preliminary data suggest that these two species of bats are slightly less efficient at extracting oxygen from a particular unit of inspired air than are birds, and both appear to compensate by over-ventilating their lungs.

Heart rates

The high metabolic demands of flight require high rates of oxygen transport by the cardiovascular (circulatory) system. In-flight heart rates are known for only two species. In *Eptesicus fuscus* (body mass, 20 g), heart rate increases from 420–490 beats min⁻¹ (prior to flight) to 970–1097 beats min⁻¹ in flight of two to four seconds duration. During two-minute flights in a large room, the heart rate of *Phyllostomus hastatus* (body mass, l00 g) increases from an anticipatory pre-flight rate of 420 beats min⁻¹ to an average rate of 780 beats min⁻¹ in steady flight (Fig. 4.9). In both of these species, heart rates return to the pre-flight rates within 10 to 20 seconds after landing. These values are only slightly higher than those observed for birds of equivalent body size and both are not substantially higher than heart rates of exercising terrestrial (non-flying) mammals. Thus, heart rate alone does not appear to account for the increased demands of oxygen transport during flight.

As we noted in Chapter 2 the hearts of bats are proportionally much larger than those of non-flying, terrestrial mammals of equivalent size. Although the cardiac output (stroke volume) has never been measured directly in either flying bats or birds, these values have been estimated. The stroke volume of *Eptesicus fuscus* has been estimated to be 1.08 cm^{3}kg^{-1} body weight and the minimum stroke volume of *Phyllostomus hastatus* has been calculated to be 1.9-2.2 cm^{3}kg^{-1} body weight. These values fall between those estimated for flying birds (2.7-3.4 cm^{3}kg^{-1}) and deer mice (1.4 cm^{3}kg^{-1}).

Since birds and bats (those studied) have similar rates of oxygen consumption and heart rates during flight and if, as the data for *Phyllostomus hastatus* suggest, their stroke volumes are lower, then bats must compensate by increasing the amount of oxygen transported by the blood. This is accomplished by raising the percentage concentration of red blood cells in the blood (high haematocrit). *Phyllostomus hastatus* has a blood oxygen capacity that is 40 to 50 per cent higher than that of either a typical bird or non-flying mammal and could, theoretically, transport 1.5 times as much oxygen per unit of blood flow as a bird or rodent. As we will note in Chapter 6 hibernating bats have the ability to regulate their haematocrit by storing red blood cells in the spleen during periods of non-activity. Although it is strongly suspected, it is not known whether bats can or do regulate their haematocrit between and during flight sorties.

Metabolic rate and cost of transport

The metabolic rate or power input is dependent on the body mass as well as on airspeed and flight angle. For birds, bats, and running mammals, metabolic rate is inversely correlated with body mass. Thus, the metabolic rate of a 100 g individual of *Phyllostomus hastatus* utilizes about 1.9 times more oxygen than does an 800 g *Pteropus alecto*. About the same relationship is found between bird species of equivalent body size (for example, budgerigar and seagull). Both birds and bats exceed the highest metabolic rates of running mammals by a factor of 2.5-3.0.

The cost of transportation is defined as the energetic cost of moving a unit of body weight over a given distance. The speed at which an animal can cover a given distance with the lowest energetic cost is its minimum cost of transportation. As might be expected, the minimum cost of transportation is also inversely related to body mass. Thus, *Phyllostomus hastatus* requires about twice the energy expenditure per unit of body weight to travel a given distance than does *Pteropus alecto*. Available data indicates that birds of comparable size are capable of a lower minimum cost of transportation than are bats. On the other hand, *Pteropus alecto* requires only one-fourth, and *Phyllostomus hastatus* only one-sixth the energy expenditure to cover a given distance than do walking or running mammals of comparable size. Thus, even though metabolic expenses of flight are high, the overall costs of this mode of locomotion are markedly lower than terrestrial forms of locomotion.

Fuel utilization

Relatively little is known concerning the utilization of carbohydrates and fats by flying bats. The data on *Phyllostomus hastatus* suggest a high reliance on carbohydrates. However, the flight sorties observed in the experimentation on this species were of relatively short duration in the laboratory and it is quite likely that, under these circumstances, they operated under carbohydrate oxidation. Other work has approached the problem of determining fuel preferences by bioassaying flight muscle tissues to determine enzyme activities. The activities of certain enzymes can be identified with aerobic processes (fat oxidation–cruising flight), whereas others are implicated in anaerobic processes (carbohydrate oxidation–sprint flight). Bats that have low aspect wings and make short dashing flights to capture insects might be expected to depend on carbohydrate utilization, whereas bats with high aspect wings and prolonged flight activity might be expected to rely more heavily on fat metabolism. No doubt this generalization will prove to be much too simplistic, but preliminary indications seem to support the notion. *Rhinolophus megaphyllus* and *Miniopterus schreibersii*, both with wings of low or moderately low aspect ratios, appear to rely heavily on carbohydrate, anaerobic metabolism. *Tadarida australis*, *Tadarida planiceps*, and *Eptesicus pumilus*, with relatively high aspect wings, seem to favour fat, aerobic metabolism. *Chalinolobus gouldii* and *Nyctophilus geoffroyi*, with wings of intermediate aspect ratio, are also intermediate in their preference of anaerobic or aerobic metabolism. There appears to be a strong correlation between food habits, activity patterns, and the relative utilization of carbohydrates and fats by the flight muscles. For example, the fruit-eating phyllostomids such as the Big Fruit-eating bat (*Artibeus lituratus*) and the White-lined bat (*Vampyrops lineatus*) appear to rely heavily on carbohydrates. On the other hand, insectivorous species such as the molossid *Eumops dabbenei* appear to depend more on fat metabolism.

Temperature regulation

During flight activity huge quantities of excess heat are generated by the metabolic activity of the flight muscles. This heat must be channelled away effectively from the animal in order to avoid overheating.

Body temperatures (T_b) of active, temperate bat species, measured over a wide range of ambient (T_a) temperatures, indicate that flight T_b is directly related to T_a in all species studied. For example, flight T_b of *Pipistrellus hesperus* is about 22°C at a T_a of −5°C and 39°C when T_a is 30°C. Thus, it appears that at least these temperate species maintain a constant flight temperature, but one that fluctuates with ambient temperature. Similar results were found with tropical species *Phyllostomus hastatus* and *Pteropus alecto*. Deep-body temperatures of *Phyllostomus hastatus* before flight are about 41°C. This temperature rises markedly at the beginning of flight. Thus, regulated temperature is just below the upper thermal lethal (42-43°C) for the species.

There are several possible routes of heat loss in animals–evaporative cooling from the respiratory tract for instance, or through the skin. Measurements from *Phyllostomus hastatus*, the only data available, indicate that it channels about 14 per cent of the total metabolic heat load generated in flight through the respiratory tract. Other mammals such as dogs and ground squirrels lose about 40-60 per cent of their excess heat load across the respiratory tract. The value for *Phyllostomus* is comparable to those known for birds that dissipate 15-20 per cent of their heat load through the respiratory surfaces.

It is not too surprising to find that *Phyllostomus hastatus* loses most of its metabolic heat load by way of non-respiratory means during flight. By virtue of their flight membranes, bats have greater body/surface areas than do small mammals and birds of comparable size. About 80 per cent of the total surface area of the Pallid bat (*Antrozous pallidus*) is contributed by the flight membranes. We have described earlier (Chapter 2) the structure of these nearly naked, thin membranes, and their rich vascular supply. For example, the Yuma myotis (*Myotis yumanensis*), dilates (expands) its wing capillaries at T_b's of 40-41°C. Similar vasodilation patterns have been reported for several species of flying foxes (*Pteropus*) and *Phyllostomus hastatus*. It is not known exactly

what proportion of a bat's metabolic heat load is dissipated through the flight surfaces, but this means would seem to account for a substantial portion of their heat loss.

ORIGIN OF BAT FLIGHT

A discussion of the early evolution and origin of bat flight can be nothing more than reasoned speculation. The fossil record has not provided much insight with regard to this evolutionary history. Until now, all identifiable fossil bats possess wings that are, without question, as refined as those of modern bats. It is conceivable, although unlikely, that the fossil record may one day produce the proto-bat or half-bat.

There can be little doubt that the impetus to develop flight in birds, bats, and pterosaurs was quite different. Throughout this chapter we have acknowledged repeatedly the marked anatomical differences between birds and bats. Ornithologists continually debate two theories for the development of flight in birds. There are those who support an arboreal theory that takes *Archaeopteryx* as its mainstay. The wing skeleton of *Archaeopteryx* is certainly intermediate between that of its supposed reptilian ancestors and modern birds. Other aspects of the skeletal anatomy of *Archaeopteryx* strongly suggest that it was not capable of the sort of powered flight possessed by modern birds. On the other hand, it may have been a proficient glider. Thus, in order to glide, *Archaeopteryx* is envisioned hopping about in trees. The point that seems to be overlooked is whether *Archaeopteryx* or its ancestor developed its wings in trees or while it was still on the ground. The ground-based, cursory theory of bird flight places the bipedal ancestors of birds on the ground. This theory seems less popular because it postulates the initial development of wings for some purpose other than flight (e.g., balancing structures used during fast bipedal locomotion or perhaps as insect catching devices). Whatever the case may have been, terrestrial bipedalism would certainly have freed the forelimbs for other purposes and it seems likely that birds started their quest for the skies from the ground.

Bats, on the other hand, have but one mode of locomotion–flight. The skeletal and muscular design of their wings is clearly a modification of the typical, quadrupedal, mammalian architecture. The occupation of arboreal niches by mammals and the relatively frequent occurrence of gliding among these mammals strongly supports the notion that the ancestors of bats were indeed arboreal quadrupeds that initially developed gliding ability. The predominance of insectivory among primitive mammals and living bats has added this further dimension to the chiropteran ancestry.

Gliding permits the development and refinement of the plagiopatagial (lifting) portion of the patagium. It does not require any special musculature other than the standard chest and back muscles typical of all quadrupedal mammals. The development of the power-generating hand portion of the wing eventually does require some specialization. However, the initial steps might have entailed no more than webbing between the relatively unspecialized digits. This, of course, would have enhanced the gliding surface area and perhaps provided some refinements for directional control. If such adaptations did provide these 'advantageous' qualities one might expect them to persist in descendants of those individuals in which they were originally developed. Living Colugos seem to be the successful beneficiaries of such ancestors.

Further refinements would have included the elongation of the fingers. Initially, this trend could have proceeded without serious problems. However, digital elongation would have reached a point where it produced an ungainly and clumsy structure that required movement as a wing rather than a fixed gliding device. With successful transition through this critical stage of wing development, bats would have been well on their way to occupying an aerial niche. Further refinements would have concerned increased manoeuverability and/or speed.

Some bat biologists have suggested that these early bats passed through a hovering stage. Certainly, some bats possess the ability to hover. However, this flight style is anatomically specialized, requiring a high aspect tip and many automatic devices. Energetically, it is the most expensive style of flight. It seems highly unlikely that the generalized wing of early bats was capable of such an aerodynamically elite flight style.

Finally, there remains the question as to whether all bats (Megachiroptera and Microchiroptera) are the descendants of a single common ancestor that developed wings or if each of these two suborders is the result of the independent acquisition of wings by unrelated ancestors.

Chapter 5 *Food habits and feeding*

"I cannot here forbear relating a singular circumstance respecting myself, viz. *that on waking about four o'clock this morning in my hammock, I was extremely alarmed at finding myself weltering in congealed blood, and without feeling any pain whatever. Having started up, and run for the surgeon, with a fire-brand in one hand, and all over besmeared with gore; to which if added my pale face, short hair, and tattered apparel, he might well ask the question,*

'Be thou a spirit of health or goblin damn'd,'
'Bring with thee airs of Heav'n or blasts from Hell!'

The mystery however was, that I had been bitten by the vampire *or* spectre *of Guiana, which is also called the* flying-dog *of New Spain, and by the Spaniards* perro-volador; *this is no other than a bat of a monstrous size, that sucks the blood from men and cattle when they are fast asleep, even sometimes till they die; and as the manner in which they proceed is truly wonderful, I shall endeavor to give a distinct account of it.— Knowing by instinct that the person they intend to attack is in a sound slumber, they generally alight near the feet, where, while the creature continues fanning with his enormous wings, which keeps one cool, he bites a piece out of the tip of the great toe, so very small indeed that the head of a pin could scarcely be received into the wound, which is consequently not painful; yet through this orifice he continues to suck the blood, until he is obliged to disgorge. He then begins again, and thus continues sucking and disgorging till he is scarcely able to fly, and the sufferer has often been known to sleep from time into eternity. Cattle they generally bite in the ear, but always in such places where the blood flows spontaneously, perhaps in an artery—but this is entering rather on the province of the medical faculty. Having applied tobacco-ashes as the best remedy, and washed the gore from myself and from my hammock, I observed several small heaps of congealed blood all around the place where I had lain, upon the ground: upon examining which, the surgeon judged that I had lost at least twelve or fourteen ounces during the night."* From J. G. Stedman, 1806. Narrative, of a five year's expedition, against the revolted Negroes of Suriname, in Guiana,... London, 2nd ed., Vol. 2, pp. 142 - 143.

Mr Stedman's vivid account and experience of a vampire attack is but one among many narratives brought back by early travellers in the tropical regions of the New World. Indeed, the European folklore concerning vampires and Stoker's 1897 tales of Count Dracula may have originated from the very earliest explorers of the New World tropics (see Chapter 10). Most people erroneously associate blood-feeding or vampirism with all bats. However, although sanguivory (feeding on blood) is a bona fide food habit of bats, it is restricted to three species that are themselves restricted, for the most part, to the New World tropics; the Common vampire, (*Desmodus rotundus*), has entered the temperate regions of North America in southern Texas.

As a group, bats possess an array of food habits that is nearly as broad as that found in all mammals. The diets of bats include: eating insects and other small arthropods (insectivory); eating flesh of other vertebrates (carnivory) and fish (piscivory); eating fruit and/or flowers (frugivory); eating pollen and/or nectar (nectarivory); and eating a variety of food items (omnivory). Although leaf-eating has been reported in some Old World fruit bats of the family Pteropodidae (*Eidolon helvum*, *Rousettus aegyptiacus* and *Epomophorus wahlbergi*, for example), there are no truly plant-eating herbivorous bats, possibly because the high cellulose content and sclerotized nature of leaves and stems require a large, pocketed stomach (rumen) for digestion and assimilation, and highly specialized grinding teeth for mastication (chewing). Surely, the size and weight factors associated with herbivory would place unresolvable constraints on the various aerodynamic and energetic aspects of flight. Finally, blood-eating (sanguivory) is a unique dietary habit of bats that is not found in any other mammal and, perhaps, no other vertebrate.

Food habits were utilized by many nineteenth century zoologists in early efforts to classify bats. The French zoologist, Cuvier, apparently regarded the general prevalence of insectivory as a form of carnivory with his placement of bats among the 'carnassiers.' Cuvier's notion prevailed in many subsequent French classifications. In 1821, J. E. Gray, an English zoologist, recognized bats as a distinct group of mammals that he divided into two orders; Fructivorae and Insectivorae. Similarly (and forty years later) the German zoologist Koch assigned bats to two suborders; Carpophagen and Entomophagen. In 1872 and 1886, another Englishman, Gill, arranged bats into two suborders; Frugivora and Animalivora. In all of these classifications, the Fructivora, Carpophagen and Frugivora corresponded to the Old World fruit bats or Megachiroptera (family Pteropodidae), and the Insectivorae, Entomophagen, and Animalivora included all other bats or Microchiroptera.

As awareness of the diversity of bats and knowledge of their natural history grew in the last half of the nineteenth century, it became clear that dietary preferences of bats, especially those of the Microchiroptera (Phyllostomidae) that consumed fruits and other flower parts, could not be used to divide the group as previously thought. Although they were never formerly classified together, the frugivorous Pteropodidae (Megachiroptera) and Phyllostomidae (Microchiroptera) were, on occasion, associated in ancestor/descendant relationships on evolutionary trees. All modern classifications of bats have largely abandoned the use of dietary habits in the formal, latinized roots of classificatory group names; only the subfamily names Macroglossinae (long-tongued Old World fruit bats), Glossophaginae (tongue-feeding phyllostomids), and Phyllonycterinae (flower-eating phyllostomids) remain as vestiges of this practice.

Real or supposed food habits are frequently used in the construction of formal generic and species names. The generic names *Macroglossus*, *Glossophaga*, and *Lichonycteris* all refer to attributes or usage of the tongue in feeding. *Vampyrum*, *Vampyrops*, *Vampyrodes*, and *Vampyressa* all erroneously refer to supposed vampire habits when indeed the latter three are frugivorous and the first is carnivorous. Other examples include *Phyllonycteris* (flower-bat), *Musonycteris* (associated with bananas, genus *Muso*), *Pizonyx* (fish-eating bat), and a true vampire, *Diaemus* (blood-stained). It is of interest to note that very few megachiropterans (frugivores) bear scientific names that connote food habits. Many common or vernacular names of bats allude to dietary preferences, for example: Cuban Frog-eating bat; Hairy fruit-eating bat; Buffy Flower bat; Black-bellied fruit bat; American False vampire; Australian False vampire, and White-winged vampire.

Most families of bats are rather stereotyped in their general food preferences; many microchiropteran families are exclusive insectivores and megachiropterans appear to be exclusive frugivores and/or nectarivores. One family, the Phyllostomidae (Microchiroptera) of the tropical and subtropical regions of the New World, combines nearly the complete spectrum of chiropteran food habits. This family includes about 240 species that are commonly classified into six subfamilies. The Phyllostominae (considered the most primitive by most bat biologists) contains a number of exclusively insectivorous species as well as species that also include fruit in their diets. In addition, some phyllostomines are carnivorous, eating frogs, lizards, small birds, rodents, and other bats. Some also include fruit and flower products on their menu. The Glossophaginae with their long tongues and noses are generally known for their pollen and nectar feeding habits; most are important nocturnal pollinators. Some glossophagines also include fruit and/or insects in their diets. The bats of the Carolliinae are similar to glossophagines with perhaps more emphasis on omnivory, including fruit and insects. Members of the Stenodermatinae are frugivorous, for the most part, but many also consume other flower products and insects. The subfamily Brachyphyllinae is confined to the Antilles and here their food habits are quite like those of stenodermatines. The Desmodontinae (three species) are vampires and consume blood meals from other warm-blooded vertebrates. The only chiropteran diet not found among phyllostomids is fish-eating (piscivory). However, this food preference is found in the family Noctilionidae which is closely related to the Phyllostomidae.

CHIROPTERAN FOOD HABITS

Insectivory

Insects and other small arthropods such as spiders and scorpions are an abundant and nutritious food resource utilized by many other mammals, some quite large. Indeed, general insectivory is a widespread feeding strategy of many vertebrates, both terrestrial and aquatic. Insects are found in huge quantities in all parts of the world except the extreme polar regions and are especially diverse in tropical regions. The primary impetus for the origin and diversification of bats (or at least the Microchiroptera) appears to have involved the exploitation of crepuscular (dusk) flying insects. With the development of echolocation, these prey items could be pursued into the night. Approximately 70 per cent of the living species of bats and the majority of those known as fossils are or were insectivores. All microchiropteran families prey upon insects to some extent.

A wide variety of insects is utilized by bats, the groups most widely used being beetles (Coleoptera); moths (Lepidoptera) and flies and mosquitoes (Diptera). Others are: cockroaches (Blattoidea); termites (Isoptera); lacewings (Neuroptera); crickets and katydids (Orthoptera); cicadas (Homoptera); true bugs (Hemiptera) and night-flying ants (Hymenoptera). The size range of insects eaten by bats also varies from gnats with a wing span of several millimetres and weighing about one fifth of a milligram to large moths with a wing span of 50 mm or more and weighing up to 200 mg.

There are three general categories of foraging styles used by bats to capture insects; aerial insectivory, foliage gleaning and terrestrial acquisition. Species may utilize one or a combination of these foraging styles, depending upon their particular flight capabilities, echolocation system, and seasonal availability of flying insects.

Aerial insectivory involves several different hunting strategies. Perhaps the most primitive of these foraging styles is the ambush strategy that is characteristic of large-sized species of *Hipposideros* and megadermatids. Individuals of these species return nightly to take up positions on specific perches in their foraging territories; there may be a scattered series of these sentry posts. From these perches, the bat scans the surroundings with its ultrasonic sounds for appropriate food items crossing into its area. When this happens, the bat tracks the prey with its echolocation system and anticipates an appropriate path of interception. At just the right moment, the bat sallies out and attempts to capture the prey item. If it is successful, it carries its meal back to the perch and consumes it. If the attack is not successful the bat returns to the perch, or another one in its territory, and waits for another opportunity. During the feeding period, attack sallies by the African Heart-nosed bat (*Cardioderma cor*) may occur at an average rate of 6-29 h^{-1} (average 13.6 h^{-1}), lasting from 1.4-7.3 seconds (average 4.07 s), and covering distances of 7-36 metres. This particular style of aerial insectivory appears to be energetically efficient, requiring input energy in quantity only during these short, rapid dashes. The echolocation system of these bats utilizes relatively low frequency acoustic signals, emitted as long, constant cries, which permit long-range target detection (see Chapter 8).

A more energetically demanding mode of aerial insectivory is that in which the bat forages, on the wing, for extended periods of time. This style of hunting may involve swift, straight-line flights along forest pathways, roadways, or other open areas that are unencumbered by obstacles. Bats of the family Molossidae and emballonurids of the genus *Taphozous*, with their high aspect wings, appear to rely on this style of hunting. On the other hand, vespertilionid bats, as well as insectivorous phyllostomids, fly less swiftly because of their lower aspect wings. These bats are, however, more manoeuverable in confined spaces and their foraging styles involve patrolling in and around vegetation for flying insects. Although there is little information available, all of these aerial insectivores appear to be faithful to

particular flyways or foraging areas and patrol them nightly. Seasonal changes in insect availability may cause them to modify their foraging pathways or restrict their activity to some portion of the foraging territory. The echolocation system of these bats generally utilizes a broad-banded sweep through a series of high frequencies. This permits short-distance detection and pursuit capabilities (see Chapter 8).

Foliage gleaning is a modification of the latter style of aerial insectivory. As the bat forages amongst the vegetation it scans for insects and/or other arthropods such as spiders sitting on the tops of leaves. When these are detected, the bat alights on the foliage and captures the prey item. Terrestrial acquisition is similar, but involves flying close to the ground in search of crawling arthropods such as beetles, crickets, and scorpions. When these are detected the bat pounces on the prey and either consumes it at the site of capture or carries it to a nearby perch. The Pallid bat (*Antrozous pallidus*), that lives in the southwestern deserts of the United States, is an example of this type of insect predator. Of course, these bats must be capable of agile terrestrial locomotion.

Relatively little is known with regard to how insects are captured in flight, but studies of bats in captivity with high-speed motion pictures suggest a variety of techniques. Small insects may be seized directly in the mouth. Other bats may use the wings like a racket to deflect the prey toward the mouth. At the same time, the uropatagium may be used as a scoop to capture the prey. The Red bat (*Lasiurus borealis*) performs an aerobatic somersault while closing the wings and tail membrane (uropatagium) around the captured insect. Before resuming flight, it tucks its head down into the pocket formed by the tail membrane to collect the insect in its mouth.

Small, soft insects are probably chewed and swallowed directly. Larger insects, especially beetles with hard, tough chitinous exoskeletons, require some handling before they can be consumed. A large rhinoceros beetle captured by a *Hipposideros diadema* will be carried to a perch. There the bat will meticulously clip off the head, legs, and hard wing covers before consuming the relatively soft abdominal portion. The wings of large moths also may be culled before eating. A field researcher may identify the roost or sentry stations of these bats by the piles of discarded insect parts.

Insects fly much more slowly than bats and must use their ability to change direction quickly to evade the pursuit of an attacking bat. Several groups of moths have developed highly specialized auditory devices ('ears') for detecting the high frequency echolocation sounds produced by hunting bats.

When these moths detect the presence of a bat, they dive swiftly into bushes or shrubs. We noted earlier (Chapter 2) that there are many species of bats with extremely long ears. Until now, no one has been able to explain the rather curious distribution of long ears among bats. Recent work seems to indicate that these especially long ears may be a device to counteract the bat-avoidance system developed by moths (see Chapter 8).

Many of the insects species consumed by bats are human pests, such as mosquitoes and flies. For example, in Papua New Guinea where copra is a primary export product, there is a virus borne by rhinoceros beetles that lay their eggs in coconut trees. The developing larvae expose the tree to this virus which lowers the productivity and eventually causes the death of the coconut trees. A number of rhinoceros beetle eradication programs have been used or are being developed to control this insect pest. However, a natural predator on these beetles is *Hipposideros diadema*. Yet continued forest clearing in and around caves where these and other insectivorous bats roost risks reducing bat populations and lowering their natural impact on the populations of rhinoceros beetles as well as those of other potentially harmful insects such as malarial mosquitoes.

Bats consume large quantities of insects. It has been estimated that they eat from one-quarter to one-half their body weight in insects nightly. Thus, a 20 g bat may eat 5-10 g of insects in one night. At this conservative feeding rate such a bat might consume 1.8-3.6 kg (4.0–8.0 lb) in one year. A colony of 100 000 individuals of this species might be expected to consume 180 000-360 000 kg (198-396 tonnes) in one year. A colony of Mexican Free-tailed bats (*Tadarida brasiliensis*) in Texas has been estimated to number 50 million individuals at times, each weighing about 20 g. This colony alone might consume as much as 6700 tonnes of insects in just one summer season. Yet, again, the populations of these bats throughout the southwestern United States are being threatened by the continued use of toxic chemical pesticides (see Chapter 10).

Carnivory

Meat-eating is found among a number of mammalian groups. By definition, members of the Order Carnivora are especially adapted for this diet and they participate at various levels in world food chains; many, such as lions, tigers and wolves, occupy positions at the top of their respective food pyramids. Carnivory does not appear to be particularly widespread among bats. Two species of False vampires of the family Megadermatidae, *Megaderma lyra* (India

and southeast Asia) and *Macroderma gigas* (Australia), regularly catch and eat other bats, small rodents and birds, or frogs and lizards. Four species of New World leaf-nosed bats of the family Phyllostomidae also are known to consume meat. All are members of the subfamily Phyllostominae and are: *Phyllostomus hastatus*, *Vampyrum spectrum*, *Trachops cirrhosus* and *Chrotopterus auritus*. Their diet is quite similar to that described for megadermatids, consisting of small vertebrates. However, they also consume insects and fruit to varying extents. Carnivory might be expected among some of the large-sized species of *Hipposideros*. Indeed, all of these carnivorous bats are characteristically large in size; *Vampyrum spectrum* is the largest microchiropteran with a wing span of nearly one metre.

Little is known with regard to the foraging behaviour of carnivorous bats. Most are thought to take their unsuspecting prey from roosting or resting places on the ground or in trees. It is not known if they actively chase flying bats or birds. The Hammer-headed fruit bat *Hypsignathus monstrosus* (west and central Africa) of the family Pteropodidae has been reported scavenging from discarded dead bird carcasses (and attacking tethered chickens) but other reports of carnivory by pteropodids refer to captive bats and may not be a true indication of their natural habits. The Short-tailed bat *Mystacina tuberculata* (Mystacinidae) from New Zealand has also been seen to scavenge meat from bird carcasses and it has been suggested that scavenging habits could provide a winter food source for this species.

Recent work on the Neotropical Fringe-lipped bat (*Trachops cirrhosus*) has prompted the discovery of some interesting evolutionary relationships between this bat and the frogs upon which it preys. Until this work began, *Trachops* was thought to capture randomly and opportunistically whatever it happened to find as it hunted. However, it now appears that *Trachops* has a considerable impact on Neotropical frog populations.

Like all sexually reproducing animals, frogs must find a mate with which to breed. Also, like many other animals, male frogs sit at a stationary location and produce species-specific vocalizations (songs) that attract females to come to their position and mate. The success of a particular male depends on how accurately he sings his song and the frequency at which he sings. Thus, all males of a species must sing their songs with sufficient accuracy so that females of the same species will be attracted and they must sing their songs with sufficient repetition so that the females can locate their position. These songs are broadcast 'for the world to hear' and, as it turns out, *Trachops* has learned to recognize the mating calls of the frog species that it eats. This, of course, presents chorusing male frogs with somewhat of a dilemma. The simplest solution might appear to be to change the song. However, marked changes result in non-recognition and therefore non-breeding. Another solution might be to call less frequently. Again, this may result in the inability of females to locate the male properly. Another solution is to call from seclusion (in bushes, under rocks, etc.), but again, this may hamper this natural game of 'hide and seek'.

Toads also vocalize to attract mates. However, most toads possess highly toxic glands in their skin which makes them either deadly poisonous or at least distasteful to the potential predator. *Trachops* also recognize and can distinguish the calls of distasteful toads from those of tasty frogs. So, another route of evasion for frogs is to mimic the songs of toads. Neotropical frogs apparently employ all of these possible means of fooling *Trachops* with varying degrees of success. In addition, prey species of frogs eaten by *Trachops* apparently can detect the presence of a hunting *Trachops*. The appearance of a foraging *Trachops* over a pond of chorusing frogs results in an immediate silence. Those who fail to heed the warning (whatever it is), or start to call again before the danger has passed, become the hapless fuel of *Trachops* energetics.

The impetus for the evolution of carnivory in bats is difficult to understand. Prey size and the energetics of this high protein diet seem to require, or perhaps permit, large body size in these predatory species; the net energy yield from relatively few captures is quite high. Carnivory in bats seems to be an extension of insectivorous food habits. Meat-eating requires an ability to chop and cut fibrous flesh as well as cut or crush bones. As we will see below, the dentitions of insectivorous bats are already well designed for cutting and chopping the hard, chitinous exoskeletons of insects. The dentition of carnivorous and piscivorous bats is only slightly modified from that of insectivorous species (Fig. 5.7). There can be little doubt that carnivory in the megadermatids was derived from insectivorous ancestors. The same may be the case for carnivorous phyllostomids, although some bat biologists imagine that carnivory in this group of bats may have involved a modification in fruit-seeking behaviour.

Piscivory

Fish-eating is really a specialized form of carnivory. It is a dietary preference limited to a small number of bat species. Most notable are the Bulldog or Fishing bat (*Noctilio leporinus*–Noctilionidae), and the Fishing bat (*Pizonyx vivesi*–Vespertilionidae); both are rather

large and occur in the tropical and subtropical regions of the New World. These bats have long legs, the feet are enormous and the toes are tipped with long, sharp and strongly-hooked claws. Both species have a long calcar that folds forward along the lower portion of the hindlimb. By doing this, the tail membrane is gathered up and held out of the way when the bat is fishing. The toes, calcar, and tibia are flattened laterally for streamlining so that they can knife through water with minimal resistance.

The foraging behaviour is similar in these two species. They fly low and relatively slowly over quiet water, almost skimming the surface (Fig. 5.1). They use their echolocation system to detect small disturbances and ripples in the surface of the water that may indicate the presence of small fish or they may detect the protrusion of fins above the water surface. In any event, once they detect a fish, they drop their enormous taloned feet into the water, like two large grappling hooks, and impale their unsuspecting victim. The fish is quickly gaffed out of the water and grasped in the mouth. Feeding may occur on the wing or they may carry the prey to a perch where it is consumed. In the laboratory, *Noctilio leporinus* may capture 30-40 small fish in an evening.

Both of these fishing bats also eat insects occasionally and the evolution of piscivory in bats is thought to have evolved from catching floating or swimming insects off the surface of water. *Noctilio albiventris* is smaller than *N. leporinus* and does not have modified feet; it is an exclusive insectivore. *Noctilio leporinus*

Fig. 5.1 The Bulldog or Fishing bat (Noctilio leporinus–Noctilionidae).

haunts caves or occasionally may be found in hollow trees. Their roost sites are characterized by a strong fishy odor and, indeed, an observer with a good sense of smell can detect the presence of foraging Bulldog bats. *Pizonyx* also frequent caves and rock crevices, but may also reside under large, flat stones by the seashore. Whereas *Noctilio leporinus* feeds on freshwater fish, *Pizonyx* is adapted to capturing marine fish over quiet lagoons and, apparently, may drink seawater on occasion. Eating marine fish and/or drinking salt water requires special physiological modifications in the kidney and urinary system to permit the excretion of high quantities of salt and the conservation of water.

Sanguivory

Feeding on the blood of other warm-blooded vertebrates is possibly the most extraordinary dietary habit of bats. As we noted in the introduction of this chapter, this food habit is unique among mammals and perhaps vertebrates. For reasons that will become obvious below, it is fortunate that this feeding preference is restricted to three species of true vampires in the subfamily Desmodontinae (Phyllostomidae). These species are: The Common vampire (*Desmodus rotundus*); the White-winged vampire (*Diaemus youngi*); and the Hairy-legged vampire (*Diphylla ecaudata*). These species are confined, for the most part, to the tropical and subtropical regions of the New World: *Desmodus rotundus* and *Diaemus youngi* (sometimes included in *Desmodus*) extend their geographic range just into the more temperate regions of North and South America.

The commonest and most widespread vampire (*Desmodus rotundus*) is a serious agricultural and public health pest (see Chapter 10). It feeds exclusively on the blood of other mammals (occasionally including human blood), whereas *Diaemus* and *Diphylla* attack birds and are both less abundant. The common vampire is a pest because, with the introduction of large numbers of horses, cattle and other domestic mammals as a result of European colonization of the New World tropics, its populations have grown markedly over the past 500 years, thanks to this greatly expanded food resource. Also, human populations in those regions have grown.

Because of the warm, tropical climate, housing tends to be rather open, and this, coupled with a general increase in the level of poverty, causes many people to sleep in open, exposed places, thereby providing an additional food source for vampires.

Mr Stedman's account of a vampire attack at the beginning of this chapter is a rather accurate one, although there are several misconceptions. Vampires are not monstrous in size; they weigh 30-35 g and have a wing span of about 30 cm. Nor do vampires suck blood from the wounds that they inflict; instead they have specially modified tongues with grooves on the sides that move the blood by capillary action as the vampire laps blood from the wound. The supposed anaesthetic cooling of the victim by fanning with the wings is also doubtful.

Vampires are quite agile on the ground or while clinging to and crawling on the victim. Their dentition is highly specialized (Fig. 5.7N). The grinding teeth are all but lost and the upper canines and incisors (one on each side of the jaw) are enlarged into razor-sharp blades; the lower canines are large, but not as blade-like. They inflict a small, V-shaped wound by biting the victim in a region where there are rich surface blood capillaries. Typical wound sites are the tips of fingers and toes (humans only), lips and eyelids, tips of the nose and ears. In domestic mammals, these sites are utilized as well as the anal region, junction of the hooves with skin of feet, and occasionally large surface vessels on face and neck. The wound is kept open and blood flowing by means of an anticoagulant in the saliva. This latter feature is in itself a serious problem both for livestock and humans because vampire wounds tend to bleed long after the bat has taken its blood meal, thus causing a continued loss of blood. Secondary infections frequently accompany vampire attacks because humans receiving such wounds are usually poverty-stricken and living under less than hygienic circumstances. Vampires do not drain their victim of blood during a feeding, but an attack by several on a young domestic animal, or small child, could result in death, due to the continued haemorrhaging of unclotted wounds. Of a more serious nature is the fact that vampires, especially *Desmodus*, are apparently vectors for rabies (see Chapter 10).

Captive vampires drink about 15 cm³ of blood per night and consume this in about 20 minutes. In the wild, vampires forage in the early portion of the night, for about two hours, during which time they may consume 30 cm³ or more (approximately one-and-a-half times their own weight). These heavy food loads often approach the lifting potential of their wings so that they have difficulty in flying. The kidneys of vampires are specially adapted to permit the rapid extraction and disposal of the large quantities of water in a blood meal. Thus, soon after feeding vampires begin to urinate continuously until they are light enough to fly. Later in the digestion of this nearly pure protein diet, the kidney must cope with high concentrations of nitrogenous wastes. At this point, the kidney switches from a water expelling mode to a water conserving mode that results in an extremely concentrated urine. Although there are no exact figures, it has been estimated that a colony of 100 common vampire bats might consume 730 litres of blood in a year, equivalent to the total amount of blood in 20 horses or 25 cows, 365 goats, or 14 600 chickens, without considering any further loss of blood after feeding has ceased.

The evolution of sanguivory also evades explanation. Some bat biologists imagine that sanguivory evolved in insectivorous species that fed on ticks and other large ectoparasites. Eventually, it is presumed that these bats began inflicting wounds themselves to feed on the host's blood. Others imagine sanguivory to have evolved in a frugivorous species that was adapted to biting succulent fruits and licking the copious juices. This habit was presumably transferred to biting other animals and lapping the blood. The fact that vampires are highly specialized for feeding on blood has led many bat biologists to regard them as a separate and distinct family. However, aside from these specializations, they are clearly members of the Phyllostomidae and, indeed most closely related to the more primitive members of the family, the phyllostomines.

Frugivory and nectarivory

Consumption of fruits, flowers, nectar, and pollen by bats is widespread in species that inhabit the tropical and subtropical regions of the world. The Old World fruit bats of the suborder Megachiroptera with but one family, the Pteropodidae, appear to be exclusively frugivores and/or nectarivores. *Nyctimene* and *Rousettus* may take insects occasionally and insect parts have been found among the stomach contents of other pteropodids such as *Cynopterus*, *Penthetor*, *Balionycteris* and *Eonycteris*, but these may have been ingested incidentally while feeding on fruit, flowers or nectar. In the New World, these vegetarian food habits evolved independently in the majority of the species of the family Phyllostomidae (Microchiroptera). There can be little doubt that the frugivorous and nectarivorous feeding behaviours of phyllostomids were derived from an insectivorous ancestor. This may have been prompted by seeking and capturing insects that feed on or otherwise visit fruits and flowers (Fig. 5.2). Presumably, these bats eventually switched over to utilizing the fruits and flower products themselves; an exclusive food source in some. The evolution of pteropodid frugivory and nectarivory seems less likely connected with an insectivorous ancestor. Whereas many phyllostomids retain their insectivorous heritage either in partial or complete insectivorous feeding habits or in various aspects of their anatomy (e.g., insectivorous or

Fig. 5.2 The Long-nosed bat (Leptonycteris sanborni– Phyllostomidae) *feeding on flowers of the Saguaro cactus.*

modified insectivorous dental morphology—Fig. 5.7I, K-M), there are no such traces that would imply insectivory in the heritage of pteropodids. We have already implied a separate and independent origin of the Megachiroptera. The impetus for the development of flight in these bats seems to have been the pursuit of arboreal frugivory and nectarivory. The fact that the wings of Mega- and Microchiroptera are similar stems from the fact that both are mammals and that both are presumed to have evolved from an arboreal ancestor through a gliding stage as discussed in Chapters 3 and 4. This seems reasonable, nonetheless speculative, since most mammalian frugivores are arboreal and that an ability to travel between fruiting tree tops, often across large distances, would have certain energetic and safety advantages.

Fruit-eating bats utilize an extremely wide array of wild fruits; many considered unpalatable by man. Among these are all sorts of wild figs (*Ficus*) in both the Old and New World, and the fruits of kapok, pepper and *Cecropia*. In addition, many cultivated fruits are eaten; some of these are commercially valuable and therefore their use by bats is considered destructive. Among these are mangos, guavas, bananas, peaches, apples, papayas, oranges, and many small berries. In Papua New Guinea and Queensland, Australia, *Pteropus* and *Dobsonia*, both large flying foxes, also eat coconut flowers and young coconut fruits; there is evidence that seems to indicate that *Dobsonia* also chews open the tough pods of cocoa.

In the tropics, there is a high diversity of plant species compared to a relatively low diversity in the temperate regions. Unlike the temperate regions where large numbers of individuals of fewer plant species are concentrated in a particular region, fewer individuals of many different species are scattered in distribution in the tropics. Whereas many pine trees are found in close proximity to one another, individual *Ficus* trees may be several hundred metres, or even kilometres, apart. In temperate regions, plant species of a particular area all flower and set fruit at about the same time. In the tropics, this is not the case and there is a fair amount of asynchrony in fruiting and ripening so that there may be several kilometres between *Ficus* trees with usable fruits. Bats and other frugivorous vertebrates are attracted to a tree or plant by the smell of its ripening fruits. It is quite a spectacle to watch a large *Ficus* come into fruit and, in a matter of two or three days, witness the feeding frenzy of all manner of diurnal and nocturnal frugivores strip it bare of all of its fruits.

At first, one might wonder how tropical plant species manage to survive and reproduce in the face of this apparently massive destruction of a fruit crop by frugivores. The seedlings of most tropical plant species will not grow and mature in the shade of the parent plant; some even produce toxins to prevent this. Thus, a means of seed dispersal beyond the influence of the parent plant is necessary. Most frugivores do not damage the seeds in the process of eating the fleshy parts of fruits. Bats, for example, may pick and carry a fruit to a perch where they eat the fleshy portion and discard the skin, fibrous pulp, and the seed(s). In the case of fig-like fruits with many tiny seeds, the bat may consume the entire fruit including the seeds. The seeds are later passed in the excreta of the bat and fall wherever the bat happens to be. The seeds of *Ficus* will not germinate unless they have passed through the gut of either a bird or bat. Thus, frugivorous bats are an important agent in seed dispersal in the tropics.

Three groups of bats feed principally on nectar and pollen. One of these includes the members of the subfamily Macroglossinae of the megachiropteran family Pteropodidae; these are found only in the Old World tropics. The other two belong to two subfamilies, Glossophaginae and Brachyphyllinae (Phyllostomidae), which live only in the New World tropics. To say that these bats resemble and behave like hummingbirds is not a stretch of the imagination; they are effectively nocturnal equivalents of these small, active birds. All are small, or relatively small, and delicate. Their muzzles are long and reduced in diameter (Fig. 5.3). The lower jaw is much reduced and frail, in marked contrast to the stout, heavy jaws of frugivorous species. Moreover, since a nectar diet is essentially aqueous, there is no need for chewing. Thus, the grinding teeth of all nectar-feeding species are greatly reduced in overall size. Also, like hummingbirds, the tongue is very long, slender, and extensible for a considerable distance. In glossophagines, the tip of the tongue has a specialized patch of elongated papillae, giving it a 'brush-like' appearance. In addition, there may be a series of grooves on the sides or lower portion of the tongue which serve to move the watery nectar into the mouth by capillary action. The upper incisors are usually large and, in most species, are thrust forward (procumbent). These are used to break open the sac-like nectar glands at the base of the flower tube. The lower incisors are frequently reduced in number and size and set to either side of the jaw axis, thereby creating a medial open space, or they are absent altogether. These modifications in the lower incisors, along with a grooved pad on the middle part of the lower lip, act as a directional guide for the tongue as it is moved in and out of the mouth during feeding. All of these adaptations for feeding on nectar are carried to an extreme in the Glossophaginae, whereas in the Macroglossinae and Brachyphyllinae they may be less pronounced. Rostral length in glossophagines closely parallels the length of the tubular flowers on which a particular species feeds. *Glossophaga soricina* has a muzzle about equal in length to its braincase, whereas the muzzle of *Musonycteris*, *Choeronycteris* and *Platalina* is several times longer than the braincase. These feed on short and long tubular flowers, respectively.

The phyllostomid nectarivores may also include insects in their diets to varying extents. Some insects may be taken in accidentally just because they happen to be inside the flowers at the time of the bat's visit. Inasmuch as most nectarivorous bats have rather weak jaws and teeth, they are not able to bite into other than very thin-skinned fruits. However, they do feed regularly on soft fleshy fruits that have been opened by other fruit-eating bats.

Nectar and pollen-feeding is not strictly confined to these three groups as some species of phyllostomines, stenodermatines, and pteropodines may, on occasion, attack flowers to reach their contents. *Phyllostomus discolor* (Phyllostominae), *Artibeus jamaicensis*

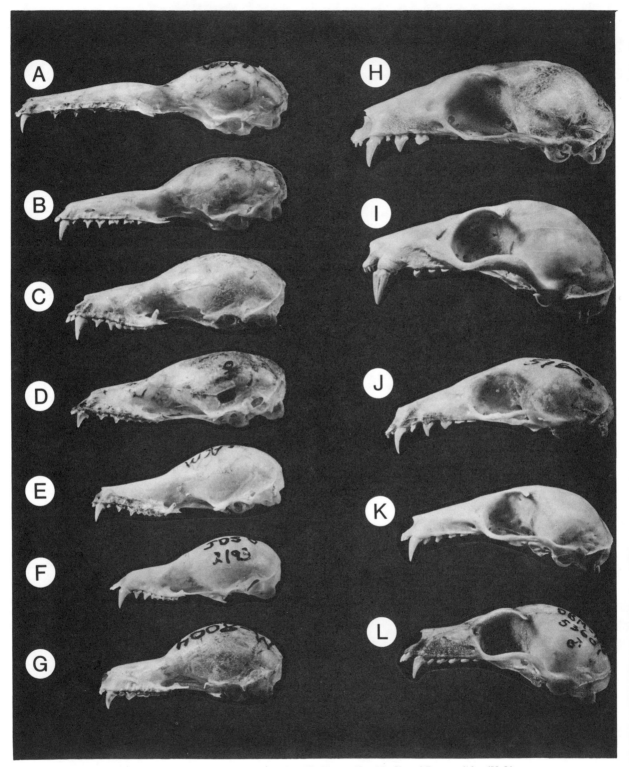

Fig. 5.3 Cranial variation of nectar-eating bats of the families Phyllostomidae (A–G) and Pteropodidae (H–L). A, Musonycteris harrisoni; B, Choeronycteris mexicana; C, Lonchophylla robusta; D, Leptonycteris curasoae; E, Anoura geoffroyi; F, Glossophaga soricina; G, Erophylla sezekorni; H, Eonycteris spelaea; I, Notopteris macdonaldi; J, Megaloglossus woermanni; K, Macroglossus minimus; L, Syconycteris crassa.

and *Sturnira lilium* (both Stenodermatinae) may consume nectar and pollen on a seasonal basis. Also, *Epomophorus* and *Nanonycteris* (both Pteropodinae) visit and consume the flower products of *Parkia*, an African tree.

All nectar and pollen-eating bats are generally slow flyers. The phyllostomid nectarivores are capable of hovering and feeding at the flower's mouth much like hummingbirds (Fig. 5.2). The pteropodid nectarivores apparently do not hover, but land on the flower heads or adjacent to flowers.

Fruits and nectar are very nutritious food items containing high concentrations of a variety of carbohydrates that are easily digestible and readily usable in various energetic cycles. The quantity of juice obtained from a fruit varies on its size and succulence. A flower may contain from 5-10 cm^3 of nectar. Some fruits also contain considerable amounts of fats and oils, whereas pollen is a rich source of protein. Studies of Long-nosed bats (*Leptonycteris sanborni*) at the University of Arizona have demonstrated that some 70-75 per cent of their diet consists of nectar, together with a much smaller quantity of pollen which nevertheless is sufficient to provide the necessary protein. Nectar-feeding bats collect quantities of pollen on the head and shoulders which in some species have hairs with a rough, scaly surface to which the sticky pollen grains readily adhere. The pollen is later loosened by grooming with the claws and collected by the tongue. The grains have a tough wax-like outer skin that resists digestion, but it is weakened by the warm mixture of saliva and nectar in the mouth of the bat so that the digestive acids of the

stomach can release the protein. The Long-nosed bat also ingests urine, possibly to further the digestion of pollen protein.

Just as many plant species depend on animal agents to disperse their seeds, many also depend on animals for pollination. No doubt the reader is already familiar with the 'birds and bees' aspect of pollination. Bats also are important nocturnal pollinating agents. Indeed, many plant species have developed specialized flowers to attract and accommodate bat visitations (Fig. 5.4). Diurnal flowering plants may have a particular structure and colour to attract bird and insect pollinators. For example, flowers that attract hummingbirds are usually red and have long, skinny carollas, while bee-pollinated flowers, such as orchids, may be white and have particular structures that momentarily trap the bee and place pollen capsules on its back. Bat-pollinated flowers, such as those of the calabash tree (*Crescentia*), sausage tree (*Kigelia*), saguaro cactus (*Carnegiea*) and agave (*Agave*) are usually white, creamy, or greenish in colour and generally have strong musky or sour scents. Of course, these flowers open at night rather than during the day. Flowers pollinated by bats may vary in size. Some are large with broad mouths, and others may have special petals that project outward and provide a landing platform or holdfast. These flowers usually possess large quantities of nectar and many springy anthers that deposit pollen on the head, cheeks, or shoulders as the bat enters to get at the nectar glands. Often these flowers grow or hang so that bats can reach them easily without being encumbered in foliage or on spines in the case of cacti.

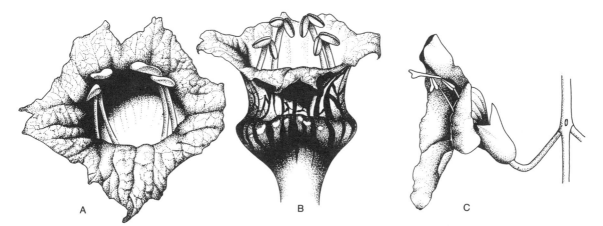

Fig. 5.4 Two of the flowers visited by bats. A, B, Calabash tree (Crescentia cujete); *C, sausage tree* (Kigelia pinnata). *The flowers are wide with a large nectary at the base. Pollen is readily deposited on to the head and shoulders of a bat while feeding, and may be eaten when groomed from the fur, or easily transferred to another flower (After McCann, 1931; Porsche, 1931).*

FORAGING AND NOCTURNAL ACTIVITY

Bats fly and feed in the nocturnal period from twilight at dusk, during the night, to the twilight just prior to sunrise. Distances travelled in one night, the size of home and foraging territories of individuals, family units, or colonies, and the activity patterns of the latter are not well understood. The nocturnal habits of bats makes the study and observation of these parameters difficult.

Technological advances in the past five years or so, in miniaturization of electronics, have made possible the development of small, lightweight radio transmitters. By attaching these to bats, researchers can effectively telemeter, by radio tracking, the nightly activity of individuals or groups of individuals. At present, the smallest radio packs (1-2 g) can only be placed on moderately large to large species with low aspect wings. In addition, costs of this equipment remain relatively high. Another somewhat cheaper, but restricted means of studying bat activity is the placement of small, luminescent chips on bats and observing them as they fly about an immediate area. Both methods become difficult when the tagged individual(s) fly beyond the area of surveillance. Still other investigators are using sophisticated (and costly) ultrasonic detectors that receive the high frequency sounds emitted by bats during their nightly activity (Fig. 5.5). Some of these detectors permit the researcher to recognize, with some practice, the distinctive vocalizations of individual species. This method can only monitor the activity of only one or two individuals. Nonetheless, in spite of these difficulties, some vital information has been gathered.

Fig. 5.5 Ultrasonic 'bat detector' used by bat biologists to recognize the signals of bats and monitor bat activity.

Nightly activity

Foraging begins a little before or at dusk and may continue throughout much of the night, interspersed with periods of rest when the bats may return to their daytime quarters or occupy a night roost in or near the foraging territory. There seems to be some indication of a differential in feeding times among bat species. Many species are most active at dusk and at dawn, whereas other species forage later in the evening. However, much of the current knowledge is based on actual captures of individuals, usually at watering sites, which may be misleading. For example, the Spotted bat (*Euderma maculatum*) that lives in the southwestern regions of the United States, was thought to be rare and out only after midnight. Studies in Utah and Nevada with ultrasonic detectors have shown that the species emerges and is active throughout the evening hours. In addition, the species seems to be more abundant than was previously supposed.

Research on the activity and feeding of the Little Brown bat (*Myotis lucifugus*) in New Hampshire has contributed some interesting information. The study was conducted in the summer months and involved pregnant and lactating females, and later the activity of the juveniles themselves. All individuals foraged for about a two-hour period just after sunset. During this time they captured from 60-65 per cent of their nightly diet; the remaining 35-40 per cent of their intake was obtained in a secondary feeding period after midnight. Lactating females captured the largest amount of insects, an average of 3.7 g per female compared to 2.5 g per pregnant female and 1.8 g per juvenile. This extra effort by lactating females was correlated with a higher energy requirement due to the necessity of periodically returning to the roost site to nurse non-flying young. It was shown that 20-30 per cent of the nightly intake was captured by all individuals in the first 20 minutes after emergence. This suggests a rather impressive capture rate. If we assume the average prey to be the size of a mosquito (the predominant, although not exclusive prey of this species), weighing 2.2 mg, the feeding rate is 140 insects in 20 minutes or 7 insects min^{-1}.

Large fruit bats (Pteropodidae) appear to fly long distances from the roost to fruiting trees and it seems that for these frugivorous species the distance flown in an evening depends upon the availability of adequate food resources. This may also be true for the New World leaf-nosed bats (Phyllostomidae). Radio-tracking studies on *Artibeus jamaicensis* suggest that the distance travelled between roost and foraging site varies greatly between habitats and is related to the density and distribution of fruiting trees. These bats were found to travel up to 10 km in areas where such trees were plentiful.

Nightly activity may be influenced by various abiotic factors. Bats tend to be somewhat more active on dark nights with little or no moonlight or when the moon is obscured by clouds. This may be in response to predator activity on well-lit nights. Bats also decrease their activity during periods of heavy rainfall or high winds. Activity may increase during light rainfall or immediately after a heavy downpour.

Seasonal activity

Bats that live in temperate regions are exposed to a wide range of seasonal temperature fluctuations. Many respond by entering hibernation during cold winter periods; others migrate to more favourable climates. These aspects of bat activity will be discussed in Chapter 6. One might think that seasonal activity would not be found among tropical species. While temperatures may not fluctuate as markedly as in temperate regions, tropical regions usually experience seasonality in the form of wet and dry periods. These periods, like temperate zone temperature fluctuations, greatly influence insect activity and availability as well as flower and fruit availability.

In temperate regions a drop in evening temperature will cause a decline in insect activity and a concomitant decrease in bat foraging activity. In the high deserts of the southwestern United States where winter temperatures may be quite cold, *Pipistrellus hesperus* may be found flying at temperatures as low as −5°C. It appears that this activity may be more concerned with replenishing water supplies than with foraging. Insects may be active at slightly warmer temperatures and foraging on warm winter nights may allow these bats an opportunity to rebuild fat stores.

In tropical regions seasonal behaviour may be expressed more in terms of diet than in foraging activity. During the wet season when fruits are readily available, most fruit-eating phyllostomids consume fruits. However, in the dry season many shift to feeding on pollen and other flower products; some take more insects during drier periods. Some species may migrate to wetter regions during seasonal dry periods. Pteropodids also seem to follow this general scheme. *Pteropus conspicillatus* normally migrates to wet highland areas during summer dry spells in the coastal regions of Queensland.

Among insectivorous species, diet and foraging behaviour may be altered by wet and dry seasons. Above we mentioned some aspects of the foraging behaviour of the Heart-nosed bat (*Cardioderma cor*).

In the dry season, *Cardioderma* feeds on terrestrial beetles and occasionally centipedes. During the wet season, there is usually an abundance and diversity of insects and katydids and sphingid moths form a large part of their diet. Also, during the dry season, *Cardioderma* may forage more on the wing, whereas less time is spent flying in the wet season. Many insectivorous bats specialize on a narrow range of prey sizes and kinds during times of plenty. For example, the Little Brown bat (*Myotis lucifugus*) appears to specialize, almost exclusively, on mosquitoes during July in New Hampshire. During winter months in Zambia, many bats consume adult moths. All (100 per cent) of the 34 stomachs from ten species, representing four families (Rhinolophidae, Hipposideridae, Nycteridae, and Vespertilionidae) contained some or many moths. Only about six per cent of these stomachs contained beetles, flies, and/or night-flying ants. During the drier summer months, the incidence of moths in 56 stomachs from these species declined to 82 per cent, and beetles and flies increased to about 25 per cent.

The reproductive cycles of many bat species are closely linked to seasonality and the availability of insects. The females of many temperate species are pregnant and/or give birth early in the spring just as insects are becoming abundant. Females of tropical, insectivorous bats achieve a reproductive effort just prior to the wet season. Pregnant or lactating females may forage earlier than males and they may forage closer to the roost or nursery site than do males. This kind of activity has been reported in Daubenton's bat (*Myotis daubentonii*), the Long-eared bat (*Plecotus auritus*), and the Long-winged Tomb bat (*Taphozous longimanus*).

Territoriality and loyalty to foraging sites

Many insectivorous bats appear to frequent individual foraging territories or beats that they patrol regularly. These foraging areas may be over a particular stretch of a stream or river, or along the margins of a lake or pond. It is not unusual to see bats flying along rows of street lights or other insect attracting lights in and around cities in the summertime. In one such situation in Las Vegas, Nevada, individuals of the Big Brown bat (*Eptesicus fuscus*) may be seen hunting along a particular series of street lights on a warm summer night. An individual will establish a repetitive circuit going from one light to another and back again. While individuals of *Myotis* or *Pipistrellus* may be tolerated in and around this hunting territory, other individuals of *Eptesicus fuscus* are briskly chased away. Recent discoveries have shown that individual Spotted bats (*Euderma maculatum*) regularly patrol a similar circuit of forest clearings, appearing at a particular clearing with a predictable frequency. We have already noted the loyalty of *Cardioderma cor* to a regular hunting territory. White-lined bats (*Saccopteryx bilineata* and *Saccopteryx leptura*) appear to visit the same areas night after night. A colony of these bats may frequent a particular foraging area that they divide up among the various harems that comprise the colony; males defend a harem's allotted territory. A close relative of these small Neotropical emballonurids—the Proboscis or Tufted bat (*Rhynchonycteris naso*)—also forages in family or harem groups rather than as individuals. Family group foraging has been suggested for the Yellow-winged bat (*Lavia frons*). Finally, *Taphozous longimanus* appears to defend a regular hunting territory against all intruding bat species.

DIGESTIVE SYSTEM

In general organization, the digestive system of bats is essentially like that of other mammals. However, as might be expected, the wide variety of food habits is reflected in the anatomy of some components, especially the stomach and intestine. Regarding these, more is known about the New World leaf-nosed bats (Phyllostomidae), that have the widest array of dietary preferences of any chiropteran family.

Stomach and intestine

The stomach may be divided into several functional regions that are defined mostly by the distribution and relative proportions of several kinds of gastric glands (Fig. 5.6). These regions include: 1) oesophageal junction, that area where the oesophagus enters the stomach; 2) cardiac vestibule, a specialized chamber near the oesophageal junction that opens into the cardiac portion of the stomach; 3) cardiac region, the large bulbous chamber of the stomach; 4) transition region, that intermediate region between the cardiac and pyloric regions; and 5) pyloric region, a generally tubular region of the stomach that opens into the upper portion of the small intestine via the pyloric sphincter. Food passes through the stomach in more or less this sequence. The relative enlargement or reduction of these regions depends on the dietary habits of the bat. These same regions may be found in other mammals and their morphology also varies with dietary preferences.

The cardiac and pyloric regions of the stomach in insectivorous bats are not much modified and they tend to be roughly equal in size. The pyloric region may be somewhat larger than the cardiac portion of the stomach in carnivorous species such as the American False vampire (*Vampyrum spectrum*). The stomachs of fish-eating species (*Noctilio leporinus* and *Pizonyx vivesi*) are essentially similar to those of carnivorous species. In *Noctilio*, there is a curious cardiac sphincter between the oesophagus and the cardiac stomach. This sphincter appears to serve as a 'cork' to block the passage of food back into the oesophagus.

The stomach is markedly modified in frugivorous species. Many of these modifications parallel those found in other herbivorous mammals. The cardiac portion of the stomach is usually greatly enlarged into a broadly tubular bag. This enlargement may also include expansion of the cardiac vestibule. The cardiac region is very large and often tubular in the Old World fruit bats (Pteropodidae). In *Brachyphylla cavernarum* (Phyllostomidae), there is a secondary pouch (cardiac caecum) at the end of the cardiac stomach. The pyloric portion of the stomach is usually short. The stomachs of nectarivorous species (Glossophaginae) are similar, but the cardiac region is not so enlarged as in frugivorous species.

The most radical modifications in the stomach are found in the vampire bats (Phyllostomidae). There is no distinct cardiac vestibule nor clearly definable pyloric region. In addition, the walls of the cardiac region are rather thin and are capable of marked expansion to accommodate the large volume of blood taken in at a feeding. There is also a remarkable network of capillaries surrounding this portion of the stomach that facilitates the rapid absorption, and ultimately the excretion, of huge quantities of excess water found in the blood meal. In the Common vampire (*Desmodus rotundus*), the cardiac region of the stomach is extremely long (approx. 80 mm) and tubular. The stomach of the White-winged vampire (*Diaemus youngi*) is somewhat different in shape. The cardiac portion is large and bag-like with a terminal cardiac caecum. The stomach of the Hairy-legged vampire (*Diphylla ecaudata*) departs even farther from that of the other two vampires. The cardiac region is large and bag-like, as in *Diaemus*, but there are many partitioned compartments. This latter vampire apparently feeds exclusively on the blood of birds.

The length of the intestinal portion of the digestive system also is correlated with differences in diet. Insectivorous species tend to have short to moderately short intestines. Food passage times are relatively short in these species. On the other hand, the gut of frugivorous species is generally long with many complex looping patterns. The distribution of specialized intestinal glands also varies according to food habit.

In the process of feeding, bats usually reject the hard parts of insects and fruits that are difficult to chew. The teeth of bats, discussed below, are designed to chop and mash the food into very small pieces or juice in the case of frugivorous species. This greatly facilitates the digestive processes and reduces the bulk of food intake. Very little is known concerning the length of time required for food passage. Some appear to be quite rapid; less than one hour in the Little Brown bat (*Myotis lucifugus*). Frugivorous species, both mega- and microchiropterans, captured in the evening will frequently be passing copious amounts of seed-laden faecal material.

Teeth of bats

The differences in feeding habits in bats are most notably reflected in differences in the structure and shape of the teeth. In addition, there is a general evolutionary trend toward a reduction in the number of teeth, with some extreme conditions associated with shortening of the face and jaws to increase the effect of the powerful jaw muscles.

The vast majority of bats are insectivorous in their food preferences and, as we have noted, insectivory appears to have been the dietary habit of primitive bats; at least those whose descendants are the Microchiroptera. This supposition is supported by the general similarity in the structure of the chewing or cheek teeth of insectivorous bats and those of the mammalian Order Insectivora (living shrews, moles, hedgehogs, etc.). The cheek teeth of insectivorous bats and other mammalian insectivores have an arrangement of three large, primary cusps and several smaller secondary cusps that are connected by high blade-like flanges or ridges (Fig. 5.7D-G, I). These ridges form a W-shaped pattern (often referred to as a W-shaped ectoloph). The upper and lower chewing teeth interlock in such a way that these complicated ridges shear against each other like many small scissor blades. During chewing or mastication the hard, chitinous exoskeletons of the insect prey are finely chopped into many small pieces. In carnivorous and piscivorous species (Fig. 5.7F, H, and J) the W-shaped pattern is little modified, being only slightly heavier in structure.

Among the New World leaf-nosed bats (Phyllostomidae) insectivory and W-shaped ectolophs are found in the phyllostomine species (Fig. 5.7I). The fruit-eating species of this family show an ever-increasing departure from this primitive tooth structure (Fig. 5.7I-N). In the stenodermatines and

brachyphyllines (nearly exclusive frugivores), only a very subtle vestige of this pattern remains (Fig. 5.7L-M). In these subfamilies, the teeth have become very broad and flat, with a high to moderately high outer blade that is oriented longitudinally rather than transversely across the teeth. These longitudinal blades facilitate chopping through the tough fibrous flesh of fruits, whereas the large flattened surfaces pulverize and squeeze the juices out of the fruit pulp. In contrast, the reduced cheek teeth of nectar-feeding glossophagines are often long and narrow.

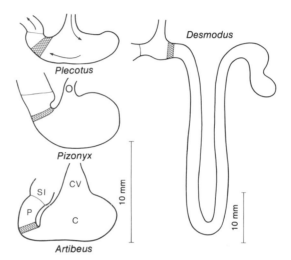

Fig. 5.6 Stomachs of an insectivorous bat (Plecotus–Vespertilionidae), *a fish-eating bat* (Pizonyx–Vespertilionidae), *a fruit-eating bat* (Artibeus–Phyllostomidae) *and a vampire* (Desmodus–Phyllostomidae). *Arrows show general passage of food through the stomach. O, oesophagus; CV, cardiac vestibule; C, cardiac stomach; P, pyloric stomach; SI, small intestine. The cross-hatched bands mark the transition between cardiac and pyloric chambers. (After Forman, 1972).*

The teeth of the Old World fruit bats (Pteropodidae) are unique in structure and bear little or no resemblance to the teeth of any other group of mammals (Fig. 5.7A-C). In addition, none shows any indication of having evolved from the W-shaped cheek teeth typical of microchiropterans. In contrast to the transversely broadened teeth of frugivorous microchiropterans, the cheek teeth of pteropodids are elongated and generally flat. The anterior portions of these teeth may be elevated as a single cusp or, in some cases, as two cusps. The most highly cuspidate teeth occur in *Pteralopex* and *Harpyionycteris*. In the former, even the upper canine teeth have many strong cusps and in both the larger cheek teeth have numerous small cusps. The pattern of cuspidation, however, appears to have no relation (homology) to the cuspidate pattern of the Microchiroptera.

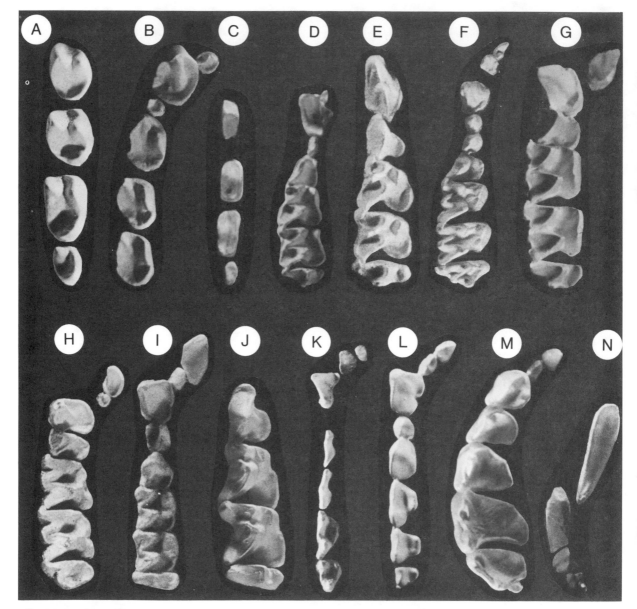

Fig. 5.7 Dentition of bats. A, Pteropus macrotis (frugivore); B, Nyctimene major (frugivore); C, Eonycteris spelaea (nectarivore); D, Taphozous melanopogon (insectivore); E, Cardioderma cor (carnivore); F, Pizonyx vivesi (piscivore); G, Cheiromeles torquatus (insectivore); H, Noctilio leporinus (piscivore); I, Phyllostomus discolor (frugivore/insectivore); J, Vampyrum spectrum) (carnivore); K, Leptonycteris curasoae (nectarivore); L, Erophylla sezekorni (nectarivore/ frugivore); M, Artibeus jamaicensis (frugivore); N, Diaemus youngi (sanguivore). Only partial toothrows (last premolar and molars) shown on A, C, and J. (A–C Pteropodidae; D, Emballonuridae; E, Megadermatidae; F, Vespertilionidae; G, Molossidae; H, Noctilionidae; I–N, Phyllostomidae).

Chapter 6 Thermoregulation

One of the many ways that animals are categorized is the degree to which they are capable of regulating their body temperature. The terms 'cold-blooded' and 'warm-blooded' are often used in this regard. However poor these terms may be, they are well established, convenient, and will suffice to introduce temperature regulation in bats. Cold-blooded animals (all animals except birds and mammals) are more or less at the mercy of their environment with respect to the body temperature they can maintain. The body temperature of truly cold-blooded animals follows rather closely that of the medium (air or water) in which they live. However, most so-called cold-blooded animals can and indeed do stay somewhat warmer than their surroundings (ambient temperature). On the other hand, warm-blooded animals (birds and mammals) generally *maintain* a constant, warm body temperature (birds, c. 35 to 41°C; mammals, c. 30 to 40°C) that is independent of their environmental surroundings. This ability to maintain a relatively constant body temperature, independent of ambient temperature, is regarded as an evolutionary specialization of these animals.

Warm-bloodedness of birds and mammals is associated with several anatomical adaptations which they share, but which they have acquired independently from their respective reptilian ancestors. These include a double circuit, completely four-chambered heart and related arterial and venous circulation. Both have an effective insulative covering; feathers in birds and hair in the great majority of mammals (a few lack fur). Both have highly efficient respiratory systems that permit a high rate of gaseous exchange. These all allow a high metabolic rate of heat generation.

In all living organisms, heat is a by-product of many biochemical reactions that occur inside all body cells as they conduct their various metabolic activities. Thus, cells can be thought of as generating metabolic heat. The management (loss or retention) of this metabolic heat, or lack thereof, directly relates to an animal's ability to control or otherwise regulate its temperature.

Physics of heat transfer

A full appreciation of thermoregulation and body temperature requires a brief consideration of the physical aspects of heat flow. Whenever physical materials are at different temperatures, heat flows from a region of higher temperature to one of lower temperature. This transfer of heat takes place by conduction (heat flow through and between physical bodies that are in contact) and/or radiation (heat flow or emission from physical bodies that are not in contact). The reader is no doubt aware of the different conductivity of different substances. For example, steel is a better conductor of heat than is glass or wood. Living tissue is less conductive than these substances and fur is even less able to conduct heat.

All physical objects that are at temperatures above absolute zero emit heat in the form of electromagnetic radiation. The intensity of this radiation (its wavelength) depends on the temperature of the radiating surface. A third means of heat transfer is evaporation which is a surface phenomenon. The changing of water from a liquid state to a vaporous state requires a great deal of heat. This heat is drawn by conduction or radiation from the areas on either side of the evaporative surface. Thus, in a sweating mammal, the heat of evaporation, at the surface of the skin, is extracted from both the warm body as well as the surrounding air.

Heat balance

All living organisms live within some range of temperatures; this range may be rather broad or extremely narrow. Nonetheless, for all organisms, there is a temperature below which they will die as well as a temperature above which they cannot survive. These two extremes are referred to as the lower thermal lethal and upper thermal lethal, respectively. In the discussion of flight physiology and temperature regulation (Chapter 4), we noted that the upper thermal lethal for *Phyllostomus hastatus* was 42 to 43°C. As we will see in this chapter, the lower thermal lethal varies among species of bats, the limit for some being quite low, whereas in others it is rather high.

The three components of heat exchange–conduction, radiation and evaporation–act on an organism between the upper and lower thermal lethals. Depending upon several factors, the most important of which is the temperature of the external environmental medium, the effect of these heat flow components may act as a double-edged blade. For example, when the external temperature is low, the direction of heat flow will be away from the organism, thereby driving its internal temperature toward the lower thermal lethal. Eventually, the internal body temperature and external temperature reach a point at which they are the same; that is, they are at equilibrium. So long as this point of equilibrium is within the survivable temperature range, there is little difficulty. If, however, the point of equilibrium is beyond its lower thermal lethal, the organism must respond either physiologically, by generating sufficient heat to stay warm; or behaviourally, by moving to a location where the equilibrium does not so exceed the lethal limit. In a situation where the external temperature is higher than the internal temperature, heat flow is toward the organism, thereby driving the internal temperature in the direction of the upper thermal lethal. Again, if the point of equilibrium is beyond the lethal limit, the organism must respond by either increasing its rate of heat loss or moving to a cooler location to maintain its temperature within survivable limits.

Thus, we see that temperature balance depends on a dynamic interaction among several factors. This dynamic interaction can be expressed by the following formula:

$H_{tot} = H_c + H_r + H_s$. Where H_{tot} represents the total heat produced as the result of cellular metabolism; this value is always positive. Under any given set of circumstances, the dynamic interaction of the various factors on the right-hand side of the formula will determine the magnitude of H_{tot}; that is, both sides of the formula will be equal or balanced. H_c represents heat lost or gained as the result of conduction (+ or increased conductance equals heat loss). H_r represents heat lost or gained due to radiation (+ or increased radiation equals heat loss). H_s represents heat lost or gained by heat storage (+ or storage equals heat gain).

Endothermy and thermal homeostasis

We have noted that most cold-blooded animals are incapable of maintaining their internal body temperatures at a level independent of the ambient temperature (ectothermy). They are called ectotherms. The sum effect of factors on the right-hand side of our formula for thermal balance is determined by external, environmental temperature. Ectotherms have little or no direct control over these factors. However, they can behaviourally move to a location of more favourable ambient circumstances. For example, a lizard may move to a sunny spot on a rock where it basks, thereby raising its body temperature both

from solar radiation as well as from heat radiated from the solar-heated rock. Thus heated, the lizard is able to forage for food and conduct other life processes. When mid day temperatures approach lethal levels, the lizard retreats to cooler spots, in shade, where its body temperature drops to more favourable levels. In this way, an ectotherm may be able to maintain its body temperature within some relatively high and, more or less constant, range of temperatures. At night, when ambient temperatures fall, or in cold seasons, the lizard is obliged to become inactive. This is a simplistic example and certainly some lizards can maintain some degree of control over their body temperature.

On the other hand, warm-blooded animals (endotherms) are capable of maintaining a constant warm internal body temperature independent of ambient temperatures (endothermy). This is achieved by physiological processes backed up by various anatomical adaptations. That is, endotherms are able to control or at least override the effects of the factors on the right-hand side of our thermal balance formula. By decreasing thermal conductance, they are able to retain heat that would normally be lost in cold ambient temperatures. Reduction of thermal conductance is accomplished by various insulating mechanisms; chief among these are feathers (in the case of birds) or furry coats (in the case of mammals). Layers of subcutaneous fat may also contribute to reducing thermal conductance as in marine mammals.

Another means of affecting internal body temperature is to simply increase the heat input by increasing the metabolic rate (heat output) of cells. This, of course, is a costly process. In order to minimize this metabolic expense, most endotherms have a range of ambient temperatures within which they expend little or no energy to regulate their internal body temperature. This range of ambient temperatures is called the thermal neutral zone. When an animal is within this thermal neutral range of temperatures, it does not have to increase its metabolic rate (oxygen consumption) above the basal level in order to maintain a constant internal body temperature. The thermal neutral zone is bounded by a lower thermal critical and an upper thermal critical temperature below which and/or above which, respectively, the endotherm must expend metabolic energy in order to maintain a constant warm internal temperature (Fig. 6.1). The maintenance of such a constant internal temperature is called thermal homeostasis.

Most tropical mammals (bats included) have a thermal neutral zone between 20 and 30°C. Most temperate species (including some bats) and all arctic species of mammals (there are no arctic bats) are able to extend their lower thermal critical temperatures

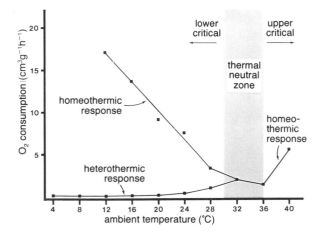

Fig. 6.1 Metabolic responses of the Western
pipistrelle (Pipistrellus hesperus–Vespertilionidae) from
southern California. See text for discussion.

and thereby increase the breadth of their thermal
neutral zone by decreasing their conductivity; that is
with heavy and dense winter coats of fur and/or
added layers of subcutaneous fat. For example, the
lower thermal critical temperature in the Arctic fox
(*Alopex lagopus*) has been found to extend at least to
−50°C. The thermal neutral temperature ranges found
in bird species also tend to be quite broad.

The Western pipistrelle – an example

The Western pipistrelle (*Pipistrellus hesperus*) is a
small-sized (3-5 g) vespertilionid that lives in the
southwestern deserts of the United States where
there is a marked annual range of ambient temperatures between −10 and 45°C. The lower thermal lethal
and upper thermal lethal temperatures for *Pipistrellus
hesperus* are −1 and 44°C, respectively. The thermal
neutral zone of *P. hesperus* lies between about 32 and
36°C (Fig. 6.1). On a warm summer night, the Western
pipistrelle has relatively little trouble staying within
its thermal neutral zone. Indeed, its major metabolic
problem is the energy expense of staying below its
upper thermal critical temperature. This is accomplished by increasing the radiation (H_r) of excess heat
from the highly vascularized flight membranes. In the
winter, *P. hesperus* faces an extreme of cold ambient
temperatures and must expend considerable amounts
of metabolic energy to remain active. Under these
circumstances, thermal conductance (H_c) and radiation (H_r) work against the Western pipistrelle. We will
return to this example in the discussion below.

Metabolic rate and endothermy

Compared to ectotherms, all endotherms have relatively high metabolic rates. Ultimately, the amount of
heat produced in various cellular processes rests on
the amount and kinds of fuels used to stoke these tiny
metabolic furnaces. This fuel is derived from the food
intake which contains carbohydrates, fats, and proteins. Carbohydrates are an immediately usable fuel,
whereas fats represent an efficiently storable, high
energy fuel. Proteins are structural items, for the most
part, and are not normally used in the heat-producing
aspects of metabolism; during starvation, however,
proteins are utilized. Recall that under normal circumstances, carbohydrates and fats are combusted
with oxygen (aerobic metabolism), but that, in some
instances, anaerobic metabolism may be accomplished.

There are two general kinds of endothermic mammals. There are those that maintain a constant
internal body temperature no matter what the daily or
seasonal ambient temperature might be. These are
called homeothermic endotherms (homeothermy)
and include humans as well as many other kinds of
mammals (including some bats). Then there are some
mammals (including most microchiropteran bats)
that are capable of maintaining a constant internal
temperature during certain portions of the daily cycle
and/or during certain seasons. However, during
some parts of the day and/or during seasons with
cold, unfavourable ambient temperatures, they allow
their internal body temperature to drop (without
metabolic maintenance) to low temperatures well
below the lower thermal critical. These mammals are
referred to as heterothermic endotherms (heterothermy).

Heterothermy occurs in some mammals that are
judged to be primitive on other grounds. Because of
this, many researchers have been led to believe that
heterothermy is a primitive feature of mammals.
Indeed, heterothermy appears to occupy a position
between ectothermy and homeothermy. However,
heterothermy is an endothermic condition that is just
as specialized as homeothermy and in some respects
it is more so. Heterothermy is much more energy
efficient in that, as ambient temperatures become
cooler (daily or seasonally), the heterotherm adjusts
its internal temperature downward and thereby
avoids the metabolic costs of maintaining a constant
internal temperature during periods of inactivity.
Heterothermy is a bona fide thermoregulatory process in that the heterotherm may spontaneously
arouse from these cooler internal temperatures. Heterothermy may be a daily process in which case we
refer to it as daily torpor. True hibernation is a special

kind of heterothermy in which torpor occurs over many days or several months during seasons of cold ambient temperatures.

DAILY THERMOREGULATORY CYCLE

The daily cycle of bats, like that of other mammals and vertebrates, is divided up into different activities. For bats, the nocturnal portion of this cycle is spent actively foraging for food, and with reproductive activities during the reproductive season. The diurnal portion of the daily cycle is spent in the day roost which may include a number of different kinds of sites ranging from caves to exposed tree branches (see Chapter 9). The majority of the diurnal cycle may be devoted to resting (sleep), although it may also include wakeful activities such as grooming, care of young, social, and/or reproductive behaviour. The energy required to accomplish or support the daily activity cycle can be placed in the economic context of a time-energy budget.

Daily energy budget

As we noted above, metabolic energy and heat are derived from the digestion and assimilation of food intake. Therefore, the total daily energy budget for an organism is directly related to the availability and acquisition of food. A large portion of the daily energy budget is expended in the pursuit of acquiring sufficient food stores to drive the organism's metabolism. In the case of a homeotherm, another substantial portion of this daily budget is involved in maintaining its thermal homeostasis. This, of course, requires that the total heat production equal the total heat flow away from (in cold ambient extremes), or toward (in warm ambient extremes) the homeotherm as the result of conduction, radiation, and/or evaporation. This expenditure of metabolic energy must continue at a relatively constant rate even when the homeotherm is at rest or occupied with minimally exertive activity.

Daily energy budgets and metabolic potential are directly correlated with body size. Small-sized organisms have proportionately greater surface areas, relative to their volume, by virtue of the fact that volume decreases more rapidly than surface area as linear dimensions decrease. This is called the surface/volume rule or ratio. Thus, for example, at any given ambient temperature a mouse will lose or gain heat at a higher rate than will an elephant under the same conditions. As might be expected, a mouse has a

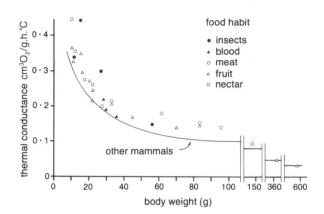

Fig. 6.2 Relationship of thermal conductance to body size in bats (symbols) compared to that of mammals in general (solid line). See text for discussion. (McNab, 1969).

higher metabolic rate and intake of food per unit of body weight than does an elephant. Likewise, a small bat, such as the Little Brown bat (Myotis lucifugus–7-8 g), has a higher daily energy budget (0.89 kcal $g^{-1}day^{-1}$) compared to that of the large-sized American False vampire (Vampyrum spectrum–170-180 g), which has a daily requirement of 0.27 kcal $g^{-1}day^{-1}$. Thus, it appears that bats generally follow what has been called the 'mouse/elephant' metabolic curve reflecting heat loss (thermal conductance H_c) and metabolic rate. However, except for large-sized species (300-1000 g), bats tend to fall slightly above this curve with generally higher values of thermal conductance (Fig. 6.2). No doubt this is due to the loss (or gain) of heat across the extensively vascularized flight membranes.

Daily torpor – optimization of metabolism

It should be clear by now that the optimal ambient situation for a homeotherm is one at thermal neutrality. In such an effective environment, metabolic energy expenditure is at a minimum. However, if the ambient conditions happen to be below the thermal neutral limit, the homeotherm must increase its metabolic rate and thereby its energy expenditure to remain at a constant, warm internal homeostasis. On the other hand, a heterotherm faced with temperatures below the lower thermal critical can opt to allow its internal body temperature to drop and thereby avoid the escalating metabolic costs of maintaining a constant warm internal temperature. When ambient temperatures exceed the upper thermal critical, both homeotherms and heterotherms actively attempt to regulate their internal body temperatures. The option not to regulate body temperature at ambient temperatures below the lower thermal critical amounts to a marked energy saving when viewed in terms of overall daily energy budget.

Precious little is known about daily energy budgets of bats. Indeed, the few daily budgets that have been proposed are rational extrapolations of measurable resting and active metabolic rates (based on oxygen consumption rates measured in laboratory experimentation), food quality (calorific value), feeding rates, and estimates of flight energetics. Such a budget has been proposed for the Fringed myotis (*Myotis thysanodes*) in early pregnancy (9 g). [The thermal neutral range for this species is 30.5 to 38.5°C.] In these bats, nocturnal activity (flight and night roost maintenance) requires 3341 calories or 0.37 kcal $g^{-1}day^{-1}$. Day-roost maintenance (ambient temperature, 20°C) for a regulating (homeothermic) female requires 1410 calories (0.16 kcal $g^{-1}day^{-1}$), whereas a non-regulating (heterothermic) female requires only one-half this amount of 690 calories (0.08 kcal $g^{-1}day^{-1}$). The total energy budget for these two groups is 4751 calories (0.53 kcal $g^{-1}day^{-1}$) and 4031 calories (0.45 kcal $g^{-1}day^{-1}$), respectively. This amounts to about a 15 per cent energy saving by not regulating.

Whereas a daily energy budget has not yet been estimated for the Western pipistrelle (*Pipistrellus hesperus*), the oxygen consumption rates ($cm^3g^{-1}h^{-1}$) of regulators v. non-regulators at 20°C further illustrates the energy optimization of heterothermy (Fig. 6.1). In this species, males are somewhat smaller (3-4 g) than females (4-5 g) which will serve to reaffirm the aspects of body size and metabolic rate (discussed above), as expressed by oxygen consumption rate. Regulating (homeothermic) males and females of *P. hesperus* consume an average of 10.01 and 8.60 cm^3 O_2 $g^{-1}h^{-1}$, respectively. On the other hand, non-regulating (heterothermic) males and females consume an average of 0.48 and 0.46 cm^3 O_2 $g^{-1}h^{-1}$, respectively. At 32°C (within the thermal neutral zone for the species), males and females average 2.43 and 1.94 cm^3 O_2 $g^{-1}h^{-1}$, respectively. Thus, for regulators at these ambient temperatures, this amounts to a 4-5 fold increase over thermal neutral metabolic rates or an 8-9 fold increase above non-regulatory metabolic rates.

Patterns of daily torpor

Laboratory experimentation has clearly shown that individuals of some species of bats can regulate their body temperatures spontaneously or facultatively in the face of low ambient temperatures; that is, maintain a body temperature well above that of ambient. At the same time, other individuals (or even the same individuals in different experimental sessions) may choose to allow their body temperatures to approximate that of the ambient temperature. Although there is clearly insufficient data on free-living individuals to permit generalization, there is interesting evidence to indicate that daily torpidity may be facultative, obligatory, or perhaps a mixture of these. Small body size and high metabolic demands may force some species into daily torpor, while somewhat larger-sized species may simply take advantage of the energy savings during mildly low ambient temperatures by relaxing their control of body temperatures. At very low ambient temperatures (those approaching 0°C), all bat species exercise some degree of homeothermy.

Daily torpor appears to be common among the temperate species of the families Rhinolophidae, Hipposideridae, and Vespertilionidae. Individuals of some populations of the Mexican Free-tailed bat (*Tadarida brasiliensis*), a molossid that occurs in the temperate portion of North America, appear to be capable of facultative torpor. Most populations of this species migrate southward in the wintertime (see Chapter 9). The populations of this species in northern California apparently do not migrate and they have been found hibernating under bridges in the area of Mt Shasta. This is rather peculiar because individuals of this species from Arizona and southern Nevada are unable to recover after being experimentally cooled to 29°C. Yet, this population also appears not to migrate. Instead they move into warm roost sites such as next to the chimneys of houses or especially warm caves and tunnels. Other populations undertake long migrations into Mexico and do not enter periods of torpor. Another North American molossid, the Western Mastiff bat (*Eumops perotis*), enters daily torpor only in the winter months. The Greater Mouse-tailed bat (*Rhinopoma microphyllum*– Rhinopomatidae), that lives in India, follows a thermal regulatory pattern similar to that of *Eumops perotis* with extended periods of torpor (hibernation) between October and March.

All of these species are insectivorous in their food habits (see Chapter 5). There appears to be a direct correlation between this dietary preference and daily torpidity. We have not yet dealt with hibernation (extended torpidity), but it too occurs in temperate bat species and also appears to be directly linked with food availability (or lack thereof). Birds do not hibernate and one might wonder how insectivorous species survive extended cold, unfavourable periods with reduced or non-existent insect availability. Those that rely exclusively on flying insects, such as swallows, migrate to warm climates where flying insects are available. Other bird species that remain in the temperate regions during these inclement periods, eat non-flying adult insects, eggs, and/or larvae that have taken refuge from the cold periods behind bark or in crevices. Some birds also switch their dietary preference to seeds or other vegetative food items. These alternative menus are not open to insectivorous bats that prey on flying insects. Some species, such as the Western pipistrelle, take advantage of periodic warm spells during the southwestern winter, when flying insects emerge, to replenish their fat stores. Daily torpor facilitates energy optimization during times of food scarcity, whether the period of scarcity is short as sometimes occurs during the summer months, or long as in winter.

Tropical insectivorous bat species also have high rates of metabolism and most also enter daily torpor to some extent. Insect availability fluctuates markedly in the tropics, although perhaps not as drastically as in the temperate regions. As we noted in the previous chapter this fluctuation is linked with the seasonality of rainfall. Here, too, if the normal feeding pattern of a bat is interrupted for more than a day or two, it is forced to rely on its fat stores. Therefore, daily torpor permits an individual to either break even or, perhaps, maintain a slight metabolic reserve, in the form of stored fat, during times of dietary poverty.

At the other extreme of thermal regulatory patterns are bats that maintain a constant warm body temperature throughout the daily cycle. All of these bats live in the tropical or subtropical regions of the world and most are frugivorous or have related diets, including nectar or other flower parts. Initial investigations on the thermal regulatory abilities of megachiropterans (Pteropodidae) were based on large flying foxes (400-600 g) such as *Pteropus* and *Rousettus*. These studies revealed that these bats were 'good' homeotherms that maintain a constant warm body temperature even at very low (experimental) ambient temperatures. At low temperatures, the Grey-headed flying fox (*Pteropus poliocephalus*) and the Collared flying fox (*Pteropus scapulatus*) wrap their wings tightly around their bodies with their heads tucked inside. This allows them to behaviourally decrease their thermal conductance (H_c) by trapping air in their fur and thereby creating an insulative dead air space. In addition, these bats increase their output of metabolic heat by increased muscular activity in the form of shivering. At high temperatures, these bats spread, and occasionally fan their wings thereby increasing their thermal conductance (H_c). Depending on the severity of the ambient temperature, they may lick their fur and/or wing membranes; open their mouths, extend their tongues, and pant; or in some cases urinate on themselves, thereby wetting their fur. All of these behaviours are directed toward

increasing heat loss by evaporative cooling (H_c). In this manner, these large flying foxes are able to regulate their daily thermal homeostasis at a rather constant level. This ability, of course, exacts a high metabolic (energetic) cost.

In view of the marked differences already noted between Mega- and Microchiroptera, the discovery of homeothermic temperature regulation in megachiropterans came with little surprise. However, recent investigations on small-sized pteropodids reveal a somewhat different picture; one that again seems to confirm the relationship between body size and thermal regulatory ability. Two Tube-nosed species (*Nyctimene albiventer*–30 g and *Paranyctimene raptor*–20 g), from New Guinea, occasionally lapse into a lethargic daily torpor (heterothermy) at cool ambient temperatures. At 25°C, homeothermic individuals of *Nyctimene albiventer* utilized 2.59 cm³ O_2 g⁻¹h⁻¹, a metabolic rate about four times higher than that of heterothermic individuals (0.67 cm³ O_2 g⁻¹h⁻¹) at the same temperature. Likewise, the small nectarivorous, African Long-tongued fruit bat (*Megaloglossus woermanni*) apparently goes into daily torpor. At an ambient temperature of 23°C, these bats relaxed homeothermic control of their thermal homeostasis and allowed their body temperature to drop to 26 to 28°C. Thus, it would appear that even though megachiropterans may be excellent regulators (homeotherms), they too may opt for the energy savings of heterothermy at cool ambient temperatures.

The daily thermal regulatory patterns of the New World fruit-eating bats (Phyllostomidae) are interesting both in terms of this discussion and in illustrating some of the pitfalls of laboratory experimentation. Two different sets of experiments were accomplished independently of each other and by different researchers using different experimental designs. One investigation utilized phyllostomids found in Brazil and Mexico, while the other utilized species encountered in Panama. Fortuitously, there was a fair amount of overlap in the species examined. One investigator captured bats in the wild, brought them into the laboratory, and maintained them in a high nutritional state on an ample diet of fruits and associated food items. Some insectivorous species also were examined, but these would not feed voluntarily on the insect diets provided by the researcher, and consequently, had to be experimented upon within 24 hours after capture and released. The nutritionally healthy frugivores responded to low ambient temperatures (down to 5°C) with a typical homeothermic pattern of thermal regulation. The insectivores generally responded with a typical heterothermic pattern of non-regulation; some regulated at mildly low ambient temperatures, but eventually lapsed into heterothermy at lower temperatures.

The other researchers utilized frugivorous and insectivorous bats captured in the wild, but they conducted their thermal regulatory experiments within 2-10 hours after capture of all individuals. Since experimentation was conducted soon after capture and the individuals were released thereafter, little effort was made to provide a maintenance diet other than sufficient water. This research provided results contradictory to those obtained by the first investigator with regard to the frugivorous phyllostomids. These bats responded heterothermically, for the most part, to a range of ambient temperatures similar to those used by the first investigator; several individuals behaved as typical homeotherms. The insectivorous vespertilionid *Myotis nigricans* responded in a typical heterothermic manner. Individuals of a molossid, *Molossus sinaloae*, and a mormoopid, *Pteronotus gymnonotus*, regulated their internal temperatures at a constant, or nearly constant, level down to about 10°C and then became heterothermic. Several individuals of both species performed more or less heterothermically throughout the entire range of ambient temperatures. Species related to these two behaved in a similar manner in the first experiments.

Thus, both groups of researchers found concordant behaviour for their respective insectivorous species, some being obligate heterotherms, while others were homeothermic or facultative heterotherms. However, their respective results for frugivorous phyllostomids were apparently conflicting. On the basis of his results, the first investigator interpreted the homeothermic responses of the phyllostomids that he tested to be a reflection of the generally abundant food resource (fruit, nectar, and other flower parts) in tropical ecosystems. The second group of researchers apparently were expecting to find homeothermic responses, for the reason given above; that is, abundance of food resource. However, their results negated this notion. They further concluded that thermoregulation (both homeothermy and heterothermy) was a non-adaptive (random) characteristic of neotropical bats.

The interesting sidelight of these investigations is that both were right to a certain extent, but for the wrong reasons. Also, both sets of experiments, by virtue of their different designs, inadvertently examined a relationship that neither knowingly intended. This relationship involves the thermoregulatory ability of bats in different nutritional states. The first investigator went to great lengths to insure that his bats were healthy throughout the experimentation. The second group went to similar lengths to guard against experimental bias by not supplementing their experimental subjects with food. This contradictory evidence remained unresolved for almost ten years before the second group of researchers duplicated the first researcher's experimental design and were able to repeat his results. Thus, nutritionally wealthy bats (both frugivores and insectivores) can afford the luxury of homeothermy, whereas bats under natural, less lucrative circumstances, must engage in more frugal means of energy conservation; that is, relaxed homeothermy or pure heterothermy. None of the frugivorous species examined had a body size large enough to outweigh markedly the constraints of thermal conductance and thereby allow homeothermy throughout the daily cycle as observed in the large-sized pteropodids.

There is relatively little information on the daily thermal regulatory cycle of carnivorous bat species. The Australian False vampire (*Macroderma gigas*–148 g) appears to be a homeotherm with a stable and constant internal body temperature over a wide range of ambient temperatures. The phyllostomid carnivores, *Phyllostomus hastatus* (80-90 g) and *Chrotopterus auritus* (90-100 g), were found to regulate their thermal homeostasis at about 36 and 37.5°C, respectively. The piscivorous bat, *Noctilio leporinus* (60 g), appears to regulate its body temperature at about 35°C, although it may occasionally relax this control and become heterothermic.

The daily thermal regulatory ability of vampire bats again illustrates the problems of experimentation on animals that have been held in captivity over an extended period of time. Early research on such vampires (*Desmodus rotundus*) indicated that they were poor regulators (heterotherms) and very sensitive to moderately high and/or low temperatures. However, more recent studies on vampires (*Desmodus, Diphylla,* and *Diaemus*) in a natural nutritive state indicates that they are capable of homeothermic regulation down to ambient temperatures near 0°C. *Diphylla* and *Diaemus*, both of which feed on avian blood, occasionally opt for a heterothermic mode of daily regulation. It may be that they are not in as good a general nutritive state as *Desmodus* simply because extracting a regular and ample blood meal from birds may be difficult on a daily basis. On the other hand, the blood reservoir for the Common vampire (*Desmodus rotundus*), cattle, horses, other mammalian livestock, and humans, may be more plentiful.

Roost selection

Bats occupy a wide variety of diurnal roosts. These are discussed in Chapter 9. Roost site selection may depend on a number of factors. These include a refuge safe from predation or one with a particular light intensity. Perhaps most important are the thermal and humidity characteristics of the roost site. Open and exposed roosting sites tend to be thermally unstable with a marked fluctuation of daily temperatures; humidity will also vary in these sites depending on climatic conditions. On the other hand, cave sites tend to remain at a relatively constant daily and/or seasonal temperature and humidity. Although we have not discussed water loss, it too is related directly to heat loss, and many of the same constraints discussed for thermal regulation also apply to water conservation.

The energetic costs of diurnal roosting can often be minimized by selecting an appropriate site. Some bats routinely select roosting sites that result in the passive entrapment of their endogenous metabolic heat. Such a site would fall within the thermal neutral zone of a particular species resulting in an economical energetic equilibrium. Some species may select roost sites that are somewhat below their thermal neutral range and thereby gain a daily energetic advantage by relaxing their thermal control and becoming mildly torpid.

Bats have been observed behaviourally to modify their roosting position in a particular roost site as daily temperatures fluctuate. For example, the Little Brown bat (*Myotis lucifugus*) frequently roosts in attics of houses or barns. Early in the morning individuals may be found tightly packed among the rafters near the peak of the attic. However, as the daytime temperature rises and begins to heat the confined attic space, these bats move down the rafters, away from the peak.

Other bats frequently form tightly-packed clusters during their occupation of a diurnal retreat. Clustering serves several energy conserving functions. For homeothermic bats, a cluster allows the group to remain at a higher overall temperature, as a result of reduced conductance (H_c), than any one individual could by itself at low ambient temperatures. Thus, a cluster of many small-sized bats effectively behaves thermally like a bat of large size. For heterothermic bats a cluster provides the same advantage. That is, a cluster at a low, energetically conservative internal temperature, tends to remain at this temperature in the face of fluctuating ambient temperatures. Many phyllostomids that roost under foliage occur in relatively large, tightly-packed clusters.

HIBERNATION

From the foregoing discussion it is clear that the energetic costs of homeothermy are extremely high. On a daily basis, bats may opt to avoid these costs by

lapsing into a daily, lethargic torpor. During favourable periods of the year and for those with ample (or at least sufficient) food availability, this mode of thermal regulation will permit the individual to survive, reproduce, and conduct other life processes.

However, temperate regions of the world undergo a marked range of seasonal variation, most becoming extremely cold during the winter months. During the winter, insectivorous bats face a major energetic crisis–declining and eventual cessation of flying insect availability. Quite simply, bats and other homeotherms that are so dependent on a particular seasonally available food source are faced with starvation that is further aggravated by decreasing ambient temperatures which, in turn, require an increased metabolic expenditure and so forth.

Under these circumstances, an organism (ectothermic or endothermic) has several choices: death; migration to a climate where there is favourable food availability; switching to a food resource that is sufficiently abundant to allow thermal maintenance; and/or entering a physiological state in which metabolic demands are reduced to minimal survival levels. Our concern here is with the survival of a species and not with individual survival. In this regard one might wonder whether death might be a viable option. For all vertebrates it is not. However, most insects do employ this strategy with the reproductive adults dying at the end of the warm season and leaving the species to overwinter as eggs or larvae in protected sites. Some endotherms (including birds and some bats) opt to migrate to more favourable climates in the winter (see Chapter 9). As noted above, some birds and mammals (not including the vast majority of bats) may switch to other food sources in the wintertime. Most ectothermic vertebrates (reptiles and amphibians) and some mammals (including many bat species) enter a long-term lethargic state called winter sleep or hibernation, in which metabolic and physiological activity is markedly lowered.

Hibernation patterns are extremely complex and a singular definition is difficult to construct. It is somewhat easier to characterize hibernation which includes the following: body temperature reduced and maintained at a level within 1 to 2°C of the ambient temperature; oxygen consumption, breathing rate, and metabolic rate reduced and maintained at a low level; reduced heart and general circulatory rate with peripheral vasoconstriction; a deep lethargic torpor more pronounced than sleep; and an ability to arouse spontaneously by major heat-producing mechanisms. The latter feature differentiates the obligatory hibernation of ectotherms from that of endotherms. Most people mistake the winter sleep characteristic of bears and other carnivores as true hibernation. This is not the case as the winter slumber of carnivores is not accompanied by the marked metabolic and physiological shutdown experienced by true hibernators such as bats and rodents.

Preparation for hibernation

All true mammalian hibernators undergo a preparatory phase before entering winter dormancy. This preparatory phase is characterized by marked increases in body weight, mostly as a result of accumulating heavy fat reserves. There are two generalizations regarding the means by which fat reserves are accumulated. One of these is simply to over-eat, thereby storing the excess. This means appears to apply to fat deposition in migratory birds. On the other hand, bats in the north temperate region do not appear to feed with any marked increase in frequency, yet they accumulate a stored fat reserve in late August and September. This is accomplished by taking advantage of the heterothermic benefits of daily torpor. In effect, by adjusting their daily energy budget and allowing their body temperatures to drop during the diurnal resting period, bats are able to deposit a small fraction of fat. It has been estimated that adults of the Fringed myotis (*Myotis thysanodes*) may store as much as 0.17 g day^{-1}. In this way bats may be able to store as much as 25-30 per cent of the total body weight in fat reserves. It is the calorific value of this fat reserve plus a markedly reduced metabolic rate that permits bats and other hibernating mammals to survive long periods of seasonal dormancy.

Some individuals, primarily young of the year, are not able to conduct their normal activity and growth processes in addition to accumulating sufficient fat reserves for hibernation. As a consequence, young of the year are often the last to enter hibernation. High winter mortality has been reported for the young of many species as a result of this insufficient fat deposition prior to hibernation (see Chapter 9).

The fat reserves accumulated in the preparatory phase of hibernation are more or less finite. Some species may be able to replenish their fat reserve by taking advantage of warm spells when insects emerge in the wintertime. However, for most hibernating bats, their fat stores are just sufficient to carry them through the hibernating period without much leeway for error.

The length of time that a bat can hibernate without supplementation has been the topic of some experimentation and logical estimation. For example, the Big Brown bat (*Eptesicus fuscus*–20-25 g), has been found to be capable of hibernating for almost an entire year (300-340 days). These bats were kept in a refrigerator, at a constant low temperature, with only water provided. However, bats never encounter such constant and controlled conditions in nature and, therefore, the potential length of hibernation is much shorter. Estimates have been derived for some species by taking into account the weight of the bat, weight and calorific value of its fat reserve, and its minimal metabolic rate. In this way, a maximum hibernation potential (in days) has been derived for three species of *Myotis*: l65 days for *M. lucifugus*, 192 for *M. yumanensis* and 163 for *M. thysanodes*. Because of size differences, males and females frequently differ in the length of their maximum hibernation potential. In November (mean temperature 6°C), males of the Western pipistrelle have sufficient fat reserves to last about 90 days; females carry enough to last about 110 days.

Onset of hibernation

The stimuli that cause mammals to enter hibernation are not well understood. In rodents the stimuli appear to involve shortage of food and shortening day lengths (reduced photoperiod). These, however, do not appear to be very important to bats. Decreasing ambient temperature seems to be a paramount factor for these hibernators. In addition, an as yet poorly understood physiological and hormonal balance must be reached before hibernation can proceed.

Once hibernation has been induced the metabolic rate is greatly reduced. The oxygen consumption rate of a Little Brown bat (8-9 g) at 2°C is about 0.030 cm^3 O_2 g^{-1}h^{-1} compared to 4.14 cm^3 O_2 g^{-1}h^{-1} at 40°C. Only about 0.00002 g fat g^{-1} body weight h^{-1} are required to sustain this low metabolic rate. The slightly larger Greater Horseshoe bat (*Rhinolophus ferrumequinum*– 20 g) uses about 0.07 cm^3 O_2 g^{-1}h^{-1} at 2°C.

Accompanying this reduction in metabolic and oxygen consumption rate is a general 'shutdown' of the circulatory system. Heart rates in the Red bat (*Lasiurus borealis*) at 5°C, have been reported at 10-16 beats min^{-1}. Comparable heart rates have been found in the Little Brown bat (24-32 beats min^{-1}), the Social bat (*Myotis sodalis*–36-62 beats min^{-1}), and the Big Brown bat (*Eptesicus fuscus*–42-62 beats min^{-1}). In addition to a drop in heart rate, peripheral circulation is shut down, thereby insuring a reduction in heat loss in the highly vascularized flight membranes. The blood composition also changes with a reduction in their red blood cell count. These are absorbed and stored in the spleen which becomes engorged in hibernating bats.

Selection of the hibernaculum

We have noted that a primary factor in hibernation is the level at which the metabolic rate is maintained– the lower the ambient temperature, the lower the metabolic rate. Since the length of time that a bat can sustain itself in dormancy depends on the rate at which it metabolizes its fat reserves, we also see that lower ambient temperatures promote longer periods of hibernation. Thus, the site of hibernation (hibernaculum) must be selected carefully to permit optimally low utilization of stored fat.

Bats hibernate in a variety of locations that are quite often different from those that they occupy in the summer season. Hibernacula include caves, mines, tunnels, cracks and crevices, unheated buildings or portions thereof, tree hollows, and, in a few cases, under loose bark. The most important criteria of a hibernaculum are firstly that it provides a low enough ambient temperature to permit an optimally low metabolic rate and secondly that the relative humidity is sufficiently high to prevent excessive water loss. In addition, it must provide protection from the weather and other disruptive factors such as light, noise, and predators.

One might reasonably expect bats to seek sites of about 2 to 5°C in which to hibernate. However, such sites in October would surely drop, slowly, to an ambient temperature of −10 or −15°C by January. A change in temperature of this magnitude would require the bat to arouse and move to a warmer location. Hibernating cave bats appear to exercise two strategies in the selection of a hibernaculum. Some bats, such as the Eastern pipistrelle (*Pipistrellus subflavus*) and the Grey bat (*Myotis grisescens*) select sites at about 10 to 15°C and remain in these hibernacula throughout the winter. During this time, the selected hibernaculum may drop to somewhat lower temperatures (0 to 5°C) thereby increasing the efficiency of hibernation by permitting lower metabolic rates. Other bats, such as the Greater Horseshoe bat (*Rhinolophus ferrumequinum*), start hibernating near the entrance of caves where temperatures may be as low as 10 to 12°C in early autumn, then, as the temperatures drop further, they move to sites deeper in the cave where temperatures have stabilized at 5 to 7°C. Likewise, the Western barbastelle (*Barbastella barbastellus*) begins hibernation in trees, but in mid to late winter it moves into cave sites. On the other hand, small *Myotis* in the Netherlands tend to concentrate and remain in the coldest parts of caves near the entrance, moving to deeper regions during winter warm spells, when locations near the cave opening become warmer. In some species, males and females appear to have different preferences. For example, males of the Big Brown bat seek out colder sites for hibernation than do females. This difference in preference appears to be reversed in the Big-eared bat (*Plecotus townsendii*) in which females occupy the coldest hibernacula.

Whereas most bats occupy hibernating positions on the walls and ceiling of caves, some seek hibernating sites in the loose rubble on the floor of caves and mines. In a West Virginia cave, the Least Brown bat (*Myotis leibii*) has been regularly encountered hibernating in the narrow cracks in the dry clay floor. In a cave in New York, both *M. leibii* and *Eptesicus fuscus* were found under flat rocks on the floor. Three species of *Myotis* (*M. daubentonii*, *M. nattereri*, and *M. emarginatus*) were found hibernating among the stones and gravel on the floor of underground limestone quarries; some individuals were excavated from as deep as 60 cm beneath the surface. These sites in the floor of caves may provide cooler, more stable ambient environments.

Perhaps the hardiest of all bats studied, with regard to hibernating ability, is the Red bat (*Lasiurus borealis*). This species is widely distributed across the Americas, but only the northern temperate populations are of interest here. These bats migrate southward in autumn from the most northerly parts of their range (see Chapter 9) and they hibernate in large numbers as far north as the Ohio River Valley where winter temperatures may fall to −25°C. In these regions, circumstantial evidence suggests that these bats hibernate in trees. They have been observed on a number of occasions flying about in temperatures of 13 to 19°C. This species appears to be rather remarkably adapted to survive at low temperatures. Red bats, and other lasiurines, are more completely and densely furred than most other bats. In very cold ambient temperatures, they curl up into a nearly spherical mass with the furred uropatagium wrapped around the belly and only the tips of the forearms, nose, and short, round ears exposed. Unlike other bats, the Red bat does not arouse from hibernation when small fluctuations in ambient temperature occur. Furthermore, they appear to be incapable of hibernating in caves. Indeed, those that have been encountered in caves were found subsequently to have perished.

Arousal during hibernation

It is becoming increasingly evident that bats frequently do become wakeful and move about during the wintertime. Such arousals are an expensive proposition as they require the metabolism of larger portions of the fat reserve to generate the heat required for the arousal and wakeful period. We have noted above that such arousal may concern moving to a more favourable hibernation site. Bats may also arouse to replenish their water balance. This seems to be the case with the Western pipistrelle that is regularly captured over watering holes throughout the winter months. Although both sexes are active in these cold temperatures, males appear to be more active than females. During warm spells when flying insects may emerge, these active pipistrelles have the opportunity to replenish their fat stores. In the Californian myotis (*Myotis californicus*), females appear to be more active than males in the winter months.

The winter activity of the Western pipistrelle is even more interesting because these bats appear to be capable of activity at reduced overall body temperatures. That is, they regulate their active body temperature at levels below that found in summer active individuals. This, of course, is a further energetically economical behaviour.

Arousal

As spring temperatures rise, hibernating bats begin to arouse more frequently and start to forage for early emerging insects. Again, the precise stimuli that trigger arousal are not well understood. Arousal commences with an increase in heart and respiratory rates. A large portion of the circulatory output is routed through a special deposit of fat called 'brown fat' because of its brownish-yellow coloration. In bats, it is a concentrated, organ-like mass located on the back between the shoulder blades; bands of this fat may extend to various other regions of the body (Fig. 6.3). The brown fat mass has been called the 'hibernating gland' because of its apparent function in arousal from hibernation. Brown fat differs from other fat by having a higher concentration of mitochondria (cellular organelles in which metabolic heat is generated). Thus, brown fat is highly thermogenic. Heat produced here warms the circulating blood which, in turn, warms other body tissues. In a matter of 10-20 minutes, the bat is fully warmed and capable of normal homeothermic activity.

Evolution of hibernation

Attempts to determine the evolution of hibernation are immediately confronted with an interesting paradox. As a physiological process it is without question a specialized phenomenon, yet its taxonomic distribution is predominantly among mammals that are judged on other grounds to be primitive. Protracted periods of torpor occur in monotremes (egg-laying mammals) and marsupials (pouched mammals). Among the seventeen orders of living placental mammals, four include hibernating species: Insectivora (moles, shrews, and hedgehogs); Chiroptera (bats); Rodentia (rodents); and a few 'primitive' Primates (Mouse lemurs). Each of these groups appears to have acquired the ability to hibernate independently. Therefore, hibernation must be regarded as a special or advanced feature of those mammals that have this ability.

In the Chiroptera, we have noted that most families have species that are capable of daily heterothermy, and hibernation has been documented in six families: Rhinopomatidae; Rhinolophidae; Hipposideridae; Vespertilionidae; Mystacinidae; and Molossidae. The hibernating members of these families are all restricted to the temperate or upper extremes of the subtropical regions of the world.

There seem to be two basic scenarios regarding the evolution of hibernation. One portrays hibernation as having evolved in temperate bats as a response to seasonally unfavourable conditions–cold temperatures and insufficient food resources. As these temperate-adapted bats invaded the tropics, they, or their descendants, lost the ability to hibernate or, at least, modified this ability to include only daily torpor. An alternative hypothesis provides that all bats evolved in the tropics or subtropics and that all were pre-adapted, to a certain extent, to exercise some degree of heterothermy. As the insectivorous bats, or their descendants, invaded the temperate regions, they simply utilized their physiologically pre-adapted heterothermic ability to hibernate.

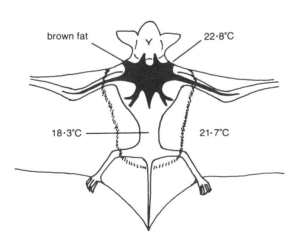

brown fat

22·8°C

18·3°C

21·7°C

Fig. 6.3 Brown fat deposit on the back of a Big Brown bat (Eptesicus fuscus–Vespertilionidae). Note differences in temperatures of the fat mass, lower body, and wing membrane. See text for discussion.

Unfortunately, most scenarios involving temperate vs. tropical species are founded on present-day distributions of these climatic regions. There is clear evidence to support the occurrence of tropical conditions and tropical biotas in the upper Ohio River Valley and northern Europe (now temperate regions where hibernating species exist) as recently as 50 million years ago. In view of this, we regard the latter scenario as perhaps the most tenable until evidence to the contrary is forthcoming.

Bats are classified as placental mammals (subclass Eutheria) and as such they share, in a broad sense, all of the reproductive features of this group. Like other eutherian mammals, young bats spend a period of time (gestation) of varying length inside their mother's womb (uterus). During this gestational or pre-natal period, the young bat progressively develops from an undifferentiated single cell (fertilized egg or ovum) to a fully formed foetus (embryo) just prior to birth (parturition). The embryonic bat is nutritionally and physiologically maintained by the placenta which is a unique organ that provides an intimate junction between the developing young and the mother. After birth, the newborn is sustained for a post-natal period of further maturation on milk produced by and secreted from the mother's mammary glands.

The reproductive system of bats is basically similar to that of other eutherian mammals. However, among bats there is about as much variation, with regard to the detailed anatomy of this system, as there is in all other mammals combined.

MALE REPRODUCTIVE SYSTEM

The male reproductive system includes the paired testes (primary sex organs), paired accessory glands, a system of ducts, and a copulatory or intromittent organ (penis).

Testes

The primary purpose of the testes (male gonads) is the production of male sex cells or gametes (sperm). Like all such gonadal organs, the gametes that are produced have one-half of the chromosomal complement and thereby one-half of the genetic complement of the parent organism. The sperm cells produced during spermatogenesis in the testes are referred to as being haploid which expresses the halved nature of their chromosomal and genetic make-up. When a sperm cell fertilizes an egg or ovum (also haploid) the newly constituted individual has two haploid complements which is a condition referred to as diploid.

The sperm cells are produced within a complex of tightly packed and tortuously coiled seminiferous tubules (Fig. 7.1). These tubules comprise about 90 per cent of the bulk of the testes. The remaining portion of the testes is made up of special interstitial cells that initiate, support, and maintain sperm cell production. These cells produce male hormones such as androgen and testosterone which in turn control various aspects of male physiology, anatomy and behaviour. Interstitial cells are themselves controlled by hormones that are produced in the pituitary gland located beneath the brain, and carried to testicular tissue by the blood vascular system. The activity of the testes (sperm and male hormone production) is thereby regulated. Later in this chapter we will discuss the seasonality of the male reproductive cycle.

During the embryonic life of males, the testes develop from specialized tissue located near the kidneys. However, after their formation the testes migrate to the lower portion of the abdominal cavity. In nearly all mammals (including most bats), the testes descend into a specialized sac called the scrotum which hangs outside the body cavity. The primary function of the scrotum is to provide the testes with a thermal environment that is 1-6°C cooler

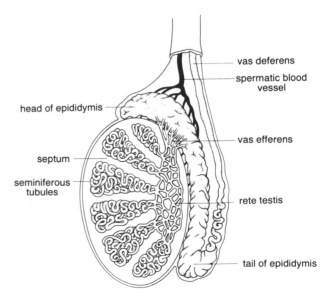

Fig. 7.1 Diagrammatic section of testis.

than the general body temperature. This is important because sperm cells are especially sensitive to warm temperatures and are inactivated or killed by prolonged exposure to normal body temperatures. In bats, the testes usually descend into the scrotum just prior to and during the breeding season; they are abdominal (not scrotal) during the non-reproductive parts of the annual cycle.

Sperm

Sperm cells consist of a head with a neck region (greatly reduced or absent in some bats), a middle piece, and a tail (Fig. 7.2). The head is tipped with an acrosomal cap that appears to function during the penetration of the sperm cell into the ovum at the time of fertilization.

The shape of the head varies among bat species and although relatively little is known, appears to be distinctive for most families of bats. In the Pteropodidae (Fig. 7.2 B-D), the head is comparatively large and rounded, with a pointed tip while in phyllostomids it (Fig. 7.2A) is broadly rounded with a blunt tip; the rear portion may be concave. In vespertilionid bats (Fig. 7.2G), the head is elongated and bullet-shaped. The attachment of the head to the neck is variable

also. In some bats such as pteropodids, vespertilionids, and rhinolophids the head is centred on the neck, whereas in most phyllostomids the head may be offset on the neck.

The middle piece of a sperm cell contains the energy-producing organelles called mitochondria. These are aligned on either side of the tail filament. The middle piece may be very long and slender as in phyllostomids; those of vampire bats are especially long. In the vespertilionids, the middle piece is moderately long and nearly equals the head in diameter (Fig. 7.2G). It is difficult to observe the tail in most kinds of sperm because they are very delicate and often fragment in microscopic preparations.

Sperm cells are produced in the seminiferous tubules during spermatogenesis which is a multi-step process. Once formed, the tiny sperm cells are stored in a collection of tubules called the epididymis (Fig. 7.1) which is located at the anterior or cranial end of the testes. The small size of sperm cells greatly restricts the amount of cellular fluid (cytoplasm) that can be contained within the cell which in turn severely limits the amount of nutrient supply that they can carry. Consequently, sperm cells must be nurtured by other specialized cells called sperm mother cells. These mother cells provide nutrient

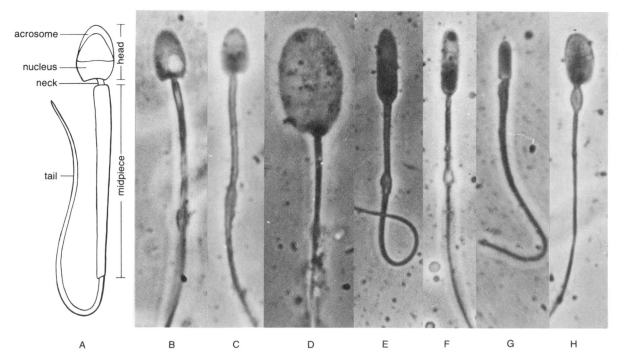

Fig. 7.2 Bat sperm cells. A, Phyllostomus discolor (Phyllostomidae); B, Pteropus neohibernicus (Pteropodidae); C, Rousettus amplexicaudatus (Pteropodidae); D, Nyctimene albiventer (Pteropodidae); E, Emballonura furax (Emballonuridae); F, Rhinolophus megaphyllus (Rhinolophidae): G, Myotis adversus (Vespertilionidae); H, Sauromys petrophilus (Molossidae).

support while the sperm cells are resting within the male reproductive tract. Once the sperm cells are ejaculated into the female reproductive tract, they are rather short-lived, surviving only about 24 hours under normal circumstances. However, in some bats the sperm cells are stored and maintained in the female reproductive tract for long periods of time. We shall discuss this phenomenon of delayed fertilization below.

Male duct system and accessory glands

The duct system in the male includes the vas efferens and epididymis which empties into the larger vas deferens, which in turn empties into the tubular portion of the seminal vesicle, the ejaculatory duct, and then the urethra (Fig. 7.3). This system of ducts serves to transport the sperm cells from the testes into the female reproductive tract. The accessory glands include the paired seminal vesicles, prostate, and paired bulbo-urethral or Cowper's glands. All of these glands contribute various constituents to the seminal plasma or semen. These constituents include

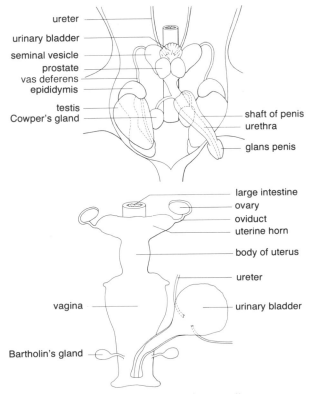

essential nutrients, fructose, and various electrolytes that aid in maintaining the seminal fluid at a nearly neutral acidity (pH) of about 7 (acid pHs are values less than 7 and alkaline pHs are above 7). In addition to being extremely sensitive to heat, sperm cells are also extremely vulnerable to slight variations on either side of a pH of 7. Some of the seminal constituents serve to neutralize the pH of the female tract which tends to be slightly alkaline.

The size and activity of the accessory glands are controlled by hormones secreted by the testes. Like the testes, their size and activity varies during the annual cycle, increasing during the breeding season. Very little is known with regard to the variation of these ducts and glands among bats. The seminal vesicles of pteropodids are very large and nearly equal the testes in size. Those of vespertilionids are also relatively large compared to their generally small body size.

Penis

The penis serves as a copulatory organ and facilitates the internal fertilization of the ovum. Since the penis is an intromittent organ it must be rather stiff or capable of erecting. Erection is accomplished in several ways among mammals. Some mammals, such as dogs, whales, and antelopes, have a fibroelastic penis that is always semierect. Others, such as rodents, have a long bone (baculum or os penis) inside the penis that creates stiffness. Still others, such as higher primates (including man) and bats, generally have paired cylindrical bodies called corpora cavernosa. These cylinders are filled with a spongy, vascular tissue that becomes erect when engorged with blood during sexual excitation.

The corpora cavernosa control the erection of the penial shaft. There is considerable variation among bats with respect to their structure. All bats have some degree of fusion between these paired erectile bodies. In pteropodids, there is considerable fusion of the corpora along most of their length, with many partitions. They are completely fused into a single cylinder along most of their length in mormoopids and some phyllostomids. In hipposiderids and rhinolophids, the distal portions of the corpora cavernosa are usually unfused and they project into the rear portion of the penial head as two separate prongs.

Many bats also possess a baculum. However, in most, this is a small bone that caps the end(s) of the corpora cavernosa. Indeed, the baculum is formed as an ossification in the tough fibrous tip(s) of the corpora cavernosa. Long bacula are unusual in bats. It is extremely long in the African House bat (*Scotoecus*)

Fig. 7.3 Top, male reproductive tract of Pipistrellus hesperus. *Bottom, female reproductive tract of* Eptesicus regulus. *(Both Vespertilionidae).*

and several pipistrelles (*Pipistrellus*). It is reduced to two paired spicules in Ghost-faced bats (*Mormoops*) and the New Zealand Short-tailed bat (*Mystacina tuberculata*). It has been lost completely in all phyllostomids and some molossids.

In addition to the corpora cavernosa, there are several other erectile bodies in the penis of bats. The urethra is surrounded by a sheath of erectile vascular tissue called the corpus spongiosum. It is present in most mammals, but its extent along the length of the penis is variable. In most microchiropterans, it extends to a level just behind the penial head. In the Megachiroptera, it extends the full length of the penial shaft then expands distally into the head of the penis. This distally expanded corpus spongiosum serves to facilitate the erection of the penial head just as it does in Primates. In fact, this structure appears to be a unique feature shared by megachiropterans, the Colugo (Dermoptera), and Primates, thereby suggesting close evolutionary kinship among these mammals.

Erection of the head of the penis in microchiropterans is achieved by a mass of spongy tissue that is independent of both the corpora cavernosa and corpus spongiosum, called accessory cavernous tissue. In many vespertilionids and some phyllostomids, the accessory cavernous tissue invades the prepuce or foreskin. In these bats, the prepuce also is erectile. The function of this specialized arrangement is not well understood. It has been demonstrated in the Little Brown bat (*Myotis lucifugus*) that the prepuce becomes erect after the penis has been inserted into the vagina of the female. This post-intromission erection causes the mating pair to be 'locked' in coitus. These vespertilionids frequently enter hibernation while copulating and it has been supposed that this holds the mating pair together in the torpid state. Some rodents, carnivores (canids), and other mammals have locking coitus; all are caused by similar erectile tissue in the prepuce.

FEMALE REPRODUCTIVE SYSTEM

The female reproductive system includes the paired ovaries (primary sex organs) and a duct system (Fig. 7.3). The duct system receives and supports the ovulated ovum and conveys it to the site of implantation (uterus) where it is sustained throughout the gestation period.

Ovary

Like the testes, the ovary has several functions. Its primary purpose is the production of mature female sex cells or ova (also haploid). The ovum or egg develops within a specialized structure called the follicle (Fig. 7.4). Similarly to that of the interstitial cells of the testes, the development and differentiation of follicular cells is regulated and controlled by hormones secreted into the blood by the pituitary gland. Indeed, these pituitary hormones are the same in both sexes. In addition to egg production (oogenesis), the ovaries produce female sex hormones such as estrogen and progesterone. These are produced by specialized cells that make up the outer layers of the developing follicle. Estrogens are secreted by the ovarian follicle early in oogenesis and these travel through the blood to the uterus. They cause the uterine lining to proliferate (thicken and become highly vascularized) in preparation for the arrival of the fertilized ovum. Progesterones are secreted by the follicle just prior to ovulation.

As the follicle matures, it moves close to the outer surface of the ovary where it can be seen as an ever-increasing bulge. At the time of ovulation, the outer surface of this bulge ruptures and the mature ovum is shot forcefully into the oviduct, where it may be fertilized. After ovulation, the remnants of the ovarian follicle differentiate further and become the corpus luteum (Fig. 7.4) which secretes large quantities of progesterone. The corpus luteum is sometimes referred to as the pregnancy gland as it remains viable, producing progesterone and some estrogen, throughout the entire gestational period. If for some reason the ovum is not fertilized, or after the birth of the young, the corpus luteum ceases to function, degenerates, and eventually becomes a corpus albicans (Fig. 7.4).

The female sex hormones produced by the corpus luteum and subsequently by the placenta serve to maintain the pregnancy. Late in gestation, the level of these hormones in the blood triggers the differentiation and development of the mammary tissue in anticipation of lactation (milk production) after the birth of the young bat.

Female duct system

Whereas the duct system of the male reproductive tract facilitates the storage and transport of sperm cells, the duct system of the female reproductive tract of eutherian mammals is regionally specialized to house and maintain the young during its embryonic development. Unlike the male duct system that is continuous with the seminiferous tubules of the testes, the female duct system is disjunct from the ovaries. In primitive mammals (monotremes and marsupials) the female duct system is completely paired, opening independently into a urogenital

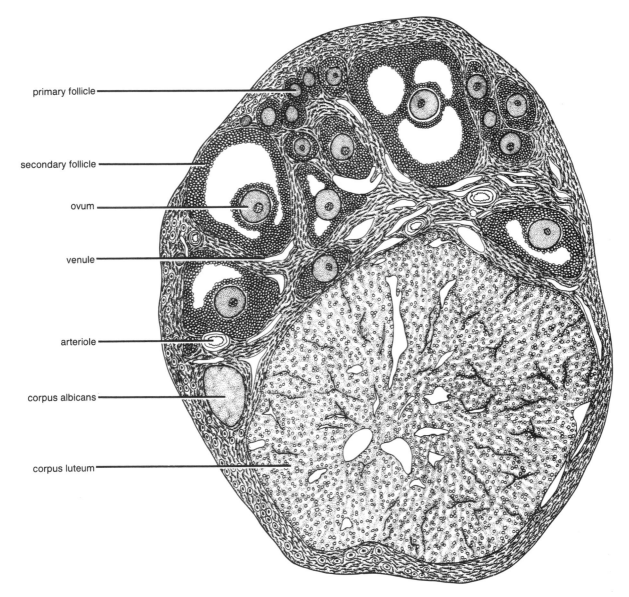

primary follicle

secondary follicle

ovum

venule

arteriole

corpus albicans

corpus luteum

Fig. 7.4 Cross-section of an ovary of the phyllostomid Sturnira lilium *showing a large corpus luteum.*

sinus or cloaca (both vestibules that receive reproductive as well as excretory products). Each of these ducts is regionally specialized into oviduct, uterus, and vagina (Fig. 7.3). Since internal gestation is much abbreviated in these primitive mammals, this regional specialization is less pronounced than in placental mammals in which internal gestation is prolonged. In all placental mammals (including bats), the vaginal portions of the paired ducts are fused (some only partially) into a common vagina that opens externally independently of the urinary and intestinal tracts.

The uterine portions of these two female ducts may remain completely unfused (duplex uterus) and open separately into the vagina (Fig. 7.5A). In other placental mammals, the uterine horns may be slightly fused (bipartite uterus) with a very short, common uterine canal (Fig. 7.5B). In still other placentals, the degree of uterine fusion may be more extensive (bicornuate uterus) with a somewhat longer common uterine canal (Fig. 7.5C). Finally in several placentals, anthropoid primates (including man) and phyllostomid bats, the uterine horns are completely fused (simplex uterus) forming a single uterine canal (Fig.

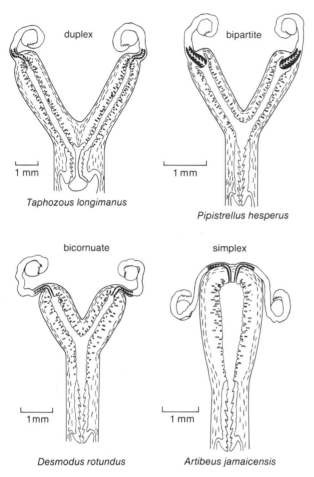

duplex

Taphozous longimanus

bipartite

Pipistrellus hesperus

bicornuate

Desmodus rotundus

simplex

Artibeus jamaicensis

Fig. 7.5 Uterine variation in bats. A, Taphozous longimanus *(Emballonuridae); B,* Pipistrellus hesperus *(Vespertilionidae); C,* Desmodus rotundus *(Phyllostomidae); D,* Artibeus jamaicensis *(Phyllostomidae). See text for discussion.*

7.5D). The form of the uterus tends to be the same among all members of a particular group of placental mammals. However, within the order Chiroptera, all four uterine forms may be encountered; the simplex uterus is thought to be the most specialized and the duplex uterus the most primitive. The oviducts remain separate in all mammals.

As noted earlier, the ovum is ovulated (released from its follicle) into the open end of the oviduct. Here it is moved along toward the uterus by the rhythmic beating of the many tiny cilia that line this portion of the female tract. Unlike sperm cells, which are mobile, the egg is immobile. In addition, the egg is many times larger than sperm cells and contains large quantities of nutrients that must supply the newly constituted blastocyst (fertilized egg) with energy prior to implantation and formation of the placenta. Fertilization occurs in the lower portion of

the oviduct and, as we will see below, several things may occur after this event. Eventually, the blastocyst is moved, again by ciliary action, into the uterus where it implants and remains throughout the gestational period.

The uterus is the most highly specialized portion of the female duct system. It comprises two general layers. The outermost (myometrium) is a heavy layer of smooth muscle fibres that run in all directions. These muscles are involuntary, for the most part, and are sensitive to various hormones that are secreted during the birth process. These cause them to contract, forcing the embryo out through the birth canal (vagina). Under the myometrium is a second layer of tissue (endometrium) which comprises numerous uterine glands, blood vessels, and connective tissue. The innermost portion of the endometrium is a dynamic layer that undergoes many marked changes during the reproductive cycle. During non-reproductive periods, this portion of the endometrium is rather thin and not particularly specialized. However, as we have already noted, the uterus is prepared for an impending pregnancy, prior to ovulation, by hormones secreted by the developing ovarian follicle. The effect of these hormones (mostly estrogens) is to cause the innermost layer of the endometrium to become quite thick as the result of cellular growth. Also, the blood vessels and glands of the deeper layers proliferate and produce a highly branched network that extends into this newly formed uterine lining. These are involved in the maternal portion of the placenta once the blastocyst has implanted itself in the endometrial lining of the uterus. Once the placenta is fully formed, the endometrial glands take over the major portion of estrogen and progesterone production; the corpus luteum, however, continues its secretory function. If after a period of time the ovum is not fertilized, or in the normal course of events at the time of birth, the innermost layer of the endometrium is sloughed off and shed. In the former case, this is referred to as the menstrual flow and the uterine lining is restored to its non-reproductive state. As we will see below, the uterus may remain in this non-reproductive state for an extended period of time or it may immediately start to undergo a new preparatory phase.

REPRODUCTIVE BIOLOGY

Estrous cycle and breeding season

Most of the emphasis in studies of reproductive cycles has been associated with events in the female reproductive system. This is because they are more apparent and often accompanied by marked changes in the morphology, physiology, and behaviour. Nevertheless, the male reproductive tract also undergoes similar, though less marked, cyclic changes.

The period of time from the beginning of follicular development of an ovum to the beginning of development of another ovum is called the estrous cycle. As we have noted above, there is a precise sequence of stages in this cycle. In the first stage (proestrum), follicular growth begins and the uterine endometrium starts to develop. During the second stage (estrous), ovulation occurs. It is during this portion of the estrous cycle, when the female is sexually receptive to the male, that copulation occurs. Ovulation may be spontaneous; that is, occurring without some prior stimulus. Or, ovulation may require provocation by some external stimulus. Very little is known regarding ovulation in bats; most are generally thought to ovulate spontaneously. However, in the Indian flying fox (*Pteropus giganteus*) and in *Rousettus leschenaulti*, ovulation must be provoked by copulatory stimulation. Some species such as Short-tailed bats (*Carollia*), appear to require copulation before ovulation can occur; other species may be found to be provoked ovulators.

Estrous is followed by a usually short stage (metestrum) in which the ovum is fertilized and travels through the oviduct; the corpus luteum develops in this phase. Pregnancy occurs in the next stage (diestrum) during which the corpus luteum matures, the uterine endometrium becomes fully differentiated, and placentation ensues. Diestrum terminates with birth or when the endometrium is shed if pregnancy does not occur. The last stage of the estrous cycle (anestrum) is a quiescent period during which the female is non-reproductive.

Bats exhibit considerable variation with regard to the number and timing of estrous cycles that may occur in the course of one year (Fig. 7.6). All temperate species have but one estrous cycle per year; that is, they are monestrous (Fig. 7.6 B-G). The estrous cycle of these bats is interesting because the length of the cycle and the necessity of having young in the earliest portions of the warm season (spring and summer), when climatic conditions and food resources are at optimal levels for growth and development, requires the intricate coordination of reproduction and hibernation. We will discuss later the special reproductive patterns that occur under these circumstances.

Monestry also occurs in some tropical species although good year-round information is lacking for most. The majority of Old World fruit bats (Pteropodidae) is thought to be monestrous, although individual bats of several species have been found to be pregnant in all months of the year. Rhinopomatids and megadermatids also appear to be monestrous with births occurring in the vernal season just prior to the beginning of the rainy season. The Neotropical bats of the family Natalidae may be monestrous with vernal births. Other tropical, monestrous species have been found in the Rhinolophidae; Hipposideridae (*Hipposideros* probably monestrous); Noctilionidae; Mormoopidae; Phyllostomidae (*Macrotus*, *Leptonycteris*, and *Choeronycteris*); Vespertilionidae; and Molossidae. Births in all of these occur prior to the rainy season.

Most of the remaining tropical bat species exhibit some degree of polyestrous reproductive cyclicity with two or more estrous cycles during the annual period (Fig. 7.6H-L). The production of several litters per year is not coincidental in these tropical species. Indeed, food and climate are less restrictive in the tropics than in temperate regions. The Common vampire (*Desmodus rotundus*) appears to be reproductive throughout the year with four continuous estrous cycles (Fig. 7.6L). However, some seasonality is expressed in the majority of polyestrous bats. Most phyllostomids experience at least two continuous estrous cycles with reproductive peaks just prior to the wet season (March-April) and toward the end of the wet season (July-August). Females of these bats are anestrous in the remaining portion of the year (Fig. 7.6I). The insectivorous Black myotis (*Myotis nigricans*) from the Neotropics, may experience as many as three continuous estrous cycles with an anestrous phase in October-December (Fig. 7.6K). The pteropodids, *Rousettus aegyptiacus*, *Epomophorus anurus*, and *Cynopterus sphinx*, have at least two (perhaps more) estrous cycles per year (Fig. 7.6H). Emballonurids exhibit seasonal polyestry; at least one Neotropical species (*Saccopteryx bilineata*) is seasonally monestrous.

From the foregoing discussion, it should be apparent that breeding is directly tied to the portion of the estrous cycle during which the female is receptive. The ultimate timing and regulation of the estrous cycle(s) in females and sperm production in males is controlled by hormones secreted by the pituitary gland. It is now known that the pituitary gland is influenced by various external stimuli. These include sensitivity to day length, temperature, rainfall, and nutritional state of the adult individual. Thus, these seasonally variable factors are intricately bound to the reproductive cycles of bats and other organisms as well. This seasonal relationship can be well illustrated by examining several species that occur in both northern and southern hemispheres where the seasons are reversed. For example, the young of the Moustached bat (*Pteronotus parnellii*) are born from April to June in Mexico and Central America, but

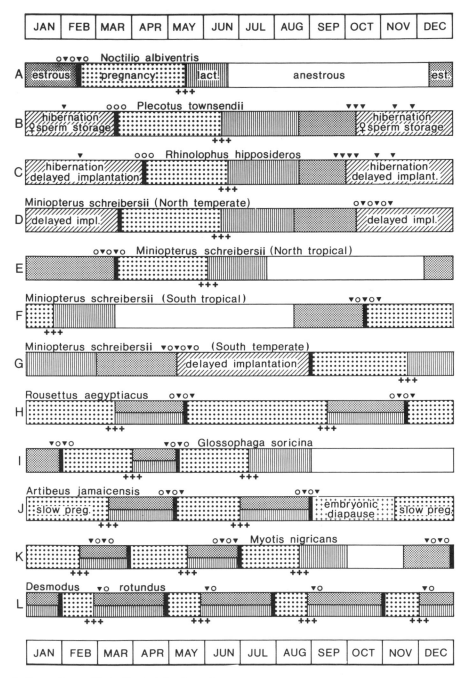

Fig. 7.6 *Reproductive patterns of bats. See text for discussion.*

births occur from September to October in Peru which is south of the equator. The geographic equator does not necessarily coincide with the 'biological equator.' In India, the young of the Black-bearded Tomb bat (*Taphozous melanopogon*) are born in the northern spring at Bombay, whereas in Sri Lanka, north of the equator, the young are born in the northern autumn. Several species of horseshoe bats (*Rhinolophus*) and an Old World leaf-nosed bat (*Hipposideros caffer*) that occur in the southern portion of Africa carry a southern reproductive pattern into the northern hemisphere in Cameroon. In the reverse fashion, Yellow bats (*Scotophilus*) in Zaire, and the Butterfly bat (*Glauconycteris argentata*) in

Kenya and central Africa, extend a northern reproductive pattern to just south of the equator.

Ovulation

Generally speaking, bats are monotocous–they produce only one ovum per estrous cycle and consequently only one young is born. Four bat families are reported to be polytocous, having two or more young. Among pteropodids, Dobson's fruit bat (*Epomops dobsoni*) and the Madagascar flying fox (*Pteropus rufus*) commonly give birth to twins. Twins also occur regularly in the Indian Horseshoe bat (*Rhinolophus ferrumequinum*). Female Californian leaf-nosed bats (*Macrotus californicus*) are frequently observed carrying two babies, like two small bombs, one under each wing. Three species of European vespertilionids–the Common pipistrelle (*Pipistrellus pipistrellus*), the European noctule (*Nyctalus noctula*), and the Particoloured bat (*Vespertilio murinus*)–tend to have two young in areas where winters are severe; only one in areas with milder winters. The noctule may, on occasion, have triplets. In North America, females in eastern populations of the Big Brown bat (*Eptesicus fuscus*) commonly have twins, whereas only a single young is born to females in western populations. Twins are usual in several other vespertilionids: *Pipistrellus subflavus* and *P. hesperus*; *Tylonycteris pachypus* and *T. robustula*; *Chalinolobus gouldii*; *Lasionycteris noctivagans*; *Scotophilus kuhlii*; and *Rhogeessa parvula*. The largest litters are found in the North American Red bat (*Lasiurus borealis*) that regularly has four young and occasionally five.

It has been speculated that multiple births are a response to a relatively high mortality rate among young bats and that more young insure a higher survival rate. This has not been effectively substantiated and if it were so one might expect a more widespread occurrence of multiple births in bats. Indeed, it is an unusual novelty. In the case of the Red bat, the more babies a female must carry and feed reduces her chances and those of her young to survive. Many female Red bats die each spring as a result of being overburdened by the weight of four or five young.

In most mammals, it is generally assumed that both ovaries are functional, even in monotocous species. In some monotocous bats, ovulation regularly alternates from one ovary to the other; implantation usually occurs in the uterine horn on the ovulating side. In others, such as the Lesser Naked-backed bat (*Pteronotus davyi*), Little Brown bat (*Myotis lucifugus*), and Common pipistrelle (*Pipistrellus pipistrellus*), the right ovary dominates with occasional ovulation from the left ovary. In some species, such as the Sharp-nosed Pouched bat (*Taphozous georgianus*), the Bicoloured leaf-nosed bat (*Hipposideros bicolor*), and the Californian leaf-nosed bat (*Macrotus californicus*), only the right ovary is functional; implantations all occur in the right horn of the uterus. The left ovary and uterine horn are dominant in the Neotropical emballonurid *Balantiopteryx io*, the Asian Greater false vampire (*Megaderma lyra*), and the Asian Dusky leaf-nosed bat (*Hipposideros ater*). In the vespertilionid Long-fingered bats *Miniopterus schreibersii* and *M. australis*, ovulation always occurs from the left ovary, but the blastocyst migrates to the right uterine horn to implant. Most polytocous species ovulate from both ovaries. However, in the Californian leaf-nosed bat (*Macrotus californicus*), twins are derived from eggs produced in the right ovary; both implant in the right uterine horn.

Special reproductive patterns of bats

As we noted in Chapter 6 many temperate bat species have the ability to undergo extended periods of facultative torpor (hibernation) during cold winter months. We emphasized the energy conserving aspects of hibernation and noted that it was accomplished by a general shutdown of body physiology. As such, hibernation exerts a profound influence on the reproductive physiology–an energetically expensive proposition–in these bats. One need only consider that daily activity, maintenance of pregnancy, and care and feeding of the young are directly tied to the availability of food resources (insects in these temperate species) to see the connection between hibernation and reproduction. A reproductive effort just prior to or during the hibernating period would have no chance of success and would therefore constitute an energetically debilitating load on the species. On the other hand, the spring and summer months are much too short for most female bats to initiate a reproductive effort, breed, bear young, and raise those young to a sufficient size and still have the ability to sustain themselves through a hibernation period. Furthermore, the adult females must wean the young early enough so that they themselves may accumulate sufficient fat stores to survive the hibernation period. Similar time and energy constraints operate on males and sperm production. Thus, reproduction must necessarily overlap hibernation. Temperate bats respond to this energetic dilemma in several ways. All involve starting an estrous and sperm production cycle in the late summer or autumn months prior to entering hibernation, with a temporary arrest in the sequence of reproductive events either before ovulation (delayed ovulation and fertilization or sperm storage); before implantation (delayed implantation); or after implantation (embryonic diapause).

We should note that, although we have stressed these special reproductive patterns in relation to hibernation and their occurrence in temperate bat species, seasonally active tropical species respond in a similar fashion. This may further support the idea that daily torpor and prolongation thereof originated in the tropical ancestors of bats that now hibernate in temperate regions.

Delayed ovulation and fertilization

This unusual reproductive pattern was thought to be a unique adaptation of bats. However, recent studies have shown that it also occurs in some rabbits and mice. It is found in temperate species of the genus *Rhinolophus* and is widespread in temperate vespertilionid species of *Myotis, Pipistrellus, Eptesicus, Nycticeius, Lasiurus, Plecotus, Miniopterus,* and *Antrozous* (Fig. 7.7). It is also found in many tropical vespertilionids such as *Scotophilus, Tylonycteris,* and *Chalinolobus*. This pattern is perhaps the most specialized, because it involves two phenomena—delayed ovulation and overwinter storage of sperm in the female reproductive tract. We distinguish the latter from sperm storage in the male reproductive tract which will be discussed below.

This pattern of reproduction has been studied in detail in the Western Big-eared bat (*Plecotus townsendii*) from California (Fig. 7.6B). Although there are slight variations, this species may be used to exemplify the pattern.

In males the testes descend into the scrotum soon after the bats leave hibernation in the spring. This is triggered by an increase in testosterone production that may have been initiated by changes in day length or other external stimuli that caused the pituitary to secrete hormones that in turn stimulated the interstitial cells to produce testosterone. Sperm production reaches a peak in late August and September. The testes begin to regress in October and by November sperm production ceases. However, viable sperm are accumulated in the tubules of the epididymis and may remain there until February. Yearling males do not undergo sperm production prior to their first hibernation.

By mid- to late summer, adult females have weaned their young and begin an estrous cycle in August. The follicle and ovum therein are fully developed by late autumn. In addition to the normal events of follicular growth, the follicle becomes vacuolated by enormous quantities of glycogen, a rich source of metabolic energy. At this stage, the estrous cycle is interrupted and the follicle overwinters in this condition.

In the meantime (mid to late autumn), males copulate with and inseminate the females. Copulation may occur during temporary arousals from hibernation throughout the winter. However, the sperm cannot fertilize the egg, because it is not present in the female duct system. Instead, the sperm are stored in the uterus, at the utero-oviductal junction, or in the oviduct; the site of storage varies among species. In *Plecotus townsendii*, sperm is stored for at least 76 days. Up to five weeks may lapse between copulation and ovulation in the Asiatic Yellow House bat (*Scotophilus heathii*) and an interval of two months occurs in the Club-footed bats (*Tylonycteris*).

Ovulation and subsequent fertilization occur in late February or March while the females are still in the hibernaculum or shortly after they leave it for their summer roosts. The young are born in May or June after a gestation period of 50-100 days. This variation reflects regional climatic variation. Yearling females may reproduce in their first year.

The ability of some bats to store live sperm in the female reproductive tract is a remarkable biological and biochemical feat. It represents nothing less than foreign cells (indeed many thousands of such cells) surviving the normal antigenic responses that usually follow invasion by foreign cells. Under normal circumstances, white blood cells (leucocytes) voraciously attack and destroy foreign cells; this is the body's first line of defence against various germs and diseases. In most mammals, including bats, there is a massive accumulation of leucocytes in the uterus shortly after insemination occurs. In those bat species that store sperm in the female tract, this leucocyte onslaught does not occur. In some human females, this assault is of such a nature that conception is difficult or impossible. Research on this phenomenon in bats has contributed much valuable medical information to fertility and birth control studies as well as to those concerning organ transplant rejection and suppression thereof.

In addition to surviving the normal antibiotic defenses, stored sperm cells apparently derive nutrition from their association with glandular cells at the site of storage in the female tract. We noted earlier that sperm cells are quite small in size and, therefore, contain relatively limited quantities of life sustaining nutrients. Indeed, sperm cells cannot survive on their own while in the male tract and must be nurtured by specialized support cells. In the uterus, or at the site of storage, individual sperm cells dock, head on with these specialized gland cells which are scattered throughout the lining of the female tract. The cells of these glands possess many microscopic, finger-like projections (microvilli) that contact and embrace the

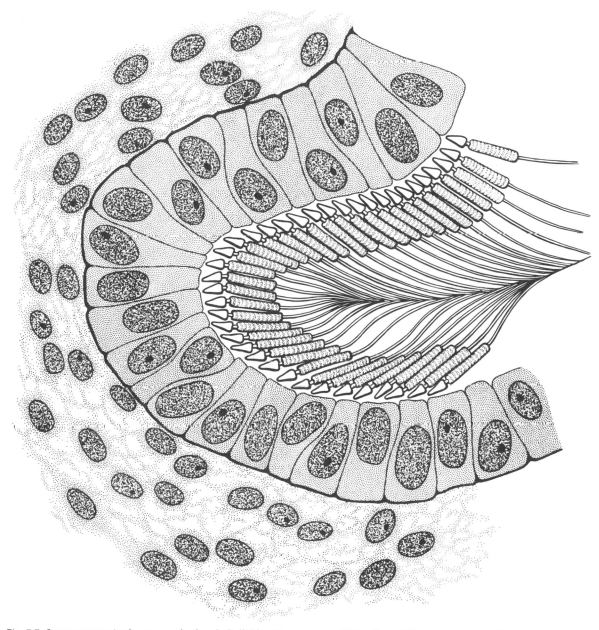

Fig. 7.7 Sperm storage in the uterus of a female Pallid bat (Antrozous pallidus–Vespertilionidae). *Sperm cells are nosed into the uterine mucosa which maintains them through the hibernation period.*

head of the sperm cell. In the Lesser Club-footed bat (*Tylonycteris pachypus*), the head of the sperm cell is embedded into tiny indentations in the oviductal lining. These intimate associations may serve as anchorages or they may facilitate nutrient transport; the mechanism is not well understood at present. It is known that sperm cells stored in this manner do conduct active metabolism. This pattern of reproduc-

tion probably evolved in conjunction with the thermoregulatory ability of bats rather than being a pattern caused by heterothermy. Indeed, the current view, relative to the uniqueness of sperm storage in the female tract, may simply reflect a rather poor state of knowledge of sperm physiology and survival; it may be much more prevalent in mammals than currently thought.

Sperm storage

This pattern is a minor variation of the previous one. In contrast to sperm storage in the female genital tract and delayed fertilization, sperm is stored in the male reproductive tract, in the epididymis, until copulation in the spring. The Mexican Free-tailed bat (*Tadarida brasiliensis*) produces sperm in the late autumn and winter months but does not copulate until early spring; populations in southern California may enter brief periods of hibernation. The Greater Mouse-tailed bat, *Rhinopoma microphyllum*, is unusual among bats in that sperm production occurs only in the winter months; copulation and fertilization occur in the spring. Sperm storage also occurs in several vespertilionid species that breed seasonally, but do not hibernate or enter long periods of daily torpor. Sperm storage in the epididymis was only recently reported in a tropical hipposiderid (*Hipposideros speoris*), a monestrous species that lives in India. Males of the Grey-headed flying fox (*Pteropus poliocephalus*) from Australia, and the Polynesian flying fox (*Pteropus tonganus*) from the New Hebrides (Vanuatu) have been found to store viable sperm.

Delayed implantation

This pattern of reproduction proceeds much like that outlined for delayed ovulation. Males reach a peak in sperm production in early autumn. Likewise, females undergo a normal estrous cycle including ovulation. Copulation and fertilization follow in mid to late autumn. However, the resultant blastocyst only undergoes the initial few stages of embryonic development, then becomes dormant. Thus, females enter hibernation in a pregnant condition, but the blastocyst remains unimplanted until the female emerges from hibernation in the spring. Several vespertilionids and at least one rhinolophid (*Rhinolophus rouxi*) exhibit this reproductive pattern. That of the Long-fingered bat (*Miniopterus schreibersii*) will suffice to illustrate both delayed implantation as well as the variability of reproductive cycles that result from differences in latitudinal occurrence (Fig. 7.6 D-G). *Miniopterus schreibersii* occurs throughout the tropical and subtropical portions of the Old World. It also extends into the north temperate regions of Europe as well as the south temperate regions of Australia and southern Africa. In the tropical parts of its range, its monestrous reproductive cycle proceeds without delayed implantation (Fig. 7.6 E-F); copulation occurs in February and March and birth in June and July in the northern hemisphere. The reproductive cycle is reversed in the tropical regions of the southern hemisphere and extends from September to early

January (Fig. 7.6 F). In Europe, this species hibernates through the winter. Here the estrous cycle, copulation, and fertilization occur from August to October (Fig. 7.6 D). The blastocysts are retained unimplanted until March when the female leaves the hibernaculum; young are born in June or early July. Five month delays have been recorded in French populations of *M. schreibersii*. Sperm are not stored by either males or females. A similar, but reversed, pattern is present in populations in the south temperate parts of its range (Fig. 7.6G). Copulation and fertilization occur in April or May, but the blastocyst does not implant until September; births occur in December or early January. The delay is somewhat shorter (2.5 to 3.5 months) in these southern populations compared to those reported for northern populations. A similar pattern exists in Australian populations of the closely related species, *Miniopterus australis*.

Again, although we are discussing these special reproductive patterns with reference to temperate species and hibernation, they also are manifested in apparent response to wet/dry seasonality in the tropics. This is best illustrated by the Straw-coloured fruit bat (*Eidolon helvum*) that inhabits East Africa. In this tropical region, there are two periods of high rainfall both of which are followed by high food productivity. In *Eidolon*, copulation takes place in April or May, during the first annual rainy season. Implantation is delayed for about three months until October or November, during the second rainy season. Young are born in February or March and are weaned by early April when ample food resources are available. Thus, an approximate gestation period of four months is added to a three- to five-month period of delayed implantation, making a total gestation of seven to nine months; perhaps the longest for any bat.

Embryonic diapause

This final special pattern of reproduction in bats, oddly enough, does not occur in any known temperate species. It was only discovered recently and is restricted to several species of New World leaf-nosed bats of the family Phyllostomidae. Its recent discovery probably best represents the wrong-minded approach to natural history; this is that harsh environments foster special adaptations, whereas tropical regions are lush shangri-las where few limitations exist. By now, it should be more than obvious that many supposed 'temperate adaptations' have their foundations in the seasonality of the tropics.

Embryonic diapause occurs in the Jamaican fruit-eating bat (*Artibeus jamaicensis*) which is polyestrous with two or more estrous cycles per year. Copulation and subsequent fertilization early in the year result in immediate implantation and embryonic development with birth in July or August (Fig. 7.6J). This birth is followed immediately by another estrous cycle, copulation, and fertilization. The resulting blastocyst implants normally, but shortly thereafter becomes dormant. Development resumes in late September to mid-November, after a pause of about two and a half months, with birth in early March or April at the end of the dry season.

The Californian leaf-nosed bat (*Macrotus californicus*) has a similar pattern except embryonic development does not stop altogether. In these bats, which commonly produce twins, the autumnal implantation is followed by very slow foetal growth until March.

Gestation

The length of intra-uterine life varies from 40 to 60 days in small vespertilionid bats such as *Myotis* and *Pipistrellus* to as much as eight months in the Common vampire (*Desmodus rotundus*). There is a general correlation between large adult body size and longer gestation periods; certainly there are exceptions. The gestation period of mid-sized bats, such as the Pallid bat (*Antrozous pallidus*), the Western Big-eared bat (*Plecotus townsendii*), the House bat (*Scotophilus kuhlii*), and the Mexican Free-tailed bat (*Tadarida brasiliensis*) varies from 50-120 days. Foetal development requires 115-125 days in the Short-nosed fruit bat (*Cynopterus sphinx*) and five to six months in large species of flying foxes (*Pteropus*). Gestation in the Straw-coloured bat (*Eidolon*) may extend to nine months including the reproductive delay that occurs in these African pteropodids.

As we have noted above, the length of foetal development may be protracted by various kinds of reproductive delays. Temperature and other environmental factors may also affect the length of gestation.

Embryological development and birth

Very little is known regarding the detailed embryology of bats. Foetal growth and development appear to follow that of the few mammals that have been studied. Pre-natal life begins as a single, undifferentiated cell and progresses to a fully formed individual that resembles a small version of the adults. The central nervous system (spinal cord and brain) is among the first systems to differentiate. Heart and somites form soon thereafter. Limb buds are visible very early in embryonic development; the wing buds proceed at a faster rate than do the hindlimb buds. Growth of the internal structure of the wing appears to be more or less isometric and final allometry of the wing is achieved in post-natal development and maturity (Fig. 7.8).

At birth, all bats are helpless and depend on the

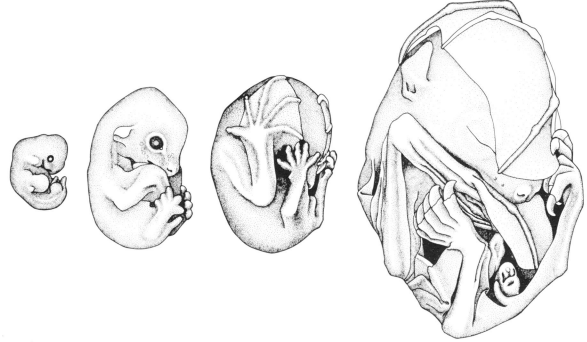

Fig. 7.8 Embryonic development in Rousettus amplexicaudatus *(Pteropodidae). These embryos were taken from wild caught females and therefore the ages are not known. Note the development of the wing and hindlimb buds. The embryo on the far right is near term.*

mother. They are capable of climbing and clinging to the mother's fur by way of strong, sharp claws and well-developed feet. All have a specialized set of milk teeth that are needle sharp and hooked at the tips. With these teeth, they are able to bite onto the mother's nipple and remain firmly anchored even when the female is in flight.

Baby megachiropterans are born at a rather advanced stage of development. Most are large-sized at term (20-30 per cent the size of the adult), well-haired, and born alert with their eyes open. The young of microchiropterans are usually less well-developed at birth; most are small-sized (10-15 per cent the size of the adult), naked and pink-skinned, and born with their eyes closed. Although they draw back when touched, they are not especially alert. The skin becomes pigmented in a day or so and hair begins to grow in several days. The ears flop and droop until the eyes open in three or four days. These young require considerable care and maintenance by the mother. Among the Microchiroptera, the young of members of the family Phyllostomidae are the most advanced. Like pteropodids, they are usually large-sized at term and haired in most cases.

Birth generally takes place in the daytime. In some species the mother may assume a horizontal posture by grasping the roosting site with both hind feet and the thumbs. In others, the female remains in the normal head down posture of bats. Birth is usually preceded by vigorous licking and grooming, especially around the genital region. Baby bats are usually born rump first (breech birth). The mother may assist the birth by licking and grooming the young bat as it emerges from the birth canal; also, she may occasionally grasp and tug at the young with her teeth or with one foot. Those bats that have a tail membrane often curl this around the emerging young and cradle it as it is being born. Soon after birth the baby bat crawls directly to a nipple where it attaches and begins to suckle.

Nursery colonies

Although certainly within the realm of reproductive behaviour (discussed below), this topic seems best considered at this point. In most temperate and some tropical bats, pregnant females congregate in unisexual groups to give birth and care for their young. During the formation and existence of these nursery colonies, adult males remain separated from the females and young. The duration, completeness of separation, and the mechanisms responsible for causing this segregation are largely unknown. In some species, such as *Rousettus leschenaulti*, *Rhinolophus lepidus*, and *Myotis nattereri*, the segregation of the sexes may be a relatively local phenomenon with females simply moving to different areas of the cave (usually warmer) or to areas within close proximity of the normal roosting site. In some hibernating bats, the males may leave the roosting site (which becomes warmer as spring temperatures rise) for cooler roosting sites where torpor can be extended. In the Big Brown bat (*Eptesicus fuscus*) and the Little Brown bat (*Myotis lucifugus*), females emerge from hibernation before males and congregate at traditional nursery colonies, sometimes several hundred kilometres away. The fidelity to maternity sites is well illustrated by some Indian populations of *Miniopterus schreibersii*. A maternity colony at Mahalleshwar services an area of approximately 15 000 square kilometres.

Segregation of the sexes may vary in different populations. For example, nursery colonies in British populations of the Long-eared bat (*Plecotus auritus*) may harbour a few adult males, whereas French and Russian nursery colonies exclude all adult males. Likewise, the nursery colonies of *Myotis lucifugus* in the northeastern United States contain no adult males; those in Illinois frequently contain a few adult males; and, in Kentucky, not only do adult males occur in the nursery colony, they also roost in clusters with females and young.

The nursery colony breaks up in several ways. Males of *Antrozous pallidus*, *Plecotus auritus*, *Eptesicus fuscus*, and several species of *Myotis* reportedly invade the nursery colony. In *Myotis velifer*, *Plecotus townsendii*, and *Miniopterus schreibersii*, the adult females abandon their young at the time of weaning and rejoin the males or live in solitude until the next breeding season. In the Large-eared Pied bat (*Chalinolobus dwyeri*), the weaned young abandon their mothers at the nursery site.

Maternal care

The care and feeding of the young bat is the exclusive responsibility of the female. The commitment of the male parent ends after copulation. In a few cases, such as among the harem groups of Neotropical emballonurids, the male may patrol and defend a feeding territory. Harem males of the Spear-nosed bat (*Phyllostomus discolor*) are often seen with a naked youngster sleeping on their backs. Whether or not this indicates a parental bond is not known. On the other hand, the bond between mother and infant is well established from birth and it carries at least through weaning and perhaps longer in a few cases.

The closeness of this bond is illustrated by the fact that mother and infant establish vocal communication soon after birth to the extent that the female is able to recognize the vocalizations of her young from among many newborn. Very young bats usually call continuously when separated from their mothers. However, as the youngsters get older and as the mother-infant bond progresses, their communications become more refined with the infants answering the specific calls from their mothers. For example, in *Pteropus poliocephalus*, females returning from foraging emit a special search call and this elicits a corresponding location call from their young. This exchange continues until the mother is close enough to either see or smell her infant. Similar mother-infant vocalizations have been reported for various microchiropteran species. In these, however, the calls are usually ultrasonic (high frequency). In the case of microchiropterans, which utilize ultrasonics (echolocation) to orientate and hunt, the mother-infant communications appear to be segments of the adult hunting repertoire; eventually the young bats learn and adopt these vocalizations. Some chiropteran biologists feel that echolocation may have evolved out of these mother-infant communications.

As we noted above, the young bat attaches immediately to one of the mother's two functional, pectoral mammae. The newborn remains in this position and is carried by the mother for a week or two. The length of time that the young is carried on the wing depends on the initial size and growth rate of the young bat as well as the lifting potential of the mother's wings. Small bats, such as Dobson's Trident bat (*Aselliscus tricuspidatus*) (3-4 g), must leave their naked, pink young hanging in the roost while the female forages for food. The young then climbs aboard the female when she returns from her feeding flight. This is interesting in that female *Aselliscus* have been observed carrying young bats that are nearly equal to them in size and weight during daily movement inside caves. Of course, their flight is laborious and clumsy; this probably is the reason why the young are detached before hunting which requires intricate manoeuvering to catch elusive insect prey. Molossids, with their high aspect, low weight-bearing potential, also abandon their young in the roost while foraging. Indeed, molossid babies are especially small-sized at birth compared to the body size of the adult female. On the other hand, most large-sized pteropodids and some phyllostomids carry relatively large-sized young on their foraging flights. These young may be set off on a branch while the female forages in the immediate vicinity.

Babies that are left in the roost often huddle together in dense 'baby clusters.' This, of course, increases the thermoregulatory potential of the group. Baby clusters are found in a number of species, such as the Mexican Free-tailed bat (*Tadarida brasiliensis*), several species of *Myotis, Macrotus californi-cus*, and the Long-fingered bat (*Miniopterus schreibersii*). In these species, the adult females roost apart from the 'baby clusters'; periodically they visit their young to nurse.

Communal care for the young has been described in several bat species. In *Myotis thysanodes* and *M. lucifugus*, two to ten adult females remain with the baby bats while the other females are away foraging for food. These 'baby-sitting' females guard the young and retrieve those that accidentally fall out of the roost. In *Tadarida brasiliensis* and *Miniopterus schreibersii*, communal care of the young is extended to communal suckling with all females nursing the young indiscriminately. Although communal care of the young may be found to be more prevalent, in the majority of bats, mothers watch after their own babies.

Juveniles begin short flying sorties in as little as two weeks after birth in small-sized emballonurids such as the White-lined bat (*Saccopteryx bilineata*). In the Large-eared Pied bat (*Chalinolobus dwyeri*) from Australia, flight commences three to four weeks after birth, and in the North American Pallid bat (*Antrozous pallidus*), flight begins in the sixth or seventh week. Large megachiropterans, such as *Pteropus poliocephalus*, may not begin flying until the third month.

For most bat species nursing lasts for one to three months. The young continue to suckle while they learn to fly, forage, and feed on their own. Relatively mature flying subadults of *Hipposideros* have been found foraging with adults, but their stomachs contained only milk.

The delay between the onset of flight and weaning may seem to be rather curious. On the contrary, a young bat, perhaps more than any other mammal, must learn to master several quite sophisticated systems. Whereas learning to walk and/or run are relatively easy tasks for young mammals, a young bat must not only learn to fly (a skill requiring considerable co-ordination), but it must master this locomotory style *in the dark*! For microchiropterans, at least, flying in the dark also requires mastery of the echo-orientation system to avoid obstacles and eventually to detect, track, and capture flying insect prey. Megachiropterans (non-echolocatory for the most part) and frugivorous microchiropterans (Phyllostomidae) are less disadvantaged with respect to the use of the echolocation system to pursue and capture food; pursuit skills are not required to catch a banana. On the other hand, young frugivores must learn how and where to find fruits.

Again, the mother-infant bond plays an integral role in this transition to adulthood. It is not clear, for most species, how much adult females contribute to the environmental education of their young. The carnivorous megadermatids, *Megaderma spasma* and *Macroderma gigas*, capture and return prey to the roost where they give it to their young. This certainly constitutes a direct provisioning of the young; it may also contribute to their education as prospective carnivores. Similarly, female vampires (*Desmodus rotundus*), have been observed offering regurgitated blood at nursing sessions to their young. In addition, young vampires may feed from a wound opened or used by the adult females on a prey animal. The young of rhinolophids and vespertilionids have been observed following their mothers on foraging flights. Similarly, young Sac-winged bats (*Saccopteryx leptura*) have been seen flying behind their mothers, meticulously mimicking her movements, as she hawked insects. This apparent copy cat learning by these young emballonurids also includes replicating the mother's echolocation signals down to the terminal capture phase. Among the Megachiroptera, mother-infant foraging has been reported in several species as evidenced by captures of lactating females and volant young.

Most young adult bats do not reproduce until the second year or late in the first. There is sufficient evidence to indicate that many young female pteropodids may initiate an estrous cycle, mate, and become pregnant before they are fully accomplished flyers. These early pregnancies probably result when sexually active males, searching for receptive adult females, encounter subadult females in close association with their mothers.

REPRODUCTIVE BEHAVIOUR

Aside from the anatomical and physiological aspects, the reproductive success of a sexually reproducing species depends heavily upon a social system of organization that ensures sexual identity of individuals and promotes the proximity of sexually active males and sexually receptive females. In a broad sense, most, if not all, social organization of sexually reproducing species is related either directly or indirectly to the promotion of successful mating. We shall discuss here only those aspects of chiropteran sociobiology that directly concern sexual identity and mating.

Bats are, without question, the most gregarious of all mammals. The breeding colonies of the Long-fingered bat (*Miniopterus schreibersii*) in Australia have been estimated to be as high as 44 000 individuals. Colonies of the leaf-nosed bat (*Hipposideros caffer*) from West Africa may accommodate up to 500 000 individuals. The Mexican Free-Tailed bat (*Tadarida*

brasiliensis) aggregates in summer colonies by the millions in caves in the southwestern United States; among these are the well-known Carlsbad Caverns in New Mexico. Although the majority of bats are known to live in moderate to large groups, remarkably little is known regarding their overall social organization, let alone those features that relate to reproductive behaviour. Until recently, most of our knowledge was based on information gathered on temperate bat species which, as we have already discussed, are influenced by rather harsh seasonal constraints. It has been wrongly presumed that the social biology typical of temperate species is equally typical of tropical bats as well. However, current investigations on tropical bat species are rapidly revealing a myriad of complexly structured mating systems.

Sexual identity

Primary sexual identity is determined by the various anatomical features discussed above. Males possess testes, a particular suite of accessory ducts and glands, and uniquely structured external genitalia (penis and scrotum). Likewise, females possess ovaries, a particular suite of accessory ducts and glands, and uniquely structured external genitalia (labia and clitoris). Except for the external genitalia, all of the primary sexual features are internal; in most cases, even the external genitalia are not particularly obvious.

The sociologically functional sexual identity is usually apparent or determined by secondary sexual characteristics. The expression of these features is directly controlled and prompted by hormonal factors released when the individual becomes sexually mature. In birds, sexual behaviour is largely prompted by visual cues. As a consequence, sexual identity and the attributes thereof (dominance, receptivity, etc.) are signalled by the presence or absence of distinctive colour patterns. These secondary sexual identifiers are often quite bold and beautiful in males and dull and sedate in females. As a rule, mammals (including bats) do not express their sexual identity by way of dimorphic variations in their overall colour pattern; there may be subtle differences in the intensity or brightness of coloration. This is the case in male Dog-faced bats (*Cynopterus*) and the Red bat (*Lasiurus borealis*).

In some mammals, as well as some bats, sexual identity (usually that of the male) is signified by a discrete area marking or badge. For example, male Three-toed sloths have a black, yellow, and white chevron patch on their lower back. Similar area patches are found in some rodents and hoofed mammals. In bats, sexual markings are generally restricted to specialized tufts of hair that are usually white and associated with specialized skin glands which may contribute an odoriferous quality to the sexual identity of the individual. Such markings are not common among bats and, when present, usually distinguish the male. The males of the African fruit bats, *Epomophorus*, *Epomops*, *Micropteropus*, and *Nanonycteris*, have plume-like epaulets of long, stiff white or yellowish hairs adorning each shoulder. These are augmented by skin glands and muscles that enable them to be erected during sexual or defensive displays. Some pteropodids, such as *Rousettus angolensis*, *R. amplexicaudatus*, *Myonycteris torquata*, and *Megaloglossus woermanni*, have a collar of specialized hairs that extends between the shoulders across the throat and upper chest; this collar is creamy white in *Megaloglossus*, but brownish in the others. A similar, but soft-textured, collar of orange fur is found in both sexes of the African Straw-coloured bat (*Eidolon helvum*); that of the male, at least, is associated with skin glands that secrete a sticky, musky fluid in the breeding season. White shoulder spots are found in both sexes of a few species of phyllostomids (*Centurio senex* and *Ametrida centurio*) and in the Indo-Australian Black-bellied fruit bat (*Melonycteris melanops*). Among male Horseshoe bats (*Rhinolophus landeri* and *R. alcyone*), axillary tufts of hair are localized in the armpits. In Tomb bats, such as *Taphozous melanopogon* and *T. theobaldi*, males possess a distinctive 'beard' of blackish or reddish brown hairs on the chin and upper throat. In the former, this 'beard' develops at the age of five to six months. The males of some African Free-tailed bats (*Tadarida chapini*, *T. pumila*, and *T. nigeriae*) have a specialized, erectile, crest of long, stiff hairs (white in some) located on top of the head between the ears. These crests develop and are displayed only during the breeding season.

The males of many bat species possess large, specialized 'scent' glands located at various positions on their bodies. Females of these species often possess an equivalent, but rudimentary, gland. The exact function of these glands is generally unknown. They are presumed to be 'scent' glands and to serve as sexual identifiers because most increase in size and activity during the breeding or rutting season. Glands of this sort are commonly located in the middle of the upper chest in some phyllostomids (*Phyllostomus* and *Phylloderma*) and molossids (*Molossus* and *Eumops*). Some species of the emballonurid genus *Taphozous* have a glandular sac on the throat, others have similar sacs in the tail membrane. Male Bulldog bats (*Noctilio*) have a gland, equipped with many fringe-like papillae, located on the outer surface of the scrotum. This gland is everted when the testes are pushed into the scrotum; it secretes an oily substance with a strong musky odour that is easily detectable over several metres' distance. A large, bulbous gland occurs on the forehead, above the eyes, of most males of the genus *Hipposideros*. This gland becomes especially swollen during the breeding season. In some species, such as *Hipposideros cyclops* and *H. commersoni*, a brush-like plume of hairs develops and protrudes from the centre of this facial gland during the breeding season. The specific name *cyclops* is derived from the one-eyed appearance manifested by these prominent glands which resemble the one-eyed giants of Greek mythology.

Perhaps the most striking instance of sexual dimorphism is found in the Hammer-headed fruit bat (*Hypsignathus monstrosus*). The rostral portion of the face in the males of this African species is longer and deeper than in females. In addition, the muzzle is highly ornamented with fleshy folds and ridges; the lips are also quite fleshy. The larynx is extremely large and extends well into the body cavity. It is used in courtship behaviour to be described later in this chapter.

For the majority of bats, secondary sexual identity is expressed by a differential in overall body size. In emballonurids, vespertilionids, and some molossids males are usually smaller than females. The reverse appears to be true for most of the other families of bats. A notable exception within the Pteropodidae is the African Long-tongued bat (*Megaloglossus woermanni*) in which females average somewhat larger than males. In the majority of those cases where males are larger than females, this robustness is especially pronounced in the size of the chest and temporal musculature. The large size of temporal musculature is often accompanied by the presence of large, blade-like bony crests that extend down the middle portion or across the back of the braincase. The canine teeth of males may also be larger than those of females. Although this area of chiropteran biology has received little attention, these differences in overall size may also relate to differences in thermoregulatory capabilities and other physiological constraints unique to each sex. These factors in turn may be related to observed differences in roost and feeding preferences.

Mating systems

Ultimately, in sexually reproducing species (bats notwithstanding), adult males and females must encounter and mate with one another with sufficient frequency that their population sizes remain stable or increase slightly. If this does not occur with some degree of regularity, population sizes decline, resulting in fewer males and females that encounter and mate less frequently, and so on. Eventually, populations may become so small that they are unable to sustain themselves and become extinct. It is presumed that the social organization of individuals within species, and mating systems in particular, guard against the eventuality of extinction.

In contrast to the majority of small mammals, very few species of bats appear to live solitary lives. Among the Megachiroptera, *Micropteropus pusillus*, *Myonycteris torquata*, *Megaloglossus woermanni*, and *Epomops franqueti* appear to live a solitary existence or occasionally they are found in mother-infant pairs. The social organization and breeding behaviour of these species are poorly known. Among the Microchiroptera, apparently solitary species are known in the Emballonuridae (*Diclidurus albus*); the Nycteridae (*Nycteris grandis*); the Rhinolophidae (*Rhinolophus luctus*); and the Vespertilionidae (*Pipistrellus nanus*, *Eptesicus minutus*, and *E. rendalli*, *Lasiurus borealis*, *L. cinereus*, and *L. seminolus*). It is not clear what factors cause or otherwise result in sexual encounters among these species. *Epomops franqueti* is apparently polyestrous and breeds throughout the year thus increasing the likelihood of productive sexual encounters. *Lasiurus*, although monestrous, frequently produces two or more young at a time (polytocous). In addition, most of these species of *Lasiurus* are migratory to some extent, and it is thought that breeding occurs along the relatively precise migratory routes travelled each autumn; mating may be initiated while the couple is on the wing.

While there is considerable variation, most temperate bats follow a general pattern of social and sexual organization. These include: aggregations of mixed sexes for the purpose of hibernation; segregated sex groups with females congregated in nursery colonies to give birth and care for young; and autumnal gathering of adults of both sexes during which time mating occurs. Nearly all of these species exhibit some interruption (delayed ovulation, delayed fertilization, sperm storage, delayed implantation, or embryonic diapause) in their reproductive cycle. We have already discussed these reproductive novelties and nursery colonies. The nature of the mating groups is of interest here. In the early autumn, adult males of the European noctule (*Nyctalus noctula*), a tree-dwelling species, begin to congregate and set up territories in hollow trees. Having weaned their young, females aggregate at these sites and enter transient harems for mating. In European populations of the Long-fingered bat (*Miniopterus schreibersii*), the sexes congregate at specific mating caves then move on to winter hibernacula. The Social bat (*Myotis*

sodalis) breeds only during a one- to two-week period in the autumn. At this time, the sexes are segregated in different portions of the hibernaculum during the day; at night, the females invade the male quarters and copulation occurs. In some species, such as the Big Brown bat (*Eptesicus fuscus*) and the Common Long-eared bat (*Plecotus auritus*), small sexually mixed groups form in late summer. Mating occurs in these small summer groups, continues throughout the hibernation period and even into the early spring.

Relatively stable, year-round harems are formed by some tropical bat species. These appear to be common among Neotropical emballonurids, such as the White-lined bats (*Saccopteryx bilineata* and *S. leptura*) and the Proboscis bat (*Rhynchonycteris naso*). It is not surprising that a great deal is known about the natural history of these bats. They roost in relatively open, well-lighted sites, such as the trunks of trees or other suitable, vertical surfaces. Several harem groups may be found occupying one tree trunk. The boundaries of each harem's territory are relatively discrete, patrolled and defended by the harem male. These males use a repertoire of visual, olfactory, and auditory displays to attract and retain one to eight females that usually comprise the harem. Stable harems have also been reported in the Spear-nosed bats (*Phyllostomus hastatus* and *P. discolor*). Harem sizes vary from 10-100 per male in the large-sized *P. hastatus*, whereas those of *P. discolor*, a small-sized species, range from one to twelve females per male. The Malaysian Club-footed bats (*Tylonycteris pachypus* and *T. robustula*) form long-term harem groups in the hollow internodes of bamboo. Harem sizes are from 1-15 in *T. robustula*. Harems of 5-12 females per male have been found in the African molossid (*Tadarida midas*) that resides in rock crevices.

A common social organization among pteropodids, and perhaps other tropical bats, is large, year-round aggregations in which breeding occurs. Many species of flying foxes (*Pteropus*) live in traditional 'camp' trees. Mating may be random among individuals of the camp, but males may tend to breed more frequently with females that roost closest to their established position in the camp.

Finally, some tropical bat species may remain in monogamous family groups. Whether these apparent family units exist over long periods of time is not known. Such groups have been found in the Nycteridae (*Nycteris hispida*, *N. arge*, and *N. nana*); the Hipposideridae (*Hipposideros galeritus* and *H. beatus*); the Megadermatidae (*Lavia frons*); the Phyllostomidae (*Vampyrum spectrum*) and the Vespertilionidae (*Kerivoula*). The Neotropical Disc-winged bats (*Thyroptera*) also appear to remain in family units. An adult male, female, and young are frequently encountered in their secretive roost inside the newly formed, rolled up leaves of bananas or *Heliconia*.

Courtship behaviour

Not only must males and females encounter each other in order to reproduce, but there must be some degree of cooperation between the mating individuals before and during copulation. Bats generally copulate from the rear with the male grasping the female with his wings and perhaps with his teeth. As we noted earlier, some hibernating bats begin copulation in a wakeful state, but lapse into torpor during coitus, being held together by special erectile tissue in the penis. Males of *Plecotus townsendii* and *Macrotus californicus* may copulate with completely torpid females.

The complexities of courtship behaviour in bats are not well known. Pre-copulatory displays frequently involve wing-shaking and mutual grooming. Males of the White-lined bat (*Saccopteryx bilineata*) shake the specialized glandular sacs in their wings at the female while singing a loud courtship song. These wing displays in courtship appear to be a carryover of individual recognition cues used in normal day-to-day encounters or vice versa. On the other hand, some male pteropodids, such as *Rousettus aegyptiacus*

and *Pteropus giganteus*, perform abbreviated courtship displays, then copulate forcefully with the female amidst loud protests on her part.

Perhaps the most interesting courtship behaviour is that performed by male Hammer-headed bats (*Hypsignathus monstrosus*), a pteropodid that lives in western Africa. This behaviour was only recently described and it represents an unusual mating system for mammals. It is called arena or 'lek' mating. Leks are not common in any group of animals. Some bird species such as sage grouse and Hermit hummingbirds form leks during their breeding behaviour. Specifically, a lek involves an aggregation of males, at a traditional site, with the visitation and selection of a male sexual partner by the female. Leks are formed for the singular purpose of mating; no other activity occurs at such aggregations. In addition, true leks usually involve: species in which there is marked secondary sexual dimorphism; extreme ritualization of male displays in the arena; a highly non-random mating success (copulatory frequency) among displaying males; and the presence of a mating centre in which the most successful males congregate. The mating behaviour of some African antelope has been characterized as arena mating. However, there is some question regarding the singular purpose of these aggregations. The mating groups of the Hammer-headed bat seem to fulfil all of

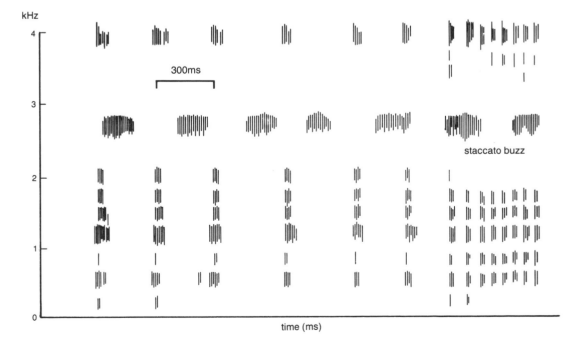

Fig. 7.9 Reproduction of a sonogram showing the display vocalizations of a male Hammer-headed bat (Hypsignathus monstrosus–Pteropodidae). *The 'staccato-buzz' is shown at the far right. See text for discussion. (Bradbury, 1977).*

the criteria of lek mating and, therefore, may be unique among mammals with respect to this form of courtship.

This behaviour was first discovered and described in Gabon along the banks and on small islands in the Ivindo River. The lek assemblage extended for about 1600 metres in the low riparian forest along the river. About 90 males were dispersed at intervals of at least 10 m in this narrow (30-40 m wide) band of forest. Male Hammer-headed bats were observed arriving at the arena at dusk and to begin 'singing' shortly thereafter. The song is a loud, throaty honk or croak not unlike the deep, hollow croak of a frog. At first, the calls are harsh and raspy, but after several renditions they take on the clear metallic note characteristic of the species. These honks are produced in a greatly enlarged, and highly specialized larynx with a large pharyngeal pouch that inflates during the call. These honks are produced at a rate of 50-120 per minute. While calling, the males extend their half-opened wings and beat them at about twice the call rate. There is considerable antagonistic behaviour between males as they take their positions in the early formation of the nightly lek. These male/male encounters drop off as the night progresses.

Next the females arrive at the arena of calling males, often carrying their young. Females cruise along the axis of the male assemblage and frequently make short, hovering inspections of particular males. When a female hovers in front of a calling male, he accelerates his wing flapping and call rate to a 'staccato buzz' which goes something like this: honk.....honk.....honk.....honk...honk...honk...honk. honk(staccato buzz)honkhonkhonkhonkhonk (Fig. 7.9). The female may alternately visit and hover in front of several adjacent males. Once she has made her choice, she may hover in front of the selected male several more times before landing next to him. Copulation is rapid, during which the male abruptly ceases all calling. The copulating pair remain in contact for 30-60 seconds and it always terminates with the female making several loud whinings before she flies off. The male resumes calling within a minute after copulation.

Lek assemblage apparently occurs, in a diffuse form, throughout the year; the duration and organization is usually short and erratic during the rainy season. The most intense activity and breeding occurs in the dry seasons: June-August and December-February.

Chapter 8   *Echolocation and vocalization*

Whether in the roost or in flight, bats produce a wide variety of sounds. Within their vocal repertoire, all bats possess and utilize low frequency sounds (below 20 kHz) which are well within the normal audible range of humans. These vocalizations are generally used to facilitate social interactions such as territorial spacing among individuals, mother/infant communications, recognition, and warning calls. Perhaps the most interesting aspects of the chiropteran vocal repertoire are those sounds that are emitted in the high frequency (ultrasonics above 20 kHz) range. These sounds are above the hearing range of most humans and they are used to navigate and avoid obstacles and capture prey in the dark. The utilization of ultrasonics for acoustic orientation (echolocation) is restricted, for the most part, to the generally insectivorous bats of the suborder Microchiroptera. These high frequency sounds are produced in the larynx (voicebox) in much the same manner as the vocalizations of humans and other mammals.

The Old World fruit bats of the suborder Megachiroptera, that feed on fruit, flowers, nectar, and/or pollen, generally lack the faculty of ultrasonic orientation. However, some members of the suborder (three species of *Rousettus* and perhaps *Epomophorus wahlbergi*) produce orientation sounds that are largely audible, but have ultrasonic components and appear to facilitate orientation. Unlike microchiropterans, the acoustic orientation sounds of *Rousettus* are not produced in the larynx, but are produced by clicking the tongue. The development of 'ultrasonic' orientation in *Rousettus* is generally regarded to be independent of that found in microchiropterans. It has been conjectured that the deep cave-dwelling habit of these megachiropterans is the cause of this independent acquisition of echolocation.

Bats are not unique among mammals in their possession of ultrasonic orientation sounds. Two other orders of mammals, the Insectivora (shrews and tenrecs) and Cetacea (whales and dolphins) utilize high frequency orientation sounds. In addition, some species of the mammalian orders Dermoptera, Marsupialia and Rodentia are thought to utilize ultrasonics. Echolocation has been described in the cave-dwelling South American oilbird or Guacharo (*Steatornis caripensis*) and in the Cave Swiftlets of southeast Asia and Indo-Australia (*Collocallia*). Unlike bats, the echolocation sounds of these birds are loud, sharp, and low frequency vocalizations. They have few, if any, ultrasonic components. Like *Rousettus*, the Guacharo and Cave Swiftlets 'turn off' their echolocation under favourable light conditions. Ultrasonic sound production is also found among some insects—moths, grasshoppers, crickets, and cicadas.

The discovery of echolocation in bats

Although the use of ultrasonic orientation by bats was demonstrated definitively only forty years ago, the mode of orientation of these nocturnal mammals had been the subject of scientific inquiry for over 200 years. This history, which began in the 1770s, is an interesting chapter in scientific discovery that contrasts its brilliant and pertinacious nature.

The Italian Lazzaro Spallanzani (1729-1799), at the age of 64 and after a long and distinguished career as a logician, mathematician and natural scientist, became interested in the abilities of nocturnal animals to move about in darkness. In 1793, he learned that owls became nearly helpless and unable to fly in a totally darkened room. On the other hand, he found that bats were not so encumbered. This prompted him to perform a number of remarkable experiments in which he learned that, unlike owls, bats did not appear to rely upon their visual sense to fly about at night. Undoubtedly his experiments, as well as those of other Europeans, were conducted with microchiropterans.

With the notion that eyesight was important to bats, Spallanzani's first experiments utilized a small lightproof hood placed over the heads of his bats with the intention of blocking their vision. Indeed, these bats were rendered incapable of avoiding obstacles in a darkened room. Thus, it would seem that he had 'proven' his point. He next conducted a control experiment in which he used a transparent hood and found that his bats were still unable to fly without crashing into obstacles. In order to settle the matter of visual orientation once and for all, Spallanzani surgically blinded some bats. To his amazement, these blinded bats, upon recovery, were as capable as normal, unblinded bats at avoiding obstacles. In another experiment, he used two groups of bats one of which he blinded and the other he left intact. He marked the individuals of both groups and returned them to the cave from which he had taken them. After several days, he recaptured his experimental subjects and found that the blinded bats had the same amount of insects in their stomachs as normal bats. From this he concluded that bats did not rely on vision to orient and capture prey in darkness. He wrote about his experiments and findings to several of his European colleagues.

A Swiss natural scientist, Charles Jurine, learned about Spallanzani's experiments and set about conducting some of his own. In these, he plugged the ears of bats with wax and found that they could no longer avoid obstacles. Jurine published his findings in 1798. In the year before his death, Spallanzani refined Jurine's experiments by fitting a small brass tube which could be plugged and unplugged into the ears of his bats. When the tubes were plugged, the bats crashed into obstacles, whereas those with unplugged tubes flew about like normal bats. Although neither Spallanzani nor Jurine could provide a plausible explanation for their results, both concluded that hearing was important in the nocturnal orientation of bats. However, these remarkable experiments and their conclusions were ignored and fell into oblivion for over 100 years.

The submersion of this important work was in large part due to a new theory proposed by the French zoologist Georges Cuvier (1769-1832) who supposed that a bat's capacity for avoiding obstacles was due to a highly specialized sense of touch. Cuvier's tactile theory was accepted, without any experimental proof, by the majority of European naturalists throughout the 1800s. Many of those who accepted Cuvier's notion fabricated explanations involving nerves and the numerous hairs on a bat's wing; all were designed to elucidate the mechanism of the 'sixth sense' of bats. However, no one was able to provide scientific substance to the tactile theory.

The possibility that bats might employ sound as the basis of a location system was resurrected in 1912 by Hiram Maxim, the inventor of the machine gun. The tragic loss of the 'Titanic' after its collision with an iceberg led him to consider a sonic warning device. He supposed that perhaps bats might utilize such a sonic device to avoid obstacles while flying in darkness. Although he correctly identified the mechanism (echo detection), he wrongly described both the source and the nature of the sound. He thought that the sound was low in frequency (below the audible range for humans) and that it was generated by the wing beat.

In 1920, the British neurophysiologist H. Hartridge reconfirmed the Spallanzani/Jurine notion that bats oriented with auditory rather than visual cues. He further hypothesized that the sounds utilized were of a high frequency nature rather than low frequency. It was not until the late 1930s that conclusive proof was finally obtained. At this time, the Harvard physicist G. W. Pierce developed a device capable of detecting ultrasonic sounds. As has been the case with many scientific discoveries, the solution to this problem hinged on the fortuitous interaction between two investigators, each concerned with independent research goals. Donald Griffin, a Harvard biology student at the time, was interested in chiropteran biology. He knew about Pierce's high frequency sound detector and it was not completely by chance that he walked into Pierce's laboratory with a cage full of bats (*Myotis lucifugus* and *Eptesicus fuscus*). When he brought the bats close to Pierce's apparatus it became clear that they were producing high frequency sounds. This, then, was the beginning of modern investigation into chiropteran ultrasonics and echolocation. This investigation has grown and diversified as technological advances have been made in the development and refinement of ultrasonic detection and recording devices.

Nature of echolocation

As visually orienting creatures, humans perceive and move about their environment by seeing things, selecting and/or avoiding these depending upon the circumstances of the encounter. Indeed, vision is the underlying basis for most aspects of human culture and society. In addition, humans fear, either consciously or subconsciously, the prospect of blindness or being trapped in darkness as a debilitated, helpless state of being as 'blind as a bat'. The often cited superiority of the human brain ultimately is a manifestation of the evolutionary development and differentiation of the visual centres of the mammalian brain.

In its simplest form, vision is the perception and interpretation of a form of energy (light energy in a variety of wavelengths and intensities) as it is reflected, or in some cases produced, by objects in the environment. This interpretation yields information concerning size, shape, colour, texture, and movement. In a similar fashion, audition (hearing) is the perception and interpretation of a form of energy (sound energy in a variety of wavelengths and intensities) as it is reflected, or in most cases produced, by objects in the environment. While one might think tone, pitch, intensity, and perhaps proximity are the only bits of information to be interpreted, sound perception can yield information concerning size, shape, texture, and movement. Colour cannot be perceived with audition.

Acoustic orientation differs from visual orientation by virtue of the fact that a sound is generated and emitted by the organism. This sound strikes an object in the environment and is reflected (bounced back) as an echo with altered sound qualities. The reception and interpretation of the qualities of the echo yield the information concerning size, shape, texture and movement. Rarely, in living systems, is light generated intrinsically by the organism for the purpose of seeing. Of course, humans may take advantage of a hand torch or other artificially generated light to find their way in darkness, and some organisms (owls) may have visual acuity such that they can function in extremely low light situations. Recall that the understanding of chiropteran acoustic orientation was not fully appreciated until the discovery was made that bats actually produced the orientation sounds themselves.

At about the same time that the mechanism of bat echo orientation was being discovered, man was designing and developing two echolocation systems —sonar and radar. Both of these systems rely on generating and beaming either sound or electromagnetic energy, respectively, at a distant object and determining its position and movement by analyzing the echo. Chiropteran acoustic orientation, and indeed that of most echolocating animals, is more akin to sonar than to radar, in that it relies on sound rather than electromagnetic energy.

Bats echolocate by producing a series of short pulses of high frequency sound. These pulses are emitted through the mouth (oral emitters) or through the nostrils (nasal emitters). As these sounds travel through air (at about 340 m s^{-1}), they spread out, three dimensionally, in the form of a cone with the long axis extending from the point of emission (mouth or nostrils). When this sound strikes an object, it is reflected as an echo. From these echoes a bat determines the presence, distance, direction and velocity of movement, size, shape, and texture of the object of interest. With this information, the bat can manoeuver to avoid obstacles as well as identify, track and intercept flying or terrestrial prey items. Thus, bats, and other echolocating animals, are able to formulate a sonic image of their immediate environment.

PHYSICAL ASPECTS OF SOUND

In order to understand and appreciate the novelty of chiropteran acoustic orientation, we must first examine some physical parameters of sound.

Wavelength and frequency

Sound, like light, heat and other forms of energy, is manifested in the form of disturbances or vibrations in a medium. The usual medium is air, but solid or liquid media may also be affected by sound vibrations. These vibrations take the form of waves, with successive peaks and troughs. Sound is measured in a number of ways. One of these is frequency, which is a measure of the rate (usually expressed as a unit of time) at which an event occurs. In the case of sound, the event is wave generation, or the length of time it takes to make a complete wave with its respective peak and trough; that is, one cycle or one oscillation (Fig. 8.1A). Thus, sound frequency is the number of oscillations (cycles) that occur in one second; this is expressed as 'cycles per second'. To honor the German physicist Hertz, cycles per second are usually referred to as Hertz (Hz). Sound frequencies may be further converted into kilocycles per second or kiloHertz (kHz); 1000 Hz being equal to 1 kHz or one kilocycle per second. The normal frequency range of human hearing is between 20 Hz to 20 kHz; hearing in the higher range of frequencies often declines with age. The frequency range utilized by bats varies from species to species, but most echolocate in a high frequency range between 20-80 kHz. Some species utilize frequencies as low as 4-5 kHz and others range as high as 120-210 kHz.

Another way in which sound is characterized is by its wavelength; that is, the linear distance between successive peaks or troughs of sound waves (Fig. 8.1A). The wavelength of a particular sound is inversely related to its frequency. Sounds with long wavelengths require longer lengths of time to repeat a cycle and, conversely, sounds with shorter wavelengths have faster repetition times. Thus, high frequency sounds generally have short wavelengths, whereas low frequency sounds have longer wavelengths.

High frequency sounds are severely attenuated (weakened in intensity) as they pass through air, whereas low frequency sounds retain their intensity over longer distances. One might wonder why bats utilize high frequency sounds rather than those of low frequency. One reason that has been suggested is that by using high frequencies bats avoid possible interference from environmental background noises such as insect songs, wind, or other nocturnal noises that are generally in the low frequency range. Utilization of high frequency signals might also provide a means of escaping detection by potential nocturnal predators. Some have suggested that utilization of high frequency sounds may be a way of detecting insect prey without being detected in turn. We will

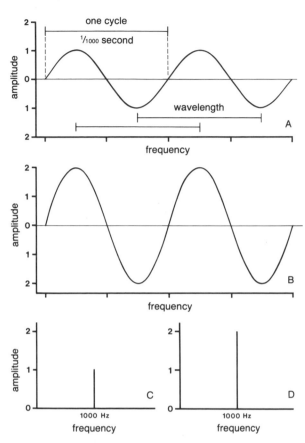

Fig. 8.1 Anatomy of a soundwave. A, 1000 Hz pure tone with an amplitude of 1; B, 1000 Hz pure tone with an amplitude of 2; C, line, sound spectrum for A; D, line, sound spectrum for B.

Amplitude or intensity

Another physical property of sound is the energy it contains; its amplitude, intensity or loudness. Amplitude is represented by the height, above and below, the zero reference line of the waveform (Fig. 8.1). It can be quantified by measuring the difference in pressure between the peak and the trough of the wave. In reality, amplitude is a measure of air pressure caused by the sound wave as it travels through air. This pressure was formerly recorded as dynes per square centimetre (dynes cm^{-2}), but it is now more usual to express the values in Newtons per square metre (N m^{-2}) (1 Newton = 10^5 dynes). The minimum sound pressure perceptible to the human ear (auditory threshold) is about 0.000 02 N m^{-2}. The human eardrum is ruptured by an absolute sound of 2 × 10^3 N m^{-2}.

Harmonics

Thus far, we have been concerned with characteristics of pure tones or sounds consisting of a single frequency with its respective wavelength and amplitude. Such sounds are rather rare in nature, although we will see that some bats utilize pure tones in their orientation sounds. For the most part, natural sounds are complex in structure and consist of a collection of several to many frequencies. Complex sounds occur as a result of structural peculiarities and/or imperfections in the design of a sound producing device. The nature of the immediate surroundings of the sound-producing device also contributes to the complexity of a sound.

Tuning forks are carefully designed and machined devices that vibrate at a specific frequency and thereby produce a pure tone. If we were to strike a tuning fork designed to produce a 'high C' and analyze the sound with an oscilloscope, we would see a simple waveform with the frequency and wavelength of 'high C'. The amplitude of this waveform would depend upon how hard we struck the tuning fork. If, on the other hand, we were to play 'high C' on a violin, clarinet, flute, and French horn, we would see a variety of waveforms with many more jagged peaks and troughs than that produced by the tuning fork. The waveform generated by each instrument would be markedly different (Fig. 8.2) because of their different structural designs and the ways in which they each produce their characteristic sound. The violin produces sounds with a tightly stretched vibrating string attached to a wooden box, whereas a vibrating reed generates and directs sounds through a wooden tube in a clarinet. More importantly, these differences in tonal quality result from the fact that

see later in this chapter that some insects (moths) that are eaten by bats can hear bat sounds and do exercise evasive manoeuvers or even produce high frequency sounds of their own to jam an approaching bat's reception.

While these may be important considerations, the most important factor seems to relate to the target discriminatory nature of high frequency sounds. As we noted earlier, high frequency sound has a short wavelength. For example, a sound with the frequency of 50 kHz has a wavelength of about 6.8 mm (340 000 mm s^{-1}: 50 000 Hz). On the other hand, a low frequency sound of 34 Hz has a wavelength of about 10 m (340 m s^{-1}: 34 Hz). The discrimination of small-sized objects (insect prey) is better as the wavelength approaches the size of the object of interest. Long waves spread in such a way that they may bend around an object without producing any appreciable reflection or echo. Thus, the use of high frequency, shortwave sounds by bats seems best correlated with size of prey items (5-20 mm in diameter).

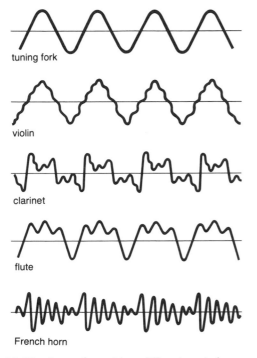

Fig. 8.2 *Waveforms of sound from different musical instruments sounding the same note.*

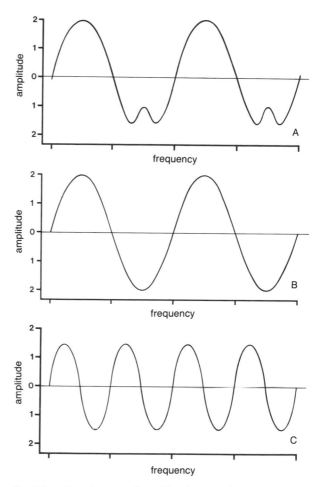

Fig. 8.3 *A, Complex wave formed by the sum of two pure tones B and C. B, fundamental, lowest frequency. C, first harmonic of B.*

vibrating structures and their surrounding areas vibrate simultaneously at different frequencies.

The different frequencies in a complex sound are called harmonics or overtones. The harmonic structure of a complex sound is not a random assortment of frequencies, but rather a precisely ordered sequence of 'related' frequencies. The component frequencies, or harmonics, of a complex sound are related by being integral multiples of a fundamental frequency (the lowest frequency in a complex sound). Figure 8.3A represents a simplistic example of a complex sound. It may be recognized as such because it is not the smooth, uninterrupted waveform that we would expect of a pure tone. This complex sound consists of two related frequencies. The lowest in this series, and thereby the fundamental frequency, is 1000 Hz (Fig. 8.3B). The second frequency, or first harmonic, is precisely 1000 Hz higher, that is, 2000 Hz (Fig. 8.3C). We would expect to find additional harmonics at 3000 Hz, 4000 Hz, etc.

Complex sounds are further complicated by virtue of the fact that each harmonic may be produced with different amplitudes or intensities. In some cases, harmonics may be 'dropped out' of the sound spectrum altogether. Indeed, the tonal quality of the instruments mentioned above is the result of this factor.

As we will see below, bats produce a variety of complex sounds in their acoustic orientation vocalizations. These include sweeps through several frequencies with accompanying harmonics. These sounds are produced in the larynx and may be filtered or otherwise altered by various resonating cavities or other peculiarities in the vocal tract or nasal passages. Thus, the acoustic sounds emitted by the bat have a particular structure. By using orientation sounds with multiple harmonics, bats increase the discriminatory ability of the sound because each harmonic represents a discrete frequency with its own wavelength and target size recognition characteristics. A range of harmonics would be of definite value in hunting in a dense, tangled environment or along solid surfaces by improving the contrast between echoes reflected from a potential prey item and its background. An abnormal range of harmonics may be produced by young bats as they learn their acoustic repertoire, by cold partially aroused bats, or by individuals in poor condition and health.

CHARACTERISTICS OF MICROCHIROPTERAN ECHOLOCATION SOUNDS

The high frequency sounds produced by microchiropterans are acoustic signals emitted by the bat for the purpose of gathering vital information about objects (potential food items or obstacles to be avoided) in its immediate vicinity. The nature of this biological imaging system, its quality and quantity, varies widely among the species of microchiropterans. As the technological sophistication of high frequency sound detection devices has improved, so has our biological understanding of microchiropteran acoustic orientation. The heavy and bulky nature of the rather crude early detection equipment restricted investigators of chiropteran echolocation to confined laboratory spaces and limited study to easily captured and maintained bats (mostly temperate species). From this early era of research, it was learned that bats varied with respect to the sounds they produced, but that groups of species tended to emit rather stereotypic acoustic signals. As detection equipment became more sensitive, lighter and more portable, and researchers began studying echolocating bats under more natural (field) conditions, it was learned that most bats produce a wider repertoire of acoustic sounds than was previously thought. Our current knowledge suggests that although some species may operate within one of several general echolocation patterns, there is considerable variation depending on changing perceptual requirements of different situations and different intentions on the part of the individual bat.

The ultrasonic vocalizations of microchiropterans may be characterized by a combination of several descriptive parameters.

1. *Duration of signal.* The duration of the orientation signal used by bats varies from about 0.2 to 100 milliseconds (ms). This range of variation may be further divided into three general groupings; those that are exceptionally short (less than 2 ms), those of moderate duration (less than 10 ms), and those that are very long (more than 10 ms).

2. *Harmonic structure of signal.* Bats may incorporate from one to perhaps five harmonics in their acoustic orientation signals. Some species include only one harmonic, often the second harmonic of the fundamental frequency which itself may be suppressed in the vocal tract. On the other hand, some species do not incorporate any harmonics in their echolocation sounds.

3. *Frequency-modulated (FM) component of signal.* Frequency-modulated components are sweeps (usually downward) from a beginning frequency, through several to many intermediate frequencies, to some other ending frequency that is (usually) lower than the beginning. FM components may be narrow in bandwidth (sweeping through relatively few frequencies, for example, 55 kHz to 40 kHz = bandwidth 15 kHz) or broad in bandwidth (sweeping through many frequencies, for example, 100 kHz to 50 kHz = bandwidth 50 kHz). In addition, FM sweeps may be linear (usually abrupt or short in duration) or they may be curvilinear (less abrupt and generally longer in duration).

4. *Constant-frequency (CF) component of signal.* Constant-frequency signals are echolocation sounds emitted at one frequency. Many bats incorporate a CF component in their acoustic orientation calls. In those species with signals that are long in duration (more than 10 ms), the CF component forms the bulk of the sound.

5. *Sequence of frequency components in signal.* Both CF and FM components are commonly encountered in microchiropteran ultrasonic sounds. Either the CF or FM component may precede the other.

6. *Amplitude (intensity or loudness) of signal.* The acoustic orientation sounds of bats appear to fall into a wide range of intensities. There has been relatively little consistent information gathered, under similar circumstances, for more than a few species of bats. Intensities of 0.1-0.32 N m^{-2} have been recorded for the Greater False vampire (*Megaderma lyra*). The Greater Horseshoe bat (*Rhinolophus ferrumequinum*) and the Mediterranean Horseshoe bat (*Rhinolophus euryale*) have been recorded at 27.0 and 2.0 N m^{-2}, respectively, 10 cm directly ahead of the bat. The Little Brown bat (*Myotis lucifugus*) produces sounds between 6.0 and 17.3 N m^{-2} 5-10 cm from the bat's mouth. Although these sounds are above the human auditory threshold, the higher intensities are comparable, in terms of energy, to those produced by jet engines and other noisy machinery. Such loud, but inaudible, sounds would be painfully perceived by most human ears, and indeed some people are especially sensitive to bat sounds or other ultrasonic noises.

As noted above, high frequency sounds tend to attenuate quickly as they pass through air. The high intensity of acoustic orientation sounds made by bats may ensure proper echo perception in a particular working space. Intensity may also vary with the complexity of the immediate surroundings. Thus, one might expect sounds of lower intensities to be used in the complex tangle of a forest canopy and those of higher intensities in more open environments. Bats of the families Nycteridae and Megadermatidae, that hunt close to the ground or around vegetation, use rather faint sounds. Some vespertilionid bats also utilize low amplitude sounds as do the fruit and nectar-feeding members of the Phyllostomidae. These bats, with amplitudes often below 0.1 N m⁻², arc sometimes collectively referred to as 'whispering bats.' Some Free-tailed bats of the family Molossidae, as well as some vespertilionids that forage high above the ground or in generally open areas, utilize loud orientation sounds. One must be careful to note that these are only general categorizations and that any one species or individual thereof may vary the intensity of its calls under different circumstances.

7. *Variations of repertoire.* An individual bat may change its acoustic repertoire along one or more of the parameters outlined above. This change may be continuous in nature, such as the case of a bat closing in on an insect in flight; these are episodical changes. On the other hand, some bats change their acoustic orientation pattern in different foraging situations; that is, 'open area' acoustic styles vs. 'cluttered area' styles. These are situational or environmentally dictated changes. With regard to this parameter, some bat species are extremely flexible, whereas others appear to be extremely inflexible.

Microchiropterans possess two general kinds of acoustic imaging systems. One is represented by a time-frequency spectrum that consists primarily of broadband, frequency-modulated signals. The other is represented by a time-frequency structure that consists mainly of narrowband, constant-frequency signals. Within each of these broad groups there are several distinctive patterns.

Broadband, frequency-modulated signals

The first broadband acoustic pattern consists of frequency-modulated signals with multiple harmonics. This pattern appears to be characteristic of the New World leaf-nosed bats (Phyllostomidae) and, perhaps, the Old World False vampire bats (Megadermatidae). The acoustic orientation of phyllostomids has been relatively well studied. Members of this family are the most diverse with regard to their feeding habits (see Chapter 5), including insectivory, carnivory, frugivory, nectarivory and sanguivory. The echolocation sounds of these bats usually contain two to four harmonics with a moderate amount of linear frequency-modulation. These ultrasonic signals are exceptionally low in amplitude (usually less than 0.1 N m⁻²) and, as noted above, phyllostomids are often referred to as 'whispering bats'. Phyllostomid acoustic sounds are especially short in duration (0.5-2.5 ms). The overall bandwidth of each harmonic may be relatively narrow (average 20-30 kHz), but the

abrupt linearity of the frequency sweep causes these harmonics to overlap thereby creating a rather broad overall bandwidth for an entire signal. For example, the carnivorous Spear-nosed bat (*Phyllostomus hastatus*) emits four harmonics (1°, 35kHz to 30 kHz; 2°, 45 kHz to 35 kHz; 3°, 60 kHz to 45 kHz; 4°, 75 kHz to 60 kHz). This results in an overall bandwidth of 40-45 kHz. The nectarivorous Long-tongued bat (*Glossophaga soricina*) apparently utilizes an exceptionally high range of frequencies in its multiple harmonic FM sweep. In this species, the fundamental frequency may descend from 104 kHz to 50 kHz which places the second harmonic at about 208 kHz to 100 kHz. These high frequency sounds would be expected to attenuate rapidly in warm, moist tropical air. However, *Glossophaga* is a hovering species and these high frequency signals are well suited for close range target discrimination. The echolocation sounds of the Common vampire (*Desmodus rotundus*) illustrate some of the possible variability of the harmonic structure of phyllostomids. The duration of its signals is very brief (1.1-2.3 ms). The signal begins with two harmonics; the fundamental frequency that sweeps from 42-38 kHz to 29-24 kHz and a second harmonic sweeping from 83-76 kHz to 54-50 kHz. At about the middle of signal emission (when the fundamental reaches about 30 kHz), a third harmonic develops at about 90 kHz and sweeps downward to near 80 kHz.

A second pattern involving broadband, frequency-modulated signals consists of a brief FM sweep (1-3 ms), followed by a short (5-7 ms) constant-frequency component. This FM/short CF pattern is found in many tropical and temperate species of the family Vespertilionidae. These bats are often called 'FM bats'. One to three (generally broad) harmonics may be present and these usually overlap. The much studied Big Brown bat (*Eptesicus fuscus*) has a short FM signal (1-5 ms) that sweeps downward in a curvilinear fashion from 50 kHz to 25 kHz. The CF portion of this signal may be shortened and deleted occasionally. A second harmonic sweeps from about 100 kHz to 50 kHz and a third harmonic (at about 60 kHz) enters in the last third of the vocalization. Members of the genus *Myotis* have somewhat shorter signals compared to those of *Eptesicus*, the downward FM sweep is more linear (usually over a slightly broader bandwidth), and the CF component is often truncated or absent. The harmonic structure is very much like that described for *Eptesicus*. Two species, *Myotis auriculus* from the southwestern United States and *Myotis septentrionalis* from the northeastern United States, have exceptionally broad, nearly linear, FM sweeps (150 kHz to 45 kHz) with a duration of 1-2 ms. At another extreme, the Hoary bat (*Lasiurus cinereus*) has a rather short (1-2 ms) narrowband FM sweep (50 kHz to 30 kHz) and a long CF component (6-8 ms).

Narrowband, constant-frequency signals

The first of these narrowband CF patterns is characterized by multiple harmonic, short CF signals. These signals are very short in duration (0.2-2 ms). Except for the lack of any substantial FM sweep, these signals are very much like those described as multiple harmonic FM signals. The fundamental frequency is emitted at or near 20 kHz and this is accompanied by up to four harmonics. These harmonics are all CF or only slightly FM. This pattern is encountered in the Rhinopomatidae, some members of the Emballonuridae, and Nycteridae. The acoustic orientation sounds of the Greater False vampire (*Megaderma lyra*–Megadermatidae) seem best placed within this group. Those of the Heart-nosed bat (*Cardioderma cor*), the only other megadermatid that has been examined, are strongly frequency-modulated, which may illustrate a subtle change of this basic pattern. Additional variation is seen in the Emballonuridae in which the Neotropical White-lined bats (*Saccopteryx*) lengthen the signal to 6-8 ms with a shallow FM tendency near its end. This is similar to the signals of the Mouse-tailed bats (*Rhinopoma*) except that in these bats there is no FM tendency. Nycterids appear to have both short CF and short FM multiple harmonic signals; these also appear to be low in amplitude. This acoustic pattern has been regarded as close to the supposed primitive echolocation system of microchiropterans.

A second narrowband CF pattern consists of a moderately short CF signal (5-7 ms) followed by a brief FM sweep (1-2 ms). There may be one to three harmonics and the FM portions of these are sufficiently shallow to prevent overlap in bandwidths. The acoustic signals of most members of the Hipposideridae are of this sort. Among the Neotropical species of the family Mormoopidae, three species (*Pteronotus gymnonotus*, *P. davyi*, and *P. personatus*) have this pattern. There is considerable variation in the length of the CF component within the Hipposideridae. In the Short-eared Trident bat (*Cloeotis percivali*), the CF component is quite short (0.5-1.0 ms), whereas in the Trident bat (*Asellia tridens*) the CF component is rather long (6-7 ms). *Cloeotis* also operates at rather high frequencies, with one harmonic, sweeping from the short CF frequency of 212 kHz to about 180 kHz. Most hipposiderids appear to operate below 150 kHz. In the mormoopids with short CF/FM signals, the durations of the sounds are rather short (1-4.5 ms); the bandwidth of the FM component ranges from 20-35 kHz. Also, these Neotropical bats

emphasize the second and third harmonics, with the fundamental frequency and a fourth harmonic being weak; there is no overlap in the FM components of the harmonics.

The third narrowband CF pattern is similar to the second except that the CF component is exceptionally long (20 to over 100 ms) in duration. This pattern is common among species of the Old World family Rhinolophidae and some members of the Hipposideridae. In the New World, it is found in Parnell's Moustached bat (*Pteronotus parnellii*–Mormoopidae). The terminal FM component is usually only moderately broad in these bats (average about 15-20 kHz), but the FM sweep of some rhinolophids (*Rhinolophus landeri*) may be as much as 40 kHz. This acoustic pattern may be accompanied by one to four harmonics, but frequency overlap does not occur in the FM sweeps. Occasionally, the long CF portion of the signal may be preceded by a short upward FM sweep. These bats are also characterized by having their inner ears (cochlea) mechanically tuned to receive the echoes from these long CF signals (see discussion below). CF signals of more than 10 ms are currently thought to be specialized acoustic adaptations to take advantage of Doppler-shifted echoes that provide target motion imagery (see discussion below).

Some species of the Emballonuridae, Phyllostomidae, Vespertilionidae, and the Fishing bat (*Noctilio leporinus*) may occasionally incorporate long CF components in their acoustic repertoire. Recent field studies on the Big-eared bat (*Idionycteris phyllotis*–Vespertilionidae) in Nevada, have found that this species frequently uses long CF signals. When flying in open areas or around vegetation, these bats emit a constant-frequency (27 kHz) signal that has a duration of 20-200 ms; durations as long as 500 ms also were recorded. A short FM sweep of 2-5 ms is emitted, but it is separated from the CF signal by a silent interval of 3-5 ms. There are two harmonics associated with the FM portion of the signal, one sweeps from 24 to 12 kHz and the second from 40 to 22 kHz. Unlike the inner ears of the long-CF bats mentioned above, those of *Idionycteris* are not mechanically tuned, but it is thought that they may utilize Doppler-shifted echoes.

Variable bandwidth, CF or FM Signals

Several insectivorous species of the molossid genus *Tadarida* appear to be quite flexible in their use of acoustic orientation patterns. Early investigations of echolocation patterns of the Mexican Free-tailed bat (*Tadarida brasiliensis*), conducted in the confined space of laboratories, suggested that these bats were 'typical' FM bats. However, recent field studies on *T.*

brasiliensis and *T. macrotis* have revealed information that clearly shows that these bats are perhaps the most versatile echolocators among the Microchiroptera. In uncluttered spaces, these bats hunt with narrowband, short CF signals with no FM component. When pursuing potential prey, they drop the CF signal while adding a broadband FM component; one harmonic accompanies this FM sweep. In cluttered or confined situations, these bats employ a multiple harmonic signal with several harmonics that overlap somewhat. The Fishing bat (*Noctilio leporinus*–Noctilionidae) also appears to shift its acoustic vocalizations from essentially FM signals to short CF/FM signals during different phases of prey pursuit. It is likely that further investigations of other kinds of bats (in natural situations) will reveal similar flexibility in their acoustic repertoire.

EFFICIENCY OF CHIROPTERAN ACOUSTIC ORIENTATION

Over the years, a great deal has been learned with regard to the efficiency of acoustic orientation of bats. Much of this knowledge has been accumulated through experimentation with free-flying bats in the 'controlled environs' of the laboratory. In recent years, experimentation has advanced markedly from rather crude and simple, yet ingenious, behavioural experiments to the use of sophisticated electronic microphonic sensors surgically implanted in various auditory regions of the brain.

Target size discrimination

Many early experiments and even some more recent studies have involved flying bats in a darkened room with a grid or series of fine wires in order to determine their ability to detect and avoid obstacles of a particular size. The Little Brown bat (*Myotis lucifugus*) is capable of detecting and flying through (in 89 per cent of the trials) an obstacle network of wires 0.28 mm in diameter. The phyllostomid, *Glossophaga soricina*, has scored 89 per cent misses with wires 0.175 mm in diameter. Other phyllostomids (*Carollia perspicillata* and *Artibeus jamaicensis*) have performed similarly, and *Macrotus californicus* readily detect and avoid wires down to 0.19 mm in diameter. The Mediterranean Horseshoe bat (*Rhinolophus euryale*) can discriminate wires as fine as 0.05 mm in diameter, and the megadermatid, *Megaderma lyra*, has the ability to avoid wires that are about as thick as human hair (0.08 mm in diameter). Figure 8.4 shows the results of an experiment demonstrating the size discriminatory ability of the Trident bat (*Asellia*

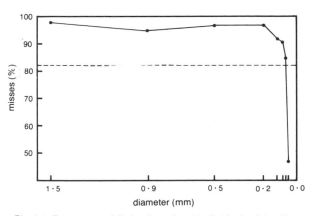

Fig. 8.4 Percentage of flights by several individuals of Asellia tridens *(Hipposideridae) without collision through vertical wire obstacles of different diameter. Wires were 20 cm apart. (Gustafson & Schnitzler, 1979).*

tridens–Hipposideridae). It performed above the level of chance (82.5 per cent misses with wires of 0.065 mm in diameter). The echolocating megachiropteran, *Rousettus*, fell below 70 per cent misses with wires smaller than 1 mm in diameter.

Target range discrimination

The range (distance to target) discrimination of echolocating bats varies, not surprisingly, with the size of the target. The Little Brown bat (*Myotis lucifugus*) can detect wires of 3 mm in diameter at about 2.25 m. This range perception drops to 1.15 m for 0.28 mm wires and 1.0 m for 0.18 mm wires. The Mediterranean Horseshoe bat (*Rhinolophus euryale*) does not detect a 3 mm wire until it is within 1.4 m of the wire, and a 0.05 mm wire is perceived at 0.2 m.

Some researchers have used small fruit flies (*Drosophila*—about 2-3 mm in diameter) in range discrimination experiments. *Myotis lucifugus* and *M. keeni* detected and pursued these small flies from a distance of about 0.50-0.75 m. The mormoopids (*Pteronotus davyi* and *P. personatus*) performed similarly, while the detection range of *Pteronotus parnellii* (a long-CF bat) was about 3.3 m. In experiments using mealworms tossed into the air, *Myotis lucifugus* and the Big Brown bat (*Eptesicus fuscus*) detected these targets about 600 ms prior to interception. In similar trials, the Red bat (*Lasiurus borealis*) detected the mealworms 375 ms before interception. Considering a flight speed of 2.4 m s^{-1} for *Myotis*, 3.3 m s^{-1} for *Eptesicus*, and 5.5 m s^{-1} for *Lasiurus*, range detection can be calculated to be 1.5, 2.0, and 2.1 m, respectively. The Fishing bat (*Noctilio leporinus*) apparently can detect small projecting pieces of fish from 1.8-2.0 m distance.

In range detection experiments of a different sort, *Eptesicus fuscus* demonstrated an ability to differentiate between two identical targets placed at different distances. These bats were able to distinguish a target as little as 12-13 mm in front of another. Similar ability has been found in the Spear-nosed bat (*Phyllostomus hastatus*–Phyllostomidae), the Big Naked-backed bat (*Pteronotus gymnonotus*– Mormoopidae), and the Greater Horseshoe bat (*Rhinolophus ferrumequinum*–Rhinolophidae).

Target shape and texture discrimination

Several experiments have been conducted with *Eptesicus fuscus* in which this vespertilionid was able to distinguish between isosceles triangles ranging in size from 10 × 5 cm to 7 × 3.5 cm. In these experiments, *E. fuscus* could recognize (as different) triangles that were 9 × 4.5 cm and 10 × 5 cm, but could not distinguish either of these from a triangle 9.5 cm × 4.75 cm. In similar experiments, the carnivorous phyllostomid, *Vampyrum spectrum*, appeared to be able to detect differences in the shape of various spheres and spheroids.

The textural discriminating ability of *Eptesicus fuscus* was demonstrated by using square Plexiglas plates drilled with a pattern of 24 holes. The depth of these holes varied from target to target from 8.0 to 6.5 mm; they were of uniform depth on any one target plate. The plates were presented for discrimination as pairs and these Brown bats were able to recognize plates with as little as 0.8 mm difference in hole depth.

Feeding rates

Finally, the efficiency of bat acoustic orientation has been evaluated by using feeding rates. In the field, this has been accomplished rather crudely by weighing bats before and after a known period of hunting activity. Dividing the weight gained in a particular period of time by the average weight of the prey gives a rough estimate of echolocation efficiency in terms of successful captures per unit of time. Individuals of *Myotis lucifugus* appear to have an average rate of insect accumulation of 1 g h^{-1}. Prey size for *M. lucifugus* varies from 0.2 mg to 3 mg with an average of about 2 mg. Thus, this species detects and captures insects, in the wild, at a rate of about 500 per hour or about one insect every seven seconds. Laboratory experiments with *M. lucifugus* foraging in a room full of *Drosophila* (weight about 2 mg) demonstrated a capture rate of 1200 per hour or one every three seconds.

TARGET IMAGERY AND INFORMATION CONTENT OF ECHOES

The special task facing an echolocating bat is acoustically to sort out objects in its immediate environment. As we have already seen, the dimensions of this 'working space' vary among species of bats from less than a metre to perhaps several metres depending on flight speed and style as well as target range discriminatory ability. Within this space, the bat must be able to discriminate potential food items that are often embedded in a complex background of potential obstacles that must be avoided. To increase further the difficulty of this task, it must be successfully accomplished in a matter of microseconds.

Each of the echolocation patterns described above (multiple harmonic FM, FM/short CF, short CF/FM, etc.) serves as a carrier of vital information about particular targets of interest to bats. Each of these acoustic patterns is limited by the kind of target imagery that it can convey. At this time, there does not appear to be any simple one-to-one relationship between the physical attributes of targets (e.g., size, shape, texture, direction of movement, and velocity) and the acoustic features of echoes (e.g., frequency, harmonic spectrum, intensity, and time of occurrence) that portray target features.

General pattern of echolocation

Although we have seen that there is an array of time-frequency patterns of acoustic orientation, there is also a generalized sequence of acoustic events that appear to be common to all echolocating bats. This generalized sequence of events may be divided into three distinct phases: search, approach, and terminal.

Each phase of echolocation is characterized by a marked quantitative change in the rate at which the ultrasonic signals are emitted by the bat and the duration of each signal. Figure 8.5 illustrates the nature of these three phases in four different species of bats, each of which uses a different qualitative pattern of acoustic orientation. In these bats, as well as most others, the search phase is characterized by a signal emission (or pulse) rate of about 10 pulses per second. In view of the fact that ultrasonic sound production is a metabolically expensive process, the repetition rate of the acoustic signals is regulated or balanced against the activity of the moment. During the search phase, signals seem to be emitted at a minimal rate, just sufficient enough to survey and screen the area ahead for potential prey items or obstacles. The rate of signal emission in the search phase also appears to be correlated with flight speed and the degree of environmental clutter. Once a target has been detected, goal-oriented flight begins with an approach phase characterized by 25-50 pulses per second, and finishes with the terminal phase during which pulse emissions may reach as high as 200 or more pulses per second. The marked rise in signal emission rate during these two, goal-oriented phases allows the bat to gather more precise information concerning the speed, direction of movement, and other acoustic imagery about the intended target or obstacle. Because of the rapidity of signal emission in the terminal phase, it is often called the 'buzz' and may be heard as such if the FM sweep passes into the human hearing range.

In many echolocating bats, the qualitative nature of each signal may be slightly modified during this continuum of ultrasonic events. For example, the duration of the signal may be shortened (*Rhinolophus*–Fig. 8.5) but the general structure of the signal remains unchanged. *Eptesicus fuscus* (Fig. 8.5) truncates and eventually drops the short CF portion of the signal and the FM sweep of the harmonics may be initially expanded in the approach phase. In the terminal phase, the overall FM sweep is lowered slightly and the bandwidth of each harmonic is reduced to the point that overlap of harmonics disappears. Nonetheless, the basic structure of the signal remains intact.

In contrast, the Mexican Free-tailed bat (*Tadarida brasiliensis*–Fig. 8.5) shows a marked change in the structure of the acoustic signal during search, approach, and terminal phases. In the search phase,

Tadarida uses a narrowband CF signal. During the transition to the approach phase and while hunting in generally open areas, they drop the CF component and add a slightly curvilinear FM component; in more complex, cluttered areas, they may add multiple harmonics as well. The Long-eared vespertilionid (*Idionycteris phyllotis*) exhibits a similar diversity of signal structure during the three phases of echolocation against different hunting situations.

Pulse/echo overlap

Initial detection of a target occurs during the search phase of echolocation. The proximity of a target is first perceived when an echo, reflected from the object, arrives back at the bat's ears. Distance can be established by evaluating the time interval between a pulse emission and the return of its echo. In some bats, the echo from a pulse arrives during the emission of the next pulse. For example, Wagner's Moustached bat (*Pteronotus personatus*) emits a search pulse of about 4 ms duration. Given that sound travels at 340 mm ms^{-1}, a pulse of 4 ms duration would be 1360 mm in length. Since the pulse/echo circuit is a two-way journey, this species would receive an echo from an object about 680 mm ahead at just about the time it was emitting the next pulse. With a flight speed of 1.7 mm s^{-1} and a search pulse rate of 18 (4 ms) pulses per second, the next echo would return (or overlap) about 0.6 ms into the succeeding pulse emission. The next echo would overlap by 0.12 ms if there were no alteration of the pulse duration.

Mormoopids and rhinolophids, all with CF components of moderate to great length, appear to rely on some amount of pulse/echo overlap. Indeed, the species of these families, with exceptionally long CF components in their acoustic signals, respond initially by lengthening the pulse duration. However, after this initial lengthening the pulse duration is shortened depending on the linear distance to the target. Although the length of the pulse/echo overlap varies among these species, all hold some overlap constant. This suggests that these bats can and do accurately measure target distance.

Most of the other species of echolocating microchiropterans appear to avoid pulse/echo overlap. Once target contact is made, pulse duration is shortened. For example, the Little Brown bat (*Myotis lucifugus*) searches with a pulse rate of about 15 per second; each pulse being about 2.5 ms duration. These bats detect targets at about two metres, but do not attend to them until about 720 mm. As the bat approaches its target, it shortens the pulse by about 1 ms per 260 mm of approach. Just before contact the pulse may be as short as 0.25 ms with the pulse rate at or near 200

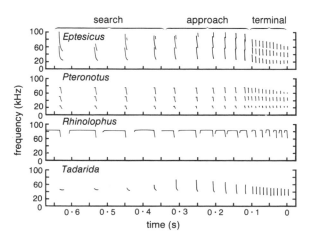

Fig. 8.5 Diagrammatic reproductions from sonograms of echolocation signals made by Eptesicus fuscus *(Vespertilionidae),* Pteronotus personatus *(Mormoopidae),* Rhinolophus ferrumequinum *(Rhinolophidae), and* Tadarida brasiliensis *(Molossidae) during search, approach, and terminal phases of hunting. See text for discussion.*

pulses per second. The Fishing bat (*Noctilio leporinus*) uses a short CF/FM signal while hawking over a water surface in search of fish or aquatic insects. These bats appear to avoid pulse/echo overlap until they are within about one metre of the target. This is accomplished by dropping the CF component in the approach phase in much the same manner as was described earlier for *Tadarida* and *Idionycteris*. From this distance to interception, the pulse/echo relationship is carefully maintained by linear shortening of the pulse and eventually overlap occurs just prior to prey capture.

Narrowband target imagery

We have previously discussed the nature and distribution of narrowband (constant-frequency) and broadband (frequency-modulated) acoustic signals in bats. Moderate to long CF signals are limited in the information they can carry and are most useful for perception of target velocity from Doppler shifts of the echo. Doppler-shifted sounds can best be illustrated with an example. Suppose we throw a rubber ball at a racket as it is being swung toward the ball. Contact results in an increase in the velocity of the ball, although it is in the opposite direction. Suppose, on the other hand, that the ball struck the racket as it was being swung away from the ball. This contact would result in reduction in the velocity of the ball. A pulse of sound striking a target that is moving toward the source is accelerated; that is, Doppler-shifted upward resulting in an echo with a higher frequency than the original sound. Likewise, a pulse of sound striking a target that is moving away from the source is Doppler-shifted downward resulting in an echo with a lower frequency than the original sound. For example, a CF signal emitted at 81 kHz and striking a target approaching at a rate of 5 m s^{-1} would be reflected as an echo with a frequency of 83 kHz; if the target were going away at the same rate the echo frequency would be 79 kHz. If the target were stationary the echo frequency would be unchanged. By detecting these small Doppler shifts in echo frequencies, bats that use moderate to long CF signals can accurately measure target velocity.

In addition to this, bats that use moderate to long CF signals tend to have their most sensitive hearing at 0.5 kHz on either side of the frequency of their CF signal; that is, they are practically deaf to their CF signal, but sharply tuned to either side of it. These bats compensate behaviourally to Doppler-shifted echoes by changing the frequency of their CF signals in order to hold the echo in their range of hearing sensitivity. Thus, an individual of *Pteronotus parnellii*, closing on an insect which was reflecting upward-shifted echoes, would lower its CF signal in order to maintain its sensitivity to the higher frequency and thereby guide itself to the interception. *Rhinolophus ferrumequinum*, with CF signals up to about 100 ms in duration, can perceive target velocities of about 0.04 m s^{-1}. *Pteronotus parnellii* (pulse duration up to 28-30 ms) can gauge target velocities to about 0.10 m s^{-1}.

In addition to Doppler information, long CF pulses (which are often of high intensity) appear to be associated with searching and target or obstacle detection at generally long distances. These acoustic signals may be more useful at high altitudes where sound attenuation is reduced. There is little doubt that these signals are of maximal efficiency in open, uncluttered situations.

Short CF signals (less than 5 ms), by themselves, are relatively limited in the information content they can carry. They are good for the initial detection of a target, but do not convey much other than the general location of the target (Fig. 8.6A). They seem to be of value chiefly in close pursuit of prey, flight in congested conditions, and perhaps in landing. Due to this ambiguity it is not surprising that there are no bats that use this kind of signal exclusively. Such short CF signals are similar to those used by *Tadarida* in its search phase. However, as we have noted above, *Tadarida* switches to FM signals in the goal-oriented portions of its echolocation behaviour.

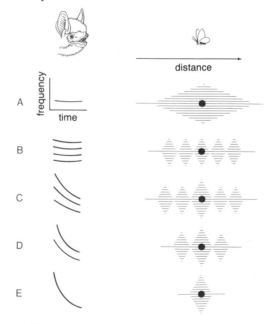

Fig. 8.6 Diagrammatic representation of the relationship between bandwidth and number of harmonics in the ultrasonic signal of a bat and the perceived position of a target or target range. Shaded area illustrates the bat's perceptual image of the target (dot). A–E are different time-frequency signals.

Adding several harmonics to the short CF signal improves the perception of the target's 'true' position somewhat by breaking up the ambiguous target area of the short CF signal into several discrete regions. The megadermatid *Megaderma lyra*, rhinopomatids, and nycterids appear to use this rather crude system of acoustic orientation.

Broadband target imagery

Many kinds of bats that move about and forage in complex, cluttered situations use multiple harmonic signals with broadband FM sweeps (Fig. 8.6C); in many, the overall bandwidth is large (Fig. 8.6D). Others may use but a single broadband, curvilinear FM sweep (Fig. 8.6E). All FM signals provide better multidimensional acoustic images than do CF signals. Figure 8.6C-E illustrates better localization of a target's 'true' position as bandwidth is broadened. Broadband FM signals facilitate the accuracy of hole depth discrimination by *Eptesicus fuscus* in the textural experiments mentioned above.

The use of multiple harmonics and the correlation with hunting situation is well illustrated in the genus *Myotis*. Species such as *Myotis volans* that hunt over open fields and in clearings use one prominent harmonic. On the other hand, *Myotis evotis* that hunt close to tangled vegetation use a narrow fundamental frequency and two harmonics.

ANATOMY AND DEVELOPMENT OF ECHOLOCATION

Although specialized in many respects, the anatomical structures associated with bat sound production and reception are basically those shared by all mammals.

Sound production

As we have already noted, the ultrasonic sounds of microchiropterans are generated in the larynx which is normal for mammals. The larynx of microchiropterans is proportionately larger than that found in megachiropterans (Fig. 8.7). The larger size and complexity of this sound-producing structure directly relates to the range of ultrasonic sounds that it produces. The high frequency signals produced by the unique echo-orienting megachiropteran *Rousettus* are generated by clicking the tongue and not in the larynx. The ultrasonics propagated in these two markedly different ways are entirely different with respect to their potential range of utility; those of *Rousettus* are extremely crude and limited.

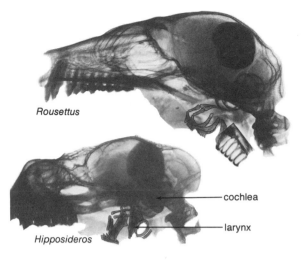

Fig. 8.7 *X-rays showing the laryngeal regions of (top)* Rousettus *(Pteropodidae) and (bottom)* Hipposideros *(Hipposideridae)*

Voiced sounds of most mammals and the ultrasonics of microchiropterans are produced when a pair of lateral membranous folds (vocal cords) are brought together like a curtain and thereby block the respiratory passage. The vocal cords are stretched taut and this tension is regulated by the muscles of the larynx. When air from the lungs is exhaled, under pressure caused by the thorax and diaphragm, these taut membranes vibrate in a manner similar to the reed of a clarinet or other woodwind instrument, producing sound. This sound is a rich composition of harmonics (complex sound) and its quality depends on tension placed on the vocal cords by the laryngeal muscles and air cavities of the vocal tract.

By contrast, the ultrasonics of *Rousettus* are limited by virtue of how and where they are produced. First, it is difficult, if not impossible, to exercise fine control of a click as it is an all or none sound. Secondly, these shock-bursts of sound are produced in and emitted from the mouth and they leave the mouth without much modification. Indeed, there is little opportunity to accomplish much in the way of filtering. Some modification may occur as the result of changing the shape of the oral cavity at the moment the sound is produced. Consequently, the acoustic sounds of *Rousettus* lack the sophistication and uniformity present in microchiropteran ultrasonic signals.

Role of the noseleaf

The role of the noseleaf in echolocation is as yet imperfectly understood. In bats such as rhinolophids and hipposiderids that have a complex noseleaf, it may serve to beam the ultrasonic sounds and thereby contribute to the directionality of the signal. The complex flaps and folds may also serve to shield the ears from the outbound, nasally emitted signals and so increase their overall sensitivity to returning echoes. The structure of the noseleaf in bats is highly variable and quite possibly its function differs from group to group.

Sound reception

The external ear conch of most echolocating bats is large and funnel-shaped. All megadermatids, nycterids, and myzopodids have exceptionally long ears. Long-eared species also occur in the Rhinolophidae, Hipposideridae, Phyllostomidae, Vespertilionidae, and Molossidae. The ears of many bats contain a short to long vertical flap (tragus) that may improve the directionality or sensitivity to inbound echoes. The tragus may also act as a deflective shield that protects the ear from the intense outbound acoustic pulses. The external ears are positioned in such a fashion as to be especially receptive to inbound echoes from 30-40° on either side of the mouth. There is some evidence that suggests that the ears act to restrict sound reception to this frontal cone rather than acting as collectors of sounds from all quarters. The direction of an obstacle or target must be enhanced by comparing the differences in the intensity and quality of echoes as they arrive at each ear. Having two ears yields stereophonic images in much the same manner as two eyes yield stereoscopic visual images. In the Horseshoe bats (*Rhinolophus*), the ears move back and forth alternately with the pulse reception rate when a roosting bat scans its surroundings.

The middle ear consists of the tympanic bone (ring) that supports the tympanic membrane and the middle ear ossicles (Fig. 8.8B). The tympanic membrane of microchiropterans ranges from 0.011 to 0.002 mm in thickness. This is relatively thinner than the eardrums of other mammals with comparable membrane areas. The area of the tympanic membrane is variable; it ranges from 1.2-2.5 mm^2 in *Glossophaga*, *Natalus*, *Myotis*, and *Rhinolophus* to 5.0-11.3 mm^2 in *Tadarida*, *Plecotus*, and *Eumops*. There is no apparent correlation between body size and tympanic area, but there does seem to be a correlation with frequency sensitivity in hearing and the acoustic signals emitted during echolocation. Bats that operate with high frequencies (50-125 kHz) generally have a smaller tympanic area than bats that operate at lower frequencies (below 50 kHz). There is a similar correlation with the mass of the middle ear ossicles; smaller

with higher frequencies. Other than minor differences, the ear bones of bats are like those of other mammals (Fig. 8.8A). There are several notable differences between the ossicles of mega- and microchiropterans. They are less massive in the Microchiroptera and the articular surfaces are more deeply grooved. In addition, the central portion of the stapedial footplate is fibrous in microchiropterans rather than bony; this is a unique feature among mammals.

There are two muscles in the middle ear (Fig. 8.8B). These are the tensor tympani (variously attached to the malleus and serving to tighten the tympanum) and the stapedius (attached to the stapes and serving to pull the stapes away from the oval window). These muscles are much better developed in the Microchiroptera than in the Megachiroptera. The stapedius muscle is especially important. The position of the larynx between the auditory regions in a bat's head presents a special problem. During pulse emission, the intensity of the signal might activate (and, in some cases, perhaps injure the ears) and interfere with echo reception. In the Mexican Free-tailed bat (*Tadarida brasiliensis*), the stapedius muscle begins to contract about 10 ms before pulse emission. This causes the stapes to be pulled away from the oval window which momentarily deafens the bat to its own pulse emission. After the pulse is emitted, the stapedius relaxes, hearing sensitivity is restored, and the ear is ready to receive an echo. In the Moustached bat (*Pteronotus parnellii*), the stapedius does not contract until the long CF component is emitted. Thus, they hear, and perhaps store, information relative to the FM component as it is emitted.

By far the most intriguing region of the ear is the inner ear with the cochlea and associated labyrinths (Fig. 8.8A-D). These sound-sensitive structures are basically similar to those found in other mammals. The cochlea is relatively simple in the Megachiroptera; this is true even in *Rousettus*. Cochlear structure in these bats generally reflects the lack of sophistication found in the Megachiroptera. The cochlea of microchiropterans is relatively larger and more complex in structure (Fig. 8.9). The number of turns in the cochlear duct in bats varies from 1.75 in the megachiropteran *Pteropus*, to about 3.5 in the microchiropteran *Rhinolophus*; most microchiropterans have 2.5-3 turns.

In those bats that emit long CF signals and are finely tuned to hear Doppler-shifted echoes, the areas of greatest sensitivity–on the organ of Corti (Fig. 8.8C-D)–are elongated and accentuated. Studies of the cochlear membrane in the Greater Horseshoe bat (*Rhinolophus ferrumequinum*), which has a large, complex cochlea and uses long CF signals, have demon-

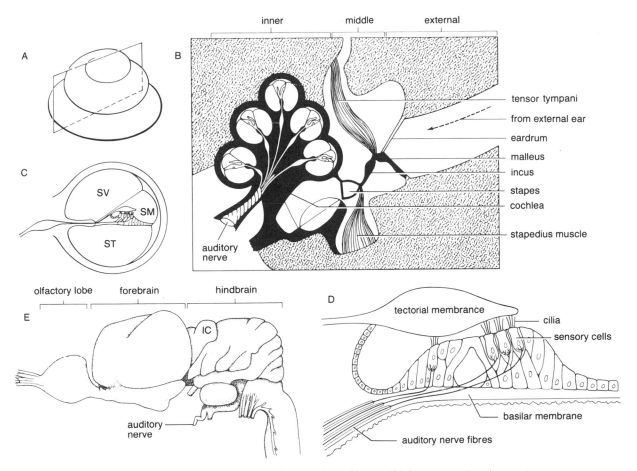

Fig. 8.8 Auditory apparatus of bats. A, Stylized cochlea showing plane of section (B); B, cross-section of ear region; C, cross-section of one cochlear loop showing the membraneous labyrinth (SV, scala vestibulii; SM, scala medii; ST, scala tympanii); D, organ of Corti; E, lateral view of brain showing inferior colliculus (IC) and auditory nerve. (B after Sales & Pye, 1974; E after Henson, 1970a).

strated that the membranous labyrinth and organ of Corti are specialized, anatomically and physiologically, for the reception of certain frequencies. In this species, more than half of the total length of the cochlea is devoted to groups of receptor cells that are especially sensitive to frequencies slightly above and below the outgoing signal. Similar specializations have been found in *Pteronotus parnellii*. These adaptations result in the cochlea being somewhat spherical rather than conical in shape.

There are also sound-dampening specializations associated with the cochlea. These are necessary because of the proximity of the sound-generating larynx to the ear region and the fact that sound is easily conducted through bone. To reduce the potential interference from outbound pulses, the cochlea is suspended loosely in connective tissue rather than being solidly fused to the bottom of the skull. In addition, the cochlea is isolated from the rest of the skull by specialized blood sinuses or deposits of fat.

The brain and its response

Electrical nerve impulses from the sensory cells in the organ of Corti are collected and travel along the auditory nerves to the inferior colliculi in the midbrain (Fig. 8.9E). Here the sounds are analyzed for their information content. As might be expected, the auditory regions and associated structures in the brains of microchiropterans are large and specialized compared to those in the brains of megachiropterans.

The location, large size, and general exposure of the inferior colliculi on the top of the midbrain has made it relatively easy to study the nature of nerve impulses in this auditory centre using microsurgically placed probes. Although the fundamental properties of various nerve cells in the bat's auditory system have been extensively studied in this way, we still do not understand fully the neural mechanisms and operational principles of echolocation. Among microchiropterans, the hearing range extends from a frequency

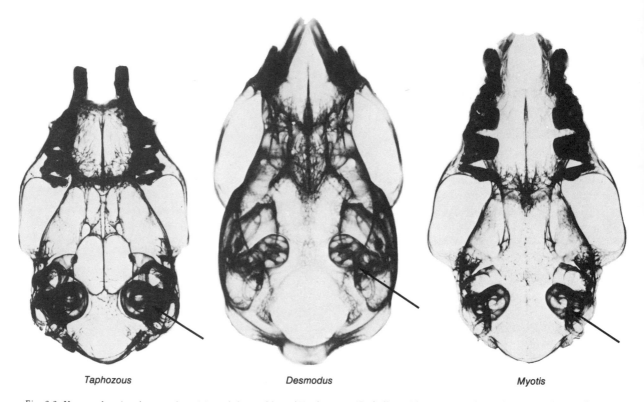

Taphozous   Desmodus   Myotis

Fig. 8.9 X-rays showing form and position of the cochlea of Taphozous *(Emballonuridae),* Desmodus *(Phyllostomidae) and* Myotis *(Vespertilionidae).*

of less than 1 kHz to about 200 kHz. Peak sensitivity in most bats includes part or all of the frequencies emitted in their acoustic repertoire. Bats that use multiple harmonics tend to have multiple sensitivity peaks which correspond to all or some of their harmonic range.

At the initiation of an outbound signal some cells of the colliculi respond weakly, but respond strongly to the returning echo. Some cells appear to require the initial sensitizing in order to respond at all. There is fairly clear evidence that certain cells of the colliculi respond to specific frequencies or to a particular sequence of component frequencies in the echo. Other cells appear to be particularly sensitive to the time delay between the outgoing pulse and the returning echo.

Ontogenetic development of echolocation

In Chapter 7, we noted that mother/infant communication appears to be an especially important means by which the young eventually develop and master the adult echolocation repertoire. For many species the crowded conditions of the nursery roost mean that the reunion between a returning mother and her infant is often difficult and must occur amidst a cacophony of other mother/infant calls. Very young bats produce many locational (or isolation) signals. These calls are characteristically lower in frequency than the adult repertoire and are repeated on a regular basis. In addition, these infant vocalizations often incorporate 'double-notes' (one long and one short modulated pulse). For example, infants of the Mouse-eared bat (*Myotis blythii*) emit pulses lasting about 25 to 50 ms. These are repeated about every 200 ms, but this interval may vary from 100 to 400 ms. The fundamental frequency range of these isolation calls sweeps from 22-24 kHz to about 14-16 kHz.

When a female returns to the roost site, she apparently picks up the isolation signal of her infant. She emits a signal which apparently triggers a vocal exchange between mother and infant very similar to the approach and terminal phases of goal-directed echolocation discussed above. The 'echoes' in this exchange are the signals emitted alternately by mother and young. As young bats grow older, they reduce the use of the isolation calls and gradually raise the frequency range of their calls closer to that of the adult repertoire. At the same time, the pulse duration and pulse repetition rate more closely approximate those of adult bats. In 20 day old *Myotis blythii*, the fundamental frequency begins at about 30 to 40 kHz and pulse duration has been reduced to 0.8 to 3.0 ms. At 45 to 50 days of age the frequency range is about 90 to 140 kHz and apparently fully capable of hunting and obstacle avoidance.

In the Greater Horseshoe bat (*Rhinolophus ferrumequinum*), which produces long CF/short FM signals from the nostrils, infants vocalize through the mouth. These isolation cries occur in groups of 3 to 5 pulses (each lasting from 5 to 20 ms) separated by an interval of 18 ms or so; the groups of pulses are separated by intervals of about 120 ms. A small portion of this vocalization series may be emitted through the nostrils. After seven to ten days of age, pulses are emitted about equally from the mouth or nostrils, but the nasal signals are higher in frequency than those emitted orally. The nasal frequency is emitted at about 30 kHz with a prominent harmonic at 60 kHz; weaker harmonics occasionally occur at 90 kHz and 120 kHz. At about 20 days, the fundamental frequency has risen to 37-40 kHz with harmonics at 74-80 kHz and 110-120 kHz. The orally emitted, low frequency signals are gradually eliminated and at 25 to 30 days the first and third harmonics are reduced or eliminated leaving the second harmonic of 81-82 kHz which is essentially that of an adult.

EVOLUTION OF ECHOLOCATION

Although the use of ultrasonic sounds has been found in a number of mammalian orders, the degree and level of sophistication found in the echolocation system of microchiropteran bats is rivalled only by that found in the toothed whales (Odontoceti). In both of these groups and, perhaps, in other mammals as well, ultrasonic echolocation seems closely tied to the exploitation of dark environments where the efficiency of visual orientation is at least reduced. In such situations, echolocation may be involved in the maintenance of mother/infant contacts, identification and capture of prey items, identification and avoidance of injury incurring obstacles, and communication among individuals for the purpose of spacing and/or contact. It is difficult to assess which of these or combination of them led to the origin of echolocation in mammals. Indeed, it is quite likely that different groups of mammals acquired and developed echolocation for different reasons.

If the two suborders of bats (Megachiroptera and Microchiroptera) are considered to be related by an immediate common ancestor, then one is almost forced to conclude that echolocation among the microchiropterans is an independently acquired ability. That is, the presumptive common ancestor did not possess this ability and, therefore, its acquisition in one descendant (Microchiroptera) constitutes an independent evolutionary event. This, of course, is possible since all mammals have the necessary anatomical features for echolocation. However, echolocation occurs also among the Insectivora (shrews and tenrecs) which are thought to be the closest relatives of bats. If this is the case, then the insectivore/bat ancestor must surely have possessed echolocatory ability. The general absence of echolocation in the Megachiroptera leads to the conclusion that the ancestral ability to echolocate was lost in this group of bats. This seems unlikely, given the extent to which echolocation is used in the Microchiroptera. One might possibly justify the above conclusion by noting that megachiropterans are generally frugivorous and perhaps did not 'need' such an acoustic orientation system. This argument is weakened by the fact that frugivorous microchiropterans (Phyllostomidae) have a relatively sophisticated echolocation system. In addition, at least one group of megachiropterans (*Rousettus*) has developed an echolocation system. The fact that the anatomical and behavioural basis of this system is markedly different from that found in microchiropterans also weakens the notion that a common ancestor of both suborders had such an ability. There is, of course, a simpler explanation that we have mentioned several times before. That is, that megachiropterans and microchiropterans did not share a common ancestor and, therefore, are not as closely related as has been generally thought.

Very little thought has appeared in print regarding the evolution of echolocation in the Microchiroptera. One author (J. A. Simmons, whose collected works and opinions have provided the basis for much of this chapter) has commented on this topic. The primitive microchiropteran is thought to have possessed an ultrasonic acoustic signal that was short in duration and composed of several multiple harmonics with very narrow bandwidth (CF). From this presumably simple beginning bats have modified and expanded their ultrasonic repertoire.

In the Rhinopomatidae (thought for other, but not necessarily valid, reasons to be the most primitive living bats), the 'primitive' acoustic pattern was extended to longer, narrowband CF signals. This was carried into the Emballonuridae to a certain extent. In one genus (*Emballonura*), the primitive pattern was altered only by increasing the bandwidth to short FM signals with multiple harmonics. This same modification occurs in the Megadermatidae and Nycteridae; *Megaderma lyra* is not much changed compared to the presumptive ancestral pattern. In the Rhinolophidae and Hipposideridae, the CF component was lengthened and exaggerated in some (*Rhinolophus*). Also, a terminal FM sweep was attached and some or all of the harmonics were lost.

In the Noctilionidae and Mormoopidae, the CF component was retained (exaggerated in *Pteronotus parnellii*) and an FM sweep added; some harmonics were dropped. The primitive pattern was converted to multiple harmonic, low intensity FM sweeps in the Phyllostomidae. This general scheme also occurs in the Vespertilionidae, but with higher intensities and with a short terminal CF component added in some cases. Long CF components apparently evolved independently in some vespertilionids (*Idionycteris phyllotis*) and the same may be true of molossids as well. The latter appear to be quite flexible in their use of various acoustic patterns.

Predator/prey co-evolution

For the most part, the interaction between a bat and its insect prey is an uncontested encounter in which the insect rarely escapes. About 20 years ago it was discovered that several groups of nocturnal moths of the families Noctuidae, Ctenuchidae, Geometridae, and Arctiidae apparently were able to sense the presence of a marauding bat and took evasive action to avoid capture. These moths were found to have a simple ear on either side of the thorax that was most sensitive to an ultrasonic sound range of 20 to 40 kHz, well within the range used by many insectivorous bats (Fig. 8.10). Among some hawk moths of the family Sphingidae, suitable sounds cause vibrations in the wall of the palps on the head that are transmitted to a sensitive organ–the pilifer–lying between the base of the palps and the proboscis. In

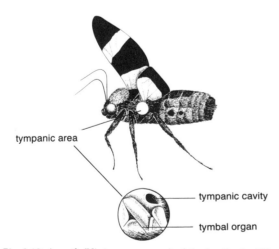

tympanic area

tympanic cavity

tymbal organ

Fig. 8.10 A moth (Viviennea moma) *of the family Arctiidae. The ridged cuticle of the tymbal organ produces a series of ultrasonic clicks when it is buckled by muscular action (see text for discussion).*

addition, experimentation has shown that some of these moths are capable of detecting the high intensity signals of many species of bats at a range of about 40 m. Upon detecting an approaching bat, they adopt a variety of erratic flight patterns including loops, abrupt turns, and vertical dives into protective vegetation.

In addition to simple detection and evasion, some arctiids and ctenuchids have developed an ability to 'jam' a bat's echolocating system or, at least, cause a pursuing bat to break off its attack. These moths produce a sequence of brief, high-pitched and rapid clicks containing ultrasonic frequencies, from tymbal organs consisting of a series of grooves or microtymbals in the hard chitin of the body surface near the hearing organ (Fig. 8.10). This striated area can be flexed or buckled so that the grooves make the sound as muscular tension is applied and released, and the effects that it produces apparently resemble the echoes that a bat would be receiving from a target at close range, the frequency-time structure of the train of clicks resembling the bat's call (Fig. 8.11).

On the other side of the coin in this game of survival, bats have apparently modified their behaviour in several ways. An obvious counter move to a prey with hearing sensitivity between 20 and 40 kHz is to simply operate outside of this hearing range. As we have noted earlier, there are many species that utilize very high frequency sounds (above 100 kHz). Still others emit orientation sounds well below 20 kHz. Another tactic is to use low intensity sounds. In either case, these bats must suffer the consequences of rapid attenuation of their signals thereby reducing their effective foraging range to distances of a metre or less.

Another curiosity that has baffled chiropteran biologists is the apparently random occurrence of extremely long ears in bats. Such ears are found in the Nycteridae, Megadermatidae, Rhinolophidae, Hipposideridae, Phyllostomidae, Mystacinidae, Myzopodidae, Vespertilionidae, and Molossidae. Many of these species are moth-eaters that use low intensity sounds of either high or low frequency. Such a correlation is not particularly surprising. What is surprising comes from some recent work that strongly suggests that these long-eared species apparently listen to and learn the communication signals of moths and are capable of locating these prey by using their own sounds. For example, the Greater False vampire (*Megaderma lyra*) apparently locates and captures its prey by using prey communication sounds alone. The extent to which this phenomenon occurs among bats is not yet known.

Until recently, our knowledge of the predator/prey interactions of bats was restricted to those involving

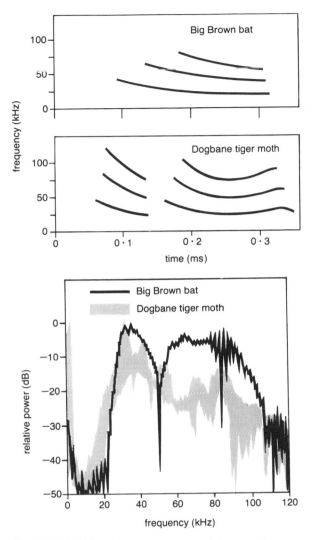

loudly than the longer, more complex, preferred call. The paradox is that the less preferable, more difficult to locate, call is used more frequently than the preferred call. Why would males seemingly want to be 'hard to find'? The answer is now clear; that is, female frogs are not the only ears listening to calling male frogs. Experimentation has clearly demonstrated that *Trachops* also prefer the more complex, easily located, mating calls. The discovery of these bat/moth (and probably other insects) and bat/frog interactions has opened new areas of study concerning animal behaviour.

AUDIBLE VOCALIZATION

In addition to the ultrasonic signals used in acoustic orientation, all bats produce low frequency vocalizations of one kind or another that are well within the audible range of human hearing. Loud, audible chirps or long squeals have been recorded for foraging *Taphozous saccolaimus* and *T. peli* (Emballonuridae); *Antrozous pallidus, Idionycteris phyllotis,* and *Euderma maculatum* (Vespertilionidae); *Phyllostomus hastatus* and *Tonatia bidens* (Phyllostomidae); and *Eumops perotis* and *E. glaucinus* (Molossidae). These sounds appear to be the lower harmonics of the echo-orientation signals of these species. They may be the result of a downward adjustment of the ultrasonics to compensate for a general tendency to attenuation of high frequency sounds in the hot and humid environments where these species live. For the most part, audible sounds appear to be associated with social behaviour rather than the complex orientation system discussed above.

By far the most audibly vocal bats are the Old World fruit bats or flying foxes (Megachiroptera). Although we have noted the use of a crude system of ultrasonic orientation in *Rousettus*, these bats, as well as other megachiropterans, are primarily vocal in their social organization. *Pteropus poliocephalus* and *P. neohibernicus* produce a wide variety of squawks and screams in the diurnal roost. Prior to leaving the day roost for the foraging site, individuals of these species fly about the 'camp' emitting specific cries, seemingly to entice their fellows to follow. At the foraging site, there is a grand clatter of noise. *Pteropus capistratus* is rather curious in that during foraging, either on the wing or from a roosting spot, it produces a melodic, bird-like trill. These bats forage in family groups and this call may serve to advertise a feeding territory, facilitate individual (mate) recognition, or other social release.

We have already discussed the mating vocalization

Fig. 8.11 (Top) Time-frequency structure of the acoustic signals of the Big Brown bat (Eptesicus fuscus– Vespertilionidae) *and those produced by the Dogbane tiger moth* (Cycnia tenera–Arctiidae) *for 'bat jamming' purposes. (Bottom) Relative power spectra of the bat and moth signals shown above. Note how closely the moth is able to mimic the bat's signals.*

insects. In the last few years some very exciting studies have been conducted in Panama with the Fringe-lipped bat (*Trachops cirrhosus*) and its prey, small pond frogs. We have already discussed some of the details of this study in Chapter 5. It is clear that *Trachops cirrhosus*, a long-eared species, is quite adept at recognizing the social calls of edible frogs. A Smithsonian biologist discovered that male frogs utilized two distinct mate-attracting calls. One is very complex and apparently is the one most preferred and most easily located by females. The other is very short and simple. It is produced less frequently and less and lek behaviour of the Hammer-headed fruit bat (*Hypsignathus monstrosus*) in Chapter 7. The Epauletted bat (*Epomops franqueti*), a close relative of *Hypsignathus*, constitutes one of West Africa's greatest nocturnal nuisances. In his book on *The Bats of West Africa*, D. R. Rosevear reports that it, 'forces itself upon the notice of thousands, driving some, in the middle of the night, to the verge of desperation by its almost ceaseless honking. It is not a matter of one solitary bat. Half a dozen, perhaps, secreted in trees close to the house may by their very proximity obtrude themselves pre-eminently upon the attention; but behind these, others can be heard; and beyond those, yet more, until into the far distance the length and depth of the darkness re-echoes to the same tireless monotonous note.'

Microchiropterans also produce a variety of audible, social vocalizations. Fishing bats (*Noctilio leporinus*) emit a loud 'honk' of descending pitch when two individuals approach each other on a collision course. When hungry and leaving the roost, *Vampyrum spectrum* (Phyllostomidae) and *Macroderma gigas* (Megadermatidae), both large carnivorous species, utter loud, characteristic cries. In captivity, the Pallid bat (*Antrozous pallidus*) has been shown to emit a variety of audible communication sounds of differing types. These include: loud, short, and rather rapid directive calls that enable individuals to locate the others in the main roosting group; squabble notes that express annoyance that are used for spacing signals in the roost; and a buzzing noise that indicates a greater degree of irritation that may be accompanied by bared teeth and aggressively spread wings. Constant 'chittering' may be heard when the colony is settled and the bats are at peace. The sharp metallic 'singing' of the African Heart-nosed bat (*Cardioderma cor*) varies seasonally in its incidence, reaching a peak during the rainy periods when food is abundant. During the dry season, 'singing' dwindles away. Possibly it is concerned with the establishment of a feeding territory before food becomes less plentiful and time and energy cannot be spared to maintain territorial boundaries. The White-lined bats (*Saccopteryx bilineatus* and *S. leptura*) 'bark' when defending a chosen roost or feeding territory.

Most of the ultrasonic vocalizations of microchiropterans have been studied from a perspective of their role in acoustic orientation. However, it is quite likely that at least some portion of these high frequency repertoires are associated with social behaviour and communications. The extent to which this is true is simply not known at this time.

The order that we observe in the natural world around us is the net product of many simultaneous interactions among collections of individuals (populations, species, and communities) with the environment in which they live. No living organism can exist isolated from the biotic and abiotic factors that surround it, and its evolutionary success or failure is governed by the extent to which it responds to these factors. The population ecology of bats is no less complicated than that of any other organism and is peculiar only in those features that combine to make bats the biological entities that we recognize them to be.

In most of the previous chapters, we have discussed specific topics (flight, food habits, reproduction, thermoregulation, etc.) and how they relate to the overall biology and natural history of bats. In this chapter, we examine the general ecological requirements and interactions of bats from the perspective of populations.

ECOLOGICAL PARAMETERS

The special place occupied by an organism in biotic communities and the relationship between an organism, its food resource, and its enemies (predators and competitors) is called an ecological niche. Bats fill an ecological niche, the nature of which is determined by several primary adaptations. These include the capacity of flight, nocturnal feeding activity, and the habit of hiding in caves and crevices. Although the latter does not pertain to certain species, especially the Megachiroptera, it is, on the whole, a feature of the vast majority of bat species. These basic adaptations account, in large part, for the uniqueness of bats and, presumably, permit them the opportunity to participate successfully in world ecosystems, more or less free from competition with other organisms.

As we have already observed, these chiropteran adaptations are not wholly without disadvantages. For example, the wings that permit a wide range of sustained flight activity, at the same time, increase the total surface area of the body. This, and the fact that the wings are highly vascularized, means that bats are constantly faced with regulatory problems of rapid heat loss and/or gain. To accommodate, bats have, in their adaptive history, developed special thermoregulatory mechanisms to help cope with these thermal problems. These adaptations are intricately bound to various metabolic energy conservation devices that may in turn relate to the daily or seasonal capacity to enter torpor or hibernation, respectively.

Adaptability of bats

The ecological factors that regulate the life cycle and numbers of bats are complex in nature and difficult to categorize. Climatic factors, in the broad sense, seem to be of primary importance to bats that inhabit the cold temperate regions of the world. On the other hand, biotic factors may be of greater importance in the ecology of tropical bats. Certainly, climatic changes, especially alternating wet and dry seasons, have similar effects in tropical ecosystems as temperature fluctuations have in temperate ecosystems. However, species diversification in the tropics may influence, to a greater extent, interspecific competition both among bats as well as between bats and other animals.

Bats are among the most extensively distributed of all land mammals, both in terms of geography and ecological diversity. They are surpassed only by rodents and man. Bats are found on all continents of the world except Antarctica, and on the majority of islands, sometimes on those from which other native mammals are lacking. Few bats have been reported north of the Arctic Circle and none dwells there all year round. To the south, they occur in Australia, Tasmania, and New Zealand, throughout South Africa, and, in South America, they extend to Navarino Island, just south of Tierra del Fuego.

Many of the families and genera of bats, and the majority of their species, are either partly or wholly tropical or subtropical. The primary radiation of bats probably occurred on tropical or subtropical landmasses. The extensive geographic distribution and diversity of habitats in which they are found shows that, in terms of evolutionary ecology, they are highly adaptable. At latitudes on either side of the equator, this ecological diversity ranges from the wet lowland rainforests of South America, Africa, southeastern Asia, and Indo-Australia to the hot and arid desert ecosystems of the Sahara, Middle East, and southwestern United States and Mexico. In the higher, temperate latitudes, bats occupy a variety of hard- and softwood forests, prairie, steppe, and montane ecosystems. However, the tropics and subtropics seem to provide a more stable and equitable environment with generally warm temperatures and availability of insects, fruits, and flowers throughout most, if not all, of the year.

Frugivorous bats are obviously restricted to regions where fruit or flowers are continuously available. The three major families of insectivorous bats (Rhinolophidae, Hipposideridae, and Vespertilionidae) are found in the temperate regions of both the Old and New World. A fourth family–the Molossidae–also occurs in temperate regions, but to a lesser extent. The Mystacinidae is the only family restricted to a temperate region, being an endemic and monotypic family on New Zealand. All temperate species overcome the problems of winter cold and the concomitant scarcity of insects either by hibernation, seasonal migration, or a combination of both.

The timberline, beyond which trees cease, usually defines the geographic and ecologic limits of bat distributions to the north and south, with the diversity of species declining rapidly towards these distributional extremes. Although temperatures may be equitable and insects may be abundant at the height of the short summer season in these subpolar regions, bats are probably excluded from them by an absence of suitable roosting sites. Short night length would lead to shortened feeding sessions and therefore might be an added restrictive factor. In this regard, it is worthwhile to note here that *Myotis mystacinus* from Finland apparently commences feeding early in the afternoon, well before sunset, in the month of May; in June and July feeding occurs in the short night. In addition, the growing season in subpolar regions is probably much too short for young bats to be born and raised before cold temperatures set in.

Timberline on mountain tops appears to have the same effect on bat distribution as latitudinal timberline. Thus, high mountain ranges are generally effective barriers to the dispersal of bats, although a few species have been found as high as 5000 m or so. Most bats that have been reported from much above 3000 m are thought to be transient visitors from lower elevations where food and temperatures are more equitable. Bats are generally found at higher elevations in the tropics than in temperate regions. For the most part, bats of the family Vespertilionidae, especially members of the genus *Myotis*, have the highest altitudinal distributions and almost without exception are also the bats that reach the north and south distributional limits. Specific information on the distribution of bats will be found in Chapter 11.

Nocturnality

Bats are nocturnal or nearly nocturnal mammals, active predominantly only in twilight (crepuscular) or in darkness; the daylight (diurnal) hours are usually spent in secluded, dark or dimly-lit roosts. Being volant and active at night has several important ecological advantages. First, the ability to fly, either in the day or night, frees any animal from most kinds of terrestrial predators. Thus, being both nocturnal and volant, bats are essentially free of heavy predation; predators of bats will be discussed below.

In addition, nocturnality in bats has the primary advantage of providing almost unlimited access to a nearly competition-free food resource. No other animals exploit this food resource to the extent that bats do and competition is limited essentially to a few nocturnal insectivorous birds. Some spiders, lizards, amphibians, and small mammals also prey on nocturnal insects, but their activity does not appear to conflict with that of bats, at least to no great extent. Fruits and flowers are largely neglected at night. Opossums and some nocturnal primates may compete with fruit- or flower-eating bats, but, again, this does not appear to be a major concern. However, there is substantial competition for this food resource exercised by diurnal animals. Unlike the diurnal and nocturnal insect faunas, which are different in these two periods of the day, a ripe fruit is exposed to whatever animal happens to eat it, regardless of the time of day. Some flowers close shortly after sunset and are therefore not available to bats or other potential nocturnal exploitation. On the other hand, some flowers open only at night and these are potential food sources for bats or sites where insects may congregate and be captured by insectivorous bats.

Aside from these two major advantages to nocturnal activity, bats profit energetically from their night-time exploitation. During the daytime, temperatures are usually at their highest and humidities at their lowest. Consequently, diurnal activity carries a metabolic energy expense of either avoiding or getting rid of excess heat and water loss. At night, temperatures are usually milder and humidities somewhat higher thereby permitting energy and water conservation.

Daytime retreats used by bats

Bats occupy a wide variety of daytime shelters or retreats (Fig. 9.1). Most people generally think of bats as inhabiting caves of various sorts and, indeed, the majority of bats are cavernicolous. Bats may also be found in mines and other tunnel-like structures such as deep wells and underground passageways, and catacombs, ancient tombs or other ruins. Some bats seek shelter under eroded cutbanks along rivers and other waterways or in natural pockets and overhangs that form during the normal erosion of granite or other stone. Deep to moderately deep cracks or crevices may also provide suitable daytime shelter. Some bats may even hide under loose rocky rubble. The vespertilionid, *Pizonyx vivesi*, sometimes may be encountered under flat rocks on the beaches of Baja California, and *Myotis leibii* has been discovered living under rocks in talus slopes in South Dakota.

Daytime retreats may be classified in a number of ways using several different features. Firstly, daytime shelters may be divided into those that are external or

Fig. 9.1 Possible roosting sites in caves, under rocks, in buildings or in trees, logs or vegetation.

exposed (outside) as opposed to those that are internal or not exposed (inside). A second level of distinction is whether the bat hangs free in the roost or is in contact with the roost substrate. Beyond these two basic levels of classification, there are three major kinds of roosts–trees and shrubs; caves and rock outcrops; and man-made structures.

External roosting sites are most frequently found in the tropics and subtropics and are usually associated with trees or shrubs. Most of the Megachiroptera occupy these kinds of roost sites. Large flying foxes (*Pteropus*) frequently occur in large, conspicuous troops or camps, hanging in the open in the tops of trees. The presence of these large numbers of bats often causes such trees to be denuded of foliage. Other smaller megachiropterans may roost singly or in small groups, hidden amongst leaves. Many of the New World leaf-nosed bats (Phyllostomidae) hide during the day in the foliage of trees and tall shrubs; aerial roots and vines may be used as well. A number of the New World species of the family Emballonuridae roost in exposed sites on the sides of trees or they may be observed resting on the shaded sides of buildings. Some of the Old World species of this family (*Emballonura*) occupy similar daytime shelters while others are found in caves. Several temperate bat species, especially those of the genera *Lasiurus* and *Lasionycteris*, roost in trees among leaves and branches. It is interesting to note here that these bats are often protectively coloured and among those that migrate to more southern regions during the cold parts of the year.

In addition to hiding in the foliage or on the external parts of trees, many bat species seek daytime shelter inside tree hollows; fallen hollow logs may also be occupied. Other cavities in trees such as those made by woodpeckers or termites are sometimes utilized for daytime shelter by bats. The environment of these usually, but not always, confined spaces may be greatly modified by the presence of bats. The accumulation of decomposing guano may raise the temperature of these roost sites and the carbon dioxide and ammonia levels in the air may be many times higher than that outside. Long-term exposure to moderate or high levels of ammonia often results in bleaching of the fur which becomes rich reddish orange; bleaching also occurs in caves with high levels of ammonia.

Other plants may be used as daytime shelters. The small Disc-winged bats of the New World (*Thyroptera*) roost in family groups inside the developing leaves of bananas (*Musa* sp.), *Heliconia*, and other similar leaves that are long, tubular, and coiled. These bats are forced to move as the leaf slowly matures and unfurls. The African bats, *Myotis bocagei* and *Pipistrel-*

lus nanus, and *Myzopoda aurita* of Madagascar utilize rolled banana leaves and those of the Giant Bird-of-Paradise (*Strelitzia* sp.) as well as human dwellings on occasion. The Lesser Club-footed bat (*Tylonycteris pachypus*) of Malaysia often occupies the hollow nodes of bamboo shoots; access to these hollow spaces is made by an insect larva. Another tree-roosting bat, *Lasiurus seminolus*, finds shelter, during the daylight hours, in clumps of the epiphytic Spanish Moss (*Tillandsia*) that hangs in profusion on trees in the southeastern parts of the United States.

As a general rule, bats do not attempt to build nests or roosts. However, several phyllostomids, especially *Uroderma*, *Artibeus*, and *Ectophylla*, do modify the leaves of palms to form a protective tent. These tent-building species systematically cut the supportive veins of palm fronds with their teeth, in such a way that the leaf collapses, folding around into a tent-like shelter. While bats do not usually build their own shelter, they frequently use those of other animals. Some African species of the genus *Kerivoula* occupy the pendulous nests of weaver birds. Other small-sized bats reportedly seek shelter in the earthen nesting galleries made by swallows. Burrows of other mammals such as foxes, wild pigs, and the aardvark have been used as daytime retreats by bats. We have already mentioned the use of woodpecker and termite nests above. Also, there is one reported instance of a bat roosting within the tangle of the large web constructed by social spiders.

By far the most common daytime shelters used by bats are caves or other similar retreats. The number of bats found in a cave is often large and on the whole, caves probably shelter more bats than most other roost sites combined. Some of the caves in the southwestern part of the United States and Mexico are thought to house some of the largest colonies of bats. For the most part, these colonies are made up of one or two species and their fame is probably due to the fact that they have been studied rather extensively by bat biologists. It is quite likely that there are other equally large or larger colonies in other parts of the world where extensive caves have not been fully explored or censused.

The dynamic nature of the cave environment offers a number of possible roost sites. Many caves have a large vestibule at the entrance which is usually well lit and generally open. Very few bats are found in this region of caves. Some 'cave-dwelling' pteropodids such as *Dobsonia moluccensis* (Fig. 9.2) and several species of *Pteropus* are frequently encountered in these places; they are rarely found in the deeper and darker parts of caves. On the other hand, species of *Rousettus*, which have a crude system of echolocation, are often found in the dark portion of caves, roosting

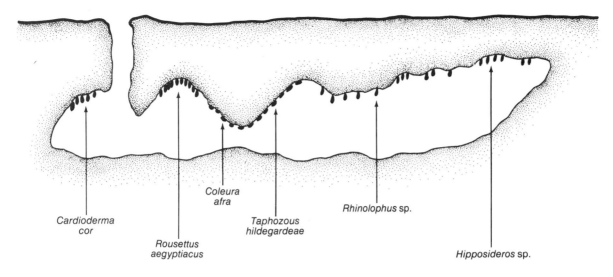

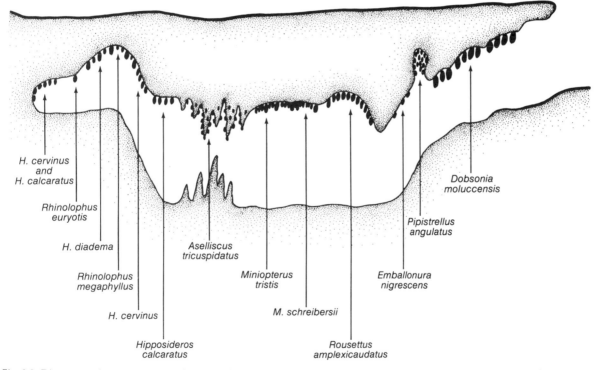

Fig. 9.2 Diagrammatic representation of the distribution of species of bats in two caves. (Top) Cave in Tanzania near the coast of the Indian Ocean. (Bottom) Cave on New Ireland Island (Bismarck Archipelago), Papua New Guinea. (H. = Hipposideros).

on the ceiling (Fig. 9.2). Some of the Emballonuridae such as *Emballonura* and *Coleura* may be found roosting on the semi-lit wall near the entrance of caves (Fig. 9.2).

Many bats utilize the ceiling portion of caves for their daytime retreat. Here, individuals may select a

promontory of some sort, such as a stalactite, or they may prefer to roost in shallow depressions and/or deep pockets in the roof. This part of a cave is where huge, tightly packed masses of bats are frequently found. However, bats may evenly space themselves on the ceiling. The walls of caves or other vertical faces are roost sites preferred by many species of bats, whereas small side passageways or galleries may be selected by others. In addition to these exposed roosting sites, many bats hide in the numerous cracks and crevices found in the ceiling, walls, and even the floor of caves.

The roost site selected by a particular individual or species of bat often depends on the environmental nature of the site. Temperature, humidity, and amount of airflow are all parameters that seem to be important in this selection. For example, members of the New World family Mormoopidae seem to prefer caves that are extremely hot and humid. Other species seek cooler, perhaps drier, shelters. Caves with streams or standing water are frequently occupied, but caves that flood regularly are not usually inhabited for any appreciable time. In temperate regions, the immediate environment of a particular roost site may change as the outside climatic conditions change. The deeper portions of caves are often very stable and less susceptible to major environmental changes. During the hibernation period, bats may move about in caves or between caves in search of favourable temperature or humidity regimes. Likewise, caves utilized as daily shelters in the summertime may not be used by the same individual or species during the cold winter months. It appears that hibernacula are selected for their stability of temperature and humidity. In the tropics and subtropics, caves are probably used throughout the year, but there may be daily, perhaps seasonal, movement within and/or between caves.

In addition to caves, bats may occupy a number of other rocky, daytime retreats besides caves. These kinds of shelter include cracks and crevices, small holes, pockets, or even shallow cave-like depressions in exposed cliff faces. Bats that occupy these shelters, many of which are found in desert regions, are often exposed to rather drastic changes in daily temperature, humidity, and light conditions. In the southwestern United States, *Pipistrellus hesperus* and *Antrozous pallidus* seem to be rather fond of these daytime shelters. The large molossid, *Eumops perotis*, another inhabitant of this region, seems to prefer roosting in semi-exposed pockets left in granite faces when the rock exfoliates as the result of natural erosion. These roosts are usually 8-10 metres above the ground and this height may be required for these bats to gather sufficient airspeed to become airborne when they drop out of the roosts at night on leaving to forage.

Man's activity has produced a number of structures that can serve as suitable daytime shelters for many bat species. The environmental qualities of tunnels and mines are essentially similar to those of caves. However, these man-made structures are often more

uniform than natural caves, with straight corridors and smooth walls and ceilings, and their environments may not be as diverse. Bats usually will not occupy these shelters permanently while man's activity continues in them, but they are inhabited fairly soon after they are abandoned. Culverts under traffic thoroughfares or bridges are common daytime shelters for bats in tropical and subtropical regions and these sites are often used as summer retreats in temperate regions.

Many bats, especially those inhabiting the cooler temperate regions, have adapted to utilizing buildings for daytime shelters. These may be occupied year-round, during the summertime, or in the winter. The adaptation process to roosting in buildings does not appear to have ended. Some species visit buildings only occasionally, whereas others seem to prefer this environment to natural shelters. The Yellow House bats, *Scotophilus*, of Africa and Asia, and the Free-tailed bats, *Tadarida* and *Molossus*, have developed a more or less permanent, yet loose, association with man. In Czechoslovakia, *Eptesicus serotinus* has been observed to take up residence in modern urban houses within five years after construction. Indeed, many bat colonies occur in houses less than 25 years old. Depending on their structure and facing, buildings may offer a wide range of ecological conditions. Some species prefer to hang openly exposed from the rafters and often in tightly packed masses. Other species may seek shelter in tight and confined spaces between joints, inside walls, and under siding or weatherboards, tiles, or shingles. Although generally dry, the accumulation of guano in buildings may be foul smelling and the scratching and squeaking may be particularly annoying to human inhabitants. In some parts of the world, there may be some public health hazards associated with these circumstances as well (see Chapter 10).

It is not uncommon for bats to occupy nesting boxes intended originally for birds. This behaviour has led some European conservationists to construct specially designed bat boxes which are placed in appropriate sites for the bats to use (Fig. 9.3). There has been a fair amount of success with these artificial shelters in Europe, but they have been less successful in the United States. The importance of bats in controlling insect populations and as a source of guano for fertilizer led some enterprising persons to construct artificial roosts or bat towers in the southern portions of the United States, but these also have not been particularly well-received by the bat populations of the region.

Generally speaking, the roosting habits of bats are related to overall body size. The majority of bats are small-sized and susceptible to predation while roost-

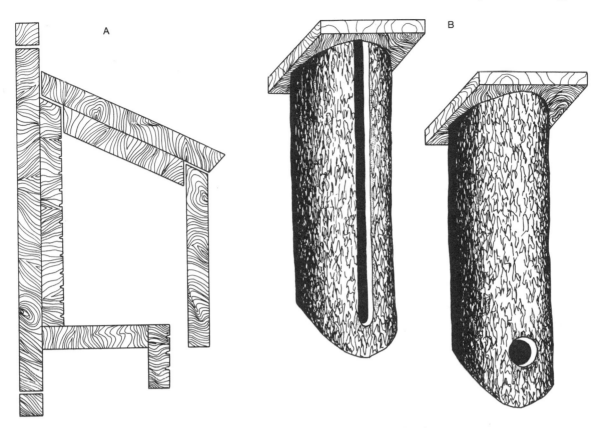

Fig. 9.3 Artificial roosts for bats. A, Section through bat box; B, hollowed logs as roosting places.

ing. In addition, these small bats, because of their size, risk high losses of body heat and moisture since their surface area is large in relation to their total volume. Consequently, only the largest of bats roost in generally open and exposed situations. Small-sized species that roost in sites other than caves usually take shelter inside tree hollows, cracks or crevices, and the like.

Finally, bats may use a convenient night roost in their foraging areas where an individual or group of individuals may stop and rest for short intervals. These sites may be used as retreats to which food items are carried and consumed or simply as spots where the bat can hang up, rest, and digest its food. Night roosts are usually characterized by small accumulations of guano and insect or fruit parts that are dropped while the bat is feeding.

Resource utilization and social behaviour

In a broad sense, a resource is anything used or needed by an organism or population of organisms to survive and reproduce. Ecological research has shown that organisms utilize resources in a non-random fashion; that is, there appear to be definite

time and space patterns of resource utilization. The exact nature of these patterns is not fully understood, but the majority of ecologists believe that there is competition among organisms for various resources such as food and shelter space. They argue that those organisms that are sufficiently adapted to utilize their resources efficiently succeed and reproduce; those that are not so adapted are either forced out or excluded from an area or ultimately become extinct. Whatever the cause, the social organization of bats does not appear to be random. Much of what is known about the social behaviour of bats has to do with roosting and, to a lesser extent, with foraging activity. It seems appropriate here to describe some of the results of the research that has been accomplished in this field.

Some of the bats that roost in open situations are solitary or nearly so. Many of the small-sized members of the Pteropodidae roost singly or in groups of two or three; usually an adult male, female, and young. These include such species as the Collared fruit bat (*Myonycteris torquata*); the Dwarf Epauletted fruit bat (*Micropteropus pusillus*); and the Long-tongued fruit bat (*Megaloglossus woermanni*). Similar solitary species are found among the Microchiroptera as well and include the Ghost bat (*Diclidurus albus*) or the Red and Hoary bats of the genus *Lasiurus*. Because of their solitary habits, little else is known about their social behaviour.

The African Banana bat (*Pipistrellus nanus*) appears to roost as solitary individuals or in small groups judging from a study conducted in Natal. The mean size of groups was 2.2-3.3 with a range of two to six. The largest groups were encountered in November and these were all maternity groups. Seventy-two per cent of all bats captured in rolled leaves were unaccompanied in the roost. Sixteen groups, half of which were male/female pairs, were captured although there were sufficient leaves nearby to house each singly. All of the bats were banded before being released. About 40 per cent of those captured in groups were later recaptured in isolation and about 20 per cent were recaptured in groups. Seventeen per cent of those captured as isolated individuals were recaptured in groups, whereas about 20 per cent returned to solitary roosting. Females were most prevalent in groups and males were commonly encountered in isolation. Of all of these recaptures, no bat was ever recaptured with individuals with which it was originally captured.

Slightly gregarious species living in small groups, often in caves or similar retreats, are common among bats. A number of species are extremely gregarious, forming huge colonies which at times may exceed many hundreds of thousands or even millions of individuals. The colonies of the Mexican Free-tailed bat (*Tadarida brasiliensis*) in Carlsbad Caverns, New Mexico or Bracken Cave, Texas are particularly good examples. These large aggregations may result from a local abundance (seasonal or year-round) of a particular food resource and/or the proximity of an adequate or suitable roost site.

It appears that definite patterns of social organization govern the relationships of bats with each other, whether within large aggregations or in the lesser context of the family unit or reproductive group. This aspect of chiropteran biology is far from fully explored, but is the subject of a considerable research effort that has suggested that social factors in bats may differ widely among species and take many diverse forms.

The existence of strictly monogamous family units has not yet been proven by year-round observation. However, there is a number of species that are frequently found in these apparent groupings. The African nycterids, *Nycteris hispida*, *N. nana*, and *N. arge*, are often encountered in male/female pairs, occasionally with young. Other pair-forming microchiropterans include: Pel's Pouched bat (*Taphozous peli*); Woolly Horseshoe bat (*Rhinolophus luctus*);

Dwarf leaf-nosed bat (*Hipposideros beatus*); Yellow-winged bat (*Lavia frons*); and American False vampire (*Vampyrum spectrum*).

A number of tropical bats associate together in harems that persist throughout the year. In Trinidad, the White-lined bat (*Saccopteryx bilineata*) forms harems consisting of one adult male and as many as eight adult females. These harem groups roost on a convenient buttress of a large tree. The male defends this roosting territory by vocalizations, chasing intruding males, or beating at them with his wings. Harem males utilize visual, olfactory, and auditory signals to attract females into their harem territory. These females may be enticed to abandon one harem male for another and thus transfer among harems. The young are born at the beginning of the rainy season, staying in the harem space in the daytime, and carried by the mother when she forages at night. Large-sized young are left alone on a nearby tree. The return of the males in the morning leads to territorial disputes accompanied by vocalization and visual displays to attract returning females before the bats settle for the day.

The Lesser White-lined bat (*Saccopteryx leptura*) in Trinidad, lives in small groups of one to five individuals. Unlike the larger *S. bilineata*, these groups are usually mixed, consisting of one or two adult males and several females. The most common group is a male/female pair, perhaps with an infant. Triads are the next most common group and these may involve two males and a female or two females and a male. Roost site selection seems less precise than in *S. bilineata*, with many sites serving the needs of the group. These roost territories are defended. Trinidad females remain in their groups during pregnancy and birth, but females of *S. leptura*, in Mexico, may form male-free groups during this reproductive period.

Among the club-footed bats of southeastern Asia, a harem in *Tylonycteris pachypus* may include as many as 15 adult females, whereas the harem size in the related species, *Tylonycteris robustula*, rarely exceeds more than six adult females. In *Saccopteryx bilineata*, unattached males (those without harems) live alone near existing harem territories, elsewhere on the same tree buttress, or on another tree buttress altogether, isolated from harem territories. In *Tylonycteris*, unattached males form small bachelor groups. Harem structure in the African Rufous Mouse-eared bat (*Myotis bocagei*) consists of one adult male and two to seven adult females with their most recent young. These harems reside inside a rolled banana leaf and each must move to other suitable leaves as these mature and unfurl. Where banana leaves are plentiful, the harem may remain in the same general area for several years. Solitary males roost alone either near harem groups or at some distance.

Larger harems have been found in colonies of the Spear-nosed bat (*Phyllostomus hastatus*), each with as many as 100 adult females. These large harems may be found in caves that also contain groups of males without harems that apparently wander from roost to roost. Males of this phyllostomid species do not display to attract females which usually remain in the same harem for long periods, perhaps a year or more. Males do, however, defend their harem territory and leave the roost to feed for only a short time while the females are also away foraging. Thus, the harem's roost site is attended for most of the time by the male. The Pale Spear-nosed bat (*Phyllostomus discolor*) is smaller in size and roosts, for the most part, in hollow trees. In these roost sites, large colonies of 200-400 individuals are formed with approximately equal numbers of males and females. Harems contain one male and up to 12 or so females; unattached males form small bachelor groups. Like *P. hastatus*, individuals roost in close contact, but with the harem and bachelor groups separated from each other. Females frequently change harems and both males and females use olfactory and vocal cues in their displays which effect these transfers. Males of both species have a very large subcutaneous gland located on the upper chest region that may be used in territory or individual marking.

In contrast to harems of this kind, a long-term breeding group in other tropical bats may contain variable numbers of males and females. The Old World fruit bat *Pteropus giganteus*, in India and Sri Lanka, forms large outdoor colonies with both sexes present throughout the year. The dominant males tend to roost near the top of the tree, whereas subordinate adult males and juveniles roost in positions lower in the tree. The males apparently tend to retain their usual place in the roost while females move around in the tree from day to day. During the mating season, the males become very possessive of adjacent females and remain with the colony throughout the pregnancy.

In Australia, *Pteropus scapulatus*, *P. alecto*, and *P. poliocephalus* form similar congregations. However, these large outdoor colonies are not maintained throughout the year. They are largest during the summer months when blossoms and fruits are abundant. Reproduction occurs at this time. As winter approaches and food abundance drops off, these large camps break up and the individuals disperse; many become nomadic or form small inconspicuous groups. This apparent disappearance led early workers to conclude that these species migrated during the winter months. While there may be some northward shift by the southernmost populations, most individuals appear to remain in reasonably close proximity to their summer roost site. This same seasonal concentration/dispersion pattern has been reported for the Insular flying fox (*Pteropus tonganus*) from the New Hebrides (Vanuatu), and *P. melanotus* from Christmas Island. With respect to the annual cycle of the colony, *Pteropus neohibernicus* from New Guinea appear to behave more like *P. giganteus* than the Australian members of the genus. Three other species, *P. hypomelanus*, *P. admiralitatum*, and *P. capistratus* which live in the Bismarck Archipelago appear to roost as solitary individuals or in small family groups. This illustrates the range of variation in social organization that can occur among several closely related species.

Females of another Australian bat, the Large-footed bat (*Myotis adversus*), form male-free groups for much of the year; males live alone or in small groups. In the autumn, when copulation takes place, the females with newborn young join the males in defended territories to form small harems of one breeding male and up to 12 adult females. Females often move from harem to harem. Shortly after copulation, these harems break up and the sexes disperse into their previous unisex groups not to reunite until the young are born in the spring. At this time, females rejoin the males and copulation occurs, thus leading to a second crop of young in the autumn when the cycle begins again.

Similar seasonally successional social organization occurs in more temperate regions where bats hibernate during the winter months. The European noctule (*Nyctalus noctula*), for example, hibernates in mixed groups. The females form nursery colonies in the spring to bear and rear the young; the males leave and become solitary. In the late summer, when the young are independent, the males set up territories in hollow trees where the females join them to form transient harems. Females may move among the harems. This is one example of a general theme that has many variations. In the Big Brown bat (*Eptesicus fuscus*) of North America, adult females emerge from the hibernaculum in early spring, prior to the males, and establish nursery colonies. The males of some species remain in the hibernation site, or, as in the noctule, share the summer range with the females. Males of the North American Pallid bat (*Antrozous pallidus*) form small groups, whereas males of other species such as *Myotis austroriparius* congregate with non-breeding females. Males of the Little Brown bat (*Myotis lucifugus*), in North America, may become solitary, form small groups, or even remain in or near the nursery colony.

This brief survey demonstrates that bats have

organized social systems that help to adapt their life to certain features of their environment, especially availability of suitable roosts and adequate food resources. Harem formation may enable successful and dominant males to control a part of the total available roosting space, gain access to greater numbers of females, and perhaps, with these females, to dominate and control a portion of the food resource. Segregation of the sexes during gestation or at birth and during the rearing of the young may reduce competition for available food or enable nursing females, at least, to utilize exclusively the foraging area in the vicinity of the nursery colony. Mixed associations of the sexes during hibernation may be a means of maximizing the resource utilization of an otherwise limited number of physiologically suitable sites.

The spacing of bats in the roost reflects their social organization, with harem groups roosting separately, for example, or with males occupying a different portion of the roost than the females. Over and above this level of social organization, bats may exhibit some degree of maintenance of individual spacing. In some bat species, there is no maintenance of individual space and individuals occupy tightly packed clusters on the roost surface. Such clusters may be incredibly dense; an average of 2000 individuals per square metre of cave surface has been estimated for the Long-fingered bat (*Miniopterus schreibersii*). In some caves in New Guinea, clusters containing this species may also contain individuals of *Miniopterus tristis* and *Myotis adversus* without any apparent individual boundaries (Fig. 9.2). Many temperate cave-dwelling bats, many of them vespertilionids, occur in such tightly packed colonies. Dense clusters are common among many phyllostomids, some megadermatids such as *Megaderma lyra* and *M. spasma*, and most molossids. Among the Old World fruit bats, *Rousettus* and *Dobsonia* include several species that may be found in tightly packed masses or clumps. Other species may occur in large colonies, but with some spacing around each individual. For example, in the Bismarck Islands, several hundred individuals of *Hipposideros diadema* may be found roosting in domed rooms (Fig. 9.2). Each individual is located at the centre of a circular space about 30 centimetres in diameter. Females may be accompanied by clinging young. These individual territories appear to be rather permanent because when the bats leave, their places are marked by a stained spot on the ceiling which could only have accumulated over time. Other hipposiderids such as Dobson's Trident bat (*Aselliscus tricuspidatus*) have similar individual spacing patterns (Fig. 9.2). Cave-dwelling emballonurids such as *Emballonura raffrayana* also roost as widely

spaced individuals. We have already mentioned the large camps formed by some of the flying foxes. In these colonies, individuals roost at intervals along tree branches. Finally, there are some species that appear to be almost intolerant of the close presence of other individuals. All of these are solitary species and some examples were given above.

Roosting bats usually engage in a certain amount of daytime activity, except when hibernating. This activity may include grooming or other maintenance behaviour or it may involve moving about in the roost. Bats frequently change their position in the roost, flying or crawling to another location during the day. In buildings, this movement within the roost may be to occupy more favourable thermal areas as daytime temperatures rise. Even hibernating bats awaken and move to more favourable parts of the hibernaculum or, perhaps, to have a drink.

Activity rhythms

A striking feature of the behaviour of animals is the regularity or cyclicity of various activities. These may be divided into two broad categories: daily activity patterns (circadian rhythms) and annual activity patterns (circannian rhythms). We have already discussed some aspects of the latter in Chapters 6 (Thermoregulation) and 7 (Reproduction and Development). Some details concerning daily activity were considered in Chapter 5 (Food habits and feeding). These patterns of activity appear to be controlled by an interaction between internal (endogenous) mechanisms and external (exogenous) stimuli.

A wide variety of biological functions in animals and plants appear to follow a 24-hour periodicity. Photoperiod (length of light and dark periods as well as quantity and quality of light or dark period) seems to be a primary factor involved in these rhythmic cycles. The majority of bats appear to be sensitive to light intensity and length of the lighted period. This appears to be especially true of those that seek daytime shelter in dim or dark retreats. On the other hand, many pteropodids regularly roost in the open, fully exposed to daylight. Still other species that occupy daytime retreats such as foliage of trees, shallow caves, hollow trees, culverts, and/or buildings may also be exposed to lighted conditions.

Although daily activity rhythms may adapt to gradual changes in local light conditions, these patterns exhibit a certain amount of regularity even when the external stimuli are removed and the organism is placed, experimentally, under constant conditions (usually constant dark). For example, when placed in total darkness for 20 days, several phyllostomids (*Sturnira lilium*, *Artibeus jamaicensis*, and *Glossophaga soricina*) still maintained a 23-24-hour circadian rhythm. In the first two species, this rhythm gradually advanced relative to the time of day and, in the latter, it was gradually delayed. Nonetheless, the general nature of the cycle remained unchanged. When these species were returned to natural light conditions, they re-established their normal pattern in a matter of a day or so; *Glossophaga* was the slowest of the three. However, these species required longer times to adjust to normal conditions after they were exposed to artificially shifted (advanced or delayed) photoperiods. Two molossids (*Molossus ater* and *M. molossus*) showed a wider range of variability in the length of their daily cycles under different light intensities. They also appear to be able to adapt to a wider range of light/dark day lengths than could the phyllostomids and they were able to readjust to normal conditions more rapidly after artificially advanced and delayed shifts in the photoperiod.

Endogenous activity rhythms have been demonstrated in several other bat species–*Pipistrellus subflavus, Myotis lucifugus, Eptesicus fuscus,* and *Rhinolophus ferrumequinum. Rousettus aegyptiacus* appears to have a rigid internal cycle similar to that described above for the phyllostomids. *Myotis myotis*, on the other hand, appears to have a more flexible cycle like that of the molossids.

Other than these few examples, little else is known with regard to the precise nature of circadian rhythms in bats. Nonetheless, the daily activities of bats tend to be at regular intervals. The time of emergence of a particular species may vary by no more than a few minutes from night to night. Species that occupy caves or other similar protected roosts become active as dusk approaches. In *Rhinopoma microphyllum* from India, nightly activity commences 2 to 2.5 hours before sunset. At this time, these bats begin to vocalize and make short flights within the roost. This activity is initiated by groups of bats located farthest from the entrance to the cave and steadily progresses to those closest to the entrance. Scouts from the deeper parts of the cave move up to positions close to the entrance and they are followed by small groups of 10-25 individuals. Although it has not been reported as such, this may be an indication of harem groups in these bats. Eventually, some scouts fly outside the cave and return and soon the whole colony begins to leave for the night. Similar activity has been observed in other cave-dwelling bats. This preliminary activity may serve to prepare the system for the demands made upon it during foraging and gradually awaken nerves and muscles to a state of full readiness. Short flights past the cave entrance may enable the bats to synchronize or otherwise adjust their internal rhythms to seasonally changing day/night cycles.

Bats leave their roosts very rapidly, sometimes in small groups that disperse quickly, perhaps to confuse waiting predators, or in a continual stream.

The timing of emergence varies from species to species and, as we have noted, appears to depend on the intensity of light. Temperature and prevailing weather conditions may also affect the timing. As a rule, bats do not normally fly, to any great extent, in heavy rain or high winds. Heavy rainfall may interfere with echolocation as well as the activity of insects. In addition, the energy expense required to dry off may preclude such activity. Whatever the case may be, there is usually a marked peak in activity shortly after a heavy downpour.

Pteropodids that roost in outdoor colonies exhibit similar preliminary foraging behaviour. As dusk approaches, certain individuals begin to fly about the camp vocalizing to the others. This activity appears to cause some to arouse and join them. They make progressively longer sorties, returning to excite more of their fellows and, eventually, the colony begins flying off to the foraging area. Presumably, these bats are affected by the photoperiod, but the nature of this influence is unknown at this time.

In addition to being sensitive to sunset, bats may also be sensitive to the amount of moonlight. In this regard, there are conflicting reports. Some bat biologists have noted an apparent drop in nightly activity of microchiropterans when the moon is full and shining brightly. Others have reported no apparent differences. On the other hand, megachiropterans appear to be more active with a full moon than with a dark moon. Whether or not there is such an effect will require further study. It seems likely that bats might avoid flying in well-lighted areas to evade possible attacks from predatory birds such as owls.

Bat predators

Although bats roost in inconspicuous places and are active mostly at twilight or at night, they nevertheless fall victim to a wide range of predators from large spiders to snakes, nocturnal birds and mammals, and even some carnivorous bats. However, with few exceptions, bats are not the regular food items for any predator and most are probably captured in chance meetings. Mammalian predators include: opossums (*Didelphis marsupialis* and *Philander opossum*); skunks (*Conepatus* and *Mephitis*); or the Long-tailed weasel (*Mustela frenata*). Occasionally, young bats that have fallen to the floor of a roosting cave are eaten by bobcats (*Lynx rufus*), feral or domestic cats, civets or genets (*Genetta*), raccoons (*Procyon lotor*), or dogs. The Potto (*Perodicticus potto*), a loris from West Africa, was observed eating an individual of the Straw-coloured fruit bat (*Eidolon helvum*) in Rio Muni. Some rodents may capture young bats that have fallen to the cave floor or they may climb to parts of the cave where bats are roosting. There are several carnivorous bat species that apparently take other bats on occasion. The false vampires (*Megaderma lyra* of India and southeast Asia, and *Macroderma gigas* of Australia) frequently feed on other bats. The American False vampire (*Vampyrum spectrum*) that lives in Central and South America is known to eat other bats. Some of the other large carnivorous bat species of the New World may also eat bats, but this has yet to be reported. A few other bat species have been reported to kill and eat smaller bats when they are confined with them in captivity; this probably does not represent a naturally occurring phenomenon.

Owls, hawks, and falcons are the most common avian predators of bats. Kestrels may also take an unwary bat that happens to venture out in the daylight or too early in the evening. The Bat Buzzard (*Machaerhamphus alcinus*) is an African member of the hawk family that waits near the mouth of a bat cave and catches bats as they emerge to forage early in the evening. Because of their nightlong activity, owls may be the most common threat to bats as they forage. Bat bones are often encountered in the owl pellets of the Barn Owl (*Tyto alba*), especially those that inhabit caves. African barn owls have reportedly captured and eaten individuals of *Rousettus aegyptiacus*. Some of the large-sized, tree roosting species of *Pteropus* from Asia and Indo-Australia may be vulnerable to the predatory attacks of some of the large eagles that inhabit these regions.

Other birds may be incidental predators on bats. The Roadrunner of the southwestern deserts of the United States reportedly has captured individuals of the Red bat (*Lasiurus borealis*). In several other cases, these bats have been attacked by Bluejays (*Cyanocitta cristata*). Daytime attacks by Red-winged Blackbirds and the Common Grackle on the Little Brown bat (*Myotis lucifugus*) have also been recorded. There is one recorded observation of a Burmese crow preying upon a free-tailed bat (*Tadarida plicata*).

Snakes are frequent predators on bats. A large Gopher snake (*Pituophis melanoleucus*) was observed crawling on the wall of an abandoned gold mine in southern Baja California and snatching individuals of the Mexican Funnel-eared bat (*Natalus stramineus*) out of the air as they flew by. An autopsy of this snake revealed six recently swallowed bats. A similar incident involving the Cuban Boa (*Epicrates angulifer*) and the leaf-nosed bat (*Phyllonycteris poeyi*) was observed in a Cuban cave. In Africa, the colubrid snake (*Boiga blandingi*) apparently feeds regularly on *Eptesicus tenuipinnis* and *Tadarida condylura*, two

common roof bats. One individual snake had eight bats and an agamid lizard in its stomach. In Panama, *Boa constrictor* and a colubrid (*Pseustes poecilonotus*) frequent the roosts of *Myotis nigricans* and are commonly found in attics containing colonies of *Molossus coibensis*. Tree-dwelling bats are probably highly susceptible to snake predation and only those bats that roost freely suspended from the high ceilings of caves are relatively safe from these predators. Unusual vertebrate predators on bats include bullfrogs (*Rana*) and the Rainbow trout (*Salmo gairdneri*).

Few invertebrates are large enough to capture and eat even the smallest bat species. However, cockroaches and driver ants have reportedly preyed on young bats. Assassin bugs may prey on young bats that have fallen to the cave floor or they may climb up into the roost and feed on them there. Large web-building spiders may capture bats in their webs. A small pipistrelle (*Pipistrellus*) was observed entangled in the sticky and rubbery web of a Golden Orb weaver (*Nephila maculata*) at the Wau Ecological Station in Papua New Guinea. This spider was about half again as big as the bat and it bit the bat before it could be freed from the web. The bat recovered and flew away after the sticky webbing was cleaned from its wings. There are several other reports of small bats becoming entangled in spider webs; one of these involved a small pipistrelle and a large Chinese spider (*Epeira bilineata*) and another concerned *Myotis nigricans* and a Panamanian orb weaver of the genus *Aerophora*. In the latter instance, the spider reportedly killed and ate the bat. Whether or not spiders regularly predate upon bats is not known. However, even if the spider just cuts the bat out of its web, it is probably doomed because of the tangle of webbing wrapped around its body. Oddly, in West Africa, the Lesser Woolly bat (*Kerivoula lanosa*) has been found roosting in the web of the social spider *Agilena consociata*. Other large cave-dwelling arthropods such as centipedes may also be potential predators on bats.

Mortality due to predation is no doubt higher among bats that roost in open situations such as trees, culverts, and other exposed places. These bats may rely more on vision to detect an approaching predator than on echolocation because of the energy requirements of the latter.

POPULATION PARAMETERS

Studying the population structure of bats is one of the most difficult tasks confronting the bat biologist because of the secretive and nocturnal habits of these mammals. As a result, attention has been directed chiefly towards studying cave-dwelling species where at least it is possible to count or estimate the number of individuals in a particular population. Large numbers of individuals in such populations can usually be captured with relative ease, especially during hibernation.

Aside from demographic information such as the total size of a population, its age structure, and sex ratio, the bat biologist often seeks additional information. For example, where and when do individuals feed? Do males and females feed in separate sites and/or at different times? Do individuals seek alternative roost sites at particular times of the year? Does the population move among various roost sites during the year? Does the population or parts thereof move long distances (migrate) during the year or is population movement restricted to relatively small local areas? These are only a few of the kinds of questions that are generally of interest in population studies involving bats.

Methods of study

Various methods have been tried to gather information on bat populations. Some have succeeded and many others have failed to produce reliable results. Most of our current knowledge about the population structure and movement of bats has been acquired by capturing individuals and marking them in some semi-permanent, non-lethal manner. The most popular marking technique has been the use of bracelet-like rings or bands placed on the forearm or ankle of the bat. These bands are usually stamped or embossed with a serial number, name, and address of the organization responsible for banding the bat. Before being released, certain critical information is gathered from the individual and recorded in a permanent diary. This information includes: identification to species; sex and, if possible, age of the individual; place and date of capture; place and date of release, if different from the foregoing; and perhaps biological information such as weight, reproductive condition, and/or nature of the roost site.

Ornithologists first used these bands to study movement of bird populations. The success of these efforts prompted an American ornithologist, A. A. Allen, to place several 'bird bands' on five Eastern pipistrelles (*Pipistrellus subflavus*) in 1916. Three of these individuals were recaptured at the same roost three years later. However, it was not until 1932 that intensive bat banding studies were undertaken. At that time, two large studies began in the eastern United States and another in Germany. By 1955, about 160 000 bats had been banded in the United States and Canada; the U S Fish and Wildlife Service reported issuing 92 844 bands for bat banding between 1952 and 1955. In 1982, the Fish and Wildlife Service reported that 1 932 000 bat bands were in use in North America. Several hundred thousand bats have been banded in large scale studies on the Mexican Free-tailed bat (*Tadarida brasiliensis*), in southwestern United States, and *Myotis lucifugus* and *M. grisescens* in eastern and southeastern United States. Because of an outbreak of rabies in the free-tail population in Carlsbad Caverns, the former study was conducted, under the auspices of the U S Public Health Services, to gather information on the movement of these bats within their geographic range of occurrence. Banding studies in Europe have focused on the population structure and movement of *Myotis myotis*, *Miniopterus schreibersii*, and *Nyctalus noctula*. These studies also have resulted in several hundred thousand bandings. Banding projects began in Mexico in the early 1960s and, in the last ten years, bat banding studies have been started in several countries in Central and South America.

In order to be effective, large numbers of individuals must usually be banded; the higher the percentage of banded bats in the population the better the chances are of recapturing a banded individual. This is the primary reason why species that congregate in caves or buildings in large gregarious populations have been the focus of most banding studies. Solitary species or species that live in small family groups outdoors in scattered roosts that are difficult to find do not make good subjects for banding studies. Once a banded bat is recaptured, a great deal of information about that individual can be determined. For example, its minimum age is the length of time between first and last capture. If the bat was a yearling banded in a nursery colony, this age may be close to its true age. If, on the other hand, the bat was an adult of unknown age at the time of banding, the span of time between captures can yield longevity information. Other information from a single recapture includes the linear distance moved by the individual bat as well as how long it took to travel that distance. Recapture of a bat several hundred kilometres removed from the original site of capture, and within several weeks of the original capture, can be quite useful in determining the migratory habits and patterns of a species. Obviously, the more recaptures made results in more information acquired. The proportion of banded bats to the total number of recaptures can be used to calculate estimates of the overall population size. The accuracy of these estimates is closely associated with the total percentage of the population banded; larger numbers result in an increase in accuracy. These calculations can be broken down into sex and age groups and, as such, begin to reveal information about the dynamics of population structure.

Small-sized bird bands were used up until about 1960 in the United States. These were issued by the U S Fish and Wildlife Service. Unfortunately, these bands had sharp edges and if improperly pinched too tightly around the forearm and wing membrane could cause serious injury (irritation, infection, and wing tearing). European bat banders did not have access to U S Fish and Wildlife bands and, therefore, had to develop their own bands. The German bat band had flat, rounded lips (rather than sharp edges) that closed flat against the wing membrane. Although not entirely free of problems, these bands caused less injury to the bat and, as a result, similarly designed, lipped bands were adopted by the U S Fish and Wildlife Service in 1958. The mortality directly due to band-caused trauma is unknown, but it, as well as possible mortality due to disturbance relating to banding activity (especially in hibernating colonies) caused the U S Fish and Wildlife Service, in 1976, to restrict issuing bat bands only to pertinent projects.

Bands are normally and most frequently recovered by the researcher or team of researchers involved in the banding study. However, a considerable number of bands are recovered by the public at large, and especially by potholers or spelunkers who frequent caves and mines. The services of organized clubs or groups of the latter are often enlisted to help with the banding operations. In the United States, the U S Fish and Wildlife Service keeps records on the bats that have been banded, processes information from public recoveries, and notifies researchers when bands from their studies are returned. Many public recoveries occur as the result of finding dead or sick bats. All bands found, either on bats or birds, should be returned immediately to the person or agency whose address appears on the band. If banded bats are observed in colonies, care should be taken, especially with hibernating bats or mothers with young, to determine the person(s) or agency responsible for the banding. They should be contacted at once, so that the proper data may be obtained.

Other methods of marking bats have been attempted. Some workers have tried tattooing numbers into the wing membrane by punching tiny holes and filling these with ink. The wound heals very quickly and a whitish scar remains for several weeks to several months. Eventually these disappear and they are also impossible to read unless the bat is in hand. Ear tags have been attached with some short-term success, but these ultimately pull out and may leave the bat with damage to the ear pinna. Other methods of temporary marking include the use of radioactive or chemiluminescent tags, or even small lights. These are usually attached to the fur of the back with glue. They fall off or are groomed free in a matter of several weeks. The largest drawback to these methods is the fact that most glues are toxic and may cause unnecessary mortality. Perhaps the most successful new technique is that currently being used by bat biologists at the Smithsonian Institution in a population study of the bats on Barro Colorado Island in the Panama Canal Zone. These researchers have taken the 'old bat band' and laced it onto a short length of beaded chain like that used for keychains and trinkets and placed this as a necklace around the neck of bats. This has several advantages over the old-style bands. Firstly, there appears to be no injury to the bat, but, more importantly, the bats cannot chew and obliterate the numbers in the soft metal of the bands. Thus far, these necklaces have been retained on bats and recovered over a period of seven years.

Small radio transmitters have been used with some success on moderate to large species of bats. These allow the researcher to track the bat to and from its roost(s) and while it forages. However, these radios and receivers are relatively expensive and monitoring can only be accomplished on several bats at any particular time and within a relatively small area; long distance migratory movement cannot be monitored. In addition, many bats are too small to carry even the smallest radio pack. Despite these disadvantages, radio-tracking has revealed some worthwhile information regarding movements within a home territory.

Population size

Various means have been used to estimate population size. The crudest of these is a simple count of the individuals at a particular place and time. This may be reasonably accurate if the number of individuals is small and if the individuals are relatively non-mobile. The population size of the Straw-coloured fruit bat (*Eidolon helvum*), in a large outdoor roost at Kampala, Uganda was estimated using two different counting techniques (Fig. 9.4). One used the number of bats in an average tree roost times the number of trees occupied by bats and the other used the number of bats occurring in a unit area times the overall area occupied by bats. These two methods yielded estimates that agreed for the most part. The differences between the two estimating techniques are probably less important than the overall population trend shown in the study; that is, the population of this species is high from October to March and then drops from June to August. This is an indication that the species either migrates away from Kampala or, at least, disperses. In some cases, researchers have used a capturing device of known size to sample groups of individuals from large clusters. With an average number of individuals per unit area, population size is extrapolated from the total area occupied in the roost. For example, North American Grey bat (*Myotis grisescens*) population sizes have been estimated by averaging representative samples taken with a hand net which covered 0.28 m² and then multiplying by total area of the roost. This method determined population sizes ranging from 5000 to 1.5 million bats in different cave sites located in the southeastern United States.

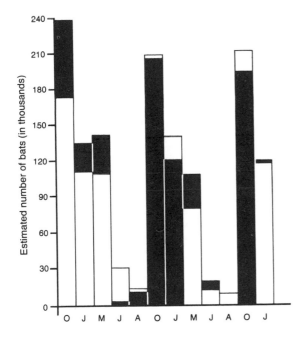

Fig. 9.4 Two different methods of counting individuals of Eidolon helvum (Pteropodidae) in a large colony at Kampala, Kenya. The black bars represent the number of individuals in an average tree times the number of trees occupied by bats. The white bars represent number of bats in a unit area times the overall area occupied by bats. These counts were taken in October, January, March, June, and August for 2½ years. Note that the two censusing techniques yield roughly the same population size. Also note that the highest number of individuals occurs October–March and that the population disperses June–August. (Mutere, 1980).

As we noted above, population size is usually estimated from capture/recapture proportions obtained in banding studies. Until recently, these kinds of studies were carried out on hibernating populations composed of adult individuals; yearlings would be indistinguishable from adults by this time. Recent studies have been conducted on summer popula-

tions, including nursery colonies, where yearlings were recognized as such. A better cross-sectional view of the population is provided by these studies. While these sorts of studies yield gross population estimates, of good to dubious value, they do not provide actual population densities; that is, number of individuals per unit area (usually measured in hectares).

Several studies have been conducted in such a way that estimates of population densities have been possible. For example, two separate studies on the Western Big-eared bat (*Plecotus townsendii*), conducted in 1952 (California) and 1976 (Kansas and Oklahoma), revealed similar estimates of population density; 0.01 and 0.02 bats per hectare, respectively. Study of the Common Long-eared bat (*Plecotus auritus*), in central Russia, found a population density of 0.1 bat per hectare. The population density of the Little Brown bat (*Myotis lucifugus*), in northeastern United States, has been estimated to be 0.1 bats per hectare. Two separate studies on the Mexican Free-tailed bat (*Tadarida brasiliensis*), in southwestern United States, found 1.4 and 0.8 bats per hectare. In Europe, the population density of the Common pipistrelle (*Pipistrellus pipistrellus*) has been calculated to be 1.1 and 3.0 bats per hectare in central Russia and Rumania, respectively. Densities of the European noctule (*Nyctalus noctula*) in these areas appear to be 0.7 and 2.0, respectively. The Marianne flying fox (*Pteropus mariannus*), studied on Guam Island, appears to occur in densities of 0.6 per hectare. On the other hand, the density of the New World Disc-winged bat (*Thyroptera tricolor*) was found to be rather high in Costa Rica, 21.6 individuals per hectare. The latter estimate must be viewed with caution, however, as this species roosts in rolled banana leaves that tend to be concentrated in clumps. Thus, this high estimate may be due to the local concentration of the roost resource and not truly represent the density of the population over its home territory.

Mortality and longevity

Bats are threatened by many natural catastrophes quite apart from the activity of predatory animals, even in the apparent safety of deep caves. Sudden rock slides or an unexpected rise in the level of an underground stream can devastate part or all of a bat colony. A change in the pattern of air circulation in a cave can adversely affect the temperature or ventilation of a cave and thereby cause casualties among the inhabitants. Occasionally, the guano deposits on the cave floor may combust spontaneously, producing lethal smoke or fumes.

Severe cold spells may be fatal to hibernating bats that, for one reason or another, cannot move to a more favourable location in the cave. Such cold spells may affect young bats more than adults because they usually have had less opportunity to gather fat reserves. Water droplets frequently collect on the fur of hibernating bats and a sharp drop in temperature may cause an icicle to form, killing and entombing the bat therein. Conversely, unusual warm spells may lead to bat mortality by causing the hibernating bats to arouse and deplete their valuable fat reserves without having sufficient opportunity or food resources to replace it. Some species, such as the Western pipistrelle (*Pipistrellus hesperus*) of the southwestern deserts of the United States, may capitalize on these warm periods to replenish water losses and/or feed on any emergent insects.

A number of apparently freak accidents involving plants and bat fatalities has been reported. There are several cases where bats (*Myotis lucifugus* and *Lasiurus borealis*) have become entangled in the long, stiff, and hook-tipped burs or flowering heads of clumps of Burdock (*Arctium lappa*). These bats may have been searching for insects when they became entrapped. Small birds also become impaled on these burs. *Leptonycteris nivalis*, a nectar-feeding leaf-nosed bat, occasionally becomes caught on the needle-sharp spines of the cacti that it visits for nectar. Likewise, the Californian leaf-nosed bat (*Macrotus californicus*) has been caught by its wing membranes on the spines of various desert shrubs around which it forages for insects. In Great Britain, there is a report of an instance where a Long-eared bat (*Plecotus auritus*) was impaled on the thorns of a rose bush. The Seminole bat (*Lasiurus seminolus*) of the southeastern United States, occasionally roosts in clumps of the epiphytic Spanish moss that hangs profusely on the trees in this region. There is one reported case in which one of these bats was entangled in the fibres of this plant and eventually died of strangulation.

Bats may also be killed accidentally by various man-made structures. It is not unusual to hear of cases where bats have been impaled on barbed-wire fencing. Electrical power lines have caused the death of some bats, but the extent of this is not known. Automobiles also take an unknown toll on the bat populations of the modern world where high speed roadways are common. Other activities of man may threaten bat survival. These include modification of the ecosystem through unwise land management or forestry practices and/or the widespread use of toxic chemicals for pest control (see Chapter 10).

On the whole, bats appear to be rather long-lived, generally living longer than other mammals of equal size. Although there are many reports in the scientific literature dealing with the longevity of bats, few are based on bats of known age. Studies on longevity of bats usually rely upon banding, release, and subsequent recapture of banded individuals. The time span between these two observations is a definite age, but it is only relative if the actual age at the time of banding was not known or determined. Based on this sort of information, the oldest recorded 'age' for a bat is 30 years. This was a male *Myotis lucifugus* from Craigmont, Ontario, Canada. Another male, 29 years of age, was also found in this same colony. There are several other reports of 20-24-year-old individuals of *Myotis* from the United States. The European horseshoe bat (*Rhinolophus ferrumequinum*) has a maximum known life span of 26 years. A number of species have been recaptured over a period of ten to 20 years. These are all 'ages' of free-living bats; a vampire bat (*Desmodus rotundus*) has been maintained in captivity for a record of 19.5 years. Other species, as well, have been housed in captivity for rather long periods of time.

Another method of determining the age of a bat is to histologically cut thin cross-sections of the teeth and count the number of layers of cementum and/or dentine, much as one would count the growth rings of trees. Recent research has shown that, while this technique reveals a 'loose correlation' between age and number of 'dental growth rings', it is generally unreliable. Young bats may be distinguished from adult bats by careful examination of the degree of fusion of the epiphyseal caps on the phalanges of the fingers. Complete fusion of all of these bones indicates adulthood, but again this information is of little use without individuals of known age and once fusion has occurred nothing, relative to longevity, may be determined.

As with most mammals, mortality in bats appears to be highest among young bats (Fig. 9.5). In this age class, the greatest loss apparently occurs in the prenatal period; that is, the period between conception and birth. Judging from the ratio of embryos to pregnant females and the ratio of young to lactating females of the Big Brown bat (*Eptesicus fuscus*) the loss in this period may be on the order of 10 per cent. Some researchers, looking at the number of mature and ruptured egg follicles in the ovary, have estimated the mortality in this prenatal period to be as high as 34 per cent. Mortality between birth and weaning is the next highest, being estimated at approximately 7 per cent in *E. fuscus*. Mortality in the first week of life of 75 per cent has been reported in the Southeastern myotis (*Myotis austroriparius*) from Florida. Many young bats of this age range simply fall out of the nursery roost and die. The circumstances of these losses are not known, although disease, physiological disorders, and/or exposure to toxic substances may be involved. As the young bats begin to fly and forage for themselves, they face another critical stage in their life history. Studies on the Grey bat (*Myotis grisescens*), in Tennessee and Alabama, revealed that the distance to the closest water source was closely associated with the survival of newly flying young. Young bats living in caves on the banks of reservoirs or close to bodies of water gained weight

faster and had higher survival rates than young bats that had to fly eight to ten kilometres to reach water. Weight gain and survival increased when some of these young bats, from distant caves, moved into caves close to water. Mortality due to avian predators may be highest at this time in the young bat's life. As we have noted previously, young bats face an additional 'uphill battle' in survival because they are usually entering the life cycle at a time when laying in

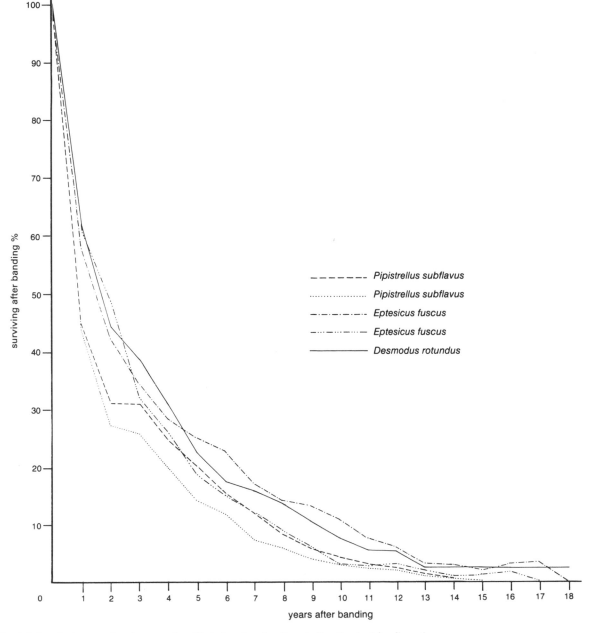

Fig. 9.5 *Survival curves for three species of bats based on banding studies. See text for discussion.*

fat stores, in preparation for hibernation, is a critical necessity. Many yearling bats simply do not survive their first hibernation period because they are unable to cope with the physiological and metabolic stresses accompanying this period of inactivity. Mortalities in this critical first year may be as high as 40-50 per cent of the yearling population.

Once a young bat has survived its first year of life, the chances of surviving to a ripe old age of seven or eight years are pretty good; between 40 and 80 per cent on the average (Fig. 9.5). Some (perhaps overly liberal) estimates of longevity based on banding data are as follows. Approximately 57 per cent of the marked individuals of *Rhinolophus hipposideros* from a cave near South Limburg, Netherlands survived one to five years after banding. About 67 per cent of the banded individuals of *Myotis dasycneme*, from this same cave, survived for that period of time, whereas 80 per cent of the banded *M. daubentonii* were recaptured in a one to four year span. The calculated average life expectancy for these three species was 1.8, 2.8, and 4.5 years, respectively.

After about six or seven years, the mortality rate of bats begins to increase again, with very aged individuals being exceptional. It may be that bat populations completely turn over, or nearly so, every six to seven years. Adult females appear to have a slightly higher death rate than do adult males, although the evidence is often contradictory. In a banded population of *Myotis lucifugus*, from Ontario, Canada female survival was 75.5 per cent and that for males was 79.9 per cent. On the other hand, females of this species from banded populations in Indiana and Kentucky had a survival rate of 85.7 per cent compared to 77.1 per cent for males. This apparent discrepancy may be due to geographical effects or it may be artificial due to the method of study. It may be too soon to make sweeping generalizations about this aspect of chiropteran biology. It is, however, reasonable to expect females to have a slightly higher mortality than males. Females must meet the physiological demands of pregnancy, parturition, and care and feeding of the young; stresses not placed on males. During this reproductive period, females often have a higher metabolic rate and infrequently enter daily torpidity to the extent experienced by males. Females of hibernating species also tend to leave the hibernaculum before males and, therefore, may be exposed to more hazardous climatic conditions. It has also been suggested that the crowded conditions in the nursery roost may be more conducive to disease transmission between individuals by various arthropod parasites. This has yet to be demonstrated.

The reasons for the relatively high survival rate and long life span in bats are obscure. Population ecologists currently believe that animals with low reproductive rates (few young over generally long periods of time) and parental care of the young are long-lived while animals with high reproductive rates (many young over relatively short periods of time) and little, if any, parental care are usually short-lived and their populations have high turnover rates. It is interesting to note that the survival rate of the bat species that have been studied are very similar to those for humans prior to modern medicine. It has been suggested that hibernation or daily torpor may be important factors in the longevity of bats. Over the course of a year, the total span of wakeful metabolic activity may be no more than a few months on the average. If indeed cellular ageing is slowed during this extensive period of metabolic inactivity, as some believe, then this may account for this longevity. At present, there is little evidence to support or refute this notion.

Sex ratio

As might be expected, the sex ratio of foetuses, newborn, and suckling young is approximately 1:1. However, the sex structure of the post-weaned populations of most bat species appears to be unequal. The biological reality of this inequality is difficult to prove. As we have noted above, there appears to be a slight differential in the survival rates of each of the sexes; males being slightly more successful. If the sex ratio of bat populations were truly 1:1, one would expect to encounter males as often as females; that is, the sexes should be randomly distributed in the environment. However, as we have already noted on several occasions, the sexes of many bat species exhibit marked behavioural differences and frequently spend large portions of the year in segregation.

Again, much of the available information is derived from hibernating populations of temperate cave-dwelling species. A midwinter population of the Little Brown bat (*Myotis lucifugus*) in Ontario, Canada, was found to contain 80 per cent males. This is much higher than 61 per cent which would be the predicted composition if the slightly higher success rate of males (79.9 per cent) was taken into account. Under similar conditions in an Indiana hibernaculum, 63 per cent of the individuals were males. The survival rate of males in this population (77.1 per cent) would have predicted 45 per cent. Similar observations have been made in hibernacula of the Big Brown bat (*Eptesicus fuscus*). In two such caves in Ohio and one in southern Indiana, the sex ratio of the population was approximately 1:1. In one other

Indiana cave, males far outnumbered the females and in another just the opposite was found.

Similar deviations from a 1:1 sex ratio have been reported in Panamanian populations of the Black myotis (*Myotis nigricans*), a non-hibernating species. The sex ratio of 159 newborn was 85 (54 per cent) females and 74 (46 per cent) males. However, adult females were found to outnumber males by two to one in the roost. This discrepancy is explained, in part, by the fact that subadult males leave the roost shortly after learning to fly and form small bachelor groups.

In contrast to these apparently skewed sex ratios, Australian populations of the Long-fingered bat (*Miniopterus schreibersii*) have been found to have statistically equal proportions of both sexes. Although there may be marked differences in the sex ratios of some species, most instances seem to be explained by behavioural or physiological preferences in roost selection, differences in foraging activity, and differences in mortality. The first two factors may exaggerate inequalities produced by the latter.

POPULATION MOVEMENT

In contrast to most other population parameters, the movement of bat populations has been studied more extensively than in any other group of mammals. Nearly all of this information has been gathered through bat banding and recovery studies and the majority of these have been conducted on temperate species in Europe and North America. Initially, most workers were interested in long distance movement (migration) of bats and some truly exceptional distances have been recorded. However, considerable information has been accumulated relative to short distance movements as well.

Population movement may be viewed and categorized in a number of different ways. The most basic category is the daily movement and activity of individual bats to and from foraging areas and within and between roost sites. We have commented on these movements in Chapters 5 and 6. In addition to these day to day local journeys, some species of bats regularly (seasonally) undertake movements of greater length. These migratory flights may be relatively short or they may cover extraordinarily long distances. Such movements may be autumnal and vernal in nature and coincide with the onset of winter and spring, respectively, in the northern extremes of the geographic range of a particular species. Or, in the tropics and subtropics, they may coincide with wet

and dry seasons and the related abundance or scarcity of a food resource such as insects or fruits and flowers. The seasonal disappearance and emergence of insects is probably as important a factor as temperature fluctuations in the migratory behaviour and patterns of temperate species. Whatever the cause, these migratory movements occur with seasonal regularity and along reasonably well-defined routes. Occasionally, an individual or small group of individuals is encountered in unusual locations. These accidental or vagrant movements may be the result of insufficiently developed homing ability in yearling bats. In addition, these oddities may be caused by man or unusual climatic conditions (high winds) during seasonal or daily flights.

Migration

Migration of bat populations was first suspected in the early part of this century, when European and North American naturalists noted the regular disappearance of temperate bat species in the winter months. The migratory behaviour of bird species was known at this time and this appeared to be a reasonable explanation for the seasonal absence of bats from this region. The migratory capacity of bats was discounted, however, when hibernating colonies were discovered. With the advent of bat banding studies, recoveries of individuals far removed from the original banding location revitalized the investigation of migration in bats. Even in the late 1960s, some workers still doubted the migratory capacity of bat populations. Indeed, the nature and extent of seasonal movements of some bat populations is not as clearcut as those of migratory birds. Nonetheless, there is a preponderance of evidence that now confirms migration as a regular part of the biological activity of some bat species.

Migration, in the sense of seasonal activity exhibited by bird species, includes two components. These involve a definite autumnal movement in a particular direction (for example, north to south) and a return, in the spring, to the original location when winter is over and conditions improve. All or some members of the genera *Nyctalus*, *Vespertilio*, *Lasiurus*, *Lasionycteris*, *Miniopterus*, *Pipistrellus*, and *Tadarida* migrate moderate (300-500 km) to long distances (1000-1500 km) in a general north/south direction with seasonal regularity. These migratory movements may be combined with hibernation in the winter part of their range. Many temperate species of the genus *Myotis* migrate generally shorter distances and not necessarily in latitudinal directions. These migratory journeys are, nonetheless, seasonal and involve moving from generally warm summer roosts (including maternity colonies) to cooler, more favourable, hibernation sites.

Bats that roost in open situations (such as trees) in temperate regions are often migratory, especially near the polar limits of their range. The European noctule (*Nyctalus noctula*) has a migration pattern in Europe that involves south or southwesterly movement in the autumn and north or northeasterly movement in the spring (Fig. 9.6). Apparently, not all individuals of a particular population migrate; some remain or move only a short distance and spend the winter in the protection of a hollow log or woodpecker hole. Migratory flights are sometimes rather short (80-160 km), but individuals of this species are known to migrate considerable distances (1000-1600 km). These long migratory flights are more generally encountered in populations living in eastern Europe and Russia where the continental winters are more severe and suitable outdoor shelters less abundant. Two exceptionally long flights from the Voronezh region of southern Russia have been recorded; one to Istanbul (*c.* 1700 km) and another to Greece (*c.* 2000 km). Two species of European pipistrelles (*Pipistrellus*

pipistrellus and *P. nathusii*), which occupy a geographic distribution similar to that of the noctule also exhibit similar migratory movements, including exceptionally long journeys.

In North America, the tree bats of the genera *Lasiurus*, *Lasionycteris*, and *Dasypterus* share migratory habits similar to those of their European counterparts. The Hoary bat (*Lasiurus cinereus*) is particularly interesting because it occurs in the temperate regions of both hemispheres and, in both, migrates to more equatorial latitudes during the cold season (Fig. 9.7). More information is available on North American populations. Nearly all recorded captures of this species from November to April are from localities south of 37° N latitude, whereas they are found in northern Canada and Alaska in the summer months. These bats have been observed travelling in migratory waves rather like some migratory birds. A rather curious point is that the Hoary bat, as well as the Red bat (*L. borealis*), Seminole bat (*L. seminolus*), and Northern Yellow bat (*Dasypterus intermedius*) may travel with migratory birds or along the same migratory routes used by birds. These bats and birds

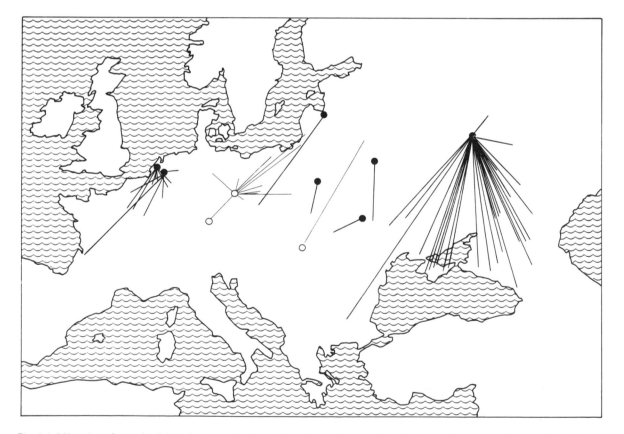

Fig. 9.6 Migration of noctules (Nyctalus noctula–Vespertilionidae) *in Europe. These bats usually move south or southwest in autumn and north or northeast in spring. (After Strelkov, 1969).*

occasionally collide with high man-made structures located in their migratory path. One such structure is the Empire State building in New York City and another is a high television tower in Florida. During the migratory season, dead bats and birds are found on and around these structures; birds usually outnumber bats and bat deaths are higher in the autumn than in the spring. *Myotis austroriparius*, *Eptesicus fuscus*, and *Tadarida brasiliensis* have also been killed in migratory collisions at the Florida television tower.

There is no clear distinction between the migratory tree bats, mentioned above, and hibernating cave bats, discussed below. For example, the Red bat migrates, but hibernates in the southern portion of its range. Some populations of the Silver-haired bat (*Lasionycteris noctivagans*) migrate in some parts of North America, whereas other populations hibernate, usually roosting in protected, but relatively open shelters in trees, logs, or buildings.

Long distance migratory movements have been amply demonstrated in the Mexican Free-tailed bat (*Tadarida brasiliensis*). These bats have received considerable attention from bat biologists because of their indirect association with rabies. They occupy a geographic range from southern Oregon, California, Utah, Nevada, southern Nebraska and Kansas, through the southwestern and southeastern United States, to Mexico, Central and South America. Four general groups of populations have been defined through the banding studies conducted on this species. One of these includes the populations of southern Oregon and California (Fig. 9.8A). These are thought to be composed of resident, non-migratory populations. There may be some local southwardly shift in the winter, but extensive migratory flights do not occur. Winters in this region are generally mild and individuals may become torpid for short periods of time; some may be active periodically during the winter months. A second group of apparently non-migratory populations occurs in eastern Nevada and California and western Arizona (Fig. 9.8B). While these populations appear to be year-round residents, they apparently are not capable of entering hibernation (see Chapter 6). Instead they seek out warm shelters such as warm tunnels or near chimneys on the outsides of houses. During the winter, they frequently move from one shelter to another. A third group of populations occupies a region from southeastern Utah, southwestern Colorado, eastern Arizona, and western New Mexico (Fig. 9.8C). These bats migrate seasonally to and from western Mexico (Sonora, Sinaloa, and Jalisco). The fourth group includes populations from Oklahoma, eastern New Mexico, Texas, and, perhaps, the remaining southeastern United States (Fig. 9.8D). The movements of these populations are generally better known because one of the resident and transitory caves in this region is the famous Carlsbad Caverns where extensive banding has been done. Perhaps less famous, but nonetheless large, populations are also housed in Merrihew Cave and several neighbouring caves near the Oklahoma panhandle, and Frio and Bracken Caves in Texas. These bats seasonally move to and from more southern locations including caves in eastern Mexico (Coahuila, Nuevo Leon, and Tamaulipas).

Many bat species that live in the temperate regions occupy caves or buildings. A number of these species, especially *Myotis*, move short to moderately long distances during the year. This movement involves seasonal journeys from hibernation caves to summer roosts (including maternity colonies) in the spring and back to hibernation caves in the autumn. The reason for these movements appears to lie in the metabolic needs of the bats. Generally warm roosts are required or preferred for the summertime activities of bearing and rearing young and breeding, whereas a stable, cool, and humid environment is required for efficient hibernation. The seasonal movements of most of the vespertilionid species of eastern and southeastern United States have been studied intensely as have those of many European vespertilionids and rhinolophids.

In North America, any number of examples could be discussed. The Little Brown bat (*Myotis lucifugus*) and the Big Brown bat (*Eptesicus fuscus*) have received much attention. However, the seasonal population movement of the Grey bat (*Myotis grisescens*) will be discussed here. These bats occur primarily in the southeastern United States, south of the Ohio River, with some populations in extreme eastern Kansas and Oklahoma, Missouri, and northern Arkansas. The population biology of this species has been studied intensely throughout the year in the Tennessee River Valley and northern Florida. Ninety per cent of the Grey bats in the southeastern states hibernate in two large caves in eastern Tennessee (approximately 375 000 bats) and one in northern Alabama (approximately 1 500 000 bats) (Fig. 9.9 and 9.10). These caves are located near the northern edge of the species range in the southeast and are characterized by stable cool temperatures and humidity throughout the year. The loyalty to a particular hibernation cave is nearly 100 per cent, regardless of where individuals spend their summertime and bats do not appear to move among these caves once hibernation begins. Of 3110 bats banded during hibernation in one of these caves, none was found wintering in either of the other hibernation caves in 14 years of study. Many of these bats were recovered with regularity in this period of

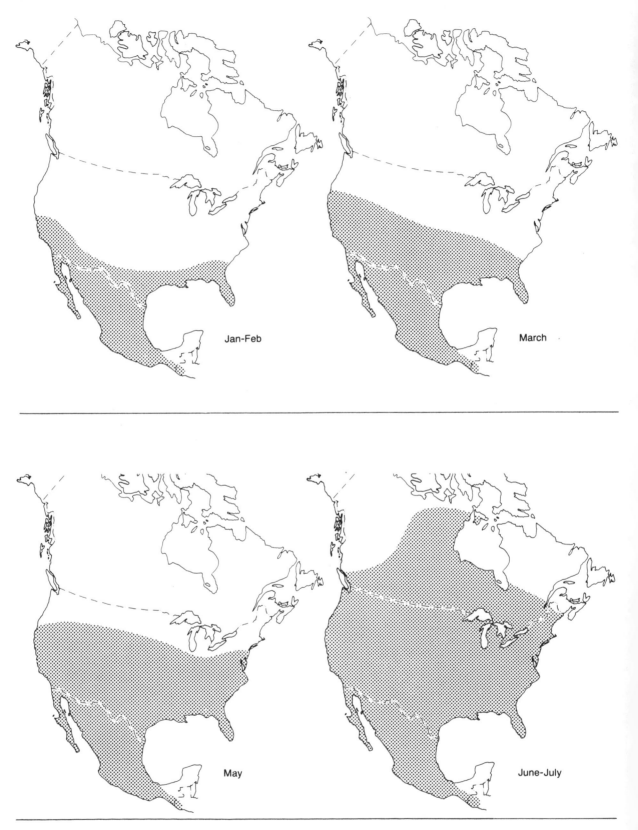

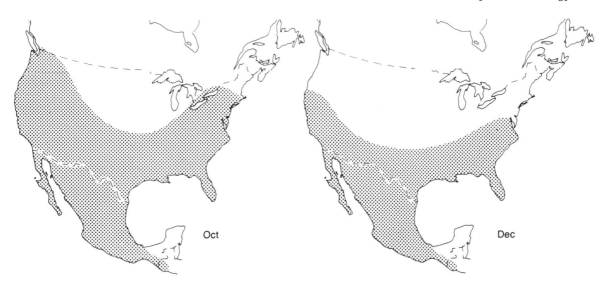

Fig. 9.7 Migratory patterns of the Hoary bat (Lasiurus cinereus–Vespertilionidae). *See text for discussion.*

time. A total of 6486 bats were banded in all three wintering caves; only one was ever recovered at more than one site.

In the spring, these bats leave the hibernation caves and disperse to their summer territories. Many bats move (100-200 km) into summer residence in caves located just south along the Tennessee River and reservoirs. The longest journeys (440-525 km) are made by the Florida Grey bats that have moved northward during the autumn. Large numbers of females were captured in waves on one night in April at a transitory cave in east-central Alabama. Some of these were again recaptured within their summer range in northern Florida. The length of time required for these flights is not known, but they may travel these distances in a matter of several days. Females usually fly to specific summer roosts where they form maternity colonies. The amount of loyalty to these caves is as marked as the loyalty to winter caves. Young bats banded in particular summer caves were captured in subsequent summers in the same cave or in a cave within the home range of that local population. Adult males disperse to summer roosts and spend most of the summer segregated from the females. Male roosts may be located in the same cave as the maternity roost, but in a different area, or they may be in different caves. In the autumn, the movement to the hibernation caves begins in August. At this time, males and females meet and fly in swarms around the entrance to the hibernation site. Mating occurs during this swarming activity.

Similar seasonal movements occur among European cave-and house-dwelling bats. The Barbastelle (*Barbastella barbastellus*) lives in trees in the summertime (sometimes under the bark) or in buildings, moving in the autumn, perhaps 100-300 km, into caves where they hibernate. They usually travel north to south or from northeast to southwest. The Long-fingered bat (*Miniopterus schreibersii*), a cave-dwelling species, is slightly migratory at the northern limit of its European range and travels 160-275 km in its seasonal journeys. European species of *Myotis* are similar to their North American counterparts in that they rarely migrate long distances; 250 km is exceptional. In England, the Greater Horseshoe bat (*Rhinolophus ferrumequinum*) usually moves little more than 30 km travelling seasonally from one limestone cave to another (Fig. 9.11). Individuals of this species often move between hibernation caves in the winter. The direction of their seasonal movement is not necessarily north to south, but seems more concerned with the location of suitable roosting sites for the respective activity.

Earlier in this chapter (social behaviour), we mentioned the seasonal congregations of Australian flying foxes. For a long time, it was thought that these Old World fruit bats migrated back and forth from summer and winter ranges. Evidence suggests that they may indeed move short distances seasonally, but that long distance movement does not occur. Instead, the summer colonies break up and the individuals disperse when blossoms and fruits are less abundant. Similar seasonal behaviour seems to occur in African populations of the Epauletted fruit bats (*Epomophorus*) and Straw-coloured fruit bat (*Eidolon helvum*). The latter species may travel moderately long dis-

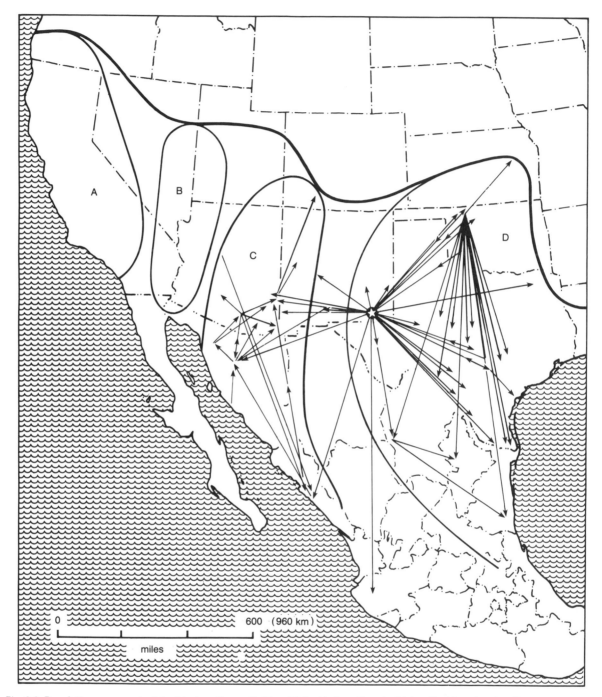

Fig. 9.8 Population movement of the Mexican Free-tailed bat (Tadarida brasiliensis–Molossidae) based on banding studies. Arrows represent movement from the banding site to a point of recovery; star represents Carlsbad caverns. See text for discussion.

tances during its seasonal movement. Fruit- and nectar-eating bats of the New World, living in northern Mexico and southwestern United States, appear to follow seasonally the fruiting and flowering cycle of the plants on which they feed. Similar local movement may be expected in insectivorous bats that inhabit these areas where pronounced wet and dry seasons occur.

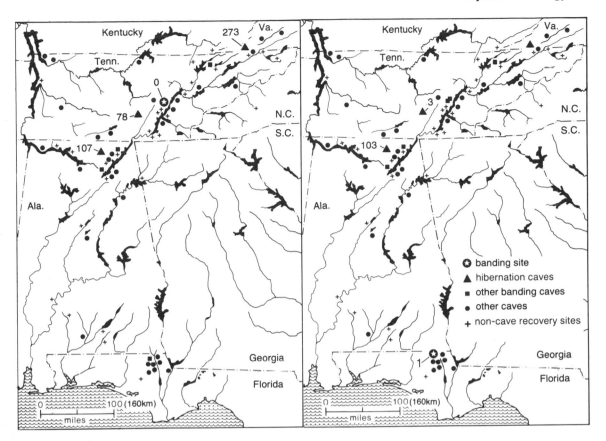

Fig. 9.9 *Seasonal movement in two populations of Grey bats* (Myotis grisescens–Vespertilionidae) *in southeastern United States. Left diagram shows the movement of individuals in a Tennessee population from one banding cave to one of three hibernacula. Right diagram shows movement of individuals from a Florida population to these same hibernacula. Numbers indicate the number of banded individuals from the original banding cave recovered in a hibernation cave. See text for discussion. (After Tuttle, 1976).*

Homing

The ability to leave the daytime retreat, travel to the foraging site, and return to that shelter after feeding, occurs day after day and may be accomplished with the aid of echolocation in microchiropterans. Often the foraging site is within several hundred metres or several kilometres of the daytime roost and familiarity with the route to and from these locations may play an important role in moving from one to the other. However, many bat species travel considerably longer distances during their daily activity. Some populations of Grey bats in the Tennessee River Valley study flew 10-15 km in order to reach their foraging areas. Some of the large pteropodids regularly fly 30-40 km to feed. There is little doubt that these megachiropterans utilize vision in finding their way to and from the roost since they lack echolocation (except in *Rousettus*). While daily movement within the familiar territory of the population may be explained by familiarity or the use of echolocation (in

those bats that have this ability) precise and repeated movement to and from migratory locations is quite another matter. This apparent homing ability of bats has occupied the interest of bat biologists since long distance movements were first discovered.

Long distance flights consume substantial energy and, therefore, should be as accurate and direct as possible to be energetically economical. In Chapter 8, we discussed the highly accurate, short-range nature of the microchiropteran echolocation system. These high frequency signals attenuate rapidly in air thereby rendering them ineffective over distances of more than 50-100 metres. Since most migratory bats fly at altitudes much in excess of this, it seems highly unlikely that echolocation plays much of a role in these seasonal movements. If echolocation were used and given this attenuation rate, bats would have to memorize an auditory corridor approximately 200 metres wide from the starting point of a migratory flight to its destination. This would be an extreme energetic luxury.

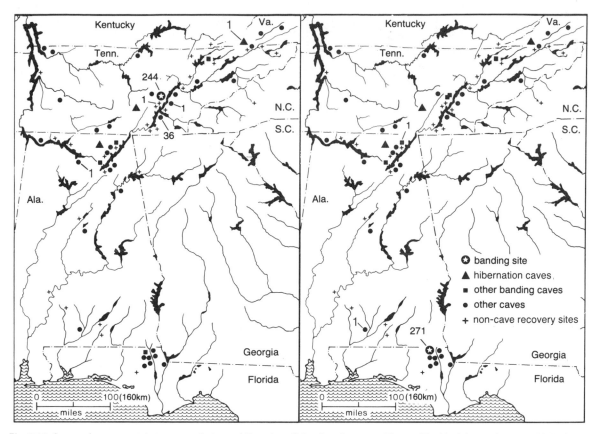

Fig. 9.10 Seasonal movement in two populations of Grey bats (Myotis grisescens–Vespertilionidae) in southeastern United States. Left diagram shows the number of reproductive females in a Tennessee population recaptured at the original banding cave early in the spring after the break up of hibernating colonies. Right diagram shows the same movement of reproductive females from a Florida population. See text for discussion. (After Tuttle, 1976).

Initial studies of the homing ability of bats involved capturing some bats at their normal roost, marking them with bands, and then transporting them to some distant location (presumably outside their familiar area) where they were released. The home roost was then monitored for any of these displaced bats that returned. Many studies of this type have been conducted in Europe and North America. Most of the species studied show a marked tendency to return to their home roost from distances of 100-150 km. Generally, the length of time required to return to the home roost varies according to the magnitude of displacement. For example, the European noctule, a known long distance migratory species, has demonstrated an ability to return from a distance of 45 km in less than 24 hours. An individual transported 237 km from the home roost was captured, halfway home, five days after being released.

In North America, individuals of the Little Brown bat have returned from about 430 km in 17-22 days, a rate of about 20-25 km per day. A female Pallid bat

(*Antrozous pallidus*) released at distances 30-110 km from her home roost in southern Arizona, exhibited a remarkable ability to return (Fig. 9.12F). She made eight consecutive homing flights between 23 May and 1 October 1960. After each return, she was captured, transported, and released from another location around her home roost. Interestingly, her two quickest returns (six days) were from distances of 89 and 95 km and her longest return (37 days) was from a location only 50 km from the home roost. All release points were thought to be well outside her area of familiarity and there was no reason to presuppose that she was familiar with the expanse of the experimental area, yet she homed in a non-random manner.

In another study involving the Little Brown bat (*Myotis lucifugus*), the homing ability of adults and juveniles was examined. Young bats were found generally to lack the ability to return to their home roost, settling instead in suitable roosts near the displacement location or wandering off to known

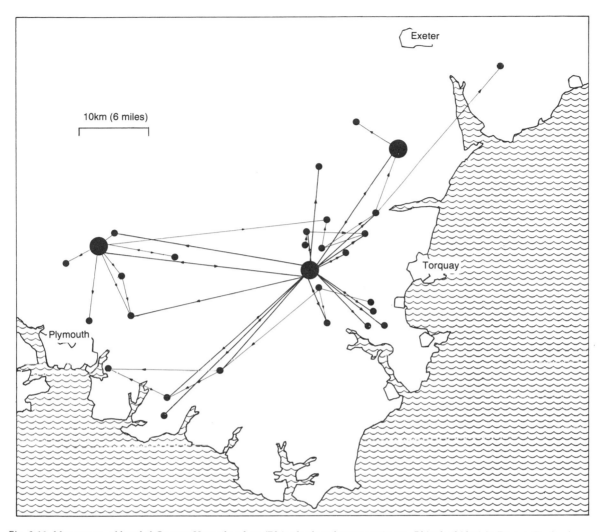

Fig. 9.11 Movements of banded Greater Horseshoe bats (Rhinolophus ferrumequinum–*Rhinolophidae) in Devon, England. Heavy lines show the journeys associated directly with the central site, lighter lines additional journeys. Double arrows indicate a return journey. (After Hooper & Hooper, 1956).*

sites. Yearling Mexican Free-tailed bats (*Tadarida brasiliensis*) have been captured flying northward during the migratory season rather than southward, the normal direction of migration.

Thus, from these many studies, it is clear that bats are capable of homing. How this and repeated movement along the migratory path is accomplished has continued to baffle bat biologists. The fact that the proportion of released individuals to returning individuals is generally low in all homing experiments has led some to imagine that homing is a random event. It is supposed that the released individual casts about, probing in different directions, and if, by chance alone, it strikes its familiar area it then returns successfully. If, on the other hand, it does not encounter familiar territory it does not return to the home roost. The success rate of returns has encouraged others to suppose that bats have an inherent ability to determine the homeward direction and thereby find their way back to the home roost. The evidence is too contradictory at this time to evaluate properly either of these notions, although there seems to be a strong indication that it is not a non-random capacity.

Whatever the cause may be, several past and recent studies clearly implicate visual orientation as playing an important role in homing. Blinded or blindfolded bats do not home as well as do bats with unimpaired vision. The use of vision has been amply demonstrated in a study on the homing ability of the Spear-nosed bat (*Phyllostomus hastatus*) in Trinidad. Individuals of this species were taken from their home roost and transported to two locations about 10 km southeast and southwest of the home cave. All were fitted with a radio pack and their movements tracked telemetrically. Some had unimpaired vision, some were fitted with special blindfolds, and a control group was fitted with goggles of the same structure as the blindfolds, but with unimpaired lenses. When released, the normal bats made several circles and then headed off in the direction of the home cave within 20-30 minutes. Those with goggles performed about as well as the normal individuals. Both usually returned to the home cave on the same night they were released. The blindfolded bats circled the release point for nearly seven hours and most did not return to the home cave. Most of those that did return to the home cave had, in the meantime, worked their blindfolds free. However, some were able to find their way back with the blindfolds still intact and effective. Beyond about 30 km, normal bats behaved in a disoriented manner typical of blindfolded bats and returns were less frequent and slower. Studies concerning the visual acuity of several microchiropteran species indicates that these small-eyed mammals are far from blind as some have thought. They are capable of discriminating among different light intensities, shapes, and some patterns. Thus,

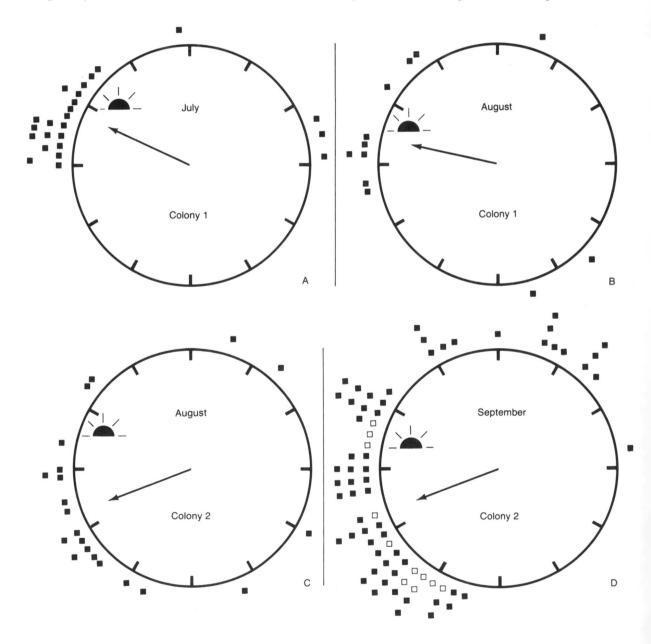

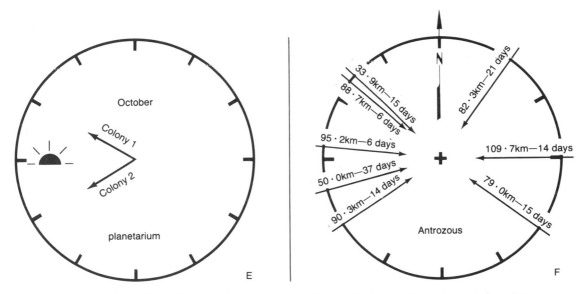

Fig. 9.12 Orientation of the Big Brown bat (Eptesicus fuscus–Vespertilionidae) relative to the post-sunset glow. Arrows (A–D) indicate the mean azimuth of departure of individuals from the roost. Direction of individual departures are represented by solid squares, open symbols represent five individuals. The average orientation of individuals from each colony inside a planetarium with artificial post-sunset glow (E). F, Distance and length of time for a female Antrozous pallidus *(Vespertilionidae) to return to her home cave after being displaced. (A–E after Buchler & Childs, 1982). See text for discussion.*

bats appear to have reasonably good vision and use it to some extent to orient in their environment. An important question remains; that is, what do bats use for cues in their visual navigation through familiar or unfamiliar territory that allows them to find their way accurately?

Several recent studies have begun to approach this crucial question. Using point light sources, several investigators have shown that the Big Brown bat (*Eptesicus fuscus*) should be able to see many bright stars in the northern hemisphere even after their intensity has been attenuated by the earth's atmosphere. Several other workers have shown clearly that the Big Brown bat uses the post-sunset glow as an orientation cue during flights from the roost (Fig. 12A-E). In this latter study, bats at two different locations were observed as they departed from the roost at sunset. Members of each colony left their respective roost sites on a generally well-defined compass heading. This heading remained more or less constant throughout the summer. Some individuals from each colony were removed from their roost and taken, under cover, to an abandoned air strip where they were released individually and the direction of their flight determined. This experimentation was timed so that the light conditions (post-sunset glow) were the same as they would experience at their home roost. Although some scattering occurred, these individuals flew in directions that closely approximated those used by their respective

colonies. To test the notion further that these bats were using the post-sunset glow, the experimenters took some bats from each colony to a planetarium where they were able to artificially create the sunset light conditions. The bats again responded in patterns consistent with those observed at each roost.

Even with this seeming wealth of information, homing and how it is accomplished remains an area of bat biology where further study is required before we can fully understand and appreciate the migratory movements of bats. Studies in planetariums, with artificially (computer-generated) created celestial patterns, may well provide new insights into this interesting chiropteran ability.

Accidental dispersals

Accidental dispersals of bats concern individuals rather than populations or groups and often involve migratory species that fly strongly over long distances. Such accidents may be caused when these bats fly in stormy or windy conditions. Strong winds are suspected in the occasional dispersal of the Australian Grey-headed flying fox (*Pteropus poliocephalus*) to Tasmania or for an isolated instance of the Australian Collared flying fox (*Pteropus scapulatus*) in New Zealand. Migratory North American bats of the genera *Lasiurus* and *Lasionycteris* provide several other examples of accidental displacement or vagrant flights to localities far beyond their usual range. All of these bats are noted for their strong, rapid flight, and indeed, *Lasiurus* is the most widespread of exclusively New World genera, reaching Hawaii and the Galapagos Islands in the Pacific Ocean. The Hoary bat (*Lasiurus cinereus*) has been reported in Iceland and the Orkney Islands off the northern coast of Scotland, probably assisted in these unusually long flights by strong winds. Together with its close relatives, the Red bat (*Lasiurus borealis*), Seminole bat (*Lasiurus seminolus*), and Silver-haired bat (*Lasionycteris noctivagans*), the Hoary bat occasionally reaches Bermuda, 800 km or so from the southeastern coast of the United States. Possibly these visitors have overflown their wintering area on the mainland; some may leave after a week or so while others may overwinter in Bermuda. The Seminole bat may have been a previous resident of Bermuda, but it no longer appears to occur there permanently as there are few trees remaining on the island. An overflight may also account for the record of a pregnant female Hoary bat on Southampton Island in the Northwest Territories of Canada where trees are scarce.

In the British Isles, Leisler's noctule (*Nyctalus leisleri*) does not normally occur further north than Northern Ireland and Yorkshire, but a single individual has been found on the Shetland Islands, having flown there, perhaps, from eastern England, assisted by a southeasterly wind. Similar circumstances may account for the occurrence of the European noctule (*Nyctalus noctula*) in the Orkney Islands. The Particoloured bat (*Vespertilio murinus*) has also been reported from Shetland, Yarmouth, and Plymouth, although this species is normally restricted to the continental mainland of Europe. There is another instance of a vagrant Particoloured bat found on an oil rig in the North Sea. Similar ocean excursions have been documented with the Long-eared bat (*Plecotus auritus*) landing on a lightship 50 km off the coast of Norfolk. The Hoary bat and Silver-haired bat have landed on ocean-going vessels off the Atlantic coast of the United States. And, the Yellow bat (*Dasypterus*

ega) landed on a ship 320 km off the coast of Argentina.

Accidental or intentional transportation of various mammals is well documented. The House mouse (*Mus musculus*), Black rat (*Rattus rattus*), and Norway rat (*Rattus norvegicus*) have followed man (accidentally transported) into nearly every corner of the world. As far as we know, there have been no intentional introductions of bats into areas of the world. However, bats have been transported accidentally by man. In November 1980, a container of timber for a furniture factory in the Netherlands left Alliston, Ontario, Canada for Halifax, Nova Scotia where it was loaded on board a transport ship bound for Holland. Two days after the container arrived at the furniture factory, it was unpacked and its stowaway, a hibernating Big Brown bat (*Eptesicus fuscus*), was discovered. This vagrant had apparently entered the container sometime in the autumn and had survived in hibernation during the transit. A freak occurrence of the Little Brown bat (*Myotis lucifugus*) in Iceland is thought to have occurred in a similar fashion. This small North American vespertilionid is apparently a regular summer passenger on a transport vessel that sails between New Brunswick and Rotterdam. Small colonies frequent the wharf area where the ship is loaded and occasionally they use the ship's hold as a night roost. Some of these stowaways have apparently disembarked in Rotterdam. The Eastern pipistrelle (*Pipistrellus subflavus*) has been found in the interior of aircraft. Another unusual case of ship transport involved an individual of the phyllostomid *Vampyressa pusilla* which probably boarded the vessel as it passed through the Panama Canal. This leaf-nosed stowaway was discovered in the chartroom as the ship was voyaging in the Bass Strait between Australia and Tasmania. With an increase in shipping and air transport between Europe and North America, it is highly likely that more instances of accidental transportations of bats will occur. This may pose some potential public health concern (see Chapter 10).

Bats have long been regarded as sinister, demoniac, and generally undesirable creatures. No other group of mammals seems so shrouded in mystery, mythical folklore, and misinformation. These qualities are represented in the modern Western expressions: 'batty' or having 'bats in one's belfry' for a crazy or irrational person; 'old bat' for an ugly or unpleasant person (usually female); 'blind as a bat' for a person with defective eyesight; or 'took off like a bat out of hell' for someone in hasty retreat. Similar, but perhaps more colourful comparisons between negative human behaviour and that of bats (flying foxes) are encountered in contemporary Fijian expressions. The flying fox is called 'mbeka' and a person not prone to regular bathing is said to 'boiboi vaka mbeka' or smell like a bat. 'Samusamu mbeka' is used for a lazy person who loafs about like a bat. Someone with bad table manners or who is just ill-mannered may be said to 'kanakana vaka mbeka' or eat like a flying fox.

FOLKLORE, SUPERSTITIONS, AND LEGENDS

Bats abound in the mythology and folklore of the world. They are most often unjustly associated with the evil and dark side of the human experience. At other times, they are portrayed as clever, sometimes comical, creatures with a double nature, being 'half bird' and 'half beast.' The general resemblance between man and bats has been recognized by many primitive cultures in tales of man's origin from bats or vice versa. Bats also appear in stories describing the origin of night, death, and/or darkness.

Witches and vampires

Perhaps the most common association of bats is with witches and vampires. These sinister beings that go about at night or dwell in dark places are a common element in the folklore of many cultures from Japan and the Philippines to Africa, Europe and the Middle East, and the Americas. In these stories, vampires, and in some cases witches, are thought to drink or suck the blood of their victims. Yet, except for the

New World tropics, there is no biological basis for the connection between bats and these malevolent spirits other than their nocturnal habits.

There is little in the way of a clear association of bats with vampires and witches in the Old World prior to the publication of Bram Stoker's *Dracula* in 1897. Stoker's main character was based on a real personage, Vlad the Impaler (*c.* 1431-1467), a Roumanian tyrant, who although known for his many wicked deeds, was not regarded as a vampire. As we noted earlier, Stoker may have been influenced by tales of vampire bats brought back to Europe by travellers in the New World.

There is a wealth of witchcraft and superstition relating to vampires in the magic and religion of the gypsies. The origin of the gypsy cult of the vampire may very well lie in India where there is a strong vampire tradition. Here, bhuta, brahmaparusha, and rakshasa are vampire-like creatures that wander about between midnight and the early hours of the morning. Although any or all of these may transform themselves into any animal, bats are never mentioned in this connection. However, there is an Indian superstition in which bats flying around a house supposedly foretell a death.

The vampires of Slavic gypsies may appear in the form of a horse, dog, cat, frog, spider, or even a flea. The Moslem gypsies of Yugoslavia believe that such animals as cocks, hens, sheep, horses, dogs, and cats may become vampires; the most fearsome, however, is the vampire snake. Even vegetables such as pumpkins and watermelons or household tools may become vampires which, although not harmful to living things, create a general disturbance.

Bats, on the other hand, appear to have been revered by gypsies as good luck or possessing beneficial magic qualities. In the ancient kingdom of Macedonia, bats were considered to be the luckiest of all animals and a person who kept a bat's bone about his person was certain to be happy. Gypsy children often wore a black bag containing the dried fragments of a bat around their necks as a talisman of good fortune. In Bohemia, the right eye of a bat, carried in the waistcoat pocket, supposedly makes the person invisible. Gypsies have long been associated with gambling and gamblers are known to be a superstitious lot. In the nineteenth century, many gamblers rode on riverboats that travelled up and down the Mississippi and Ohio rivers and it was believed by some of them that carrying parts of bats brought good luck. This practice may have its origin in the gypsy folklore of southern Germany where a gambler who wanted to win tied a bat's heart to the arm with which he dealt cards.

There are several associations of bats with witches in African folklore. Among the Nupe of west-central Nigeria, witches are said to breathe fire from their mouths, and to suck their victim's blood like a vampire. These witches are not directly identified with bats, but they are said to meet and talk in baobab and iroko trees. Both of these trees are pollinated by fruit bats that make a clatter like people ('witches') talking. The Azande of Central Africa believe that bats can be vehicles of the souls of witches. When a crop is attacked by bats it is thought to be an act of witchcraft. To discover the perpetrator, the owner of the crop must catch one of the bats, burn it, and mix the ashes in beer which other members of the tribe are invited to drink. Upon drinking the beer, the guilty party is betrayed when he vomits.

In the New World, bats were associated with death and darkness by the ancient Maya. 'Zotz' is the Mayan word for bat and 'Zotziha' (bat house) was one of the regions of the underworld through which a dying man had to pass on the way to the depths of the earth. This kingdom of darkness was inhabited by the Vampire Bat God or Death Bat called 'Camazotz' who decapitated his victims and was responsible for killing the young hero Hunahpu. He and his brother Xbalanque had been travelling in the underworld to avenge the death of their father at the hands of the evil Lords of Xibalba. While in the Bat House, they slept inside a blowgun for protection from the bats in the night. Hunahpu lost his head when he stuck it out in the morning to see if it was light. His head was later restored when he and his brother emerged from the underworld. The bat deity, Zotz, was often depicted in the codices of these ancient people as its representation was also the symbol for one of the Mayan months of the year (Fig. 10.1). These depictions all bear a striking resemblance to the leaf-nosed bats of the family Phyllostomidae.

Even today, in certain parts of Mexico, there is continued worship of bats or bat gods. For example, there is a large cave in Veracruz where pregnant women go to give offerings to the vampire bats and pray for successful deliveries of their babies. The people in the village may also call upon the bats to protect them from enemies and general bad luck, or ensure the harvest of bountiful crops. Offerings may be food, flowers, or in some cases, money.

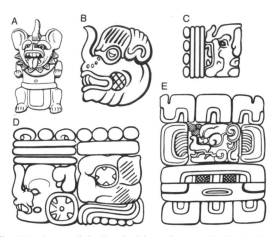

Fig. 10.1 A, urn of the Bat God from Oaxaca; B, Glyph 'Zotz' from the Mayan calendar; C, Mayan calendric glyph with the Zotz symbol and the number 19 from a stone tablet in the Temple of the Sun at Palenque, Mexico; D, Mayan calendric glyph with the Zotz symbol and the number 18 followed by another glyph and the number 9 from a stela at Quirigua, Guatemala; E, Mayan glyph from stela at Quirigua, Guatemala.

There are several stories involving man-eating or blood-sucking bats in the folk tales of the Arawak Indians of northern Guyana in South America. In one of these, a group of men have set out on a long journey in search of stone axes. Along the way they have to cross through the country of the Bat Tribe where the bats were as large as cranes. In order to protect themselves during the night, the men built an enclosed corral. One young man was slothful and unwilling to help in the construction of the shelter because he did not believe that the bats, however big they were, would harm him. Of course, he slept outside the protective compound that night. Late in the night, when it was quite dark, his companions heard him begging to be let in, but, in fear, they refused to open their shelter. The next morning, all that was left of the young man were his bones—the bats had sucked him dry.

Another story told by the Makusi tribe of the Arawak concerns an immense monster bat that lived on Bat Mountain in the Pakaraima range. As the story goes, this bat would swoop down on the village at night and carry off anyone who it found outside. It carried the hapless person in its powerful claws to its nest where the individual was devoured. This continued for some time and the men of the village tried, in vain, to locate the monster's nest and kill it. Finally, an old woman declared that she was willing to sacrifice herself for the good of the tribe. That night, before stationing herself in the middle of the village, she took from the cooking fire a stick smouldering with sparks. This she concealed under her shawl. The bat came and seized her in its powerful talons and carried her aloft toward its hidden nest. However, she uncovered the smouldering stick which burst into flames and left a glowing trail like a comet providing the men of the village with the direction to the nest. The bat's nest then caught on fire and the high flames served as a gliding beacon. The bat was killed, but the fate of the heroine went untold.

In yet another Arawak tale, the owl (Boku-boku) married the sister of two bats. Thereafter, the owl took his two brothers-in-law hunting and taught them how to steal cooked fish from the village folk. The villagers cooked their fish outdoors over an open fire and the owl and his two in-laws would swoop down shouting 'Boku! Boku! Boku!' This frightened the villagers who fled into the forest leaving the fish for the owl and the bats. One night, the owl had other business to attend to and, before leaving, he told the two bats to stay home and not go hunting. The bats, of course, saw no reason to do so and as usual they swooped out of the night screaming 'Boku! Boku! Boku!' Their voices, however, were neither as loud or as thunderous as that of the owl and the villagers were only mildly frightened. They saw that it was only bats stealing their fish and one man took up his bow and arrow and shot one of the bats. The bat fell, stunned, and the people ran after and caught him while his brother escaped. The brother went in search of the owl and after finding him, he recounted what had happened. Together they returned to the village and this time the booming voice of the owl frightened the people. They rescued the wounded and unconscious bat and carried him home. There the owl slapped him where the arrow had struck, bringing him back to life. Unfortunately, the two bats did not learn from this lesson and the next time that the owl left on business they tried again to steal fish from the village. Once again the villagers were not scared by the weak voices of the bats and again one was shot. He was caught and placed over the fire with the fish. Again the brother escaped and fetched the owl. This time, after they had rescued their fallen comrade, the owl was unable to revive him as the fire had dried the life out of him. From that time on, the bat that lived has gone out to avenge his brother's death. This he does by drinking the blood from the livestock and chickens that belong to the people and sometimes from the people themselves. It may be from such tales as this that the vampire associations with bats started.

There was apparently no direct association of bats with vampires and witches in the writings of the ancient Greeks. Nonetheless, bats were associated with the underworld and were considered sacred by Persephone, the daughter of Zeus, wife of Hades, and ruler of the subterranean world of the dead.

A legend about bats and death

As we have seen, it is not unusual for bats to be associated with death. They are sometimes viewed as forewarning an impending death or other misfortune. In the case of vampires and witches, they are often portrayed as the agent of death. Aside from these, there is an Australian aboriginal legend that curiously parallels the story of Adam and Eve.

When the first man and woman were put on earth, they were told to stay away from a large bat as it was venerated by the spirits and was not to be disturbed. Just as Eve became curious about the apple, this woman also became curious about the large bat. Ultimately, she could no longer control her curiosity and she approached the bat for a closer look. The bat was frightened and flew away from its perch. It had been guarding a cave in which death dwelled. When the winged sentry abandoned its guardian vigil, death crawled from its dark prison into the world and, since then, men have died.

The origin of night

Many of the evil qualities wrongly attributed to bats seem to be related to the fact that bats are creatures of the night; a time when most disasters, even death, befall man who, by his nature, is a diurnal creature. Night-time or darkness are awkward environs for us and so it would seem natural that these would be the habitat of the things that we fear most—ghosts, demons, devils, and witches. It is interesting to note in passing that owls are also associated with these fearsome beings. Many of man's folk tales seek to explain how the night came to be separated from the day and some of these tales involve bats. An example of one of these legends comes from the aboriginal mythology of Australia.

At the beginning of time, birds and animals often gathered together for feasts and dancing. There was much vying among the tribes at these festive occasions. The Cockatoo, who was quite vain, was casually talking to the Eagle-hawk, the leader of the bird tribes, and he noted that the birds were better performers than the animals. The Eagle-hawk agreed. In addition to his vanity, the Cockatoo was also a bit of a gossip and he soon had told many of his bird friends that the Eagle-hawk had said that birds were better than animals. Before long, the word spread and soon the Kangaroo, the leader of the animal tribes, heard what the birds were saying. He went to the Eagle-hawk to protest and asked for an apology. The Eagle-hawk was stubborn and, confronted in this way, he refused. Soon, the Kangaroo and Eagle-hawk were quarrelling. Tempers rose, others joined in, and soon blows were struck and a battle began. As the battle raged, the only ones who were uncertain about the dispute were the Flying Fox and the Owl. They conferred and decided that the sensible thing to do was to wait and join the winning side. So they watched the war from the shade of a tree.

The birds and animals fought back and forth as their fortune ebbed and flowed; weapons flashed and were dulled with blood. By and by, the animals were pushed back and the birds, cheered by their success, redoubled their efforts. At this point, the Owl shouted to the Flying Fox, 'Come on, we are bird-men' and the two conspicuously joined the side of the birds. However, the Kangaroo had wisely mustered a fresh band of highly-trained warriors in the rear and soon the course of the battle swayed to the animals. The Flying Fox hissed at the Owl that he had been wrong. The Owl shrugged and replied, 'Do not worry,' as he turned and began bludgeoning the birds with his club. Reluctantly, the Flying Fox followed the Owl's example.

Presently, the Kangaroo and the Eagle-hawk met in combat. Both were so exhausted from the fighting that they could scarcely raise their clubs. The Eagle-hawk said, 'What are we really fighting about, Kangaroo? If I have offended you with my boasting, I am sorry.' The fighting stopped and everyone made up and became friends again. The Flying Fox and the Owl quickly realized the awkwardness of their position, having switched sides in the heat of the battle. To avoid the scorn of their fellow creatures, they went off to hide in the bush. As they went, the light paled and soon the darkness was impenetrable. They did not know that Yhi, the Great Ruler, had been grieved by the fighting among the tribes and had hidden the light as punishment. The Flying Fox and the Owl were puzzled by the darkness, as sunset was many hours away, but neither was distressed because they were both quite comfortable in the darkness. The other creatures, however, soon began to wail because they could not see to gather food or find their way home. Presently, they decided to start fires and were able to find some food within the dim glow of their campfires.

The birds and animals were soon gathered in council to discuss what to do about the darkness. The Flying Fox and Owl were in hiding and, therefore, did not attend. The Lizard was sent to fetch them as the creatures thought that they might be able to help solve the dilemma. Eventually, the Lizard found the Flying Fox and the Owl and asked that they come back with him to the council fires. The Owl refused and said that he was quite comfortable in the darkness. The Flying Fox, feeling guilty for his actions, said he would come to the meeting. Once

there, he confessed that he had been overly influenced by the deceitful Owl. All the creatures forgave him and asked him to help bring back the light. He said that since he was half bird and half animal that he was related to everyone and would help, but that all must remember that the darkness came because of the evil in their hearts. He then asked to borrow a boomerang. The Lizard gave him his. The Flying Fox threw the boomerang to the north and it flew straight and true around the earth and soon returned from the south. Next, he threw the boomerang to the east and it soon returned from the west. Just as he was about to throw the boomerang again, the Laughing Jack (Kookaburra) caught him by the shoulder and asked, 'Why do you keep throwing the returning boomerang? Anyone can do that. What we need is the light to return.' The Flying Fox replied that he was cutting the darkness in two and that he would give the light to the creatures and keep the darkness for himself. He then threw the boomerang with a mighty heave to the west. It flew swiftly and, as it returned from the east, it brought with it the light. The birds and animals thanked him as he flew off into the departing night. The Owl was never forgiven and, to this day, when he flies out in the early dusk, he is mobbed by the other birds.

Why bats inhabit the night

A wealth of human legends and myths attests to man's creative imagination and his attempts to explain occurrences in the natural world around him. In this regard, there are many stories telling why bats are creatures of the night.

One such African myth not only explains why bats occupy the night, but also gives us some insight into the nature of bats. In the beginning of the world, the King called the 'people' together to be given their tasks. The dove was sent to call the Moon and the bat to call the Sun to this meeting. The dove returned promptly with the Moon, but the bat tarried and caused the Sun to arrive very late. The King did not know that the bat was the cause of the Sun's tardiness and, in punishment, he gave the hardest tasks to the Sun and the easiest to the Moon. This angered the Sun who waited for his chance to get revenge on the bat. By and by, the bat's mother became ill and only the Sun had the power to cure her. When the bat asked the Sun for help, the Sun told him to come back before he left his house to start his daily journey across the sky. As was his nature, the bat tarried and so did not arrive at the appointed time. Since the Sun had already started his trek across the sky, he refused to return home to fix the medicine for the bat's mother. Without the healing medicine the bat's mother died. The animals refused to help the bat bury her because the bat had wings, and therefore was not one of them. The birds also refused to help because the bat had teeth, and therefore could not be a bird. Thus, furious with the Sun for having let his mother die and with the animals and birds for not helping bury her, the bat decided to go about at night, rather than the day, lest he meet either the Sun or the other 'people.'

The Kanarese of southwest India believe that long ago bats were a kind of bird. The bats were unhappy with their lot and they went to the temples to pray that they be made into men. After a time, their prayers were answered and they were transformed, but only in part. They acquired hair, teeth, and faces like men, but they retained other aspects of their bird-like appearance. Ashamed to be seen by other birds, they went abroad only at night and, by day, they returned to the temples to pray that they be changed back into birds; people called them bats.

Several tales that concern bats are attributed to Aesop, the famous Greek teller of fables who lived five hundred years before Christ. It is not known, with certainty, that Aesop in fact wrote these anecdotes that portray animals in human situations as a vehicle of imparting insightful virtues and morals. One of these stories provides further insight into the nature of bats and presents another explanation of why bats fly at night rather than in the day. In this story, a bat, a bramble, and a cormorant went into business together to make a fortune through a voyage. The bat borrowed money for the venture, the bramble brought clothes to sell, and the cormorant added brass as his part of the ship's cargo. They set out, but on the voyage the ship encountered a terrible storm and was overturned. The three would-be merchants reached land safely, but the ship and its cargo sank. Ever since, the cormorant flies out to sea and dives in search of his brass. The bramble stands beside the path and catches hold of the garments of those who pass with the hope of finding those clothes that he lost. The bat, for fear of meeting his creditors, never ventures about until night. The moral of this story is: the impression of any notable misfortune will commonly stick by a man as long as he lives.

Another of Aesop's tales resembles the one mentioned above about the bat and owl, the war between the animals and birds, and the separation of night from day. In Aesop's story, the birds and the beasts had a war and the bat, at first, was neutral. When it looked as though the birds would win, the bat joined forces with the birds. However, the beasts rallied and eventually won the war. The bat was brought before a tribunal and was found guilty of desertion. The

sentence of the war council was that the bat be condemned never to see daylight again.

In the religious literature of the Muslims, there is a story that involves Jesus and a bat. Ramadan is a month-long period during which the Muslims observe a fast; they neither eat nor drink water during the hours of sunlight. A Muslim author apparently mistook the fast of Jesus to be an observance of Ramadan; he assumed that the son of God ate after dark. According to the story, Jesus retired, with his disciples, to a secluded spot in the mountains outside of Jerusalem. The mountains obscured the sunset and so it was impossible to determine when the sun sank below the horizon. With God's permission, Jesus fashioned a clay image of a winged creature and breathed life into it. This creature was the bat and it fled immediately into one of the dark caverns of the mountains where it hid so long as the sun shone. Every night, at the moment of sunset, this bat fluttered around Jesus, who then prepared himself and his disciples for prayer after which they supped.

The origin of bats

Just as modern day scientists seek to comprehend the origin and evolution of bats, primitive man also endeavoured to explain the origin of bats in his myths and folk tales. Some of these are quite novel and all are certainly more colourful than the scientific interpretations.

An African legend tells about two sisters who, thousands of years ago, were placed in the world by the gods to create beasts and birds. One of the sisters made gaily coloured birds with beautiful songs to sing and lovely butterflies with gorgeous flowers to eat from. The other sister also made these things, but her birds were drab and plain and the songs that they sang were coarse like that of the crow. Nothing that she made was as perfect or as attractive as the creations of her sister. In a fit of jealousy, she made all sorts of ugly creatures—toads, ugly-faced apes, and bats—to offset the perfections made by her sister.

Stories of conflict or competition between animals and birds seem to be common in man's mythology. We have already described examples of 'animal and bird wars' as found in the aboriginal tales of Australia and the fables of Aesop. The Cherokee Indians of North America explain the origin of bats in another competitive scenario involving a ball game between the animals and birds. In this story, the animals challenged the birds to a great ball game. The captain of the animal team was the Bear, who was so strong and heavy that he could tackle anyone who stood in his way. As he went to the appointed place for the game, he tossed huge logs in the air and boasted about what he would do to the birds when the game began. Likewise, a large Terrapin, with a shell so hard that the heaviest blows could not hurt him, bragged that he would crush anyone who tried to take the ball away from him. He demonstrated by lifting himself, repeatedly, onto his hindlegs and then crashing to the ground with a mighty thud! The Deer proudly proclaimed that he could outrun every other animal.

The birds had the Eagle as their captain as well as the Hawk and Swallow, all swift and strong of flight and unafraid of the boastful animals. Two small creatures, hardly larger than field mice, climbed up the tree where the Eagle and Hawk were perched. They asked the Eagle if they could join the birds' team. The Eagle, seeing that they were four-footed, suggested that they should join the animals. The two creatures said that they had tried, but that the animals had laughed and made fun of them because they were so small.

The Eagle and the Hawk were puzzled about how these tiny creatures could join the birds when they had no wings. At last it was decided that they would make some wings for the little fellows. They remembered that the drum, used in the dance before the ball game, was covered with the skin of a groundhog. From this they cut two pieces of leather which they stretched between cane splints and fastened to the forelegs of one of the small animals. Thus, he became the bat. He took off and the Eagle threw the ball to him. He caught it in his mouth and by the way he dodged and darted, keeping the ball always in the air, the birds realized that he would be one of their best men.

Not enough leather remained to make another pair of wings for the other animal, so the Eagle and the Hawk took hold of him, from opposite sides, and pulled on his skin until it was stretched between his fore and hindfeet. In this way, they made the Flying Squirrel. He, too, proved to be quite agile at carrying the ball from tree to tree.

The ball game began with the birds getting the ball almost at the first toss. The Flying Squirrel caught the ball and carried it up a tree where he threw it to the birds who kept it in the air for some time until it dropped. The Bear rushed to get it, but the Swallow beat him and threw the ball to the Bat who grabbed it and by flying swiftly and dodgingly outmanoeuvered even the Deer and eventually threw it between the poles and won the game for the birds.

The Creek Indians had a similar, but slightly different version of this story. In their tale, the Bat first tried to join the birds, but was driven away. The animals took pity on the Bat and let him join them. In order to make the Bat more like themselves, the animals gave him teeth which allowed him to hold the ball better than the birds. Ultimately, the Bat carried the day for the animals by winning the game.

A Fijian folk tale explains the origin of flying foxes (Mbeka) in a story about a rat and a heron. In this story, the Rat is jealous of the Heron's ability to fly and sets out to trick the Heron and steal his wings. One day while watching the Heron fly over the lagoon, the Rat called out to the Heron. When the Heron came to stand by him on the sandy beach, the Rat giggled about how dull it must be to have to fly everywhere he wanted to go. The Heron expressed surprise and said that he would have thought the Rat would gladly exchange his four short legs for his lovely wings. The Rat said, 'No!' and continued his ruse by proclaiming the virtues of scrambling about on the ground and how sad it was that the Heron could never experience these delights. The Heron replied that slithering about in the dirt and mould was not something that he wished to experience. He told the Rat that he could fly as swift as the wind and boasted that he could fly to a nearby tree, take a short nap, wake up, and fly to the end of the beach before the Rat could run there, no matter how fast he ran. The Rat's heart pounded with anticipation as he accepted the Heron's challenge to the race. Soon they set off; the Heron to nap under the nearby tree and the Rat, supposedly, running to the end of the beach. As the Rat came upon the tree, he found the Heron, fast asleep as he had hoped. He crept up to the sleeping bird and, ever so carefully, began nibbling at the base of its wings. Before long, the Rat had chewed off both wings and with a strong vine he lashed them to his own forelegs. Soon he was flying above the sandy beach. As the sun began to set, the Heron woke up and realized that he had slept longer than he had intended. He got up and started to stretch his wings before taking off for the far end of the beach. To his surprise, he found that his wings were gone and when he looked up he saw the Rat, now a Flying Fox, and knew that he had been tricked.

There is a similar Samoan folk story in which the Rat tricks a winged creature called a 'Peka' into letting him borrow his wings. Once the bargain had been made the Rat, now transformed into a Flying Fox, departed leaving the unhappy Peka without wings. Another Fijian tale illustrates yet another variation of this story. In it, the Rat was the first animal to have wings and the 'Mbeka' (flying fox) was a four-footed animal. Ultimately, through trickery, the Mbeka fooled the Rat into letting him try his wings. After the trade, the Mbeka refused to return with the Rat's wings and the Rat swore he would get his revenge by climbing up into the trees and eating the young of the Mbeka. For this reason, the mother Mbeka always carries her young with her so the Rat will not be able to make good his threat.

Bats as symbols

In addition to being the subject of many of man's myths and superstitions, bats have also played an important role in man's symbolism. The bat is considered to be a 'sex animal' among many of the aboriginal tribes of Australia. Here man is regarded as the brother of the bat and women are usually regarded as sister to a bird such as the Night Jar, Fern Owl, or Superb Warbler. In the Murray River region of New South Wales, it is thought that to kill a bat results in the death of a man. Likewise, to kill a female sex animal, such as a Fern Owl, will result in the death of a woman.

The regard for bats held by the Chinese stands in sharp contrast to that of nearly all other cultures of the world. In the Chinese language, the characters for bat and luck are different, but both are pronounced 'Fu'. By substitution, the figure for a bat stands for good luck and happiness. It is often worked into the designs in Chinese art, handicraft, embroidery, jewellery, and the like (Figs. 10.2 and 10.3). Two bats drawn on a gift signifies good wishes from the giver. Another common talisman, frequently encountered in Chinese designs, is the figure of five bats surrounding the symbol for a peach tree which signifies life. This figure is called 'Wu-fu' and stands for the five great happinesses sought by man: health, wealth, good luck, long life, and tranquillity.

The European distaste for bats caused many Chinese artisans to remove them from goods traded with the western world. In some cases the bat symbols were made so stylized that they were no longer recognizable as bats. With the founding of the People's Republic of China, this and other symbols from the so-called 'old culture' have been systematically suppressed.

In Scandinavia, Germany, and Great Britain, bats were used to drive bad luck away from homes. This was accomplished by nailing a live bat over a doorway or window in much the same manner that some folk hang a horseshoe over such a passageway. In some cases, the power of the charm could be enhanced by carrying the bat three times around the house before it was impaled.

The use of bats as totems is not entirely restricted to primitive societies. Bats, as well as many other animals, are frequently displayed on the coats of arms of a number of European families (Fig. 10.4). In Great Britain and Ireland, the bat or 'rere-mouse' may be found in the heraldic crests of the Baxters, Babington, Stainings, Atton, Josue, Blake, and Wakefield fami-

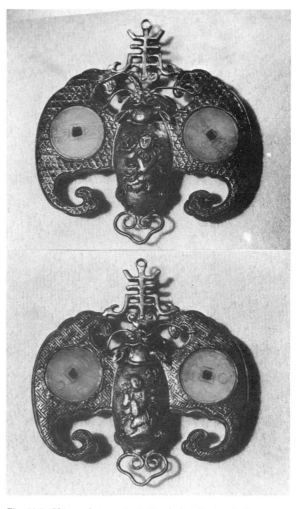

Fig. 10.2 Chinese bat pendant. Symbol at the top is the character for happiness. The jade coins in the wings of the bat indicate wealth. The figure of a boy holding a basket on the bat's body (top) symbolizes prosperity. The figure of a woman holding a lotus flower on the bat's body (bottom photo) symbolizes raising oneself from humble beginnings to the heights of purity.

lies. In the crest of the Daunscourt family, bat wings are shown protruding from the sides of the head of a negroid woman, while in the Bateson family crest, a single outstretched bat wing arises from the coronet. Three bats are displayed on the achievements of the Heyworth and Bascombe families. There does not seem to be any significance associated with the use of the bat in these heralds. On the other hand, the use of a bat in the family crest for the Swiss Schaffhausen family does seem to have an understandable reason. Schaffhausen means 'sheepfold' and perhaps this family adopted the bat symbol from the custom of impaling a bat, for good luck, over the doorway of a house.

Fig. 10.3 (Top) Antique Chinese teapot with Wu-Fu symbol of five bats (only three are shown). (Bottom) Chinese jade bat symbol that was sewn onto clothing.

Finally, several squadrons of the Royal Air Force include bats in their badges. The 153rd Fighter Squadron shows a bat on a six-pointed star from the arms of Northern Ireland where this group spent most of their operational life. Their motto 'Noctividus' means 'We see by night.' The badge of the 9th Bomber Squadron has a bat and the motto 'Per Noctem Volamus' or 'By night we fly.'

BATS AND PUBLIC HEALTH

Ranking high with the general misconception that most bats are bloodthirsty vampires is the quite erroneous notion that bats are filthy, disease-ridden animals that seriously threaten human health and well-being. Indeed, some bats are involved in the epidemiology (incidence and distribution) of several important diseases, such as rabies and histoplasmosis, which may be transmitted to humans, directly or indirectly, as well as to other warm-blooded animals.

But the general attitude that all bats are the bearers of rampant human pestilence is simply not true, and although they have been found to harbour a variety of harmful or potentially harmful organisms, disease transmission to humans is rare. Despite this, sensational, careless or inaccurate accounts of bats can stimulate public antipathy to the point where they may be unnecessarily harassed or even destroyed.

For the most part, the biology of disease-causing microbial agents is no different from that of the host organisms in or on which they occur. Just as the populations of host organisms are controlled and regulated within the context of a natural, dynamic state of equilibrium, so too are the populations of microbial agents. The manifest expression of a disease is the self-limiting consequence of imbalances in this dynamic equilibrium. Such imbalances occur when the populations of the host organism, vector, or the microbial agent itself, increase beyond their natural bounds. This causes an increase in the infection or reinfection rate due to an increase in the likelihood of exposure. Aside from the obvious effects of overcrowding and stress, an overly large population may over use a food resource and cause it to fail which in turn may trigger an epidemic manifestation of disease. Most natural populations of wild animals, bats included, exist within these dynamic limits. The fact that many species of bats live in large masses of hundreds, thousands, or in some cases, millions, of individuals, without being destroyed by infectious diseases, attests to this equilibrium between hosts and their microbial community.

Humans and their domesticated animals are in equilibrium with certain epidemiologic agents, but frequently become susceptible to others of which they are not the natural host organism. Such is the case with a few bat-borne conditions, since bats are a native faunal element often encountered by man and/or his livestock. Bats, and some kinds of rodents, are of particular interest because they are so ubiquitous, highly mobile, and often take up residence in human dwellings thus increasing the likelihood of epidemiologic contact. Another factor of interest is the fact that bats being mammals, are distantly related to man and therefore susceptible to some human diseases. As a result, bats may become the inadvertent vector for some human illness.

Microbial, disease-causing organisms that have been found in bats or guano (faecal deposits) in bat roosts fall into several classes. These include bacterial agents, fungal or mycotic agents, and viral agents. In addition to these potential disease-causing microorganisms, bats harbour an array of endo- and ectoparasitic organisms that may cause diseases or carry one or more of the above listed microbial agents.

Wakefield   Heyworth

Fig. 10.4 (Left) Herald of the Wakefield family showing a bat crest. (Right) Herald of the Heyworth family showing three bats on the achievement and bat wings in the crest.

These include protozoan parasites, parasitic flatworms and roundworms (helminthic parasites), and arthropod parasites.

Bacterial diseases

Very little investigation of the bacterial community of bats has been accomplished. A number of human and livestock disease-causing bacteria have been found in bats, but the extent to which these pose a serious epidemiologic public health threat is not known. Generally non-pathogenic, gram-negative, and short rod bacteria (*Klebsiella, Aerobacter, Serratia*) have been isolated from the intestines of *Pteronotus parnellii* (Mormoopidae), *Carollia perspicillata* (Phyllostomidae), and *Molossus major* (Molossidae). These are widespread soil bacteria and their occurrence in bats is not unique or especially surprising.

Eight serious to moderately serious human pathogenic bacterial agents have been isolated in some bats. The incidence of these bacterial organisms appears to be quite random and sporadic. *Salmonella*, which causes typhoid and related diseases, has been found in several phyllostomids (*Glossophaga soricina, Sturnira lilium*, and *Artibeus lituratus*) and in *Molossus*

major. Several individuals of an Australian species of *Pteropus* were fatally infected with *Salmonella typhimurium*, in the laboratory, but attempts to cause contagion among individuals were largely unsuccessful. This study was conducted in an effort to find a disease-causing agent that could be used to control crop pest populations of *Pteropus*.

The dysenteric bacteria *Shigella* has been isolated in one individual of *Molossus bondae*. The African molossid, *Tadarida pumila*, and the European noctule (*Nyctalus noctula*) have been infected experimentally (in the laboratory) with the plague-causing bacteria *Yersinia* (=*Pasteurella*). Bacilli of the bovine-type have been found in several captive individuals of an Indian fruit bat (*Pteropus giganteus*). This variety of tuberculin bacteria usually reaches man through unpasteurized milk from tubercular cows. The source of the infection in these captive bats was not determined, but it may be transmitted by an airborne route. Some wild-caught specimens of the Mexican Free-tailed bat (*Tadarida brasiliensis*), from a single cave in Arizona were found to have a rather high, asymptomatic, incidence (approximately 10 per cent) of another variety (Group III) of *Mycobacterium* in their livers. *Mycobacterium* causes tuberculosis and leprosy. The incidence of tuberculosis in bats might well have resulted from cross-infection by an avian strain from birds inhabiting the same cave. The leprosy bacillus (*Mycobacterium leprae*) has not been isolated from bats, but vampire attacks on leprotic persons have been recorded in French Guiana. It is possible that vampires might mechanically transport this disease from one person to another.

Leptospirosis (Weil's disease) is a bacterial disease found throughout the world in man and in many wild and domestic animals. Among other symptoms, this bacterium causes severe fever, jaundice, haemorrhaging of skin and mucous membranes and may result in death. Various species of *Leptospira* have been reported from pteropodids (*Pteropus* and *Cynopterus*) and a handful of vespertilionid bats. The epidemiological role of bats in leptospirosis is not clear and the evidence seems to suggest that bats, like man and domestic animals, are incidental hosts of this microbial agent.

Relapsing fever in man is caused by several varieties of the bacterial organism *Borrelia recurrentis*. It is transmitted, mechanically, by parasitic arthropods such as ticks and body lice. Rodents and other wild mammals apparently comprise the major natural reservoir for this infection. A number of species of *Borrelia* (with unknown relationships to human disease) have been isolated in bats. In Europe, these include: *Rhinolophus ferrumequinum*, *Nyctalus noctula*, and *Pipistrellus pipistrellus*; in Africa, *Eidolon helvum*, *Cardioderma cor*, and *Scotophilus kuhlii*; and in the Americas, *Antrozous pallidus* and *Natalus tumidirostris*. Other species of bats have been experimentally inoculated with *Borrelia recurrentis*. Notable among these is the Common vampire, *Desmodus rotundus*. However, laboratory attempts to cause contagion between vampires and pigs have been unsuccessful.

Finally, there is a large group of bacterial agents that are obligate intracellular parasites; that is, they live and reproduce only inside living cells. These are called rickettsial bacteria; not to be confused with 'rickets' which is a disease caused by a vitamin deficiency. Many rickettsial bacteria are transmitted, mechanically, by arthropods. *Bartonella bacilliformis* causes Oroya fever in humans living in the Andean region of South America. This bacterium has not been reported in any bats, but another species *Bartonella rochalimai* is known from the red blood cells of *Carollia perspicillata* (Phyllostomidae). *Grahamella* is a bacterium related to *Bartonella* and it occurs in many non-human mammals including a number of bat species. None is known to cause human disease. *Coxiella burneti* is the causative agent of the severe, but rarely fatal 'Q' fever. It has been isolated in an *Eptesicus serotinus* from Morocco and a bat (species

unknown) from Tashkent in southern USSR. Rocky Mountain Spotted fever, *Rickettsia rickettsi*, caused death in two Brazilian bats, *Carollia perspicillata* and *Histiotus velatus*, and a Mexican species, *Artibeus lituratus*, which had been experimentally infected. Similar inoculations of this rickettsial pathogen in the Common vampire (*Desmodus rotundus*) failed to cause any reaction.

Although it is apparent that the causative agents of a number of bacterial diseases have been isolated from bats, it cannot be stressed too strongly that so far as is known there is little evidence that their possible transmission from bats to man poses a serious health hazard. Many are common to other mammals as well, and infect bats in just the same way that other mammals, including man, become infected. In other words, bats are victim to this natural event, and in this respect are no different from their other mammalian relatives.

Fungal or mycotic diseases

The most common fungal or mycotic disease shared by bats and man appears to be histoplasmosis, a respiratory illness caused by inhaling the spores of the soil fungus *Histoplasma capsulatum*. The fungus is not transmitted directly, but is found in soils containing much organic matter, especially in sheltered spots such as the roosts of birds and bats. It produces a respiratory infection that may prove fatal to humans although serious infections are rare. It has been reported from the United States, Mexico, Central and South America, and Africa. The fungus has also been isolated from bat guano in Roumania and Malaya. Human infection is common in some areas, usually as a mild respiratory illness. The fungus does not survive as a rule in hot dry attics and human infection from bats occurs most frequently in dusty caves. The most important sources of infection appear to be bird roosts. Histoplasmosis is almost certainly the 'cave disease' or 'mine fever' contracted by Mexican guano diggers in the past. The high mortality among these miners probably resulted from the thick, spore-burdened dust produced in mining and the deep breathing involved in heavy work. The fungus is more common in tropical, humid conditions and may be found in an enclosed roost, for instance in a cave, a building, or in a hollow tree. Such roosts should only be entered or disturbed with great care and suitable precautions. The use of a mask or respirator that can remove particles as small as two microns in diameter in such places or when removing guano from a roost will reduce the risk of infection.

A number of other disease-causing fungal organisms are associated with guano deposits of bats although none is uniquely involved with bats. Blastomycosis causes a highly dangerous granulomatous disease of mucous membranes (gastrointestinal tract, lymph nodes, skin, and lungs). The agent has been reported in many Latin American countries and has been recovered from the faeces of *Artibeus lituratus* and *Natalus tumidirostris*. *Tadarida brasiliensis* has been experimentally infected and found to pass viable yeast cells in its faeces. Similarly, *Scopulariopsis* has been found in the guano deposits of some Colombian bat species. Spores of *Cryptococcus neoformans* also may be found in dusty guano deposits; it causes a chronic, usually fatal, meningitis. A new species of yeast-like fungus (*Candida chiropterorum*) has been described from the organs of *Mormoops megalophylla*, *Desmodus rotundus*, and *Natalus tumidirostris* from Colombia. It is thought to be pathogenic for humans from studies based on infection responses in laboratory animals. Another nonpathogenic species, *Candida parapsilosis*, has been recovered from the liver of a *Leptonycteris sanborni* in the southwestern United States. *Torulopsis glabrata*, a common fungus of skin and mucous membranes of humans, was also found in this individual of *Leptonycteris*. Dermatophytes (ringworm agents) have been found on several bat species of the New World, Great Britain, and western Europe.

Many of the fungal agents mentioned above are endemic soil saprophytes in the areas where they are found. They are not specifically associated with bats and may be found in any soil environments enriched by animal faeces. Nonetheless, they may cause public health concern especially in situations where large groups of bats occupy human dwellings but apart from their reported occurrence there is no evidence to support this notion.

Viral diseases

Bats are also infected by a wide variety of different types of viruses, at least 28 having been reported. In addition, antibodies for another 32 viruses have been discovered in the blood serum of bats. The virology of bats is virtually in its infancy and is further confounded by the fact that most bats are small in size and samples of blood serum are frequently too small to permit extensive assay.

The colonial habits of many bat species provide a highly efficient arena for the transmission of viruses from bat to bat by arthropods such as biting or blood-sucking insects and ticks, through aerosol suspension in the atmosphere of poorly ventilated roosts, or through casual bites inflicted during the aggressive activity that occurs among densely crowded individuals. Many of the viruses encountered in

bats are not often pathogenic and many are not pathogenic in man or only mildly so. However, some such as Venezuelan equine encephalitis, Western equine encephalitis, and Yellow fever virus may cause death in man or domestic mammals. Most bat viral agents occur only in specific and frequently very localized regions of the world as indicated by their names; for example, Chikungunya virus (Asia and Africa), Rio Bravo virus (southwestern United States), Japanese B encephalitis virus (western Asia), Mount Suswa bat virus (Kenya), Tacaribe virus (Trinidad), Montana *Myotis* leukoencephalitis virus (Montana).

Bats may be important in the natural history of various arboviruses (viruses transmitted by biting or blood-sucking arthropods). These viruses reproduce and multiply in the arthropod vector and are reintroduced into a host (bat, other mammal, or bird) when it is subsequently bitten. A number of experiments have been performed, in which bats, of various species, were inoculated, either by aerosol or injection, with viruses. Virus-free mosquitoes were then allowed to feed on these infected bats. After a period of time, the mosquitoes were examined and found to be infected. It was also found that uninfected bats could become infected by eating infected mosquitoes. Many viruses apparently are capable of overwintering in hibernating bats.

So far as man is concerned, the most important virus carried by bats is that which causes rabies, an acute and extremely serious disease of the nervous system that is one of the most terrifying and unpleasant of human infections. Once clinical symptoms have developed, the disease is almost always fatal.

Rabies virus is found almost everywhere in the world except Great Britain, Australia, Hawaii, and certain other Pacific islands. The disease is most frequently observed in wild and domestic carnivores (dogs and cats); although any warm-blooded animal is susceptible to rabies. It is transmitted in the saliva of an infected animal, usually through a bite. The virus migrates to nerve tissue where it travels along the centre of the nerve fibre to the spinal cord and finally to the hippocampal region of the brain. Here it multiplies and eventually spreads outward along other nerve tracks to infect almost all other body tissues including the salivary glands. Incubation periods in most mammals usually vary from one to three months, but extremes of ten days to 15 months have been reported. The symptomatic phase of the infection may be expressed in one of two ways or, in some cases, both. The aggressive or excitative phase is one most commonly associated with rabies. During this phase the infected animal wanders aimlessly and viciously attacks any object. This phase is often accompanied by a frothing of the mouth and an aversion to water (hydrophobia). The paralytic phase is a more docile phase in which the affected animal is listless. The symptoms may last for three to four days and eventually the animal becomes convulsive and dies. It is not hard to imagine that an infected animal or human might appear to be possessed by demons. Also the aggressive behavioural transformation of a person bitten by a rabid animal might well be the basis for many tales concerning werewolves and vampires.

The rabies virus or similar viruses have been found in numerous species of bats in the New World, with many fewer reports from Europe and Asia. Onward transmission of the virus by bats is generally confined to other bats. However, because of their blood-feeding habits, infected vampire bats of Latin America are responsible for the direct infection of humans and domestic livestock. Very rarely indeed, rabies may be contracted directly (through bite) or indirectly (through aerosol) from other species of bats. The disease usually, if not always, takes a paralytic course when contracted from a bat bite. Again, there are reasonable parallels between this biological observation and the listless, 'undead' victims of Stoker's Count Dracula.

European colonists attributed deaths among humans and livestock in the New World to the 'venomous bites' of vampire bats as early as the sixteenth century. However, it was not until the early part of the twentieth century that the role of these bats in the epidemiology of rabies was fully recognized. Since then, the incidence of vampire-borne rabies has been demonstrated in many lowland areas of the Neotropics from Argentina and Chile to north-western Mexico. Vampire bats are especially important vectors of rabies virus since it can be present in their saliva for long periods and is readily transmitted to the vampire's victim in the course of normal feeding. The Common vampire (*Desmodus rotundus*) is a serious pest of domestic livestock, especially cattle, because they are usually gathered together in large herds and easily accessible to vampires. It has been suggested that there has been a general increase in the size of vampire populations since the introduction of large numbers of domestic animals into Latin America by European colonization.

The World Health Organization has shown that vampire-borne rabies and other vampire-borne livestock diseases are a major cause of death in cattle in Latin America in addition to being an important obstacle to the economic expansion of agriculture. Estimates of the annual cattle mortality due to vampire-borne rabies range from one-half million head (approximately $50 million) to several million head (approximately $100 million). These are direct costs and costs due to indirect losses, including malnutrition, may approach a quarter of a billion dollars. Prior to 1950-1960, human mortality to vampire-borne rabies was relatively high in certain areas; 89 cases reported in Trinidad 1925-1937 and 31 cases in Mexico 1951-1961. Fewer cases of human rabies attributed to bats have been reported from areas where vampire bats do not occur, the United States reporting a total of no more than nine in 30 years, while only one case is known from Canada. Public health measures, including prophylactic immunization, have reduced human deaths considerably. Likewise, vaccination has been the most effective method of combating the problem of rabies in livestock. Other control measures include destroying vampire roosts, by trying to repel them, or by bat-proofing to deny them access to potential victims. Unfortunately the former approach, like so many other attempts to exterminate a specific pest species, indiscriminately sacrifices many beneficial species. For example, cave fumigation or cave destruction has been employed for vampire control in Venezuela. This practice kills vampires as well as many insectivorous bats which are important in the natural control of insects in these regions which are often malarial areas. Furthermore, vampires also roost in trees and other non-cave sites which are not affected by cave-control measures.

The rabies virus has been detected in 26 out of 40 insectivorous species of bats in the United States with reports from every state except Hawaii and Alaska. However, it is probably true to say that the incidence of rabies in the bat population of America is no higher than the incidence of rabies among the remainder of its mammal population. For example, an informed estimate suggests that about 1 in every 1000 bats in California has rabies. In addition, rabies has been found in many non-vampire species in Latin America. Outside of the New World, rabies virus has been reported in several insectivorous bats from Germany, Yugoslavia, Turkey and possibly Hungary, and from a fruit bat (*Cynopterus brachyotis*) in Thailand. There is some doubt attached to the German, Yugoslavian and Hungarian reports. A human death in India in 1955 was attributed to a bat bite, and there is a report of a similar human infection from Africa. There does not appear to be a widespread infection of rabies in the bat populations of the Old World and here they are not considered important vectors of the disease. Although initially bats and especially vampires were thought to be immune and therefore far more dangerous carriers of rabies, current evidence suggests that bats succumb to the disease just as do other warm-blooded animals and do not act as an immune reservoir of the virus.

Nor do bats other than vampires appear to be seriously implicated in the transmission of rabies to other wildlife.

No more than eight human deaths have been directly attributed to insectivorous bats in the United States and Canada in the past 30 years. Most of these have resulted from bites received while handling a moribund bat. A second means of transmission, exposure to airborne virus in a densely crowded and poorly ventilated bat cave, has been blamed in two human deaths in Texas. The low incidence reported for human aerosol transmission suggests that the risk is low. Certainly it does not seem a major public health hazard except where an enormous population of bats is concentrated into a relatively small area. Unfortunately, there seems to be a lack of objectivity in considering the implications of bat rabies, especially in the United States. These figures suggest that at least in that country the intensity of public fear and feeling in relation to this possible threat is exaggerated. In fact, more people have died annually as a result of attacks by dogs, bee stings, or lawn mower accidents than this 30-year total of deaths through bat rabies. These experiences suggest that sick bats, lying on the ground, should not be handled, particularly in North and South America. And, caves or other roosts in which there are dense populations of bats, especially those of the Mexican Free-tailed bat (*Tadarida brasiliensis*), should be avoided.

The introduction of strict quarantine regulations for imported dogs and cats together with measures to control the dog population led to the disappearance of rabies from Great Britain by 1903 although the disease was formerly widespread. Since then there have been only a few, sporadic occurrences in illegally imported pets or in dogs either infected in quarantine or in which the virus may have survived the quarantine period. The theory has been advanced that bats might introduce the disease into Great Britain from France, where it is spreading. This appears to be a possibility, but the likelihood of such an introduction seems small and remote. It involves not only the occurrence of the virus in the bats of the adjacent parts of continental Europe, but also the possibility that rabid bats would migrate or be blown across the Channel to transmit the disease further by biting other bats, or, falling moribund to the ground and biting an inquisitive fox, dog, cat, or human.

Protozoan diseases

Many protozoan (single-celled) organisms have been found as natural parasites of bats; many more will undoubtedly be discovered by future study. Relatively few chiropteran protozoan parasites are known

to be harmful to man or to domestic animals. Most of these protozoans are transmitted mechanically by way of an intermediate insect vector such as a mosquito, kissing bug, or fly. A number of malarial parasites (*Plasmodium*, *Hepatocystis*, *Nycteria*, and *Polychromophilus*) have been found in the blood of bats throughout the world. However, none of these species appears to be involved in human malaria which is caused by *Plasmodium vivax*, *P. malariae*, *P. falciparum*, and/or *P. ovale*. The flagellated protozoan *Trypanosoma* is associated with a number of human and livestock diseases such as sleeping sickness, Chagas disease, murrina, and Mal de Caderas. Nineteen species of trypanosomes have been reported in 52 species of bats representing ten families of tropical and subtropical regions of the world. Chagas disease is caused by *T. cruzi* and many bat species have been found to harbour *cruzi*-like parasites. The pathogenicity of these *cruzi*-like parasites is not well understood; they do not appear to cause human infection. On the other hand, *T. hippicum* and *T. equinum* (protozoan agents for murrina and Mal de Caderas, respectively) have been found in the vampire bat *Desmodus rotundus*. Again, the blood-feeding habit of these bats makes them an efficient vector for the transmission of these two diseases that infect cattle and horses. Apparently, vampires are infected when they take a blood meal from an infected victim. The trypanosome then reproduces in the vampire and invades various organs, including the salivary glands. The parasite is then reintroduced into uninfected horses or cattle via vampire attack.

Helminthic parasites

A wide variety of parasitic flatworms (Trematodes and Cestodes) and roundworms (Nematodes) have been reported from bat species. These are all internal parasites with complex life cycles. Tapeworms are usually found in the intestine, whereas flukes (Trematodes) may also reside in the gall bladder, liver, or lungs. Roundworms may occupy these same body regions as well as the general body cavity, urinary bladder, or bloodstream. The life cycle of flukes usually involves one or more intermediate hosts which may be an insect or, in some cases, a mollusc (snail or clam). In the case of bats, these parasites are acquired when the bat eats an infected insect. Others of these helminthic parasites have direct life cycles or have larval stages in soil or other organic material such as guano. Infection from these may occur as the result of grooming behaviour. Many of these parasites are specific to bats, although several human or domestic animal helminths have been encountered in bats. The latter are thought to be either accidental or spurious. Some bat trematodes have been recovered from bat predators such as the raccoon which presumably acquire these by eating infected bats. A fluke (Trematode) known to occur in *Tadarida plicata*, *Rhinopoma microphyllum*, and *Scotoecus pallidus* of India has been found in some Indian dogs. Likewise, a snake endoparasite was recovered from the carnivorous phyllostomid *Phyllostomus discolor*. Generally, insectivorous bats have a richer fauna of these endoparasites than do exclusively frugivorous species. At any rate, bats do not appear to be a significant reservoir for any human helminthic parasites.

Arthropod parasites

Bats are parasitized by a wide array of ectoparasitic arthropods. Many of these parasites such as bat flies (Nycteribiidae and Streblidae) and various groups of mites (Spinturnicidae, Macronyssidae, and Laelapidae) are tightly associated, or nearly so, with one to several bat species. Other arthropod parasites are not so host specific. These include mosquitoes, assassin bugs, ticks, and fleas. Many of the arthropod parasites may be important vectors (intermediate hosts) or mechanical transporters of the bacterial, viral, or protozoan agents discussed above.

Arachnids. These include ticks and mites. Some mites spend their entire life cycle on the bat host, whereas, others may spend only a portion of their life cycle on the host. For the most part, mites occupy specific sites on the bat host. For example, gastronyssids, ereynetids, and some trombiculids occupy feeding sites in the nasal passages of bats. Certain macronyssids (*Radfordiella*) feed on the periodontal tissue between the teeth and gums of phyllostomids such as *Leptonycteris nivalis* (but not *Leptonycteris sanborni*), *Monophyllus redmani*, and *Anoura geoffroyi*. These infections may ultimately result in the loss of teeth. Other mites may be found in tightly packed clusters in the ears, at the base of the tail, around the eyes, or on the wings. The unusual antibrachial sacs in the wings of some New World emballonurids are frequently filled with small red or yellow mites. Wing mites are rarely found on the furred parts of the body and mites found in body fur usually do not wander onto the wing membranes.

Occasionally, bat mites may find their way onto humans. This may occur in situations where bats occupy human dwellings or when humans intrude into bat roosts. These displaced mites may bite their accidental host and there are records of reactions to these bites ranging from mild dermatitis and, very rarely, to rather serious, but undiagnosed diseases.

Hard- and soft-bodied ticks have been reported on many kinds of bats. These usually occupy feeding sites on the lower back, tail and wing membranes, and occasionally on the face and ears. These bat ticks may attack humans and inflict painful bites. Such attacks may occur when bats occupy human dwellings or when people enter bat caves. Several rickettsial bacteria have been found in bat ticks in Egypt and several arboviruses have been found in bat ticks in Malaysia and India.

Hemipterans. These insects are generally referred to as 'true bugs.' Several species of assassin bugs have been found in association with bats in Brazil and Colombia. It is rather curious, but it has been suggested that bats may have been the original hosts of the insect family Cimicidae that includes the 'bedbugs.' Three species of bedbug are currently shared by bats and man. These are the cosmopolitan *Cimex lectularius*, the tropicopolitan *C. hemipterus*, and the west African *Leptocimex boueti*. It is speculated that *Cimex lectularius* became adapted to man when caves and similar shelters were major human

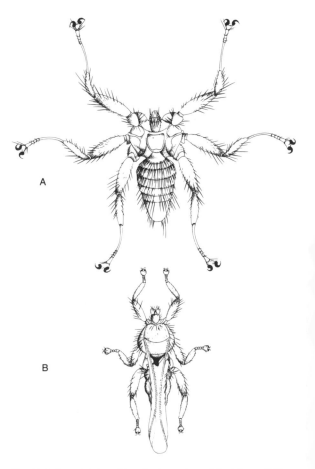

Fig. 10.5 Parasitic bat flies. A, A member of the Nycteribiidae, Penicillidia fulvida; B, a member of the Streblidae, Brachytarsina africana.

habitations. Although *Cimex lectularius* has been shown to be associated, naturally or experimentally, with 28 human disease agents, there is no evidence to suggest that it is an important vector between bats and man. Some other cimicids may be important vectors in transmitting trypanosomes between bats.

Diptera. Two families of flies (Nycteribiidae and Streblidae) are specially adapted to live on bats (Fig. 10.5). The former have lost their wings and crawl, spider-like, on and in the fur of their host. Streblids have reduced wings and are capable of short flights. They, too, scramble, spider-like, on the membranes and fur of the bat. Both families feed on the blood of their host and are therefore potential vectors or mechanical transporters of various disease agents. The females of these two families retain the eggs within the abdomen until they hatch. The larvae are then deposited on the host, an adaptation increasing their chances for survival. The genus *Ascodipteron* is an interesting extreme in dipteran parasitism (Fig. 10.6). After mating the female makes a small hole in the skin of the host, behind the ear, in the genital region, along the forearm, or one of the phalanges. It enters this hole, head first, sheds its wings and all but the basal joint of the leg. The body enlarges enormously and eventually produces a single larva to continue the life cycle.

The Mystacinobiidae are very exceptional among bat flies. The single genus and species, *Mystacinobia zelandica*, has been found solely in association with the Short tailed bat (*Mystacina*), the only representative of the family Mystacinidae, which is completely restricted to New Zealand. Unlike the true bat flies, *Mystacinobia* lives in the bat roost and not on the bat; it lays eggs instead of producing live larvae. The eggs are laid in fissures and beetle tunnels in the hollow trees where *Mystacina* roost. The flies and developing larvae live on the organic material that accumulates in the guano in which yeasts and other fungi can grow. Also unlike other bat flies, *Mystacinobia* is not adapted to sucking blood from the host. The claws, however, are adapted for movement over and in the fur. The bat roost evidently provides an ideal environment. Since they lack wings, these bat flies are entirely dependent on their bat hosts for transportation; those left in an abandoned roost die. There is no indication that any of these bat flies are involved in disease transmission to man. However, there is strong evidence that a Malayan streblid may be a vector for the bat malarial protozoan *Hepatocystis*.

Malarial organisms may be transmitted between bats by certain cave-dwelling mosquitoes. Other human diseases with which bats have been associated may also be carried by mosquitoes. Several

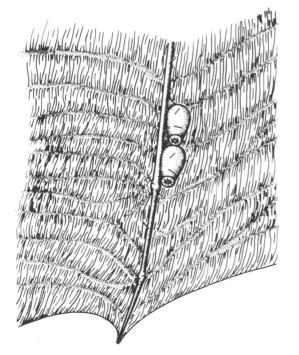
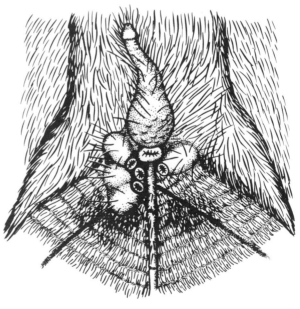

Fig. 10.6 Two Ascodipteron *along the fourth finger of* Emballonura furax–(Emballonuridae). *Four* Ascodipteron *embedded in the skin around the tail and genitalia of* Hipposideros diadema (Hipposideridae).

species of blowflies reportedly lay their eggs on bats which result in myiases; that is, larval invasion of living tissue. These are of little consequence as disease agents in humans. However, wounds caused by vampire bats are frequently invaded by the larvae of the Screwworm Fly (*Callitroga*). Livestock infected by screwworms invariably die and occasionally humans are fatally infected. In some parts of Latin America, livestock mortality due to screwworm invasion of vampire wounds may be as serious as rabies.

Other arthropods. Fleas are rather common on bats, especially those that live in large closely packed colonies. Normally these do not leave their bat host but, *Ischnopsyllus elongatus*, a bat flea commonly found on the European noctule (*Nyctalus noctula*), has also been found on a dog. One species of bat flea, *Rhynchopsyllus pulex*, represents another extreme in parasitism. It lives on free-tailed bats of the genus *Molossus* in South America. The adult female burrows into the skin of the bat and then sheds her legs so that any further movement on the host is impossible. An African bat flea, *Lagaropsylla anciauxi*, found on the Free-tailed bat (*Tadarida ansorgei*) reportedly has attacked man.

A rather different association exists between the earwig *Arixenia esau* and its host, the Hairless bat (*Cheiromeles torquatus*) of southeastern Asia. This insect lives in the roost of these bats and evidently feeds on the fragments of skin and body secretions of its hairless host. This is probably a symbiotic relationship, one of mutual benefit to both organisms, rather than a parasitic relationship. These earwigs also occur on two other furred species of bats that also roost with *Cheiromeles*. There is no indication that there is any pathology associated with this relationship.

Finally, the guano deposits of some bats support large populations of dermestid beetles. These carrion feeders eat fresh guano and any sick or dead bats that happen to fall to the floor of the roost. It is quite possible that these beetles could be contaminated with rabies virus when they feed on infected carcasses and thus become a potential mechanical transport agent for the disease.

OTHER NUISANCES

Bats in buildings and caves

Bats roosting in buildings can occasionally pose considerable problems and not uncommonly form quite substantial colonies that can become a nuisance through noise, smell, and droppings. Depending on the site of the colony, the accumulation of guano and urine may become quite large, piling up on attic floors and perhaps falling into inaccessible parts of the building such as wall spaces. The accompanying odour can be quite pungent, but it is not dangerous. In addition, the excreta may seep through cracks and crevices causing brown stains on ceilings and walls. More importantly, cockroaches and other insects may be attracted to these guano deposits and further perpetuate the nuisance. Risk of food contamination may occur when bats take up residence in hotels, restaurants, or warehouses. Although there may be certain potential human health risks (as discussed above) associated with bat occupation of buildings, the greatest annoyance is usually the noise and/or unsightly odours and stains that they cause.

This said, it has to be pointed out that factors such as these usually apply only to very large colonies, especially in hot, humid climates, and, so far as health risks are concerned, basically only to areas where rabies is an important consideration. Most colonies of bats in houses or similar buildings are small or relatively so; their droppings are usually dry and harmless (and can be sometimes collected on a polyethylene sheet beneath the roost) and the bats themselves do no damage to timber, paintwork or to other parts of the structure of the building. Many people whose houses or outbuildings are colonized welcome the presence of the bats and recognize their value as an integral part of the environment, rather than as a nuisance to be eliminated as quickly as possible.

Maternity colonies in buildings often disperse once the young bats are weaned and independent. In temperate regions, bats may occupy buildings during the summer months and depart when temperatures become colder. Some hibernating species may move into buildings during the late fall and winter. In tropical and subtropical regions, many species of Free-tailed bats of the genus *Tadarida* frequently reside in human dwellings as do a number of other bat species.

Bats living in caves are not a usual nuisance for the average citizen. However, persons who enter bat-inhabited caves may face a number of potential hazards. By their nature, caves are inherently dangerous places that should not be entered casually. Thick, fermenting, and foul-smelling deposits of guano may cause treacherous footing and conceal rocks and pitfalls. These organic deposits usually support a rich flora of fungal organisms such as *Histoplasma capsulatum*. In areas where rabies is endemic in the bat populations, the virus may be present as a pathogenic aerosol. Also, these guano accumulations may support a wide variety of arthropods ranging from mites and millipedes to cockroaches and dermestid beetles.

Bites from any or all of these arthropods may transmit various pathogens to the unsuspecting visitor.

The atmosphere of poorly ventilated bat caves often contains high levels of ammonia produced by the decomposing guano. Ammonia and/or carbon dioxide concentrations may be so high as to impede normal breathing and cause nausea. Humans can endure ammonia concentrations of 85-100 parts per million (ppm) for a one hour period of time. The Californian leaf-nosed bat (*Macrotus californicus*) reportedly can tolerate 3000 ppm and the Mexican Free-tailed bat (*Tadarida brasiliensis*) can live in caves with ammonia concentrations as high as 5000 ppm. Experimental studies on *T. brasiliensis* and the Little Brown bat (*Myotis lucifugus*) have shown that, in these high levels of ammonia, the mucous in the respiratory tract tends to neutralize it. The mechanism by which this occurs is not well understood, but it is thought to be influenced by carbon dioxide retained in solution or, perhaps, by protein action. In addition, carbon dioxide may be retained in the blood where it may serve to neutralize alkali concentrations resulting from inhaling ammonia. This physiological adaptation apparently maintains an equilibrium between carbon dioxide and ammonia thereby protecting the respiratory and circulatory systems from the corrosive and toxic effects of these poisonous gases. In addition to these physiological effects, ammonia concentrations (even low levels) may enhance the susceptibility to airborne disease agents. Chickens were found to be doubly susceptible to airborne Newcastle virus exposure after several days in an ammonia (20 ppm) atmosphere. Rabies, histoplasmosis, and perhaps other airborne pathogens might be expected to be similarly augmented.

Bats and fruit crops

Fruit-eating bats belong to two different tropical and subtropical families: the Phyllostomidae (Microchiroptera) in the New World and the Pteropodidae (Megachiroptera) in the Old World. Although the members of these families consume many native fruits not generally used by man, their tastes occasionally include fruits that are raised commercially or used by local human populations. These include mango, guava, banana, papaya, breadfruit, avocado, and sapota. While fruit-eating bats may cause local damage to fruit crops, research suggests that they do not cause widespread damage and are, perhaps more of an annoyance than a serious pest. A manager of a cocoa plantation in New Guinea was concerned about damage to ripening cocoa pods by birds and bats. He painstakingly recorded, on a daily basis, the damage done over an entire year. Calculations considering the average market value of the cocoa for that year indicated a loss of between $100 and $200 per month. This is a pittance compared to the thousands of dollars lost to *Pantorhytes* (a flightless weevil) and a fungus that causes 'cocoa die back.'

Balanced against the apparent agricultural nuisance, is the fact that many tropical and subtropical fruit plants are either pollinated by nectar-eating bats or their seeds are dispersed by fruit-eating bats. Some tropical trees have flowers that are especially adapted for bat pollination. Other plants owe their distribution and dispersal to the tastes of bats for their large fruits which are often too heavy to be transported by birds or too pendulous for many arboreal mammals to reach.

Bats and aircraft

High speed collisions with birds are well known hazards to aircraft in flight. Collisions with bats are generally a rarer event and usually cause little damage to the airframe. However, there is at least one serious case where bats have caused considerable damage to aircraft. This involved Randolph Air Force Base in Texas. Randolph Field is located approximately 20 km northwest of Bracken Cave which is occupied by a huge population (40 million at peak times) of Mexican Free-tailed bats (*Tadarida brasiliensis*). Many jet engine failures occurred when one or more bats were ingested by the engines and occasionally windscreens were shattered. The majority of the bat strikes (99 percent) occurred during take-off and landing, below 2500 feet (over half of these were below 1000 feet). The loss of a number of multimillion dollar fighter jets prompted the United States Air Force to finance a study of the Bracken Cave bats. The researcher used the Randolph Field radar to study the flight behaviour of these bats and found there were predictable patterns. At dusk, when the bats left the cave to forage, they formed a radar-detectable cloud about 32 km in diameter. Eventually they dispersed. By slightly modifying its evening flight activities and using radar to alert departing or inbound pilots, the Air Force has been able to co-exist with the bats.

CONTROL MEASURES

It is sometimes necessary to try to prevent or reduce public health risk from bats or the damage that they cause. Ecologically sound and effective control of bat populations is difficult and as a result there are several different approaches that may be employed. All aim basically either to discourage or to destroy bats, although destruction is rarely necessary or justified. In the majority of cases, it is totally unwarranted, sometimes based on false premises or antipathy, and not infrequently counter-productive. The majority of species are beneficial rather than harmful and at most cause little more than a nuisance when roosting in human habitations. Strong control measures are essential, however, to protect humans and livestock from the ravages of vampire bats and are occasionally warranted to prevent depredation of fruit crops.

Vampire control

Vampire bats have proven to be an extremely resilient and formidable foe. Sleeping in the presence of a light or placing a light in livestock corrals is commonly used to repel vampires. This control measure has had limited success and frequently vampires attack on the shaded side of the intended victim. Humans also may sleep under mosquito netting which affords protection from both vampires and malarial-infected mosquitoes. Bells or other noisemaking devices, in and around livestock compounds, have had some success. Of course, seeking night shelter inside bat-proof buildings is the best means of escaping vampire attack, but this is not always an economically feasible alternative in these generally poor regions of Latin America.

Bounty systems have been tried with some success, but indiscriminate killing of bats may result. Newcastle virus, a deadly pathogen for poultry, was used in a cave in Colombia to kill vampires. Some were killed, but this virus also caused illness in the personnel which were accidentally exposed during its application. While disease-causing agents may seem to be a reasonable measure, it can often backfire and spread rampantly in non-pest species. Disease resistance has provided another hard lesson learned initially with the use of myxomatosis virus to control rabbit populations in Australia or in Great Britain where resistance has enabled the rabbit population to survive, even if in reduced numbers. As we have already noted, cave fumigation and/or cave destruction has been used. These drastic and indiscriminate methods, however, risk destroying many harmless and otherwise beneficial bat species.

The major problem is that there does not appear to be a readily identifiable natural control of vampire bats that can simply be enhanced as an effective means of control or eradication. At the moment, there appear to be several potentially vulnerable links in the vampire's natural history. Firstly, only one or occasionally two young are born each year. This means that a substantial depletion in the reproduc-

tive adult population could drive it to extinction or at least reduce its impact. Secondly, a large portion of the vampire population is concentrated around domestic livestock nightly. Thirdly, vampires often visit the same wound in livestock on several successive nights and, like other bats, they are quite fastidious animals with a habit of grooming each other by licking in the roost. One or the other of these habits might be exploited as a control measure.

With this in mind, several new techniques have been tried with a promising amount of success. Strychnine-laced syrup mixtures have been applied around fresh wounds. Also, attack sites on livestock are smeared with petroleum jelly mixed with an anticoagulant. The former is aimed at killing an individual vampire bat by direct poisoning. The latter measure is designed to soil the fur of one individual which may come into contact with several others during grooming. The ingested anticoagulant causes death by internal bleeding. A drawback with these two poisons is that any animal that eats a poisoned vampire also may be killed.

House bat management

Many insectivorous bats roost or, more often, form colonies in the cornices and crevices around the roof of a house or other building, in attics or lofts, or in spaces between a ceiling and the floor, above or between an external cladding of boards or tiles and its supporting walls. Frequently these colonies occupy difficult to reach or inaccessible places. They may be more of an annoyance than a serious health risk; although, as we have noted, in some parts of the world it is possible that potentially dangerous organisms may accompany colonies of bats. The vast majority of colonies are harmless and at most no more than a mild nuisance. Occasionally, however, they occur in hospitals or food stores where some form of management becomes necessary.

Different people react differently to the presence of bats in buildings. Often bats that are a nuisance to one household may be encouraged by a neighbouring household. In the United States, house bat problems have an interesting distribution. Complaints have been recorded in nearly all states and southern Canada. The largest number of complaints originate from the northeastern states; New England and adjacent Canada, New York, New Jersey, Pennsylvania, and Maryland. The area also loosely corresponds to an area where news media coverage often exaggerates or sensationalizes human/bat encounters and the incidence of rabies. By comparison, house bat colonies are about as common in Florida as in the northeastern United States, but very few complaints originate from this state. This may be due to the fact that Florida residents are used to the abundance and variety of Florida wildlife living in close proximity to people.

The usual initial reaction to the presence of bats in buildings is to kill the uninvited intruders. Often this response is irrational and enforced by a latent bat prejudice derived from phobias based on myth and ignorance. The killing may be accomplished by various mechanical means, but, more often than not, the distraught resident resorts to applying some chemical toxicant; usually in the form of an aerosol spray. Attempts to kill house bats are counter-productive for several reasons. First, it is a waste of time and energy, because the animals are usually replaced promptly by other individuals. Secondly, killing house bats is only a temporary treatment of a symptom and falls short of effecting a permanent solution which is physical exclusion. Thirdly, killing house bats is difficult to justify given the relatively low incidence of rabies in these animals which are otherwise important and valuable agents in the natural control of insects. Indeed, in most parts of the world, rabies does not occur in bat populations. Finally, killing house bats with chemical agents such as DDT and other organochlorine insecticides has the effect of scattering sick bats over wide geographic areas. Indeed, this may raise the likelihood of human/bat encounters and 'bat bite' incidences, especially to children, as well as increase the likelihood of human exposure to these persistent and bioaccumulating toxicants. Another consideration is that many bat species are protected by law and killing them may carry the possibility of substantial penalty or imprisonment.

Various methods have been used to evict house bats. Repellents such as naphthalene flakes, burning sulphur candles, or other strong aromatic substances are often ineffective and may be dangerous or irritating to human occupants. Floodlights, spotlights, or fluorescent lights may be used to illuminate roosting sites in attics or other spaces. This method is cleaner and safer than most other methods, but its cost may be exorbitant and its efficiency low. Bats tend to avoid draughty locations for roosting. Thus, opening doors and windows or artificially creating a draught with electric fans is possibly an effective means of evicting house bats. High frequency sound such as that produced by dog-training whistles has been used with some success. High frequency rodent control devices do not appear to be effective for bat control. Various sticky-type repellents (ROOST-NO-MORE, TANGLE FOOT, and TACKY TOES) have been used in situations where roost surfaces and bat accesses may be coated. These sticky deterrents are

not very effective because bats are able to avoid them and they must be continually re-applied.

The most effective and environmentally sound method of evicting unwanted house bats is to simply deny them access to human habitation. The method may not be as simple as it sounds, but a diligent effort to locate and block all possible entrances will be rewarded with success and the satisfaction of having solved the problem without wastefully destroying an otherwise valuable resource. Unless it is totally unavoidable a colony should not be evicted in the breeding season (for example, in the temperate summer) when it may contain young bats that cannot fly and will be trapped in the roost to die and decay. Likewise, eviction efforts should not be conducted during cold seasons (late fall and winter) when lethargic bats may be entrapped or expelled into climatic conditions where survival is unlikely. Thus, bat-proofing activities should be limited to late summer and early fall. All accesses, except one or two should be plugged with mortar, plaster, pieces of wood or metal, rags or other pliable material, or fine metal mesh over holes and ventilators. The unsealed accesses are left open for two or three days so that the bats become accustomed to the restricted route of entering and leaving the roost. Once the bats are accustomed to this, the final access holes are sealed, after dusk when the bats have left to forage. The hole may be reopened on several subsequent evenings to allow stragglers the opportunity to escape. In the United States, bat-proofing efforts may be coupled with improving the energy efficiency of a home by insulating, weather stripping, and caulking around windows, doors, or other passages. These energy conservation measures are eligible for Federal Residential Energy Tax Credit as provided by the Energy Tax Act 1978 and in 43 states there are additional tax benefits. For additional details, United States citizens may want to obtain *House Bat Management: Resource Publication No. 143*, published by the United States Department of the Interior, Fish and Wildlife Service, Washington, DC. In Great Britain, the Wildlife and Countryside Act 1981 provides that the Nature Conservancy Council (19/20 Belgrave Square, London, SW1X 8PY) must be notified of any proposed action to get rid of bats in any part of a house or other property (including outbuildings), except from a living area, or of any action that is likely to disturb them or their roost. The Nature Conservancy Council must then be allowed sufficient time to advise on whether the action or operation should be carried out, and, if so, on the method to be used and its timing. The Council also publishes a booklet *Focus on Bats* which British readers will find informative and helpful. It may be obtained from the Interpretative

Branch, Nature Conservancy Council, Attingham Park, Shrewsbury SY4 4TW.

Control of fruit-eating bats

Controlling marauding fruit bats is limited by many of the same constraints discussed for controlling vampire bats. Unlike vampire bats, fruit bats do not appear to pose serious public health or economic problems. Crop destruction is usually restricted to local areas and general control measures have been neither effective nor economically feasible. Physical disturbances that have been used as deterrents in orchards and plantations include noise or odour making devices and lights. These are moderately successful. More drastic measures include destruction of flying fox 'camps' or the indiscriminate destruction of caves. The destruction of caves for vampire control is often further justified by arguments that fruit crop pests are also destroyed. To a certain extent this is true, but populations of fruit-eating bats are usually broad-based, in terms of overall size and reproductive potential, making their local destruction a fruitless folly. Ultimately, it is the destruction of the beneficial insectivorous species, some of which occasionally eat fruit (omnivorous phyllostomids), that is ecologically unsound.

Bounty systems and massive shootings have been attempted, but these are generally not economical and usually the destruction is wrought on the wrong species. Poisonous gases, flamethrowers, and explosives have also proven unsatisfactory; the latter resulting in more tree damage than bat control. The introduction of pathogens such as the typhoid bacteria (*Salmonella typhimurium*) has been tried in the control of *Pteropus* in Queensland, Australia, but has been found to be ineffective as well as imprudent because of the disease risk to the general public. Strychnine-laced baits were effectively employed against *Pteropus* in Australia and used subsequently against *Artibeus* and *Carollia* in Trinidad. However, this method is limited in use because poisoned fruits may also be eaten by unsuspecting humans (children) or non-pest animals.

BENEFICIAL ASPECTS OF BATS

Bats and arthropod control

It is clearly evident that insectivorous bats are much involved in maintaining the balance of insect populations. Unfortunately, a proper assessment of this biological interaction is not possible, in other than general terms, because of a lack of good qualitative and quantitative data. As noted in Chapter 5, insectivorous bats utilize a wide variety of arthropod prey items. The choice of prey seems not to be random and there is considerable evidence to suggest a fair amount of prey selection among species or groups of species.

Bat researchers have measured the feeding rates in some species of bats by weighing individuals before and after feeding. These measurements have provided a means of conservatively estimating or generalizing about the quantity of insects consumed by bats. For instance, individuals of the Mexican Free-tailed bat (*Tadarida brasiliensis*), returning to their roost from feeding, were found to have stomach contents weighing 1 gram more than before their departure. Taking this as an average and considering the number of individuals in the colony (approximately 50 million), feeding for an average of 120 nights in the summer, an estimate of 6700 tonnes of insects consumed has been calculated. It is quite likely that this figure could be three, four, or, perhaps, more times higher given the fact that food captured and passed through the digestive tract was not measured. Another estimate suggests that a colony of some 20 million Free-tailed bats might eat a quarter of a million pounds (112 500 kg) of insects in a single night, or, in other words, some 13 000 tonnes in the same period of 120 days. Similar estimates have been calculated for other bat species and there can be little doubt that the insectivorous bat fauna of the world consumes huge quantities of insects and other arthropods on a nightly and annual basis. Many of these insects are pests such as mosquitoes, various moths and beetles with known plant, animal, and/or human disease associations, and others generally regarded as nuisances. It should also be noted that some of the arthropods consumed by bats may be beneficial as well.

Guano

The accumulations of guano in bat caves have been exploited as a source of organic fertilizer for many years, especially where extensive deposits occur. The use of guano, while still used in some local areas, has generally declined in the last twenty years due to the emergence of cheaper synthetic fertilizers. Also, much of the resource has been depleted, but guano continues to be a valuable source of fertilizer in some underdeveloped countries.

Bats as a food source

Large fruit bats are often cooked and eaten in many parts of Africa and Asia. *Pteropus vampyrus* from

Timor were first given the Latin name *'Pteropus edulis'* in reference to their use as food. Writings from the Middle Ages attest to the use of bats as food by Babylonians and fruit bat remains from kitchen middens in New Guinea suggest that these bats were an important food source for the aboriginal inhabitants some 10 000 years ago. Fruit bats are considered a great delicacy by the Chinese and in other oriental cultures particularly on Guam Island, for example, and large numbers may be harvested annually from a single roost in eastern Asia and the Pacific. Although the generally small-sized microchiropterans may be less palatable than the large fruit bats or even too small to offer much in the way of sustenance, there are a few accounts of these being eaten.

Bats, remedies, and medical research

Bats have long been associated with medicine, formerly as the mystical ingredients of supposed remedies and poultices, for a variety of ailments. Gypsy doctors used the blood of bats in 'cures' for various human ailments. Bats' blood was also used by the ancient Egyptians to treat diseases of the eyes. As recently as the 1920s, a concoction of bat's blood and fat could be purchased in the state of Indiana (USA) as an aid for rheumatism.

Bats are often associated with baldness. In a common old wives' tale, a person was expected to go bald after a bat had become entangled in his or her hair. Primitive witch doctors boiled the naked wings of bats in brews and patients smeared these on the areas from which they wanted to remove hair. Blood or the brain of a bat, mixed with the gall of a hedgehog or goat's milk was also regarded as an excellent depilatory agent. In contrast to these hair removal remedies, bats wings have also been used to restore or prevent the loss of hair. In India, the dried and crushed wings are still sometimes used in the preparation of a hair wash along with coconut oil and other ingredients. This mixture is stored in a sealed vessel, underground, for several months before it is used. The fat of flying foxes is also considered to be a strong preventative of baldness in India, as well as useful in the treatment of rheumatism.

Bat guano has been used in some rather curious ways. Some Arab groups mixed bat guano in vinegar to be taken internally for the cure of tumours. This same mixture could also be applied externally. Bat urine was thought to have certain medical qualities. The ashes of burned bats, mixed and drunk with wine, was thought to promote lactation. If a nursing mothers' milk had stopped, it was thought that bathing the nipples in this same tonic would restore the flow of milk.

The potent and magical brew containing 'Eye of newt and toe of frog; wool of bat and tongue of dog,' stirred by the witches in *Macbeth* was no less intricate than some of the remedies prescribed by early physicians. Gout supposedly was relieved by a poultice made from three bats boiled in rainwater with one ounce of flax seed, three raw eggs, a cup of oil, dung of an ox, and one ounce of wax. This concoction was applied to the affected area. These are but a few examples of the various ways that bats were used by man in his medieval medical practices.

More recently, bats have become the subjects of serious medical research. The growth of bacteria and other microorganisms in circulating blood can be studied quite easily by transilluminating the thin wing membrane of bats. Similarly, the wing membranes may be used to determine the effects of alcohols and other drugs on the blood vessels and nerves or on muscle regeneration and tissue repair. Echolocation in bats has provided analogues for the construction of functional ultrasonic orientation systems for the blind. The mechanism of thermoregulation may have a bearing on studies of infection and virulence of various microbial disease agents. In addition, the ability of some bats to survive for long periods of time at low temperatures and lowered metabolic rates may further the development of surgical techniques involving lowering the temperature of the human body. Medical study of hibernation may be relevant to space biology since, when dormant, bats tend to age more slowly and they resist or defer radiation pathology more effectively. Bats may become a factor in vaccine development because some at least seem to be able to resist viruses and other infective organisms. Bats may be more sensitive to DDT and other chlorinated hydrocarbons than any other mammals making them valuable indicators of these toxic substances in the environment. Various aspects of chiropteran social organization and behaviour may provide useful insights into the psychological stresses associated with overcrowded conditions.

Bats as pollinators and seed dispersers

Nectar-feeding bats are responsible for the pollination of many bat-adapted tropical and sub-tropical trees and shrubs, and as we have noted, although some fruit-eating species may at times be local pests of fruit crops this is off-set by their value in the dispersal of seeds. Bats play an important part in both pollination and seed dispersal, and many trees and shrubs that they visit are commercially important as a food resource or for other purposes. They include avocados, bananas, figs, guavas, and mangos among fruit, nuts such as cashews, spices such as cloves, manila and sisal for rope-making, kapok, and balsa wood and other timber. The extent to which bats are involved in these natural processes is not fully appreciated and is just now being investigated by tropical biologists.

Bats at war

It may seem improbable that bats might be enlisted in wartime activities. However, bat guano and guano-enriched soil is a rich source of saltpetre (sodium nitrate) which is used in the production of gunpowder and other explosives. During the latter portion of the American Civil War, the Confederate states were forced to utilize bat guano to make gunpowder and several large caves in northern Texas were held and guarded as valuable military resources. Bat caves have also been considered as possible bomb shelters in the event of nuclear attack. However, the discovery of airborne rabies virus and histoplasmosis in some caves has largely discouraged this notion. Bat caves were used extensively as underground shelters by the Japanese in the Second World War. Bat populations in certain areas of the South Pacific have profited from the wartime activity of man. For example, the Japanese excavated many kilometres of tunnels in New Guinea. These tunnel systems now provide extensive roost sites for large populations of bats.

Perhaps the most bizarre involvement of bats in human warfare was a scheme developed by the United States Armed Forces during the Second World War. This plan, called 'Project X-Ray', proposed using large numbers of Mexican Free-tailed bats (*Tadarida brasiliensis*), each carrying a small incendiary bomb attached to its belly by a short string and a surgical clip. The planners of this scheme imagined parachuting cages, containing large numbers of these 'free-tailed bombers', over enemy territory. These cages were specially designed to open at a particular altitude thereby releasing the armed bats that would then disperse to buildings. Once in their new roosts, they would chew through the string releasing the bomb which would detonate after a period of time. The potential effectiveness of this project was decreased when it was found that the bats tended to aggregate at one or two sites rather than disperse. Also, several hundred bomb carrying bats escaped the southwestern desert test range and took up residence under an elevated gasoline tank in a nearby town. In addition, several military buildings were accidentally incinerated by stray bats. The project was eventually abandoned just prior to the advent of the atomic bomb.

PROTECTION AND CONSERVATION

There is growing evidence that populations of some temperate bat species have experienced a marked decline in numbers in recent years. In western and central Europe, bat species (*Rhinolophus hipposideros* and *R. ferrumequinum*) that were once common are now encountered only infrequently, although in some instances such variation in population levels may be the result of natural processes when bats exist at the limits of their range where they may be susceptible to natural changes in climate and environment. *Myotis sodalis*, *M. grisescens*, and *M. austroriparius* are regarded as endangered in the eastern United States. In addition, many bat colonies in the Los Angeles Basin and around other metropolitan centres are no longer present. These are only a few examples. There is little information on tropical and subtropical bat populations, but the extensive destruction of tropical forest ecosystems surely jeopardizes many of these species as well. Fruit bats in eastern Asia and in the Pacific region are often hunted for food and this is causing concern for their survival in some cases. Perhaps more than most other mammals, bats are vulnerable to a wide range of factors, often resulting from direct or indirect human activity, that can modify or otherwise alter their environment.

One of the most important factors in the decline of bat populations in the United States and Europe is the destruction of roost sites. Mineshafts are sometimes intentionally sealed or unintentionally modified when they are used as rubbish depositories. Quarry operations frequently destroy or otherwise modify cave environments rendering them unusable by bats and other cavernicolous organisms. Urban renewal has resulted in the destruction of many old buildings that served as roost sites for large bat colonies. This is certainly the case in the Los Angeles area where old styled churches with steeples and belfries (favoured roost sites of *Eumops perotis*) have been replaced with more modern architectural styles. Forestry practices in both Europe and the United States often dictate the removal of old hollow trees. This practice in the southeastern United States may be affecting many already sensitized tree bat species. Clearing trees from around cave or mineshaft entrances may not appear to cause any noticeable damage. However, this may result in an overall increase in summer temperatures or decrease in winter temperatures, both of which may render the cave uninhabitable. In addition, the natural airflow in and out of the cave or its humidity may be altered to such an extent that the inhabitable portions are reduced or eliminated.

Bats are also put at risk by unnecessary disturbances, especially when they are hibernating and dependent upon their accumulated fat reserves to maintain their reduced metabolism through the winter. These arousals make extra demands on this critical energy reserve that often cannot be replaced and may cause sufficient depletions so that not enough remains for survival until spring. Frequent disturbances of a summer roost may cause the bats to abandon it or at least lead to a decline in numbers. In the case of nursery colonies, mothers may leave non-flying young when they abandon a disturbed roost. These disturbances are usually caused by mindless vandals, unscrupulous collectors, or naive potholers or spelunkers. Many national and international speleological societies are cognizant of the danger of disturbing bat colonies and exercise considerable care when in caves occupied by bats. These groups have also contributed substantially to the general education of the public regarding the benefits of bat conservation.

Efforts to reduce disturbance to bat roosts include attempts to restrict access to caves and mines by fitting the entrances with a locked iron grille that allows bats to enter and leave, but prevents interference by unauthorized persons. This has been reasonably effective in the southeastern United States and Great Britain. However, these grilles occasionally increase the hazard of predation to bats. At one cave in Missouri, a raccoon was observed clinging to the grating and easily grabbing bats as they negotiated their way through the metal blockade.

Indiscriminate or unnecessary bat-banding is also a threat to bat populations, undertaken sometimes for no real reason or to further a project of dubious value. Banding not only involves disturbance and stress for the bats but also carries the very real danger that badly designed bands or bands that are put on without proper care will injure the flying membrane. As a result, banding studies should not be undertaken except by properly competent workers in pursuit of clearly defined, essential, relevant, and worthwhile objectives. Even so, the recognition of banding as a major cause of disturbance has recently (1976) led the United States Fish and Wildlife Service to impose a moratorium on the issue of bands and on banding studies in the United States, and to limit bands for studies already begun only to those involving bats whose populations are not reduced. Bat boxes similar to those used for birds have been provided in the forests of several countries in an effort to conserve or increase the bat population, especially for its potential value in the control of insects. Bat towers constructed for this purpose in the southern United States met with only limited success in encouraging further colonization. The preservation

and conservation of existing roosts, especially of caves, is perhaps the most important facet of this aspect of bat conservation, since many are traditional and used by successive generations of bats over many years.

Perhaps the most insidious factor threatening world bat populations is the continued use of persistent and bioaccumulating organic pesticides such as DDT and other related chlorinated hydrocarbons. The usage of these toxic substances has proved to be a many-headed hydra. While killing the intended pest, they also kill beneficial insects. The pest populations almost always develop resistance to the chemical agent and come back in larger numbers than before the pesticide application. These toxic chemicals, however, continue to be accumulated in the fatty tissues of insects and these toxic concentrations are passed up the food chain to bats, birds, and other organisms that participate in these food webs. The dosages received by adult bats may be sublethal, but deadly to nursing young. Recent studies of massive die-offs of nursing baby Mexican Free-tailed bats (*Tadarida brasiliensis*) at Carlsbad Caverns suggests that these deaths may be linked to the detrimental effects of pesticide residues on the developing nervous systems of these young bats. Such large-scale failures in the reproductive efforts of the Carlsbad population may have contributed significantly to the reduction in their numbers over the last ten years or so. This, of course, leads into a never ending spiral; fewer bats eating fewer insects resulting in more insects to be controlled by chemical means, and so on. Adults may experience a delayed response. For example, these fat soluble compounds may be taken in and deposited in fat stores during the summer months and have no appreciable effect. However, in the fall, when migration flights tax these fat stores, the accumulated toxins may be released in lethal or physiologically debilitating quantities, both resulting in the death of the individual. Similarly, the toxic spectre may come out of hiding when fat stores are metabolized during hibernation.

Bats seem especially at risk from organochlorines such as DDT and related substances because their relatively high metabolic rates demand a correspondingly high food consumption, thereby increasing the quantity of toxic material ingested. Also, many bat species tend to form large colonies in the diurnal roost, for maternity purposes or for hibernation and are particularly vulnerable when in these retreats to direct application by misguided persons.

In addition to accumulation in the diet, bats may be exposed to chemical toxins in other ways. Bats may be exposed directly to deleterious chemicals used to treat roof timbers in lofts and attics against wood-boring insects or fungi that destroy wood. DDT and other related chemicals, or anticoagulants such as chlorophacinone, are regularly used to eliminate house bat colonies. Indeed, some preparations of the latter may be indicated as suitable for this purpose. It is, however, also very hazardous to humans. This results in scattering sick bats and thereby increasing the likelihood of human or pet encounters with bats which may result in bat bites and subsequent precautionary rabies treatment. Also, slow biodegradable toxins such as DDT are introduced into the ecosystem where they may travel when the bat dies and decays or is eaten by some other animal. We cannot yet fully assess the impact of these toxic substances in world ecosystems. There is no doubt that they cause massive destruction of sensitive wildlife such as bats and birds. This alone seems to be reason enough to stop and contemplate our actions and responsibility to other living organisms.

Current public attitudes toward bats also threaten their survival, especially since the first reaction of many to their presence in houses or buildings is to eliminate or remove them as quickly as possible. We have tried to show, repeatedly, in this chapter, that most popular beliefs about bats are founded in myth, superstition, on fear, or are irrational and not factually based. Some, such as the belief that most bats are rabid and that they are important reservoirs of rabies, are extensions from the known fact that vampires, and especially *Desmodus rotundus*, can be vectors of the disease, and that some individuals of other species can also be infected, especially in the Americas. Moreover, recent studies have concluded that bats are not an immune reservoir of rabies, but are susceptible to it in the same way as other mammals. Antipathy to bats seems to have roots deep in human history, and misconceptions serve only to reinforce it. Another false belief is that bats are filthy animals likely to infest houses with dangerous parasites—in fact they are scrupulously clean animals that groom themselves regularly, and their parasites rarely create problems since they survive for only a relatively short while once divorced from their host. We have already indicated that the supposed necessity of poisoning bats in houses is counter-productive and likely to cause more problems than it solves, apart from the risk of exposing humans to powerful and virulent chemical substances. The belief that bats are aggressive and likely to attack people, children and pets is also ill-founded. In normal circumstances healthy bats do not attack people and even rabid vampires do so only rarely. Some alleged attacks blamed on bats have been found to be the result of encounters with screech owls, and alleged bites to be inadvertent scratches, or insect bites. Finally, the belief that bats

regularly become entangled in women's hair is also without foundation—in normal circumstances the bat would easily avoid such an event.

Bats also receive what is colloquially called a 'bad press'. Newspaper and other media reporting of alleged bites, colonizations, and indeed almost any event concerning bats, not infrequently dwells on their allegedly dangerous aspects; such reporting is often sensational and generally has little regard for accuracy or for facts. In turn it reinforces public antipathy and can lead to demands for totally unnecessary control and destruction. Bats have been and still are the subject of highly coloured fictional tales that may be best categorized as 'bat scare-stories'. Public portrayal of bats as horrendous creatures, ravaging and rampaging around and in houses, or attacking humans, serve only to propagate and perpetuate the myth that bats are dangerous, disease-infested creatures that must be destroyed at all costs. This kind of image is also furthered by pest control literature that employs it to justify the products that it extols.

Bats are protected to a greater or lesser extent by legislation or other regulations in several European countries, in Russia, Australia, Mexico, and parts of the United States. In Great Britain, for example, the Wildlife and Countryside Act 1981 makes it illegal for anyone without a license intentionally to kill, injure, or take a wild bat of any species; to possess a bat whether alive or dead (unless legally obtained) or to disturb a bat while it is roosting. Ringing, marking, or photographing bats (except in outdoor flight) thus requires a license from the Nature Conservancy Council (19/20 Belgrave Square, London, SW1X 8PY). It is also an offence in Britain to sell, hire, barter, or exchange any wild bat, whether alive or dead without a license. The law only allows a disabled bat to be tended until it can be released when recovered or to be killed if disabled to the point where recovery is unlikely. Bats in Britain have been given special protection because of their roosting needs; it is also an offence to damage, destroy or obstruct access to any place that a bat uses for shelter or protection, or to disturb a bat while it is occupying such a place, a provision that, as we have indicated above, applies even to houses and outbuildings (except for living areas).

While legislation can and does give bats more protection and clearly assists in their conservation, it is clear that much remains to be done. To this end a number of leading bat biologists have formed an organisation called 'Bat Conservation International'. Based at the Milwaukee Public Museum, Milwaukee, Wisconsin 53233, USA, this organization is a group of the Fauna and Flora Preservation Society, founded recently with the aims of raising funds for bat conservation projects throughout the world, to prevent the extinction of species, to ensure the survival of viable populations, and to improve public awareness and appreciation of the role of bats. It is intended to implement conservation measures, to educate society at all levels in matters concerning bats, and when required, to carry out relevant research. In order to draw attention to the many misconceptions concerning health risks and bats, especially in the United States, the organization has already produced a valuable account 'Bats and Public Health' in the journal *Contributions in Biology and Geology of the Milwaukee Public Museum* (No. 48, 1981) by M. D. Tuttle and S. J. Kern. This has been distributed to health officials throughout the United States and also internationally, and has attracted favourable comment. A more popular leaflet and other articles have

also been prepared and published, and surveys of conservation projects in Thailand (the protection of Kitti's Hog-nosed bat, *Craseonycteris thonglongyai*) and in the Pacific (to assess the implications of the commercial trade in fruit bats, *Pteropus*, which are exploited for food) have been undertaken.

Protection and conservation depend often on public attitudes, and much might be achieved by wider recognition of bats as an outstanding example of evolutionary development and adaptation, of their part in the ecosystem, and of their real and potential value to man as a unique, irreplaceable natural resource. Once achieved, such an understanding might well lead to the further development of legislation intended to protect bats from disturbance and destruction, and to the eventual formulation of programmes designed to conserve these important and fascinating animals.

The classification of living bats is based chiefly on the studies of G. S. Miller, Jr whose formal arrangement of families and genera was published in 1907. Although original in many respects, Miller's classification of bats rests firmly on a classificatory foundation established by a number of European zoologists/taxonomists in the eighteenth and nineteenth centuries.

The practice of classifying things is, perhaps, as much a characteristic of humankind as is speech and the use of tools. Classification has the practical feature of effectively conveying information about groups of things; that is, a common feature of a group of things stands as an identifier of the group in question. Thus, the 'identifying feature(s)' convey information about the group of things being classified. Given the external appearance of bats it is not at all surprising that many early classifications grouped bats with birds. The biblical prohibition in Leviticus XI, 19-20 'And the stork, the heron after her kind, and the lapwing, and the bat. All fowls that creep, going upon all fours, shall be an abomination unto you' (that is, not to be eaten) adds bats to an assemblage of birds. Indeed, many of man's early classifications portrayed attributes such as edible vs. inedible or dangerous vs. harmless. However, the science of classification (Taxonomy or Systematics) endeavours to group organisms on the basis of evolutionary kinship or phylogenetic relationships. Ultimately, the members of a group are supposed to share a common ancestor. Thus, a scientific classification is a hierarchic arrangement of groups of species nested within increasingly larger groups of species all of which are bound together by common ancestry. Of course, the whole notion of evolution grew out of the need to classify organisms by their natural affinities and was gradually developed by Darwin, his predecessors, and those who followed. John Ray's 1693 classification was, perhaps, the first to place bats correctly among the mammals. However, it is clear that the winged nature of bats confused Ray as he considered them to be anomalous and his classification was vague with regard to the affinity of bats to other mammals. The science of classification takes as its arbitrary beginning the arrangement proposed by Carl Linnaeus in the tenth edition of his *Systema naturae* published in 1758, one hundred years before

Charles Darwin's *On the origin of species*. Seven species of bats were known to Linnaeus and these he classified, along with humans, some other primates, and the Colugo, in his Order Primates. In the next 150 years, the 'Age of Discovery' unfolded in which European naturalists visited or received collections of specimens from nearly every corner of the world. In the process of identifying and cataloguing these collections, the knowledge of bats, as well as that of other organisms, grew by 'leaps and bounds' and the classification of these organisms began to take shape. Noteworthy among the early classifications of bats are those by the French zoologists de Blainville, Lacépède, E. Geoffroy Saint-Hilaire, and Georges Cuvier; the German zoologists Blumenbach, Wagner, and Peters; and the British zoologists J. E. Gray, G. E. Dobson, and K. Andersen.

The broad outlines established by Miller remain basically unchanged nearly 75 years after they were proposed. Some of the groups that he recognized have been modified and an additional new family (Craseonycteridae) was added in 1974. Of course, many new species and genera have also been added. The total number of families of modern bats recognized today varies from sixteen to nineteen since the definition of such groups still remains somewhat subjective with some authorities combining one or more families while others fragment one or more. Bats are represented in the fossil record by a number of species from as early as the early to middle Eocene of Europe and North America. These too have been subjectively grouped into three or fewer families. Several living families extend far back into geological time, some being reported as early as the late Eocene or early Oligocene of the Old World and Oligocene of the New World.

We hasten to point out that these early fossil bats are 'fully fledged' in the sense of being bats and that the naive, yet common, practice of ascribing a date of origin to the oldest fossil representative of a group is truly an illogical exercise. These fossils simply stand as irrefutable evidence of the antiquity of the group that certainly must extend farther back into evolutionary history. The extent and nature of this history is, as we have already noted in Chapter 3, highly speculative at best.

FAMILIES AND GENERA OF BATS

The Order Chiroptera divides emphatically into two suborders; the Old World fruit bats or flying foxes (Suborder Megachiroptera) are represented by one family (Pteropodidae) and the rest are the basically insect-eating bats (Suborder Microchiroptera). The modern Microchiroptera are usually divided into four superfamilies to indicate evolutionary affinities among the remaining families. The combination of the two suborders (Megachiroptera and Microchiroptera) into the Order Chiroptera may, as we have noted earlier in this book, unduly convey the notion that these two diverse groups share a common ancestor. This seems weakly founded on the fact that both have wings and we believe that there are serious reasons to question the justification of this notion. It is not our purpose here to present a new classification of bats. Therefore, we will represent the classification of bats more or less as it is currently understood. This classification may be summarized as follows:

Order CHIROPTERA
    Suborder MEGACHIROPTERA
        Family Pteropodidae
    Suborder MICROCHIROPTERA
      Superfamily EMBALLONUROIDEA
        Family Rhinopomatidae
            Emballonuridae
            Craseonycteridae
      Superfamily RHINOLOPHOIDEA
        Family Nycteridae
            Megadermatidae
            Rhinolophidae
            Hipposideridae
      Superfamily PHYLLOSTOMOIDEA
        Family Noctilionidae
            Mormoopidae
            Phyllostomidae
      Superfamily VESPERTILIONOIDEA
        Family Natalidae
            Furipteridae
            Thyropteridae
            Myzopodidae
            Vespertilionidae
            Mystacinidae
            Molossidae
      Superfamily *PALAEOCHIROPTERYGOIDEA
        Family *Palaeochiropterygidae
            *Archaeonycteridae
            *Icaronycteridae

* Known as fossil only.

The classification shown above is relatively conservative and has been adopted chiefly so that the general reader may recognize families, subfamilies, and genera as they have appeared in the literature of the past half century or so. It must be realized that classifications are rarely completely stable, but are subject to change as new knowledge is gathered. The classification of the New World leaf-nosed bats illustrates the instability of chiropteran systematics. Until the early 1970s, the Mormoopidae was considered to be a subfamily within the family Phyllostomidae and the vampire bats were thought to represent a separate and distinct family (Desmodontidae). However, close study has shown that quite the opposite appears to be true. The vampires, although bizarre in their food habits, are indeed phyllostomids, whereas the Mormoopidae seem to represent a separate and distinct family. Likewise, the subfamilial classification of the Phyllostomidae remains tentative at best.

In the tables that follow we have attempted to indicate, where appropriate, relevant changes in the classification so that these lists can be used as a guide both for the older literature as well as that published more recently. Also, the symbol * preceding a name indicates that the genus or family is known only from fossil material. The number of species ascribed to a large genus is sometimes an approximation, since, as yet, a precise classification of the genus may be lacking or the validity of some of its species may be uncertain.

THE FAMILIES OF BATS

It is not always easy, at first sight, to decide to which family a particular bat belongs. Thus, we include here a brief but useful description of each family.

MEGACHIROPTERA

Ear simple, its edge forming an unbroken ring; second finger relatively independent of the third finger and usually bearing a small claw.

Pteropodidae Small to very large (forearm *c.* 40-220 mm); no noseleaf or tragus; second finger with three bony phalanges, the last very small or rudimentary; third finger with two bony phalanges; tail membrane usually narrow; tail generally short or absent (moderately long in *Notopteris*), when present tail not at all involved with membrane.

MICROCHIROPTERA

Ear often complex, its edge interrupted, never forming a complete ring; second finger scarcely independent of third finger, without a claw.

Rhinopomatidae Small to medium (forearm *c.* 46-75 mm); sides of muzzle swollen, a slight transverse fleshy ridge above the slit-like, oblique nostrils; ears large, joined anteriorly at the base by a low fleshy band over the forehead; a small tragus; second and third fingers each with two bony phalanges; tail membrane narrow, a long thread-like tail projecting freely from its posterior edge; no calcar.

Emballonuridae Small to medium (forearm *c.* 35-66 mm); ears variable, often joined anteriorly at the base over the forehead; a small or moderate tragus; second finger lacking bony phalanges, third with two bony phalanges, the first reflexed above the wing when at rest; sometimes a glandular pouch or area on throat; a glandular sac often present in the antebrachial membrane or propatagium near elbow of New World species; tail partially enclosed in moderate tail membrane, its terminal part projecting from the upper surface.

Craseonycteridae Very small (forearm 22.5-26 mm); muzzle with low transverse dermal ridge above nostrils; ears very large; tragus with a swelling in its anterior part; second finger with one bony phalanx, third finger with two bony phalanges; the last phalanges of the third and fourth fingers reflexed under the wing when at rest; often a small glandular swelling at base of throat; tail membrane extensive; no external tail; calcar absent.

Nycteridae Small to medium (forearm *c.* 35-65 mm); muzzle with complex folds and outgrowths of skin flanking a deep longitudinal groove on its upper surface; ears long and large, joined anteriorly at the base by a low band of integument over the forehead; a small but well-developed tragus; second finger lacking bony phalanges, third finger with two bony phalanges; extensive tail membrane totally enclosing tail which has a T-shaped cartilaginous tip at the posterior edge of the membrane.

Megadermatidae Medium to large (forearm *c.* 50-115 mm); muzzle with conspicuous, long, erect noseleaf; ears large, joined anteriorly at the base by a high band of integument over the forehead; tragus prominent, bifurcated; second finger with one bony phalanx, third finger with two bony phalanges; tail membrane extensive; tail short or absent.

Rhinolophidae Small to medium (forearm *c.* 30-75 mm); muzzle with complex noseleaf consisting of an anterior horseshoe-shaped structure, a triangularly pointed, pocketed lancet posteriorly and a narrow, strap-like median sella above the main leaf from the nostrils to the lower part of the lancet; ears large; no tragus; second finger lacking bony phalanges, third finger with two bony phalanges; tail membrane moderate, totally enclosing tail.

Hipposideridae Small to large (forearm *c.* 32-114 mm); muzzle with complex noseleaf consisting of an anterior horseshoe-shaped structure as in Rhinolophidae, but lacking a vertical posterior lancet, the rear upper edge of the leaf semi-circular, with folds, pockets, or sometimes swollen vertical projections; no strap-like sella above and behind nostrils; ears moderate; no tragus; second finger lacking bony phalanges, third finger with two bony phalanges; tail completely enclosed in moderate tail membrane or absent; second, third, and fourth toes with only two phalanges each.

Noctilionidae Medium to large (forearm *c.* 55-90 mm); pointed muzzle with anterior pad; lips forming cheek pouches; no noseleaf; ears large, slender, pointed; a small tragus with tiny finger-like projections; second finger with one bony phalanx, third finger with two bony phalanges and a terminal cartilaginous phalanx; distal phalanges of third and fourth fingers reflexed below wing when at rest; moderate tail membrane also completely enclosing tail, the tip emerging from the upper surface of the membrane about halfway along its length; calcar long and blade-like; toes of *N. leporinus* (a fish-eating species) long and tipped with sharp, recurved claws.

Mormoopidae Small to medium (forearm *c.* 35-65 mm): no noseleaf, but chin and lips with many complex plates and folds of skin; ears large, joined anteriorly at the base over the forehead in *Mormoops*; tragus complex with fold in front edge; second finger with one bony phalanx, third finger with three bony phalanges; extensive tail membrane with about one-half of tail protruding from its upper surface, rear, tail–less portion of tail membrane folded forward when at rest; wing membranes attached high on the flanks, in subgenus *Pteronotus* wing membranes attached at the dorsal midline giving a naked-backed appearance.

Phyllostomidae Very small to large (forearm *c.* 25-110 mm); muzzle usually with rather simple, spear-shaped erect noseleaf, occasionally small or reduced; ears variable; tragus present, simple and blade-like, sometimes elongate; second finger with one bony phalanx, third finger with three bony phalanges; tail membrane and tail variable; tail when present completely enclosed in tail membrane, occasionally tail extends slightly beyond posterior margin of membrane or is slightly shorter than the rear extent of the membrane; calcar present or absent; teeth variably modified, upper incisors and canine blade-like in the vampires.

Natalidae Very small to small (forearm *c*. 27-41 mm); body slender; nostrils closely adjacent, near upper lip; no noseleaf; ears large, funnel-shaped and directed anteriorly; tragus more or less triangular, variously distorted and thickened; second finger lacking bony phalanges, third finger with two bony phalanges; extensive tail membrane enclosing long tail; hindlimbs long and slender.

Furipteridae Small (forearm *c*. 30-40 mm); no noseleaf; ears large, funnel-shaped and directed anteriorly; tragus small, triangular; forehead high and domed; rudimentary thumb enclosed in fold of antebrachial membrane to base of minute, functionless claw; second finger lacking bony phalanges, third finger with two bony phalanges; tail enclosed in moderate tail membrane, not reaching its posterior edge.

Thyropteridae Very small to small (forearm *c*. 27-38 mm); muzzle long and slender; no noseleaf; ears large, funnel-shaped and directed anteriorly; forehead high and domed; tragus prominent; second finger lacking bony phalanges; third finger with three bony phalanges; large sucker-shaped adhesive disc at base of thumb and side of foot; extensive tail membrane enclosing long tail which projects slightly beyond its posterior margin; second, third, and fourth toes with two phalanges each.

Myzopodidae Medium (forearm *c*. 46 mm); no noseleaf; ears very long, slender; tragus small, square-shaped, its anterior edge and part of its upper edge fused to rear of anterior edge of ear conch; a mushroom-shaped process consisting of a short stalk supporting a flat, kidney-shaped expansion developed from the base of the posterior edge of the ear to partially block the ear opening; thumb small with vestigial claw; second finger lacking bony phalanges, third finger with three bony phalanges; medium-sized, sucker-shaped adhesive disc at base of thumb and side of foot; tail membrane extensive, enclosing tail which extends slightly beyond its posterior margin; second, third, and fourth toes with two phalanges each; toes united by webbing almost to the base of claws.

Vespertilionidae Very small to large (forearm *c*. 24-80 mm); no noseleaf, at most rarely no more than a low transverse dermal ridge above nostrils; ears variable; tragus short, moderate or long and pointed; second finger with one bony phalanx, third finger with three

phalanges, terminal phalanx almost entirely cartilaginous; distal phalanges of third and fourth fingers sometimes reflexed below the wing when at rest; extensive tail membrane enclosing tail to its posterior margin; occasionally adhesive pads present on wrist, sole of foot, or both.

Mystacinidae Medium (forearm *c*. 40-49 mm); muzzle obliquely truncate anteriorly; no noseleaf; ears large, pointed; a long narrow tragus; second finger with one bony phalanx, third finger with three bony phalanges; wings thick and leathery; tail membrane thin, enclosing short tail with its tip protruding from the upper surface; legs short, the outer and inner toes longer than the other toes; claws with small talon on lower surface; sole of foot wrinkled.

Molossidae Very small to large (forearm *c*. 27-85 mm); muzzle broad, obliquely truncate anteriorly; lips often wrinkled; no noseleaf; ears usually moderate, thick, often joined anteriorly over forehead or upper part of muzzle by integument; a small tragus; antitragus often well-developed; second finger with one bony phalanx, third finger with three phalanges, terminal phalanx almost entirely cartilaginous, the first reflexed above the wing when at rest; flight membranes thick and leathery; tail membrane relatively narrow, enclosing stout tail which extends considerably from the posterior margin; legs short and strong; toes often swollen with glandular structures.

SUBORDER MEGACHIROPTERA

This suborder contains only the Old World fruit bats or flying foxes of the family Pteropodidae. They differ from all other bats in several important respects, and in some ways they seem less specialized. Sophisticated flight styles are rare among these bats that live on fruits and flowers or flower products. The architecture of the shoulder joint is relatively simple and the wing itself is simple compared to that of other bats. Yet many are large, strong flyers capable of travelling long distances to obtain food and shelter. With few exceptions, echolocation is unknown among members of the suborder. The acoustic orientation signals of those that do echolocate (*Rousettus* and perhaps *Epomophorus*) are rather crude and are produced by an entirely different mechanism from that used by all microchiropterans. The eyes are unusually large and sight as well as smell appears to be the major means by which these bats orientate and navigate within their environment. All have teeth that are specially adapted to frugivory as a dietary habit.

Family Pteropodidae

Old World fruit bats, flying foxes

Undoubtedly of ancient origin among bats, the Old World fruit bats are distributed throughout the tropical and subtropical regions of Africa, Asia, and Indo-Australia (Fig. 11.1). They are especially diversified in southeast Asia and Indo-Australia where over 200 species make up more than half of the bat fauna of the region and constitute approximately 70 per cent of the living species of pteropodids. The family includes some of the few kinds of bats that populate islands in the mid-Pacific Ocean. Here they occur on the Caroline, Tonga, and Samoan Island groups and Niue Island, and they have been reported from as far east in the Pacific as Cook Island. As fossils, pteropodids are known from the middle Oligocene and Miocene of Europe, the Miocene of Africa and from the Pleistocene of Madagascar and the East Indies. The family includes the largest of living bats with several species of *Pteropus* and *Acerodon* having a wing span of perhaps 1.5 m or a little more; most species are small to moderately large in size.

All pteropodids consume fruits, flowers, and/or flower products. As a rule, the muzzle and jaws are strong and massively built. In some genera, the jaws are rather short and stocky to increase their power when biting and chewing the tough-skinned fruits that they eat. Some also have a strong, bony mid-sagittal crest which provides additional surface area for the attachment of the extensive jaw muscles. In others, the braincase may be elongated and deflected downward to serve the same functional purpose of increasing the size and efficiency of the jaw musculature.

The grinding teeth of most species are large and flat to provide ample area for chewing their fruit diet. Those species that have adopted flower- or nectar-eating habits tend to have more lightly built jaws and smaller teeth. In many of these species, the muzzle is narrow and elongated thereby allowing them to probe deeply within the flower and their tongues are also long and especially equipped with brush-like papillae to collect pollen or nectar from the flowers that they visit.

Another aspect of the dentition is that the incisor teeth are usually small, often reduced in number. In the Tube-nosed bats (*Nyctimene* and *Paranyctimene*), the lower incisors are completely absent. The canine teeth are usually strong and in the genus *Pteralopex*, these teeth are particularly massive and armed with many strong cusps. Generally, the crowns of the chewing teeth are often rather flat, usually with a centrally located, shallow furrow along their length. This furrow is flanked by low ridges and sometimes there are small, pointed cusps. In *Pteralopex* and *Harpyionycteris*, these teeth have many strong cusps which presumably serve to facilitate the chewing of hard, coarse and fibrous fruit pulp.

Most fruit bats roost in trees or other foliage. Some species of *Pteropus* are especially gregarious and form large, noisy colonies or 'camps' that are easily

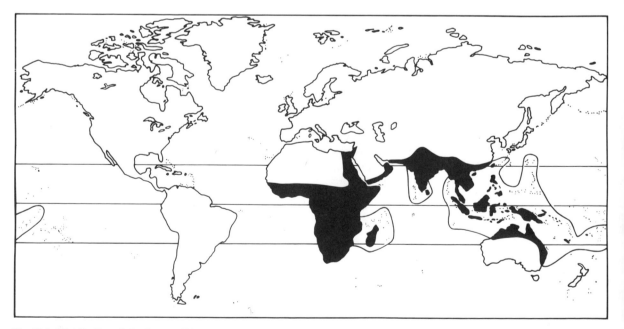

Fig. 11.1 Distribution of the Pteropodidae.

*Fig. 11.2 Representative pteropodids. A, Spectacled flying fox (*Pteropus capistratus*), B, Geoffroy's Rousette (*Rousettus amplexicaudatus); C, Bismarck Tube-nosed bat (*Nyctimene vizcaccia*).*

spotted. One such camp of the Bismarck flying fox (*Pteropus neohibernicus*) in Madang, Papua New Guinea contains several thousand individuals and is a local tourist attraction. In the early evening, the sky is blackened as these large bats (wing span 1.3 m) depart for a night of foraging. Other species form smaller, more secretive groups and some such as *Melonycteris* and *Nyctimene* may hang solitarily or as a mother-infant pair among the leaves of trees. Only a few species occupy caves. Large colonies of the Greater Naked-backed fruit bat (*Dobsonia moluccensis*) frequently occupy the twilit gallery near the cave entrance, whereas the echolocating species of *Rousettus* may be encountered in the deeper, darker portions of caves or tombs. Occasionally, but as a rule less frequently than by microchiropterans, human habitations may be occupied by pteropodids.

The foraging behaviour of pteropodids is rather interesting and spectacular to witness. Flowering and

fruit setting of tropical trees is typically asynchronous. These bats appear to monitor the flowering or fruiting progress of a particular tree or stand of trees. When the time is right, they congregate in hordes over several nights in a feeding frenzy during which time they ravage and literally strip the tree of fruit or flowers. The composition of visiting bat species may change as the tree goes through its reproductive cycle of producing flowers and fruits. For example, *Melonycteris melanops*, *Macroglossus minimus*, *Pteropus capistratus*, and *Pteropus hypomelanus* have been observed feeding on the open flowers of kapok trees in the Bismarck Archipelago. Later in the season, after fruits have set, these pteropodids disappear and they are replaced by *Pteropus neohibernicus* and *Dobsonia moluccensis* which feed on the tough-skinned kapok fruits. Some pteropodids, such as the Grey-headed flying fox (*Pteropus poliocephalus*) or the Collared flying fox (*Pteropus scapulatus*) in eastern Australia migrate seasonally to follow the ripening of fruit in different regions.

Fruits are occasionally carried to a convenient perch where they are consumed. Since the seeds are generally discarded along with the fibrous pulp or passed through the intestinal tract, many members of the family are involved in the important ecological function of dispersing the seeds of fruiting trees and shrubs. Indeed, many tropical plants such as fig (*Ficus*) require the passage of their seeds through the digestive tracts of either bats or birds before proper germination can occur. The nectar or pollen-feeding pteropodids, not surprisingly, are important pollinators of many tropical trees and shrubs.

As might be expected, the frugivorous habits and tastes of many pteropodids extend to fruiting trees utilized by man as a food source. The havoc and devastation wreaked by these bats on such fruiting trees frequently puts them in direct conflict with man as fruit crop pests. They are especially fond of succulent, sweet fruits such as mangos, and in regions such as Egypt and the Middle East they are serious crop pests and must be controlled. On the other hand, many flying foxes are large and constitute a readily available and easily obtainable animal protein resource for man. They are eaten regularly by local populations in Africa and Asia and, indeed, are considered a delicacy by some Asian cultures to the extent that commercial exploitation may well be a threat to some. The skeletal remains of *Dobsonia* in kitchen middens in New Guinea suggest that these bats were an important food source for aboriginal inhabitants some 10 000 years ago. Even today, it is not uncommon to find flying foxes trussed up in banana leaves in native markets alongside other indigenous mammal species.

Breeding appears to occur throughout the year, although there may be one or several peaks in reproduction associated with rainy seasons and/or food abundance. One newborn is the rule, but

occasionally twins may occur. The young is carried by the mother as she forages, until it becomes too heavy, and it is frequently carried to the feeding site where it is put off on a branch while the mother continues to feed.

Most pteropodids are quiet and secretive. However, others are especially vocal and create considerable noise and racket in and around the roost or feeding site. One species, the Hammer-headed bat (*Hypsignathus monstrosus*) has an enormously developed larynx which occupies the upper chest as well as the throat. These bats are very noisy and, perhaps, belong to one of two mammalian species that gather together in groups (leks) for the purpose of attracting mates.

The faces and heads of most pteropodids are dog-like in appearance, hence the name 'flying foxes.' Most species are reddish brown or brown and rather mundane in general appearance. Other pteropodids are truly bizarre and spectacularly coloured. Among the more curious are the Tube-nosed bats (*Nyctimene* and *Paranyctimene*) which have a short, tubular extension on each nostril that is directed laterally. The Hammer-headed bat (*Hypsignathus monstrosus*) lives up to its latinized name with a long, deep muzzle that is decorated with many bumps and folds of skin. Some pteropodids (many species of the genus *Pteropus*) possess richly coloured mantles over the shoulders and upper back. This is often in striking contrast with the grey or greyish brown coloration of the head. White markings occur on the faces of the Stripe-faced fruit bat (*Styloctenium wallacei*) and *Scotonycteris*, while others such as *Epomops*, *Epomophorus*, or *Nanonycteris* have white spots at the base of the ear. White tufts of specialized glandular hairs may adorn the shoulders of some species. The Spotted-winged fruit bat (*Balionycteris maculata*) has white or yellowish spots or blotches on the wings. *Nyctimene* has similar mottled yellow or whitish markings on the wings as well as spots and blotches on the face, ears, nose, and tail membrane. In the Black-bellied fruit bat (*Melonycteris melanops*), these markings are similar, but bright reddish orange.

Two, three, or four subfamilies of Recent pteropodids are recognized by bat biologists, together with one fossil subfamily. Among extant subfamilies, the Pteropodinae are the more generalized, including the more strictly flower- and fruit-eating genera. The subfamily Harpyionycterinae includes only the rather aberrant Philippine and Sulawesian genus *Harpyionycteris* which is sometimes included in the Pteropodinae. The subfamily Nyctimeninae contains the Tube-nosed genera *Nyctimene* and *Paranyctimene* both of which are occasionally incorporated in the Pteropodinae. Finally, the Macroglossinae includes

*Fig. 11.3 Common Long-tongued fruit bat (*Macroglossus minimus*).*

Table 11.1   Common name, genera, number of extant species, and distribution of the Pteropodidae

Common name	Genera	Species	Distribution
Subfamily: Pteropodinae			
Straw-coloured Fruit bat	*Eidolon*	1	SW Arabia; Ethiopia; Africa S of Sahara; Madagascar
Rousettes	*Rousettus* (incl. *Lissonycteris*)	9	Africa; Comoro Islands; Cyprus; S Asia to Philippines and Solomon Islands
Collared Fruit bat	*Myonycteris*	3	W and S Africa from Sierra Leone to Zambia
None applied	*Boneia*	1	N Sulawesi
Flying foxes	*Pteropus*	65	Madagascar; islands of Indian Ocean; India; SE Asia to Australia; islands of the W, SW, and S Pacific
Woolly flying foxes	*Pteralopex*	2	Solomon Islands; Fiji Islands
None applied	*Acerodon*	6	Lesser Sunda Islands; Sulawesi; Philippines; N Moluccas
Small-toothed Fruit bat	*Neopteryx*	1	W Sulawesi
Striped-faced Fruit bat	*Styloctenium*	1	Sulawesi
Naked-backed Fruit bats	*Dobsonia*	11	Lesser Sunda Islands to Sulawesi, Philippines, Australia, New Guinea, and Solomon Islands
Anchieta's Fruit bat	*Plerotes*	1	S Zaire; Zambia; Angola
Hammer-headed Fruit bat	*Hypsignathus*	1	C Africa from Gambia to Kenya, Zaire, and NE Angola
Epauletted Fruit bats	*Epomops*	3	Africa S of Sahara to Angola and Botswana
Epauletted Fruit bats	*Epomophorus*	9	Africa S of Sahara
Dwarf Epauletted Fruit bats	*Micropteropus*	3	Africa from Senegal to Ethiopia, Tanzania, and Angola
Veldkamp's Dwarf Fruit bat	*Nanonycteris*	1	W Africa from Guinea to Cameroon
None applied	*Scotonycteris*	2	W Africa from Liberia to Zaire and Gabon
Short-palate Fruit bat	*Casinycteris*	1	W Africa from Cameroon to Zaire
Dog-faced Fruit bats	*Cynopterus*	5	India to China, Java, Timor, Sulawesi, and Philippines
Tail-less Fruit bats	*Megaerops*	4	NE India to Sumatra, Java, Borneo, and Philippines
None applied	*Ptenochirus*	2	Philippines
None applied	*Dyacopterus*	2	Malaya to Sumatra, Borneo, and Philippines
Black-capped Fruit bat	*Chironax*	1	Thailand to Sumatra, Java, and Sulawesi
None applied	*Latidens*	1	S India
Lucas' Short-nosed Fruit bat	*Penthetor*	1	Malaya; Borneo
Swift Fruit bat	*Thoopterus*	1	N Sulawesi; North Moluccas (Morotai Island); Philippines (Luzon Island)
None applied	*Aproteles*	1	E New Guinea
Blanford's Fruit bat	*Sphaerias*	1	NE India to NW Thailand
Spotted-winged Fruit bat	*Balionycteris*	1	S Thailand; Malaya; Borneo
Pygmy Fruit bat	*Aethalops*	1	Malaya; Sumatra; Java; Borneo
None applied	*Haplonycteris*	1	Philippines
None applied	*Alionycteris*	1	Philippines (Mindanao Island)
Small-eared Fruit bat	*Otopteropus*	1	Philippines (Luzon Island)

Table 11.1   *continued*

Common name	Genera	Species	Distribution
Subfamily: Harpyionycterinae			
Harpy Fruit bats	*Harpyionycteris*	2	Sulawesi; Philippines
Subfamily: Nyctimeninae			
Tube-nosed Fruit bats	*Nyctimene*	13	Timor; Sulawesi; Moluccas; Philippines; New Guinea; Bismarck and Solomon Islands; Santa Cruz Island; N Australia
Lesser Tube-nosed Fruit bat	*Paranyctimene*	1	New Guinea
Subfamily: Macroglossinae			
Dawn Fruit bats	*Eonycteris*	4	Burma to Java and Lesser Sundas (Sumba and Timor Islands); Sulawesi; Philippines
African Long-tongued Fruit bat	*Megaloglossus*	1	W and C Africa from Guinea to Uganda and Angola
Long-tongued Fruit bats	*Macroglossus*	3	NE India through SE Asia, Indonesia, and Philippines; New Guinea; Bismarck and Solomon Islands; N Australia
Blossom Fruit bats	*Syconycteris*	2	Moluccas; New Guinea; Bismarck Islands; NE Australia
Greater Long-tongued Fruit bats	*Melonycteris* (incl. *Nesonycteris*)	3	Bismarck and Solomon Islands
Long-tailed Fruit bat	*Notopteris*	1	New Hebrides (Vanuatu); New Caledonia; Fiji Islands
Subfamily: Archaeopteropodinae			
None applied	*Archaeopteropus*	–	Oligocene (N Italy)
Subfamily: incertae sedis			
None applied	*Propotto*	–	Miocene (Africa)

* Known as fossil only.

the nectar- and pollen-eating genera. Thus, the subfamilial classification of the Pteropodidae reflects the major evolutionary trends among fruit bats. The Pteropodinae, including Harpyionycterinae and Nyctimeninae encompass the general fruit eaters with their relatively strong jaws and massive dentitions. On the other hand, the specialized nectar- and pollen-eating species are placed in the Macroglossinae.

SUBORDER MICROCHIROPTERA

In striking contrast to the Suborder Megachiroptera which is a rather stable group of bats, the suborder Microchiroptera is a much more diverse assortment including many families with a wide variety of food specializations ranging from insects to flesh, fruit, nectar, flowers, pollen, and blood. Members of this assemblage also employ a wide variety of flight styles from erratic fluttering to swift, efficient flight in their daily activity. These different flight styles are provided by different wing morphologies and widely varied shoulder architecture. All living species lack a claw on the second finger. At least one fossil species (*Icaronycteris index*, early Eocene of Wyoming) possessed a claw on this digit. Nearly all microchiropterans have small, insignificant eyes and, so far as is known, echolocation is universal within the suborder. This mode of acoustic orientation is sometimes associated with a complex of noseleaves or specialized ears. In all but the species that are adapted to diets of fruit, pollen, nectar, or blood, the crowns of the chewing teeth have a complex W-shaped pattern of ridges and blades to facilitate the cutting, slicing, and crushing of food.

Family Rhinopomatidae
Mouse-tailed bats

This family includes but one genus, *Rhinopoma*, with no more than three species. These three species occur in the arid and semiarid parts of northern Africa, southwestern Asia and India to Thailand and Sumatra (Fig. 11.4). Mouse-tailed bats have a rudimentary noseleaf consisting of a transverse dermal ridge above the valvular nostrils which can be closed, possibly to prevent sand and dust from entering. These bats have soft greyish brown or dark brown fur on their backs and are slightly paler on their bellies. Mouse-tailed bats are gregarious and colonial, roosting in caves or openings in rock walls and in many man-made structures including houses, wells, tunnels, tombs or pyramids. Rhinopomatids are quite agile and use the thumb as well as the feet to scramble about the roost. At least one species appears to utilize a specialized flight style that consists of a series of alternating rising and falling flutters punctuated with short intervals of gliding.

In some parts of their geographic range, they are known to become torpid for long periods, moving to a definite winter roost not far from the roost occupied during the summer, but offering a different and more suitable environment for the cooler months. Stores of fat are accumulated beneath the naked area on the lower back and at the base of the tail to provide for this torpid period.

Family Emballonuridae
Sheath-tailed bats

Sheath-tailed bats occur throughout the tropical regions of the world from the islands of the Pacific Ocean through Australia, Indonesia and the Philippines to Africa and the New World (Fig. 11.6). The family is known from fossils in the Miocene of Africa and the late Eocene or early Oligocene of Europe. These bats are called Sheath-tailed bats because the tail is partially and rather loosely enclosed in the tail membrane with the tip projecting from the upper surface. Many of the New World species have a small pocket or sac in the antebrachial membrane or propatagium joining the shoulder and forearm; they are often referred to as sac-winged bats. These curious pockets are generally larger in males than in females and often they produce a secretion with a strong musky odour. They are thought to contribute to marking of territories which are defended by harem males. *Taphozous* has a small wing pocket beneath the base of the metacarpals, and many also have a glandular sac at the base of the throat. This throat sac is usually less developed or absent in females. Emballonurids have long, narrow wings and when at rest in the roost they fold the tip of the wing over the upper surface, perhaps to protect it from damage.

As a rule, emballonurids are brown or greyish brown, but some are blackish. The Ghost bats (*Diclidurus*) are pure white or greyish white; the wing membranes, facial skin, and ears are pink with a pale yellowish tinge. Some of the New World species (*Saccopteryx*) have a pair of white stripes running down the back. *Taphozous* frequently has white spots on the body, or is pale cream or whitish underneath.

Table 11.2 Common name, genera, number of extant species, and distribution of the Rhinopomatidae

Common name	Genera	Species	Distribution
Mouse-tailed bats	*Rhinopoma*	3	NW and N Africa from Morocco and Nigeria to Thailand and Sumatra

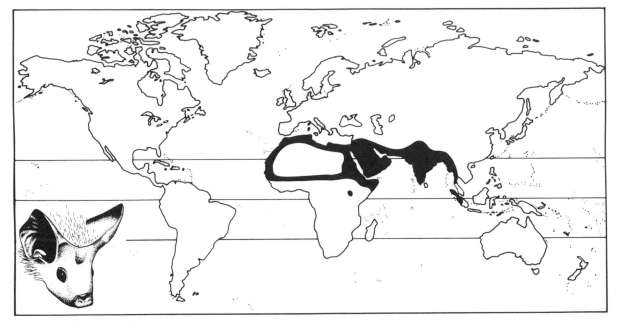

Fig. 11.4 *Distribution of the Rhinopomatidae.*

Fig. 11.5 *Greater Mouse-tailed bat* (Rhinopoma microphyllum*).*

The Proboscis bat (*Rhynchonycteris naso*), an inhabitant of the New World tropics, is yellowish, grizzled grey in colour with an indistinct white stripe down the back. The forearm of this species is clothed with grizzled fur and tufts of yellowish white hair. These bats frequently roost in the open, hanging from branches or exposed roots over or near streams. Their curious coloration is thought to provide a degree of protective camouflage, perhaps giving them the appearance of lichen.

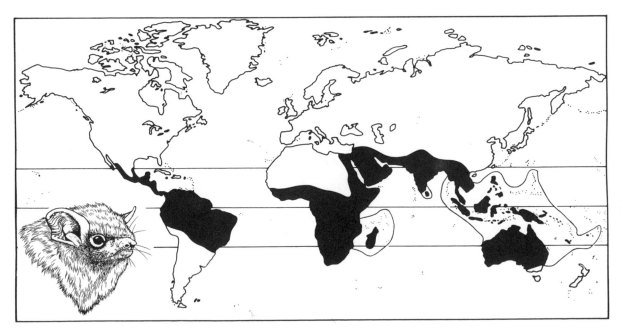

Fig. 11.6 *Distribution of the Emballonuridae.*

Fig. 11.7 *Emballonura* nigrescens.

The different members of the family occupy a wide variety of roosting sites ranging from caves, crevices, foliage and hollow trees to man-made structures. In the Old World, the Tomb bats (*Taphozous*) are usually found in secluded roosts in caves or rock openings and as the common name suggests, they are frequently found in tombs. At least one species has been found in coconut palms and another in hollow logs. The Old World genus *Coleura* is primarily cavernicolous, but may be found in sizeable colonies in human habitations. Members of the genus *Emballonura* occur in a wide range of roosts. Most are found in caves where several species may occupy different parts of the cave. For example, *Emballonura raffrayana* is usually found on the walls of the cave, near the entrance and in the well-lighted zone. *Emballonura furax* seems to prefer the darker portions of the cave, but almost always is found on the wall as opposed to the ceiling. *Emballonura nigrescens* is similar to many of the New World species in that it is usually found hanging in pairs or family groups under the leaves of ginger plants or other low shrubby vegetation; occasionally it is found in caves or under rocky overhangs that are shaded. These bats are usually active throughout the day in these low light, shaded situations. New World species occupy a similar range of roost sites with a large majority being found in non-cave sites.

The social organization of the New World species appears to be rather complex. Males form harems during part of the year and these harems defend a roost territory as well as a feeding territory. A tree trunk may provide several roosting territories and harem males patrol the boundaries between territories keeping marauding intruders out. Casual observation of some of the Old World species of *Emballonura* would seem to suggest similar social organizations.

Emballonurids are agile bats, crawling easily in the roost and scampering about on the vertical walls of caves or tree trunks. They subsist entirely on an insect diet, although there are several unconfirmed reports that they occasionally eat fruit. The species of *Taphozous* are generally large in size and hawk insects on the wing. Breeding may occur throughout the year, but most have a distinct breeding season associated with rainy seasons and/or food abundance.

The most diverse emballonurid fauna is found in

Table 11.3   Common name, genera, number of extant species, and distribution of the Emballonuridae

Common name	Genera	Species	Distribution
Subfamily: Emballonurinae			
Old World Sheath-tailed bats	*Emballonura*	10	Madagascar; Burma to islands of W, SW, and S Pacific
African Sheath-tailed bats	*Coleura*	2	S Arabia; Africa S of Sahara to Angola and Mozambique; Seychelles
Proboscis or Tufted bat	*Rhynchonycteris*	1	Mexico to Bolivia and Brazil; Trinidad
White-lined bats	*Saccopteryx*	4	Mexico to Bolivia and Brazil; Trinidad
Wagner's Sac-winged bat	*Cormura*	1	Nicaragua to Peru and Brazil
Sac-winged bats	*Peropteryx*	2	Mexico to Peru and Brazil; Trinidad; Tobago; Grenada
None applied	*Peronymus*	1	Venezuela; Surinam; Brazil; Peru
Shaggy-haired bat	*Centronycteris*	1	Mexico to Ecuador and Brazil
Least Sac-winged bats	*Balantiopteryx*	3	Mexico to Costa Rica; Ecuador
Pouched or Tomb bats	*Taphozous*[1]	20	Africa to SE Asia and Australia; Philippines; Solomon Islands
None applied	*Vespertiliavus*	–	Late Eocene or early Oligocene (Europe)
Subfamily: Diclidurinae			
Ghost or White bats	*Diclidurus*	4	Mexico to Peru and Brazil; Trinidad
None applied	*Depanycteris*	1	Venezuela; Brazil
Short-eared bat	*Cyttarops*	1	Nicaragua and Costa Rica; Guyana

* Known as fossil only. [1] Includes *Saccolaimus* and *Liponycteris*.

the New World tropics. Two of the three Old World genera (*Taphozous* and *Emballonura*) have numerous species. The distributional pattern of *Emballonura* is rather curious from a biogeographic point of view. All but one species are found in the Pacific and Indo-Australian regions. One species, *Emballonura atrata*, is isolated on Madagascar.

The family is currently divided into two sub-families–the Emballonurinae which includes the majority of species and the Diclidurinae which includes three genera of New World emballonurids. This arrangement is certainly incorrect and further study is likely to find another classification to be more appropriate. The intriguing problem that has been ignored until now is the fact that the New World species form a group that has had a common ancestor. This New World group seems more closely related to *Emballonura* and *Coleura* than to *Taphozous* which appears to form a distinct group of species of its own. The resolution of this problem will no doubt shed considerable light on the overall evolution of world bat faunas.

Family Craseonycteridae
Hog-nosed bat; Bumblebee bat

The Craseonycteridae include only a single genus with one species. The family was discovered in Thailand (Fig. 11.8) in 1973 and so it is therefore the most recently described family of bats. The most distinctive features of *Craseonycteris thonglongyai* are its very small size, its vertical, rather pig-like nose surmounted by a low transverse dermal ridge, large ears with swollen tragus, its extensive tail membrane, and the complete absence of an external tail or of calcars. It is brown or reddish brown in colour, sometimes greyish; the underside is slightly paler than the back. In some ways it resembles the mouse-tailed bats of the family Rhinopomatidae, while in others it is similar to the sheath-tailed bats of the Emballonuridae. It differs widely from the members of either family in several important respects, especially in the structure of the wing which is long and broad and may be adapted for hovering flight. The premaxillary bones which carry

Table 11.4 Common name, genera, number of extant species, and distribution of the Craseonycteridae

Common name	Genera	Species	Distribution
Hog-nosed bat	*Craseonycteris*	1	S Thailand

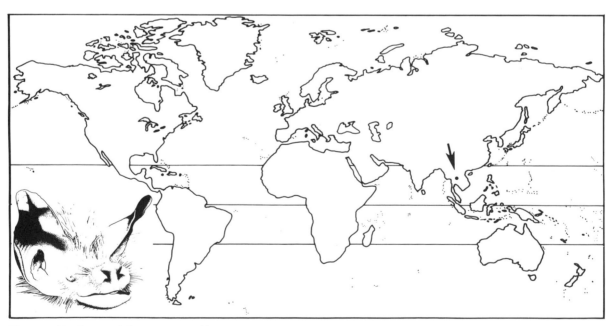

Fig. 11.8 *Distribution of the Craseonycteridae.*

Fig. 11.9 *Kitti's Hog-nosed bat* (Craseonycteris thonglongyai).

the upper incisive teeth are tubular and ring the narial opening to support the flattened narial pad at the front of the muzzle.

Very little is known of the biology of *Craseonycteris thonglongyai,* which so far has been found only in a limited area of Thailand. It roosts in extensive limestone caves where it appears to prefer the high ceiling. Individuals roost separately at some distance from each other. These bats have been observed flying around the tops of bamboo clumps and teak trees on several occasions. The stomach of one individual contained the remains of small beetles, other small insects, and a small spider. These food items would seem to indicate that these small bats capture prey on the wing as well as picking them off foliage. The echolocation sounds of *Craseonycteris* appear to be similar to those reported for rhinopomatids and emballonurids, being constant in frequency with a shallow downsweep of about 3 ms duration. The fundamental frequency is 35 kHz with a strong harmonic at 70 kHz and a weaker harmonic at 105 kHz.

With a forearm length of 22.5-26 mm *Craseonycteris thonglongyai* is probably the smallest known bat, although the Asiatic Lesser Club-footed bat (*Tylonycteris pachypus*), the Asian Funnel-eared bat (*Kerivoula minuta*), African Banana bat (*Pipistrellus nanus*), and/or the American Little Yellow bat (*Rhogeessa parvula*) are only slightly larger. Wingspan aside, this tiny bat also qualifies among the smallest mammals; other likely candidates are the Asian Pygmy shrew (*Crocidura etrusca*) and/or the American Pygmy shrew (*Microsorex hoyi*). This tiny bat is apparently a rare species and is under threat from a variety of factors. Active steps have been taken by the Thai administration and by conservationists to ensure its survival.

Family Nycteridae

Slit-faced bats; Hollow-faced bats

This family includes only the genus *Nycteris* which contains twelve species. Most are found in the tropical forests and semi-arid regions of Africa and adjacent Arabia and Palestine. Curiously, one species of *Nycteris* is isolated in Indonesia, from southern Burma, Malaya, Sumatra, Java, Borneo, to perhaps Sulawesi and Timor Island (Fig. 11.10). All have a characteristic deep longitudinal furrow or slit along the top of the muzzle behind the nostrils. This furrow is bordered and partially concealed by large fleshy outgrowths. There is an extensive concave hollow at its upper end. The cranium has an extensive large concave plate that rests on top of the rostrum and presumably supports this curious pouch. The function of this facial apparatus is not known, but some bat experts suspect that it is involved in echolocation. All species of *Nycteris* also have very large, oval-shaped ears.

Most nycterids vary in colour from brown to reddish brown or pale grey; one is rather orange. Not much is known with regard to their natural history. They appear to occupy a variety of roosting sites ranging from caves and abandoned tunnels to tree holes, human habitations, hollow logs, and tree branches. They have also been reported to use the burrows of digging mammals such as aardvarks and porcupines. Occasionally, they are found roosting with other bats such as *Rhinopoma* and *Hipposideros*. The majority appear to be rather gregarious and colonial, although colonies are typically small consisting of 20 or so individuals. Some species appear to roost as solitary individuals or in groups of two or three.

Slit-faced bats are insectivorous for the most part and may specialize on moths during some portion of the year. They also have been found to eat scorpions which they capture on the ground and appear to search for food close to walls, rock faces, or around bushes.

Family Megadermatidae

False Vampires; Yellow-winged bats

The Megadermatidae includes four genera and five species. These bats are confined to the Old World tropics where they are found in Africa, India, and Sri Lanka to the Philippines and Australia (Fig. 11.12). The family is represented in the fossil record

Table 11.5 Common name, genera, number of extant species, and distribution of the Nycteridae

Common name	Genera	Species	Distribution
Slit-faced bats	*Nycteris*	12	Israel; SW Arabia; Africa S of Sahara; Madagascar; S Burma to Java and Borneo; Timor

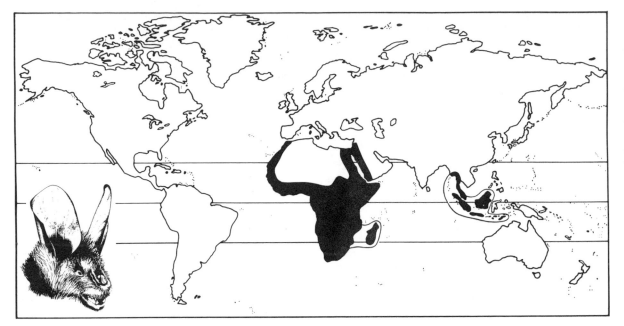

Fig. 11.10 Distribution of the Nycteridae.
Fig. 11.11 Egyptian Slit-faced bat (Nycteris thebaica).

back to the late Eocene or early Oligocene of Europe and the Miocene of Asia. All members of the family have a large, erect cutaneous noseleaf and their ears are also very large and connected for about half of their length. These bats were thought to lack pre-maxillary bones, a truly unusual feature. However, they do possess premaxillae, but these are very tiny, thread-like bones that are often lost when the cranium is prepared for museum study. They do lack upper incisor teeth which is unusual for bats.

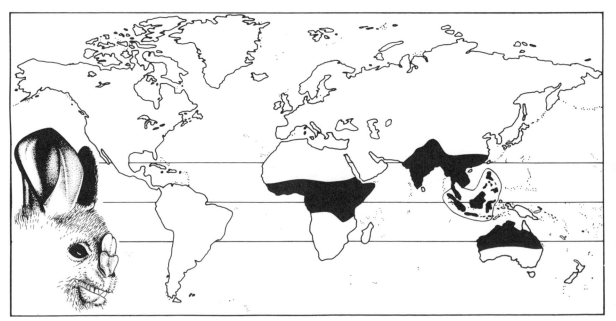

Fig. 11.12 Distribution of the Megadermatidae.
Fig. 11.13 Heart-nosed bat (Cardioderma cor).

The colour of these bats is variable. For example, the Greater False vampire (*Megaderma lyra*) is blue grey or pale greyish brown. The Australian False vampire (*Macroderma gigas*) has whitish hairs on the back that are tipped with greyish brown; the underparts, head, noseleaf, ears, and flight membranes are more or less whitish. In life, these whitish skin areas are coloured by the blood capillaries that lie just below the surface which gives these bats a powdery pinkish colour. The Yellow-winged bat (*Lavia frons*) is perhaps one of the 'prettiest' bats because of its colour. These bats are pale bluish grey or sometimes bluish brown. The noseleaf, ears, and other skin areas are yellowish and the colour of these areas is also enhanced by the underlying blood capillaries. In addition to these striking colours, the fur itself is usually very long and lax.

Some megadermatids roost in caves, rock openings or hollow trees in small colonies. Others roost alone in the open in trees or other vegetation. The false vampires, *Megaderma lyra*, of southern and southeastern Asia and *Macroderma gigas* of Australia are so called because it was long thought that they lived on blood. However, this is not the case. Megadermatids are truly carnivorous bats and they eat small vertebrates including other bats, small rodents, birds, frogs, and fish. They also eat a variety of large insects. While foraging they fly close to the ground and near trees and bushes. The Heart-nosed bat (*Cardioderma cor*) usually flies to an established hunting ground where it hangs up and scans the area for passing insects. When prey is spotted, the waiting bat flies out to intercept the passing meal. Megadermatids usually carry their prey to a favourite perch where they consume it and leave various discarded parts strewn on the ground below. As might be expected, they do not make cordial neighbours and other bats when roosting in the same cave usually seek shelter in the deeper portions of the cave or in inaccessible rock crevices.

Family Rhinolophidae

Horseshoe bats

The bats of this family are found throughout the Old World from Europe and Africa to Japan, Philippines, and Australia (Fig. 11.14). They are known from fossils in the late Eocene of Europe. As their common name implies, these bats have a characteristic noseleaf with a horseshoe-shaped cutaneous plate that surrounds and surmounts the nostrils. This noseleaf is further complicated by two other noseleaf elements. The horseshoe merges with a triangular, pointed and pocketed structure called the lancet which stands erect behind the horseshoe and above the tiny eyes. The third element of the noseleaf is called the sella. It is a flat, strap-like structure that rises from behind the nostrils and stands erect in the middle of the noseleaf. The sella is attached to the lancet by a connecting process that acts like a buttress. The noseleaf is highly characteristic and may be used to identify species as well as groups of species. Its form ranges from relatively simple to a truly bizarre and ornate ornamentation. The precise function of this curious nasal decoration is not fully understood, but it may be associated with beaming or otherwise directing the high frequency orientation signals of these bats.

Table 11.6 Common name, genera, number of extant species, and distribution of the Megadermatidae

Common name	Genera	Species	Distribution
Asiatic False Vampire bats	*Megaderma*[1]	2	E Afghanistan to Sri Lanka, Java Sulawesi, N Moluccas, and Philippines
Australian False Vampire bat	*Macroderma*	1	N and W Australia
Heart-nosed bat	*Cardioderma*	1	Ethiopia to N Tanzania; Zanzibar
Yellow-winged bat	*Lavia*	1	Africa S of Sahara to Zambia
None applied	*Necromantis*	–	Late Eocene or early Oligocene (Europe)
None applied	*Miomegaderma*	–	Miocene (Europe)
None applied	*Provampyrus*	–	Oligocene (Africa)
None applied	*Afropterus*[2]	–	Miocene (Africa)

* Known as fossil only.

[1] Includes *Lyroderma*. [2] *Afropterus* may represent *Megaderma*.

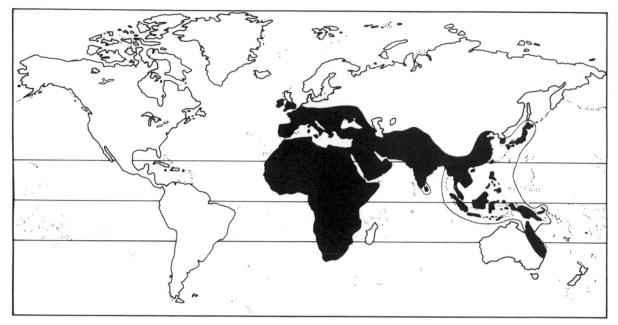

Fig. 11.14 *Distribution of the Rhinolophidae.*

The noseleaf of rhinolophids superficially resembles that of the closely related family Hipposideridae, yet there are pronounced differences between the two.

There is only one modern genus–*Rhinolophus*–in the family which includes approximately 70 recent species. In addition to their unique noseleaves, these bats have large, highly mobile ears and broad wings. Their flight is characteristically slow and fluttery; they are also capable of hovering. Most species are brown or reddish brown in colour. Their hair appears to be particularly susceptible to bleaching and it is not uncommon to find bright, rich orange individuals.

Fig. 11.15 *Representative rhinolophids. A, Broad-eared Horseshoe bat* (Rhinolophus euryotis); *B, Maclaud's Horseshoe bat* (Rhinolophus maclaudi).

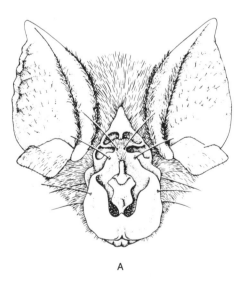

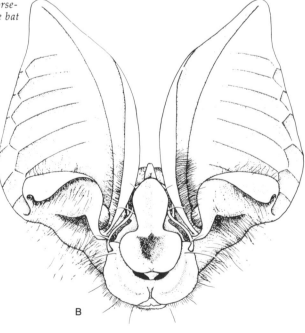

A

B

Table 11.7   Common name, genera, number of extant species, and distribution of the Rhinolophidae

Common name	Genera	Species	Distribution
Horseshoe bats	*Rhinolophus* (incl. *Rhinomegalophus)*	69	Europe and Africa to Japan; SE Asia to Australia, New Guinea, Bismarck Islands, and Philippines
None applied	**Palaeonycteris*	–	Oligocene (Europe)

* Known as fossil only.

Rhinolophids may be found roosting in caves, hollow trees, or, on occasion, in human habitation. They may be found in large gregarious colonies, as solitary individuals, or small groups. They are frequently found roosting among species of *Hipposideros* which are usually found in the same caves. They often forage near the ground or among leaves and foliage, gleaning insects or other arthropods such as spiders. They may land to capture or consume a prey item. Many species appear to specialize on moths at least during some portions of the year.

Although the majority of rhinolophids are tropical, many species occur in the temperate regions of the Old World where they hibernate during the winter months in caves and other similar retreats. They occasionally wake during this hibernation period and move about in the hibernaculum. Hibernating species copulate in the autumn and the female stores the sperm; fertilization occurs in early spring. Young are born in late spring or early summer when food is abundant.

Family Hipposideridae
Old World leaf-nosed bats

The members of this Old World family, rather like their close relatives the rhinolophids, are distributed throughout the tropics and subtropics from Africa to Australia and the New Hebrides (Vanuatu) (Fig. 11.16). Likewise, they are known as fossils from as early as the middle or late Eocene of Europe. Hipposiderids also possess a complicated and ornate noseleaf. There is a horseshoe-shaped portion similar to that of rhinolophids. However, Old World leaf-nosed bats do not have a definite lancet and there is no structure which might be construed to be equivalent to the sella of rhinolophids. Behind the anterior leaf, there is an intermediate swollen area which sometimes has a small central projection. The intermediate leaf forms a base for a thinner, more elaborate, erect posterior element.

This posterior leaf is not pointed, as in rhinolophids, but is usually rounded or flat across the top. In addition, the face of the posterior leaf may have several cell-like compartments separated by thin divisions. There may be a central finger-like tubercle arising from the upper edge of the posterior leaf or in some species there may be several spike-like projections. The complexity of the noseleaf may be further enhanced by secondary foliations of skin from under the edges of the horseshoe. Hipposiderids are differentiated from rhinolophids by other features such as the foot morphology which is rather unusual for bats. Hipposiderids have two phalanges in each toe of the foot instead of two in the first toe and three in the others. There are also major differences in the shoulder joint and the pelvic girdle.

Like that of their relatives, the rhinolophids, the noseleaf of hipposiderids may be rather simple or extremely complex; it too is a valuable feature used to identify species and species groups. In the principal genus *Hipposideros*, the noseleaf is usually comparatively simple, and its posterior element has, at most, a small central projection or is pocketed. In the trident bats (*Asellia* and *Aselliscus*), the top edge of the posterior leaf is divided into three small upstanding points. This pattern is carried to an extreme in the African Trident bat (*Triaenops*) or in the African Short-eared Trident bat (*Cloeotis*). The Flower-faced bat (*Anthops ornatus*) has a quite different arrangement; the upper edge of the posterior element has three rounded cells that face rearward. In the Australian Orange leaf-nosed bat (*Rhinonycteris aurantius*) and the African genera *Cloeotis* and *Triaenops*, there is a small strap-like structure over the centre of the horseshoe in front of the nostrils; the face of the posterior leaf is honeycombed with many cells. In yet another genus, *Coelops*, there are lappets extending over the upper lip from beneath the horseshoe and a small, flat projection on the posterior part of the leaf. There may be a large frontal sac located behind the posterior noseleaf in some species of *Hipposideros*; this is usually more developed in males than in females. Occasionally,

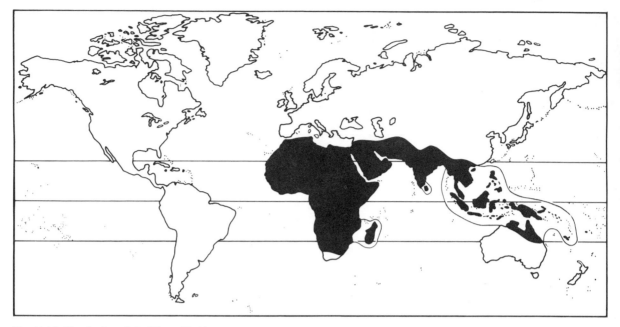

Fig. 11.16 Distribution of the Hipposideridae.

there may be a tuft of stiff white hairs protruding from the centre of this glandular structure.

In general, most hipposiderids are some shade of brown or reddish brown. They, too, seem to be highly susceptible to bleaching and it is not uncommon to find reddish or rich reddish orange individuals. The fur of *Rhinonycteris* is silky and golden yellow or yellow orange and it is one of the most strikingly coloured Australian bats. Some species of *Hipposideros* have extremely large funnel-shaped ears.

As a rule, Old World leaf-nosed bats are found in caves or tunnels. Occasionally, they may be encountered in hollow trees or the burrows of digging mammals. They may roost in very large colonies or separately as solitary individuals. *Hipposideros caffer*, a small African species, may, on occasion, become a pest when it roosts in human habitations.

Fig. 11.17 A, Commerson's Leaf-nosed bat (Hipposideros commersoni); B, *noseleaf of Persian Trident bat* (Triaenops persicus); *noseleaf of Tail-less Leaf-nosed bat* (Coelops frithii).

Table 11.8 Common name, genera, number of extant species, and distribution of the Hipposideridae

Common name	Genera	Species	Distribution
Subfamily: Hipposiderinae			
Old World Leaf-nosed bats	*Hipposideros*[1]	48	Africa; Madagascar; SE Asia to N Australia, Philippines, and New Hebrides (Vanuatu)
Trident Leaf-nosed bats	*Asellia*	2	N Africa to NW India
Trident Leaf-nosed bats	*Aselliscus*	2	Burma and SE Asia to New Hebrides (Vanuatu)
Flower-faced bat	*Anthops*	1	Solomon Islands
Short-eared Trident bat	*Cloeotis*	1	Kenya to Mozambique and S Africa
Orange Leaf-nosed bat	*Rhinonycteris*	1	N and NW Australia
Trident Leaf-nosed bats	*Triaenops*	2	E Africa; Madagascar; Seychelles; SW Asia
Tail-less Leaf-nosed bats	*Coelops*	2	India to Java, Bali, Philippines, and Taiwan
None applied	*Paracoelops*	1	Vietnam
None applied	*Pseudo-rhinolophus*	–	Eocene, Oligocene, Miocene ? (Europe)
Subfamily: *Palaeophyllophorinae			
None applied	*Palaeophyllophora*	–	Eocene, Oligocene (Europe)
None applied	*Paraphyllophora*	–	Late Eocene or early Oligocene, Miocene ? (Europe)

* Known as fossil only. [1] Includes *Brachipposideros*.

Family Noctilionidae

Bulldog bats; Fisherman bats

This family contains one genus–*Noctilio*–with two species (*N. leporinus* and *N. albiventris*). These bats live in the tropical and subtropical parts of the New World (Fig. 11.18). One of the two species is unusual, but not unique in catching and eating fish. Noctilionids have large swollen lips that suggest the common name of Bulldog bats. The sexes are dimorphic in colour, with the males being reddish or slightly orange on the back in contrast to females which are generally brown or greyish. Males are often covered with an oily secretion that has a very pungent fishy odour. The tail membrane is supported by strong calcars. These are especially well developed in the fishing species, *Noctilio leporinus*, which also has long legs and enormously developed feet with strong gaff-like claws.

Small fish are detected by the high frequency signals emitted by the bat as it skims over the surface of quiet water. They detect an exposed fin or perhaps ripples in the water as the fish swims just beneath the surface. Fish are caught by trailing the feet through the water like two large grappling hooks. The calcars lift the tail membrane away from the surface of the water while these bats are fishing. Once they have captured a fish, it is carried to a convenient perch where is is consumed. *Noctilio leporinus* catches fish up to 100 mm in length from as much as 25 mm below the water surface. These bats also catch and eat small crustaceans and aquatic insects floating on the water surface. This fishing activity usually takes place along stream or river margins, but they also fish over brackish water as well. *Noctilio albiventris*, the second species, is a miniature version of *N. leporinus*. Its feet are not so enormous as those of its fishing relative and insects are its primary food source.

Both species may be found roosting as small groups in caves, rocky crevices or hollow trees. Occasionally, small groups are found roosting in human habitations. The roosts of *N. leporinus* are characterized by a strong musky odour. Both species forage over water and both are good swimmers, capable of taking flight from water.

The classification of the Noctilionidae has been uncertain in the past but they are now regarded as being close relatives of the Mormoopidae and Phyllostomidae. Indeed, these three families may be the oldest bats in the New World.

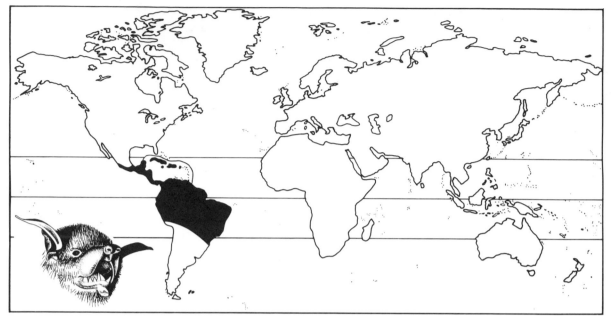

Fig. 11.18 Distribution of the Noctilionidae.
Fig. 11.19 Mexican Bulldog bat (Noctilio leporinus).

Table 11.9   Common name, genera, number of extant species, and distribution of the Noctilionidae

Common name	Genera	Species	Distribution
Bulldog bats	Noctilio	2	Mexico to Argentina; Antilles

Family Mormoopidae

Moustached bats; Naked-backed bats; Ghost-faced bats

This small family includes two tropical New World (Fig. 11.20) genera; the Naked-backed and Moustached bats (*Pteronotus*) and the Ghost-faced bats (*Mormoops*). Until the early 1970s, they were placed in the Phyllostomidae as the subfamily Chilonycterinae. The name *Chilonycteris* has been applied to the Moustached bats, but they are now classified within the genus *Pteronotus*. Unlike the phyllostomids, mormoopids have only a rudimentary noseleaf which is little more than a bump on the nose. Similar to the noctilionids, the lips are rather large and the lower lip and chin bears an ornate array of plates and folds. These ornamentations give the mouth a distinct funnel-like shape when it is opened. In addition, there is a moustache of many stiff hairs near the end of the muzzle. These structures further enhance the funnel-shape of the mouth. Since these bats emit their acoustic signals from the mouth, these curious structures may facilitate the focus of these sounds. Also, the funnel-shaped mouth may aid in the capture of insect prey as these bats feed on the wing much like swallows.

The wing membranes of mormoopids attach high on the flank. In two species, the wing attachments have migrated to the centre of the back. The result of this is that the back appears to be naked which is unusual for bats. Such an arrangement is found only in one other genus, *Dobsonia* (Pteropodidae) and in one species of another pteropodid genus, *Rousettus*, in which effectively the wings reach the midline of the back. In a few others such as the species of *Pteralopex* (also a member of the Pteropodidae) the wing junctions may be higher than usual or approach the centre of the back. The function of this curious wing attachment is not known, but it may serve to

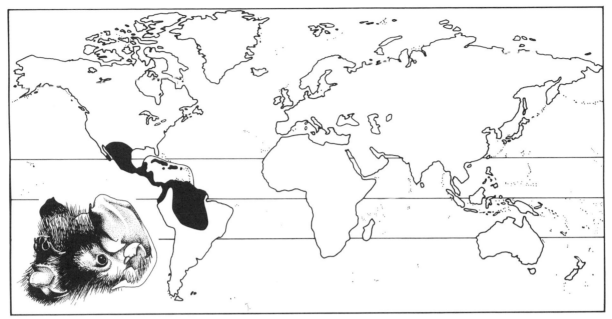

Fig. 11.20 *Distribution of the Mormoopidae.*
Fig. 11.21 *Peters' Ghost-faced bat* (Mormoops megalophylla).

Table 11.10   Common name, genera, number of extant species, and distribution of the Mormoopidae

Common name	Genera	Species	Distribution
Moustached and Naked-backed bats	*Pteronotus*[1]	6	Mexico to Peru and Brazil; Trinidad; Antilles
Ghost-faced bats	*Mormoops*	2	S Arizona and SW Texas to Venezuela, Colombia, and Ecuador; Trinidad

[1] Includes *Chilonycteris* and *Phyllodia*.

increase the lifting area of the wing without increasing its length or width. The back is normally covered with fur beneath the fused wing membranes. Mormoopids are generally brown or reddish brown in colour. Occasionally, bleaching will cause the fur to become bright reddish orange. An individual in the process of molting to its new fur may be quite striking in colour with its back covered with new brown fur rimmed with old, bright orange fur. The ears may be ringed with orange and the muzzle may also have an orange patch. The fur of *Pteronotus* tends to be short, whereas the fur of *Mormoops* is long and lax.

Mormoopids are often found near lakes or streams and as a rule they roost in caves or tunnels. Some species of *Pteronotus* may be found roosting in foliage. Generally, these bats are gregarious and roost in moderate to large colonies. They appear to prefer very hot, humid caves. On the whole, the family has a wide range of ecological tolerances and occupies habitats varying from hot, wet tropical forests to drier and much more arid areas. Most mormoopids are swift flyers that forage close to the ground; *Mormoops* is perhaps the best adapted for rapid flight with its long, narrow wings.

A number of morphological, chromosomal, and biochemical features suggest that the mormoopids are closely related to the Noctilionidae and Phyllostomidae. It is possible that these three families evolved from a common ancestor that lived in the New World in the middle to late Palaeocene.

Family Phyllostomidae
New World leaf-nosed bats

The Phyllostomidae is among the three largest chiropteran families with approximately 50 genera and 140 species. This is only slightly fewer species than found in the Pteropodidae. The Vespertilionidae, the largest bat family with approximately 320 species, has slightly fewer genera than the Phyllostomidae and Pteropodidae. Phyllostomids are confined to the tropical and subtropical environs of the New World (Fig. 11.22). They are represented in the fossil record as early as the Miocene of South America. Although not the largest family, phyllostomids are without rivals in terms of their diversity of food habits. Many species are insectivorous, but many others consume flesh, fruits, flowers and flower products such as pollen and nectar. And, of course, the vampires feed on blood.

Most phyllostomids have a relatively simple, lanceolate noseleaf and for this reason are often referred to as Spear-nosed bats. In a few species, the noseleaf is low and reduced; it is extremely rudimentary in the vampires. In addition to the noseleaf, many phyllostomids have an array of warts and tubercles that adorn the face and lips. The ear and tragus are generally simple, often pointed rather than rounded, and perhaps narrower than in most other bats. In several species, the ears are quite long. The tail and the extent of the tail membrane vary widely. Some phyllostomids lack a tail altogether and the tail membrane is extremely narrow or non-existent. In others, the tail is long and enclosed in an extensive tail membrane. Yet again, the tail may be short and not extend to the full length of the tail membrane.

The colour of the fur is also quite variable and usually is some shade of brown or reddish brown. One species, *Ectophylla alba*, is white. Many species have a pattern of white facial stripes and a few have a mid-dorsal stripe on the back. These markings are thought to provide protective camouflage for species that roost in trees or other exposed situations. The wing membranes are usually black or greyish. In *Ectophylla*, they are quite black and stand in sharp contrast to the white fur. The ears and noseleaf may be rimmed in yellow giving an overall striking appearance to these bats. And finally, the wing tips are often tipped with white patches.

As might be expected in such a large family, phyllostomids occupy a wide range of environments ranging from hot, wet tropical lowland forests, or moist, cool montane forests, to drier savannahs and semiarid deserts. They also occupy a variety of roosts including caves, tunnels, road culverts, hollow trees and logs, among branches and leaves, and human habitations. Members of the subfamily Stenodermatinae are often found clustered in small groups under palm leaves. A few, such as *Uroderma*, *Ectophylla*, and several species of *Artibeus* construct a protective shelter by systematically biting the main ribs of a palm frond thereby causing it to droop and fold around forming a crude 'tent.' This might be considered a form of nest-building, although no bats

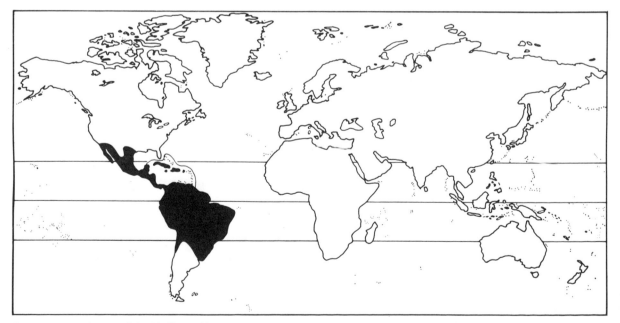

Fig. 11.22 Distribution of the Phyllostomidae.

actually construct a nest like birds or other vertebrates. Phyllostomids may be encountered as very large gregarious colonies or they may be found in small groups or even as solitary individuals.

The classification of the family is in a state of flux at the present time. The group has and continues to attract the attention of most American bat specialists. It is this interest and a wide variety of study techniques being used by these researchers that has caused this healthy confusion. As many as eight or nine subfamilies have been recognized at one time or another. At this time, six seem appropriate to discuss. These subfamilial rankings are generally based on the dietary specializations of their member species or morphological characteristics associated therewith.

Phyllostominae

This subfamily is often regarded as the most primitive of the phyllostomid subfamilies. The Miocene fossil *Notonycteris magdalenesis* from South America (Colombia) is clearly assignable to it. Many of these bats are more or less omnivorous, eating a variety of insects and fruits and their teeth are perhaps less specialized for frugivorous diets than those of other phyllostomids. This subfamily contains the carnivorous members of the family, which include *Phyllostomus*, *Chrotopterus*, *Trachops*, and *Vampyrum*, all preying upon small vertebrates such as birds, other bats, rodents, lizards, and frogs. In addition, they may capture and eat insects and other arthropods as well as eat fruit on occasion. *Vampyrum spectrum* is the

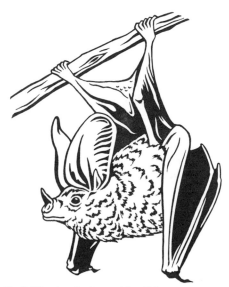

Fig. 11.23 *Californian Leaf-nosed bat* (Macrotus californicus).

Fig. 11.24 *Mexican Long-nosed bat* (Choeronycteris mexicana).

largest of the New World bats with a wing span of about 1 metre.

Glossophaginae

Members of this subfamily are highly specialized to eat diets of fruit pulp, nectar, and pollen, and their adaptations for these diets are parallel to those discussed for the Old World fruit bats of the subfamily Macroglossinae. The muzzle is moderately long and narrow in many glossophagines, reaching an extreme in *Platalina* and *Musonycteris* which have very long noses. Accompanying the elongation of the snout, glossophagines also have very long and extensible tongues. Most are tipped with a brush-like patch of papillae that facilitates the collection and transfer of pollen and nectar to the mouth. The lower lip is frequently grooved and the lower incisors are reduced or absent to allow the easy movement of the tongue in and out of the mouth. In addition, the complicated structure of the teeth, essential for insectivory, has been replaced by reduced, narrow teeth which lack much in the way of cusps and ridges.

This group has attracted considerable attention from bat biologists because it seems to split into two groups that appear to share different ancestors and have different affinities within the family. The major problem is that no two workers seem to be able to agree on the composition of the two groups in question. The question of interest is of course whether or not the observed specializations for pollen- and nectar-feeding in this group are the result of common ancestry or were independently evolved within the family. A similar, but as yet unstudied, problem exists within the Macroglossinae. The Indo-Australian species seem to be related, but the African *Megaloglossus* seems to have affinities within the Pteropodinae and not with the other macroglossines. The resolution of these problems will make a marked contribution to the knowledge of chiropteran evolution.

Carolliinae

The members of this small subfamily are chiefly frugivorous. They appear to be related to the glosso-phagines, but they do not possess the marked modifications of the muzzle or tongue. The teeth are somewhat reduced, but they still retain much of the insectivorous morphology. These bats frequently attack mangos and banana crops and therefore may become pests in many tropical regions of the New World.

Stenodermatinae

These bats are primarily frugivorous, although they may take insects during some parts of the year. In most, the face has been shortened and flattened thereby causing the mouth cavity to become rounded. The dentition is modified for fruit-eating with the molar teeth becoming flat and broad, filling the rounded oral cavity. Much of the insectivorous crown morphology has been lost or reduced so that the teeth are low and flat. There may be a high cutting blade retained on the outside margin of the tooth which may facilitate the cutting and chopping of coarse fruit fibres. These dental adaptations are tied to the frugivorous habit and in that respect coincide with similar modifications in the Old World fruit bats of the family Pteropodidae. However, their degree and form is quite different in the two groups which have been erroneously related in the past.

Many stenodermatines such as *Uroderma*, *Vampy-rops*, *Vampyrodes*, and *Artibeus* have a pattern of white facial stripes and sometimes a white mid-dorsal stripe is present on the back. This subfamily also contains the grotesque Wrinkled-faced bat (*Centurio senex*) which has an extremely flat, naked face covered by an intricate array of cutaneous folds and flaps. These bats roost on low hanging branches and, while at rest, a fold of skin on the chin and throat is extended down over the face with only the tips of the ears visible. There are two naked, translucent patches on this fold of skin that correspond to the position of the eyes. Thus, while covered, these bats may be able to distinguish light and dark or detect movement.

Fig. 11.25 *Jamaican Fruit-eating bat* (Artibeus jamaicensis).

Brachyphyllinae

These bats are confined to the islands of the West Indies and until recently were referred to as the 'Phyllonycterinae.' They are chiefly fruit and nectar feeding species. They, too, appear to be related to the glossophagines, but they are specialized in different ways. The muzzle is rather long, but not nearly as long as in the glossophagines. The teeth are reduced in size and crown complexity and their tongues are extensible. *Brachyphylla* is the least specialized member of the subfamily and has been placed in the Stenodermatinae or, more recently, has been assigned to a subfamily of its own, separate from other 'phyllonycterines.' However, a collection of features clearly suggests that it is most closely related to these other 'phyllonycterine' flower bats.

Desmodontinae

This subfamily includes the true vampires. These bats live on the blood of other warm-blooded vertebrates. Until recently, they were considered to be a distinct family, although related to the Phyllostomidae. This arrangement was justified largely on the basis of their unique food habit and associated specializations. Included among these adaptations are highly modified upper incisors and canines which are long and razor sharp. Most of the remaining teeth are reduced in size. In all other respects, they share the features of phyllostomids and they are now generally regarded as members of this family.

Vampires are very agile, both in the roost and on the ground, crawling easily on their thumbs, forearms, and feet. When foraging, they land on or near their intended and unsuspecting victim. They seek out a relatively naked area of skin where there is an ample blood supply close to the surface. Such areas are around the eyes, lips, ears, feet or fingers, base of the tail, and anus. Here they use their specially designed teeth to make a wound which may be about 10 mm in length, 6 mm wide, and perhaps 5 mm deep. This wound is inflicted in such a manner that it does not awaken the sleeping victim. The saliva of vampires has an anticoagulant that causes the blood to flow freely from the wound. The tongue has grooves along the side and along its ventral surface and is moved rapidly in and out of the mouth. In this fashion, blood is drawn, by capillary action, into the mouth. A feeding session may last for half an hour after which time the vampire is usually gorged with blood. In many cases, it is too heavy to fly properly and may crawl off to a protected place where it waits for some digestion to occur. The specialized kidney facilitates this digestive process by eliminating most of the water that is a large proportion of the blood volume.

Vampire attacks can be dangerous for two reasons. First, vampires are a common vector for rabies and the unsuspecting victim is inoculated with the virus when it is bitten. Ultimately, the victim dies of rabies. As a result of this, large quantities of livestock and some humans are lost every year in regions where vampires occur. In addition to transmitting rabies, vampires leave a wound that, because of the anticoagulant, continues to haemorrhage long after the bat has taken its blood feast. These wounds often become infected and the victim may die or become debilitated as a result of secondary diseases. Young victims may simply bleed to death. Thus, vampires are a serious public health and agricultural pest in those parts of the tropics where they are abundant.

There are three species of vampires, only one of which is a serious pest. This is the Common vampire (*Desmodus rotundus*) which is widespread throughout tropical America. It attacks livestock, humans, and other mammals. The other two species are the Hairy-legged vampire (*Diphylla ecaudata*) which seems to prefer the blood of birds, and the White-winged vampire (*Diaemus youngi*) which attacks birds and mammals to a lesser extent than *Desmodus*.

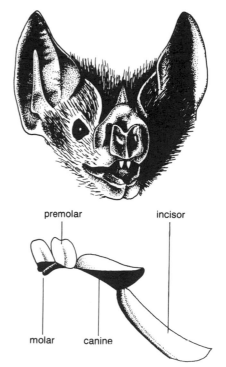

Fig. 11.26 *(Top) Common vampire bat* (Desmodus rotundus); *(Bottom) right upper toothrow of vampire.*

Table 11.11 Common name, genera, number of extant species, and distribution of the Phyllostomidae

Common name	Genera	Species	Distribution
Subfamily: Phyllostominae			
Little Big-eared bats	*Micronycteris*[1]	9	Mexico to Peru and Brazil; Trinidad; Tobago; Grenada
None applied	*Barticonycteris*	1	Costa Rica to E Peru and Guyana
Big-eared bats	*Macrotus*	2	SW United States to Guatemala; Antilles; Bahamas
Sword-nosed bats	*Lonchorhina*	3	S Mexico to Peru and Brazil; Trinidad; Bahamas (accidental)
Long-legged bat	*Macrophyllum*	1	S Mexico to N Argentina
Round-eared bats	*Tonatia*	8	S Mexico to Argentina; Trinidad
Gray's Spear-nosed bats	*Mimon*[2]	3	S Mexico to Bolivia and Brazil
Spear-nosed bats	*Phyllostomus*	4	S Mexico to N Argentina
None applied	*Notonycteris	–	Miocene (South America)
Peters' Spear-nosed bat	*Phylloderma*	1	S Mexico to Peru and NE Brazil
Fringe-lipped bat	*Trachops*	1	S Mexico to Bolivia and S Brazil
Peters' Woolly False Vampire bat	*Chrotopterus*	1	S Mexico to N Argentina and Paraguay
False Vampire bat	*Vampyrum*	1	S Mexico to E Peru and C Brazil; Trinidad; Jamaica (?)

Table 11.11   *continued*

Common name	Genera	Species	Distribution
	Subfamily: Glossophaginae		
Long-tongued bats	*Glossophaga*	5	Mexico to N Argentina; Trinidad; Lesser Antilles; Bahamas (?)
West Indian Long-tongued bats	*Monophyllus*	2	S Bahamas; Antilles
Saussure's Long-tongued bats	*Leptonycteris*	3	S Texas to Venezuela and Colombia; Aruba and Curacao Islands
None applied	*Lonchophylla*	8	Nicaragua to Bolivia and Brazil
None applied	*Lionycteris*	1	Panama to E Peru and N Brazil
Geoffroy's Long-tongued bats	*Anoura*	3	Mexico to Peru and NW Argentina; Trinidad; Grenada
None applied	*Scleronycteris*	1	Venezuela; Brazil
None applied	*Lichonycteris*	2	Guatemala to Peru and Brazil
Underwood's Long-tongued bat	*Hylonycteris*	1	W Mexico to Panama
None applied	*Platalina*	1	Peru
Godman's Long-nosed bats	*Choeroniscus*	4	Mexico to Peru and Brazil; Trinidad
Long-nosed bat	*Choeronycteris*	1	S California and Arizona to NW Venezuela
Banana bat	*Musonycteris*	1	Mexico
	Subfamily: Carolliinae		
Short-tailed leaf-nosed bats	*Carollia*	4	Mexico to Peru and Paraguay; Trinidad; Tobago; Grenada
None applied	*Rhinophylla*	3	Venezuela and Colombia to Peru and Brazil
	Subfamily: Stenodermatinae		
Yellow-shouldered bats	*Sturnira* (incl. *Corvira* and *Sturnirops*)	12	Mexico to N Argentina and Uruguay; Chile(?); Trinidad; Lesser Antilles; Jamaica
Tent-building bats	*Uroderma*	2	S Mexico to Bolivia and Brazil; Trinidad
White-lined bats	*Vampyrops*	9	S Mexico to N Argentina and Uruguay; Trinidad
Great Stripe-faced bats	*Vampyrodes*	2	S Mexico to Peru and Brazil; Trinidad; Tobago
Yellow-eared bats	*Vampyressa* (incl. *Vampyriscus* and *Meta-vampyressa*)	5	S Mexico to Peru and Brazil
White-lined bats	*Chiroderma*	5	S Mexico to Peru and Brazil; Trinidad; Lesser Antilles
White bat	*Ectophylla*	1	Nicaragua to W Panama
McConnell's bat	*Mesophylla*	1	Costa Rica to Bolivia and Brazil; Trinidad
New World Fruit bats	*Artibeus*	15	Mexico to Peru and N Argentina; Trinidad; Antilles; Bahamas
Hart's Little Fruit-eating bat	*Enchisthenes*	1	NE Mexico to Bolivia; Lesser Antilles

Table 11.11 *continued*

Common name	Genera	Species	Distribution
Tree bat	*Ardops*	1	Lesser Antilles
Falcate-winged bats	*Phyllops*	2	Cuba; Hispaniola
Jamaican Fig-eating bat	*Ariteus*	1	Jamaica
Red Fruit bat	*Stenoderma*	1	Puerto Rico; Virgin Islands
Ipanema bat	*Pygoderma*	1	Surinam to N Argentina and Paraguay
Short-faced Fruit bat	*Ametrida*	1	Venezuela; Brazil; Trinidad
None applied	*Sphaeronycteris*	1	Venezuela; Colombia; Peru; Bolivia
Wrinkle-faced bat	*Centurio*	1	Mexico to Central America; Trinidad
Subfamily: Brachyphyllinae			
None applied	*Brachyphylla*	2	S Bahamas; Cuba and Isle of Pines; Hispaniola; Puerto Rico; Virgin Islands; Lesser Antilles
Brown Flower bat	*Erophylla*	1	Bahamas; Greater Antilles
Pallid Flower bats	*Phyllonycteris*[3]	4	Greater Antilles
Subfamily: Desmodontinae			
Common Vampire bat	*Desmodus*	1	Mexico to Chile, Argentina, and Uruguay; Trinidad
White-winged Vampire bat	*Diaemus*	1	Mexico to Bolivia and Brazil; Trinidad
Hairy-legged Vampire bat	*Diphylla*	1	S Texas to E Peru and S Brazil

* Known as fossil only. [1] Includes *Xenoctenes, Lampronycteris, Neonycteris, Trinycteris* and *Glyphonycteris.*
[2] Includes *Anthorhina.* [3] Includes *Reithronycteris.*

Family Natalidae

Funnel-eared bats; Long-legged bats

This small family contains only the single genus *Natalus.* These bats are restricted to the tropical lowlands of the New World from northern Mexico to Brazil, and on the islands of Trinidad, Curacao, and the Antilles (Fig. 11.27). Natalids are rather small, slim bats with a high, domed head. Their ears are large and funnel-shaped and their legs and wings are long and slender. Adult males have a curious, bulbous 'natalid' organ that lies just below the skin of the forehead; its function is not known. The fur is long and lax and varies in colour from grey or yellowish to rich reddish brown or chestnut. Funnel-eared bats generally roost in caves or tunnels, but have been found under overhanging rock ledges. Their flight style is fluttery and erratic, and in some ways parallels the flight styles of the Old World Funnel-eared bats of the vespertilionid genus *Kerivoula.* Natalids feed on a variety of small insects.

The Natalidae are probably related to two other small New World families, the Thyropteridae and Furipteridae. These three families are currently regarded as being most closely related to the large, cosmopolitan family Vespertilionidae.

Table 11.12 Common name, genera, number of extant species, and distribution of the Natalidae

Common name	Genera	Species	Distribution
Funnel-eared bats	*Natalus*[1]	4	Mexico to Brazil; Trinidad; Antilles; Bahamas

[1] Includes *Chilonatalus* and *Nyctiellus.*

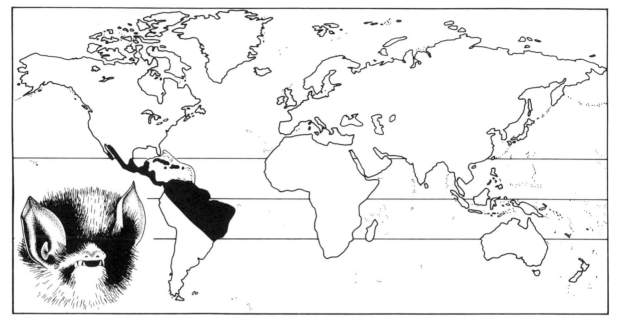

Fig. 11.27 Distribution of the Natalidae.

Fig. 11.28 Mexican Funnel-eared bat (Natalus stramineus).

Family Furipteridae

Smoky bats

The members of this small family occur in tropical South America (Fig. 11.29). They resemble the bats of the family Natalidae and Thyropteridae in many respects. They have a high, domed crown and large, separate and funnel-shaped ears. The head is covered with dense fur. Although the thumb is present, it is so small and almost entirely enclosed in the antebrachial membrane that they are sometimes called 'thumb-less' bats. The fur is generally rather coarse and greyish or brownish grey in colour. Very little is known about the biology of the family. They appear to prefer roosting in caves, but have been found in man-made tunnels or storehouses. The genus *Amorphochilus* is one of the few bats known to inhabit the dry, low country lying between the foothills of the Andes and the west coast of South America.

Family Thyropteridae

Disc-winged bats; New World Sucker-footed bats

Thyroptera is the sole genus of this family and is distributed from Mexico to the northern part of South America (Fig. 11.31). The muzzle of these bats is long and slender, with small warts above the nostrils. As in the Natalidae and Furipteridae, the crown of the head is high and domed; the ears are funnel-shaped. Thyropterids have a circular adhesive disc or sucker-shaped cup at the base of the thumb and on the sole of the foot just in front of the heel. There is a short stalk associated with the disc on the thumb. There are only two phalanges in each of the toes and the third and fourth toes are fused together to the tips of the claws. The fur is generally reddish brown or light brown with the underside being whitish in one of the two species and brownish in the other.

Table 11.13 Common name, genera, number of extant species, and distribution of the Furipteridae

Common name	Genera	Species	Distribution
Smoky bat	*Furipterus*	1	Costa Rica to Peru and Brazil; Trinidad
None applied	*Amorphochilus*	1	W Ecuador to N Chile

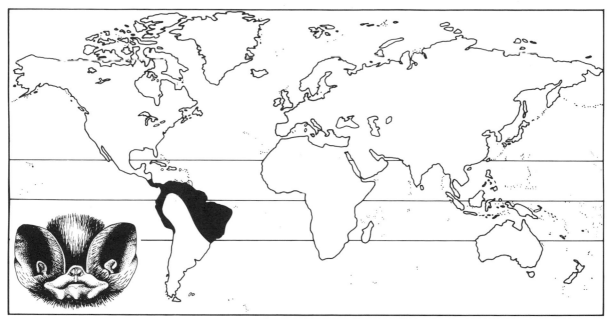

Fig. 11.29 *Distribution of the Furipteridae.*
Fig. 11.30 *Smoky bat* (Amorphochilus schnablii).

Table 11.14   Common name, genera, number of extant species, and distribution of the Thyropteridae

Common name	Genera	Species	Distribution
Disc-winged bats	*Thyroptera*	2	S Mexico to Peru and Brazil; Trinidad

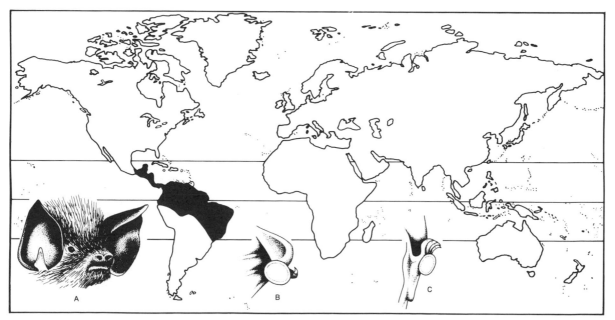

Fig. 11.31 *Distribution of the Thyropteridae.*
Fig. 11.32 *A, Spix's Disc-winged bat* (Thyroptera tricolor); *B, C, discs on thumb and foot.*

These bats frequently roost as family groups in a rolled leaf or frond, often those of banana trees or other plants that produce new leaves as long cylindrical shoots. The sucker-like discs are used to adhere to the sides of such leaves. Unlike most bats, these bats do not hang with their head downward, but instead face upward towards the entrance of their tubular retreat. As the leaf matures and unfurls, they have to seek other new shoots for roosts.

These bats are thought to be related to the previous two families, Natalidae and Furipteridae, and all have been treated as relatives of the large family Vespertilionidae. Recent studies of the uterine morphology of thyropterids strongly suggest a relatively close tie with the Phyllostomidae which is a further indication of how little is really known with regard to the evolutionary relationships among bats.

Fig. 11.33 Distribution of the Myzopodidae.

Fig. 11.34 A, Sucker-footed bat (Myzopoda aurita); B, adhesive sucker on thumb.

Family *Myzopodidae*
Old World Sucker-footed bats

This family is represented by but one species and one genus, *Myzopoda aurita*. Individuals of this species are extremely rare and the family is now restricted to Madagascar (Fig. 11.33), but is also represented in the early Pleistocene deposits at Olduvai in eastern Africa. *Myzopoda aurita* resembles the New World species of *Thyroptera*, with a high, domed crown and large ears, although these are not funnel-shaped. Myzopodids have a sucker-like disc at the base of the thumb, but it does not have a stalk or pedicle and there is a similar disc on the sole of the foot. The tragus of *Myzopoda* is rather curious in structure, being mushroom-like with a kidney-shaped fleshy expansion surmounting a short stalk. Like furipterids, the thumb is quite small and the claw is vestigial. The toes of the foot have but two phalanges and are united for much of their length. There is very little known about the biology of this rare bat. One was captured in a rolled leaf and another was reportedly found in the axil of a Traveller's palm leaf, suggesting roosting habits similar to thyropterids.

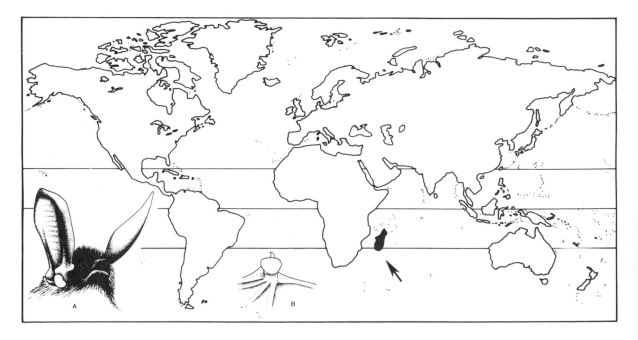

Table 11.15   Common name, genera, number of extant species, and distribution of the Myzopodidae

Common name	Genera	Species	Distribution
Old World Sucker-footed bat	*Myzopoda*	1	Madagascar

Family Vespertilionidae

Evening bats

With nearly 320 species, this family is the largest among bats. Among mammals, it is second only to the rodent family Muridae (*c.* 1000 species) in overall size. In addition to being one of the two largest families, vespertilionids are among the most widely dispersed of mammals. They occur almost everywhere in the world, to the limits of tree growth, being excluded only from the Polar and near Polar regions (Fig. 11.35). They are also found on some isolated oceanic islands and island groups. As fossils, the family is known from the Eocene of Europe, the Oligocene and Miocene of North America, the Pliocene of Asia, and the Pleistocene of Africa and South America. Its members are found in a wide variety of environments ranging from tropical forests to arid semi-desert and desert regions as well as throughout the cool temperate regions of the world. As might be expected, this large and adaptable group of bats displays a correspondingly diverse range of variation. Generally, the muzzle is simple, although members of the subfamily Murininae have tubular nostrils similar to those found in the pteropodid genus *Nyctimene*. The facial region may have a variety of swollen glands and related structures. A true noseleaf is absent in all, but the members of the subfamily Nyctophilinae have a small rudimentary and fleshy nasal flap. The eyes are usually quite small and often hidden by the thick fur on the face. The ears of vespertilionids are generally small and simple in structure, but some species have very long ears. In the genera *Plecotus*, *Idionycteris*, and *Euderma*, the ears are rolled up around the head when the bat is at rest, but they are inflated by blood pressure when the bat is active. The tragus is usually a simple tongue-shaped structure, but it too may be long and variable in form. Occasionally, the lower margin of the ear is attached low on the side of the head just behind the corner of the mouth. In the Lobe-lipped bats of the genus *Chalinolobus*, the lower lip sometimes has a small, fleshy lateral lappet on each side of the head in front of the insertion of the posterior edge of the ear. As a rule, the tail membrane is extensive and encloses the tail which extends to its posterior border. Small suction pads, similar to those described for the Thyropteridae and Myzopodidae are found in *Eudiscopus*, *Glischropus*, *Tylonycteris*, and a few isolated species of *Myotis*. There is a similar pad at the base of the thumb in one species of *Hesperoptenus*, and the base of the thumb and the sole of the foot is thickened in some *Pipistrellus*.

The skull of most of the small-sized vespertilionids, such as *Kerivoula* and *Pipistrellus*, is delicate and lightly built, whereas the skull of larger species, such as *Scotophilus* and *Lasiurus*, is heavy and relatively massive. In some species, such as the Bamboo bat (*Tylonycteris*) and Moloney's Flat-headed bat (*Mimetillus moloncyi*), the skull is extremely flat; indeed, not much thicker than several coins. There is a general trend throughout the family to shorten the jaws to increase the effectiveness of the chewing muscles. This, of course, results in a reduction in the number of teeth which varies from a total of 38 to as few as 28 within the family. This reduction involves losing premolars for the most part, although incisors may be reduced to one above and two below on each side of the mouth. The molar teeth are always three above and below, but the last molar in each series may be quite short.

Most vespertilionids are monotonously brown, grey, or blackish brown in colour. *Rhogeessa*, *Baeodon*, *Antrozous*, and *Scotophilus* are predominantly yellowish brown. All tend to be slightly paler on the underside. While most vespertilionids are rather dull and often referred to as 'little brown bats', there are a few species which are truly spectacular and beautiful in colour and colour pattern. The Painted bat (*Kerivoula picta*) is one of the most beautiful of all bats with its brilliantly orange coloured fur. This reddish orange colour extends along the forearm and digits and contrasts markedly with its jet black wing membranes. The African myotis (*Myotis welwitschii*) is similarly coloured as is the African Woolly bat (*Kerivoula argentata*). In the latter, the orange fur is frosted with whitish tips. The American Red bat (*Lasiurus borealis*) is bright red and its close relative *Lasiurus cinereus* is hoary. All of these species roost in trees and this coloration is thought to provide some degree of camouflage. The butterfly bats (*Glauconycteris*) display other striking colour patterns of white, pale yellow, grey, and black spots and stripes. In addition, the wing membranes of these bats are often mottled or reticulated. There is an irregular pattern of white spots and markings on an orange-red background in the Harlequin bat (*Scotomanes ornatus*) which is said to resemble hanging fruit when roosting. *Euderma* is reddish brown or black with two pure white spots on the shoulders and a third white spot on the back. This colour pattern, coupled with its pink face and enormous pink ears makes it one of the prettiest American bats. The colour pattern is thought to aid the concealment of these bats in conditions of changing light and shade which are encountered in their rocky cliff-face retreats.

The majority of vespertilionids are wholly insectivorous, catching insects on the wing or picking them from the surface of leaves and other vegetation. These bats may capture insects in the mouth, but frequently they use their wings like a tennis racket to bat the

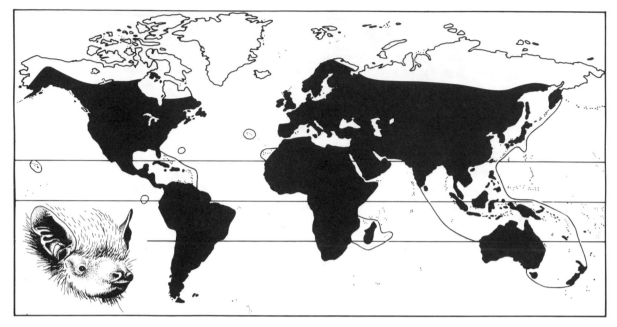

Fig. 11.35 Distribution of the Vespertilionidae.
Fig. 11.36 Nathusius' pipistrelle (Pipistrellus nathusii).

prey into the tail membrane. In addition, the capture of an insect is often accompanied by an aerobatic somersault in which they tuck their head down into the tail membrane to retrieve the captured food item. Some species, such as the Pallid bat (Antrozous pallidus) of the southwestern deserts of America, land on the ground and stalk scorpions and other large arthropods. The Fish-eating bat (Pizonyx vivesi) of western Mexico, and several species of Myotis catch and eat small fish. These fish-eating vespertilionids have adaptations similar to those described for the Bulldog bat (Noctilio leporinus), including large feet with sharp claws. Captured food items may be eaten while foraging for more food or they may be carried to a convenient perch where they are dismembered and eaten at leisure. Foraging may take place in open spaces or in cluttered spaces around low bushes and tree branches. Most species appear to patrol definite feeding territories and some defend these hunting areas from other individuals of the same species or from individuals of different species.

Vespertilionids may be found in nearly every conceivable roosting site. They are frequently found in caves, mines, wells, tunnels, and rock crevices. Pizonyx may be found in sea caves; at one location in Baja California they take shelter in the rocky rubble on the beach. Other vespertilionids also take refuge in cracks in cave floors or under loose gravel. Many species roost in open situations such as trees, tree holes, road culverts, and even inside large flowers.

Abandoned birds' nests, such as those of the African weavers, may be used. Other species find a favourite retreat beneath loose tree bark or behind the shutters of houses. Many vespertilionids of the eastern United States are rather unjustly considered pests because they roost in human dwellings. The southeast Asian Club-footed bats (Tylonycteris) roost inside bamboo stalks once they have been opened by boring insect larvae. Several species, Myotis bocagei, M. mystacinus, and Pipistrellus nanus roost singly or in small groups inside rolled banana leaves. Male and female vespertilionids may roost apart during most of the year, gathering only to reproduce; mothers and newborn frequently occupy nursery roosts. Colonies may be very large, or composed of small groups of individuals. Tree dwelling species often roost as solitary individuals or mother/infant pairs.

Much of the success of the family in extending throughout the temperate regions of the world is due to their ability to adapt their thermoregulation and metabolism to hibernation during the winter months when temperatures are low and insects are scarce or unavailable. Many species migrate long distances or move to more favourable hibernation sites to avoid the cold winter temperatures. Hibernation sites are usually different from those used during the warmer months and are generally caves with stable cool temperatures and equitable humidities. Reproduction in all vespertilionids is, as a rule, a seasonal phenomenon and those that hibernate have reproductive behaviours that are geared around this period of inactivity. Thus, some store sperm over the hibernation period, while others have delayed implantation of the fertilized blastocyst or delayed embryogenesis of the implanted embryo.

The classification of this large family is in dire need of re-evaluation. Currently the family is divided into five subfamilies. The Vespertilioninae include the least specialized species and is composed of the majority of genera. The subfamily Miniopterinae contains only the Long-fingered bats of the genus *Miniopterus*. These bats are peculiar in that they have a very long third finger of which a large percentage of the length is made up by the second phalanx. The Tube-nosed bats (*Murina*) and the Hairy-winged bat (*Harpiocephalus harpia*) are assigned to their own subfamily, the Murininae. These bats have curious tube-like extensions on the nostrils. The Kerivoulinae includes the funnel-eared bats of the genera *Kerivoula* and *Phoniscus*. *Antrozous* and *Nyctophilus* have a rudimentary leaf-like flap on their noses and are consequently placed in the subfamily Nyctophilinae. Finally, the Tomopeatinae contains the genus *Tomopeas* whose placement within the family Vespertilionidae has been questioned recently. Its ears are

similar to those of the Molossidae, but in other respects it resembles other vespertilionids. There are other aspects of the classification that should be noted. These include different generic assignments and are here included for the general reader who might encounter these variations in other reading. The genus *Pizonyx* is often placed in the genus *Myotis*; *Scotozous* and *Ia* are sometimes included in *Pipistrellus*; *Scotoecus* may be placed in *Nycticeius*; and *Glauconycteris* may be referred to *Chalinolobus*. *Eptesicus* is sometimes placed in *Pipistrellus* or both may be assigned to *Vespertilio*. Some specialists go even further and place *Glischropus, Laephotis, Histiotus, Philetor, Tylonycteris, Mimetillus*, and *Hesperopterus* in the genus *Vespertilio*. *Baeodon* is frequently united with *Rhogeessa*; *Dasypterus* with *Lasiurus*; and *Idionycteris* is often placed into *Plecotus*, whereas other American representatives of this genus are sometimes referred to *Corynorhinus*. The above variations, some of which bear some validity or are at least worthy of consideration, all involve vespertilionine genera. The classification with the other subfamilies is more or less stable. Occasionally, *Phoniscus* is united with *Kerivoula*.

Table 11.16 Common name, genera, number of extant species, and distribution of the Vespertilionidae

Common name	Genera	Species	Distribution
Subfamily: Vespertilioninae			
Mouse-eared bats	*Myotis*[1]	94	Europe; Asia to Japan, Australia, and New Hebrides (Vanuatu); Africa; Azores; Canada to Argentina and Chile; Lesser Antilles
Fish-eating bat	*Pizonyx*	1	NW Mexico
Silver-haired bat	*Lasionycteris*	1	Alaska; S Canada; United States to NE Mexico
Disc-footed bat	*Eudiscopus*	1	Burma; Laos
Pipistrelles	*Pipistrellus*	48	Europe; Asia to Australia and Tasmania; Africa; Madagascar; S Canada to Honduras
None applied	*Scotozous*	1	India
Noctules	*Nyctalus*	5	SW Europe, Azores, and N Africa to N India, China, Korea, and Japan
Thick-thumbed bats	*Glischropus*	2	Burma to Java, Borneo, and Philippines
Brown bats	*Eptesicus* (incl. *Rhinopterus*)	33	Europe; Africa; Asia to Australia; Alaska to Argentina; Antilles
Great Evening bat	*Ia*	1	Assam to S China and Vietnam
Particoloured bats	*Vespertilio*	3	Europe; N Asia to Japan
Long-eared bats	*Laephotis*	4	Ethiopia to Angola
Big-eared Brown bats	*Histiotus*	5	Colombia to Argentina and Chile

Table 11.16 *continued*

Common name	Genera	Species	Distribution
None applied	*Philetor*	1	E Nepal; Malaya; Sumatra; Java (?); Borneo; Philippines; New Guinea; Bismarck Islands
Club-footed or Bamboo bats	*Tylonycteris*	2	India to Sulawesi; Timor; Philippines
Flat-headed bat	*Mimetillus*	1	W Africa to W Kenya and Angola
Narrow-winged bat	*Hesperoptenus* (incl. *Milithronycteris*)	5	India to Malaya, Borneo and Sulawesi
Butterfly bats	*Glauconycteris*	10	Africa S of Sahara to Namibia
Lobe-lipped bats	*Chalinolobus*	6	Australia and New Guinea; New Caledonia; New Zealand
Light-winged Lesser House bats	*Scotoecus*	4	Africa S of Sahara to Mozambique and Angola; Pakistan; N India
Evening bats	*Nycticeius* (incl. *Scoteanax* and *Scotorepens*)	6	SW Arabia; Africa to Mozambique and Namibia; Australia; United States to Mexico; Cuba
Little Yellow bats	*Rhogeessa*	5	C Mexico to Ecuador, Bolivia and S Brazil; Trinidad
Allen's Little Yellow bat	*Baeodon*	1	W and C Mexico
Harlequin bats	*Scotomanes*	2	N India to Vietnam
Yellow bats	*Scotophilus*	9	Africa S of Sahara; Ethiopia, Somalia, Aden; Madagascar; Reunion Island; Pakistan to Timor; N Sulawesi; Philippines
Long-eared bat	*Otonycteris*	1	Algeria and Tunisia to Afghanistan, Turkestan, and Kashmir
Red or Hoary bats	*Lasiurus*	5	S Canada to Paraguay, Argentina, and Uruguay; Bahamas; Greater Antilles; Trinidad; Galapagos Islands; Hawaii
Yellow bats	*Dasypterus*	4	New Jersey to Argentina and Uruguay; Trinidad; Cuba and Isle of Pines
Barbastelles	*Barbastella*	2	Europe; N Africa; N India; Asia to Japan
Long-eared bats	*Plecotus*[2]	5	Europe; N Africa; Asia to Japan; SW Canada to Mexico; Cape Verde Island
Big-eared bat	*Idionycteris*	1	SW United States to Mexico
Spotted bat	*Euderma*	1	C Canada to W and SW United States and NE Mexico
None applied	*Pareptesicus*	–	Miocene (Europe)
None applied	*Stehlinia*	–	Late Eocene or early Oligocene (Europe)
None applied	*Oligomyotis*	–	Oligocene (North America)
None applied	*Suaptenos*	–	Miocene (North America)
None applied	*Miomyotis*	–	Miocene (North America)
None applied	*Samonycteris*	–	Pliocene (Europe)
None applied	*Simonycteris*	–	Pliocene (North America)
None applied	*Ancenycteris*	–	Late Miocene (North America)

Subfamily: Miniopterinae

Long-fingered bats	*Miniopterus*	11	S Europe; Africa; Madagascar; S Asia to Philippines; New Caledonia; Loyalty Islands, and Australia

Table 11.16   *continued*

Common name	Genera	Species	Distribution
	Subfamily: Murininae		
Tube-nosed bats	*Murina* (incl. *Harpiola*)	12	India to Japan; Java; Borneo; Sulawesi; Moluccas; Philippines; N Australia, New Guinea, and Bismarck Islands
Hairy-winged bat	*Harpiocephalus*	1	India to SE Asia, Sumatra, Java, and Moluccas
	Subfamily: Kerivoulinae		
Painted or Woolly bats	*Kerivoula*	16	Africa S of Sahara; India and Sri Lanka to S China; SE Asia to Sumatra, Java, Lesser Sundas, Borneo, Sulawesi, N Moluccas, Philippines, New Guinea, Bismarck Islands, and NE Australia
Groove-toothed bats	*Phoniscus*	4	S Thailand to NE Australia; New Guinea, and Philippines
	Subfamily: Nyctophilinae		
Pallid bats	*Antrozous*	2	SW Canada to Mexico; Cuba
Van Gelder's bat	*Bauerus*	1	Tres Marias Islands; S Mexico; Honduras
Long-eared bats	*Nyctophilus* (incl. *Lamingtona*)	7	Timor (?); E New Guinea; Australia; Tasmania
None applied	*Pharotis*	1	SE New Guinea
None applied	**Anzanycteris*	–	Pleistocene (North America)
	Subfamily: Tomopeatinae		
None applied	*Tomopeas*	1	NW Peru

* Known as fossil only. ¹ Includes *Selysius, Isotus, Paramyotis, Chrysopteron, Leuconoe, Rickettia* and *Cistugo*.
² Includes *Corynorhinus*.

Family Mystacinidae

Short-tailed bat

The family Mystacinidae currently includes a single genus and species, *Mystacina tuberculata* but recent evidence suggests that there may be two species in the genus, rather than one. It is restricted to New Zealand (Fig. 11.37). In the past, this bat has been called *Mystacops* with the family designation then being Mystacopidae. The species name *tuberculata* is shared with the only other bat now living on New Zealand, *Chalinolobus tuberculatus*. The muzzle of *Mystacina* is rather long; the nose projects beyond the lower lip and the nostrils are set in a rudimentary narial pad which has many short, stiff bristles. The tongue can be protruded to a certain extent and it has a rough, transversely ridged surface with a small

patch of brush-like papillae at its tip. The ears are separate, quite long and slender with a long, pointed tragus. The tail emerges through the tail membrane so that its tip lies on the upper surface of the membrane. The Short-tailed bat has short, dense, rather velvety fur which led an earlier writer to propose an appropriate, but invalid name, *Mystacina velutina* for this species. The fur is greyish brown, brown, or blackish brown with a subtle greyish frost.

In many ways, *Mystacina* is an unusual and unique bat. It is quite agile on the ground and there are indications that it frequently uses this mode of locomotion. The wing membranes are especially tough and leathery near the body and legs. The wings can be furled slightly to reduce the risk of damage by folding the phalanges of the third, fourth, and fifth digits so that they lie close to the side of the lower

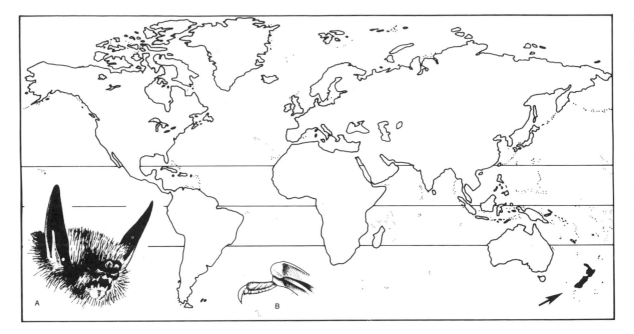

Fig. 11.37 Distribution of the Mystacinidae.

Fig. 11.38 A, New Zealand Short-tailed bat (Mystacina tuberculata); B, thumb, with talon at base.

Table 11.17 Common name, genera, number of extant species, and distribution of the Mystacinidae

Common name	Genera	Species	Distribution
Short-tailed bat	Mystacina	1	New Zealand; Stewart Island; adjacent small islands

body with the terminal parts of the digits tucked into a small cutaneous pouch that extends along the flank just in front of the leg and along the underside of the thigh. As a result, the wing tips and delicate portions of the wing are concealed. The tail membrane may be rolled forward so that the area beyond the tail disappears under the protective inner band of tougher membrane. The legs are short and stout with large, broad feet that turn slightly outward when the bat is on the ground. The soles of the feet are soft and deeply wrinkled with the grooving extending onto the lower surface of the leg and ankle and across the underside of the toes. The thumb has a strong claw with a small, subsidiary talon or denticle near the base of its ventral surface. There is a similar subsidiary talon on the claws of the toes. The degree of terrestrial adaptation in this peculiar species is unusual for bats.

Mystacina is chiefly an insectivorous bat. These food items are captured on the ground or while moving about in trees as well as in flight. Other food sources are also used. These bats have been observed scavenging flesh, and certainly fruit is eaten at some times of the year. Nectar and pollen may also make up part of the diet during some parts of the year.

Short-tailed bats do not apparently undergo prolonged hibernation, but arouse spontaneously to feed in warmer spells in winter. They usually roost in small groups in hollow trees. The presumed antiquity of *Mystacina* is supported by its commensal relationship with an equally unusual family of bat flies—the Mystacinobiidae—whose sole genus and species, *Mystacinobia zelandica*, lives on the fungi and yeasts growing on the guano deposits beneath the roosts of *Mystacina*.

The phylogenetic relationships of the Mystacinidae are not well understood. Most bat specialists treat the family as an archaic relic and suggest that it is closely related to the Vespertilionidae or Molossidae. This seems questionable and recent studies suggest a closer relationship with the phyllostomoid families, Noctilionidae, Mormoopidae, and Phyllostomidae.

Family Molossidae

Free-tailed bats

Members of this family are found throughout the warmer parts of the world from southern Europe and southern Asia to Africa, Australia and the Fiji Islands, and from the central part of the United States through Mexico, Central America and most of South America including the West Indies (Fig. 11.39). The fossil record of the family extends back to the late Oligocene of Europe. Molossids have quite distinctive heads and faces and the lips are often thick and wrinkled. The muzzle is truncate with the snout often projecting beyond the lower lip and the nostrils open in a fleshy, sometimes raised, narial pad that may be covered with many short stout bristles. These bristles have curious spoon-shaped tips. The ears vary in size and shape and they often lie forward obscuring most of the face and eyes; they may also be joined for part of their length by a band of skin. There is frequently a hollow pocket between the joined ears that is sometimes the origin of a seasonal tuft or crest of erectile hairs. The wing and tail membranes are usually rather tough and leathery; the wings are also very long and extremely narrow. The first phalanx of the third finger is reflexed over the wing when it is at rest. The tail is very thick and stout and it always projects considerably from the posterior margin of the tail membrane thereby giving these bats their common name–'free-tailed'. The legs are strong and robust and the feet are short and broad with fleshy soles. The foot usually is fringed by many long sensory hairs that have spoon-shaped tips like the facial bristles. Some molossids have throat or chest glands that sometimes have a central tuft of special hairs. These glands are usually more pronounced in males than in females and it is thought that they function in sex recognition or territorial marking. Some species such as the Flat-headed bat (*Platymops setiger*) have strongly flattened skulls. These Flat-headed bats roost under rocks and in narrow cracks and crevices.

As a rule, the fur of molossids is very short and velvety and brown or blackish brown in colour. Some species have distinct reddish or blackish colour phases although these may also result from bleaching. The bellies of some species are whitish or greyish white. The wing membranes of several species are cream white in colour giving these bats a very striking appearance. The two species of *Cheiromeles* are completely naked with only a few scattered hairs here and there. As well as being naked, *Cheiromeles* also has wing pouches along the sides of the body, formed by a fold of skin that extends along the flanks under the wing from the upper arm to the upper part of the leg. When folded the outer part of the wing is pushed into this pouch with the foot which has an opposable first toe.

Molossids are strong, fast-flying bats that live on insects caught chiefly on the wing. They are frequently found in caves, tunnels, under bark and

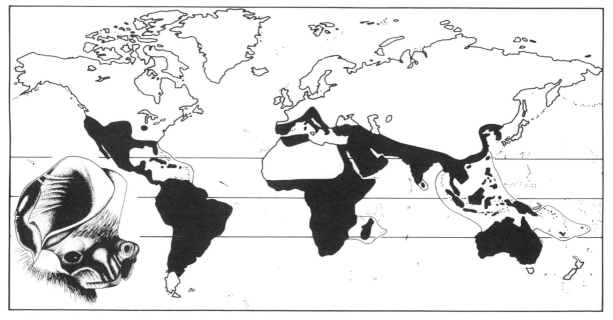

Fig. 11.39 Distribution of the Molossidae.

*Fig. 11.40 Big Free-tailed bat (*Tadarida macrotis*).*

Table 11.18   Common name, genera, number of extant species, and distribution of the Molossidae

Common name	Genera	Species	Distribution
Free-tailed bats	*Tadarida*[1]	52	S Europe; Africa; Madagascar; Aldabra Island; Mauritius; Reunion; S Asia to Philippines, Australia, Solomon Islands, and Fiji Islands; United States to Argentina, Chile, Antilles, and Bahamas
Flat-headed Free-tailed bat	*Sauromys*	1	Namibia to Zimbabwe, Mozambique, and S Africa
Flat-headed bat	*Platymops*	1	Ethiopia, Sudan, and Kenya
Big-eared Free-tailed bats	*Otomops*	5	Africa S of Sahara to Angola and Natal; Madagascar; S India; Java; New Guinea
None applied	*Myopterus*	3	Senegal to Zaire and Uganda
None applied	*Molossops*[2]	6	Mexico to Argentina and Paraguay; Trinidad
Rough-winged bat	*Neoplatymops*	1	Venezuela; Guyana; Brazil
None applied	*Cabreramops*	1	W Ecuador
Mastiff bats	*Eumops*	8	S United States to Argentina, Paraguay, and Uruguay
Dome-palate Mastiff bats	*Promops*	2	Mexico to Argentina and Paraguay; Trinidad
Velvety Mastiff bats	*Molossus*	6	Mexico to Argentina and Paraguay; Trinidad; Antilles
Naked Free-tailed bats	*Cheiromeles*	2	Malaya to Sulawesi and Philippines
None applied	*Molossides*	–	Pleistocene (North America)

* Known as fossil only. [1] Includes *Mops, Mormopterus, Chaerephon* and *Xiphonycteris*. [2] Includes *Cynomops*.

rocks, hollow trees and logs, and in dense palm fronds. They are also frequent residents in human habitations, under shingles, eaves, roof tiles, attics, and outbuildings. Some species seem able to tolerate or even prefer high temperatures in the roost. They have been found under galvanized iron roofing where the midday temperatures may reach 54° C. A few species are solitary or live in small groups, but most are highly gregarious and live in very large colonies; the world famous colony at Carlsbad Caverns in New Mexico may have contained several hundred thousand or even millions of individuals of *Tadarida brasiliensis* before its decline. Members of this species, at least, are migratory to a greater or lesser extent; some populations of this species migrating from the central United States far south into Mexico while others do not move as far. Molossids do not hibernate in the strict sense, although there are short periods of winter torpidity in some such as *Tadarida* and *Eumops* where they occur in more temperate areas.

Fossil families

Many fossil bats belong to the same genera as modern bats, or to genera that can be allocated to one or another of the extant bat families. Three further families that are known only from fossils have been recognised, all from the Eocene period of Europe or North America and so including the earliest bats so far discovered. These three families are currently placed together in the superfamily Palaeochiropterygoidea: their relationships are not yet fully understood and some authorities consider that they should be united into a single family, the Palaeochiropterygidae, possibly as three subfamilies. In addition, three genera of fossil bats have been described from deposits of similar age in Europe, but their affinities have yet to be properly established and they have not been allocated to a particular family. There is some evidence that suggests that *Hassianycteris* among these should be associated with the Emballonuroidea or the Rhinolophoidea, unlike the Palaeochiropterygidae, Archaeonycteridae and Icaronycteridae which seem to have affinities with the Vespertilionoidea. As might be expected, none of these bats has a common name.

Table 11.19 Genera and distribution of the fossil bat families, with the unallocated genera

Family: *Palaeochiropterygidae	
Palaeochiropteryx	Eocene (Europe)
Cecilionycteris	Eocene (Europe)
Matthesia	Eocene (Europe)
Family *Archaeonycteridae	
Archaeonycteris	Eocene (Europe)
Ageina	Eocene (Europe)
***Family *Icaronycteridae**	
Icaronycteris	Eocene (North America, (?) Europe)
Family incertae sedis	
Paleunycteris	Eocene (Europe)
Paradoxonycteris	Eocene (Europe)
Hassianycteris	Eocene (Europe)

* Known as fossil only.

Bibliography

GENERAL BOOKS

Allen, G. M. 1939. *Bats*. Harvard University Press, Cambridge, Massachusetts. (Reprinted as a Dover Paperback, 1962).

Brosset, A. 1966. *La biologie des Chiroptères*. Masson et Cie, Paris.

Fenton, M. Brock. 1983. *Just bats*. University of Toronto Press, Toronto, etc.

Griffin, D. R. 1958. *Listening in the dark*. Yale University Press, New Haven, Connecticut.

————— 1959. *Echoes of bats and men*. Anchor Books, New York; also 1960, Heinemann, London.

Jones, G. S. & Jones, D. B. 1976. A bibliography of the land mammals of southeast Asia 1699-1969. *Special Publication of the Department of Entomology, Bernice P. Bishop Museum with the U S Naval Medical Research Unit No. 2 and Asia Foundation*, 1-238. (Large bibliography on bats included).

Kunz, T. H. (Ed.). 1982. *Ecology of bats*. Plenum Press, New York & London.

Kuzyakin, A. P. 1950. *Letuchie Mishi (Sistematika, obraz zhizni i pol'za dlya sel'skogo i lesnogho khozyaistva)* [Bats (Systematics, life-history and utility for agriculture and forestry)]. 'Sovetskaya Nauka', Moscow.

Lauber, P. 1968. *Bats: wings in the night*. Random House, New York.

Matthews, L. H. 1969. *The life of mammals*. Weidenfeld & Nicholson, London.

Mohr. C. E. 1976. *The world of the bat*. J. B. Lippincott Co., Philadelphia & New York. (Living World Books, (Ed.) Terres, J. K.).

Novick, A. & Leen, N. 1969. *The world of bats*. Holt, Rinehart & Winston, New York. Also Edita Lausanne (Production Edita, S. A.).

Nowak, R. M. & Paradiso, J. L. 1983. *Walker's Mammals of the World*. 4th Ed. John Hopkins University Press, Baltimore & London.

Peterson, R. 1966. *Silently by night*. Longmans, Green & Co. Ltd, London.

Ripper, C. L. 1954. *Bats*. William Morrow & Co., New York.

Ryberg, O. 1947. *Studies on bats and bat parasites*. Bokförlaget Svensk Natur, Stockholm.

Salvayre, H. 1980. *Les chauve-souris*. Collection faune et flore de France. Balland.

Schmidt, U. 1978. *Vampirefledermäuse*. Die Neue Brehm-Bucherei, A. Ziemsen Verlag, Wittenberg Lutherstadt.

Turner, D. C. 1975. *The vampire bat. A field study in behavior and ecology*. John Hopkins University Press, Baltimore; London.

Wimsatt, W. A. (Ed.). 1970, 1977. *Biology of bats*. I, II, III. Academic Press, New York, etc.

Yalden, D. W. & Morris, P. 1975. *The lives of bats*. David & Charles, Newton Abbot, London, etc.

REGIONAL STUDIES

North America and Caribbean

Banfield, A. W. F. 1974. *The mammals of Canada*. National Museum of Natural Science, University of Toronto Press, Toronto.

Barbour, R. W. & Davis, W. H. 1969. *Bats of America*. University Press of Kentucky, Lexington.

Felten, H. 1955–1957. Fledermäuse (Mammalia, Chiroptera) aus El Salvador. Teil 1–5. *Senckenbergiana Biologica*, 1955, **36**: 271–285; 1956, **37**: 69–86; 179–212; 341–367; 1957, **38**: 1–22.

Findley, J. S., Harris, A. H., Wilson, D. E. & Jones, C. 1975. *Mammals of New Mexico*. University of New Mexico Press, Albuquerque.

Goodwin, G. G. 1946. Mammals of Costa Rica. *Bulletin of the American Museum of Natural History*, **87**: 271-473.

————— **, & Greenhall, A. M.** 1961. A review of the bats of Trinidad and Tobago. *Bulletin of the American Museum of Natural History*, **122**: 187-302.

Hall, E. R. 1981. *The mammals of North America*. John Wiley & Sons, New York, etc.

Handley, C. O. 1966. Checklist of mammals of Panama. Pp. 753-795 of *Ectoparasites of Panama*, Wensel, R. L. & Tipton, V. J. (Eds.), Field Museum of Natural History, Chicago.

Jones, J. K., Jr. 1966. Bats from Guatemala. *University of Kansas Publication, Museum of Natural History*, **16**: 439-472.

─────, **Smith, J. D. & Turner, R. W.** 1971. Noteworthy records of bats from Nicaragua, with a checklist of the chiropteran fauna of the country. *Occasional Papers, University of Kansas Museum of Natural History,* **2**: 1-35.

Koopman, K. F. 1968. Taxonomic and distributional notes on Lesser Antillean bats. *American Museum Novitates,* No. **2333**: 1-3.

Silva Taboada, G. 1979. *Los murcielagos de Cuba.* Editora de la Academia de Ciencias de Cuba, La Habana, i-xvi + 1-423.

Villa-R, B. 1966. *Los murcielagos de Mexico.* Universidad Nacional Autonoma de Mexico.

South America

Albuja, L. 1982. *Murcielagos del Ecuador.* Departamento de Ciencias Biologicas, Escuela Politécnica Nacionál, Quito.

Anderson, S., Koopman, K. F., & Creighton, G. K. 1982. Bats of Bolivia: An annotated checklist. *American Museum Novitates,* No. **2750**: 1-24.

Cabrera, A. 1958, 1961. Catalogo de los mamiferos de America del Sur. *Revista Museo Argentino de Ciencias Natural,* 1958, **4**: i-xvi + 1-308, 1961, **4**: xvii-xxii + 309-732.

Husson, A. M. 1962. The bats of Suriname. *Zoologische Verhandelingen, Leiden,* No. **58**: 1-282.

───── 1978. *The mammals of Suriname.* Zoologische Monographieen van het Rijksmuseum van Naturlijke Historie, No. 2. E. J. Brill, Leiden.

Tuttle, M. D. 1970. Distribution and zoogeography of Peruvian bats, with comments on natural history. *University of Kansas Science Bulletin,* **49**: 45-86.

Europe

Corbet, G. B. & Southern, H. M. 1977. (Eds.). *The handbook of British mammals.* Blackwell Scientific Publications, Oxford, etc.

Pucek, Z. 1981. (Ed.). *Keys to vertebrates of Poland. Mammals.*(Klucze do oznaczania kregowców Polski. Ssaki - Mammalia). Polska Academia Nauk, Zaklad Zoologii Systematycznej w Krakowe. Pánstwowe Wydawnictwo Naukowe (Polish Scientific Publishers), Warszawa. (First published in Polish, 1964, Kowalski, K. (Ed.).).

Saint-Girons, M-C. 1973. *Les mammifères de France et de Benelux (faune marine exceptée).* Doin, Paris.

Salvayre, H. 1980. *Les chauve-souris.* Collection faune et flore de France. Balland.

Africa

Aellen, V. & Brosset, A. 1968. Chiroptères du sud du Congo (Br.). *Revue Suisse de Zoologie,* **75**: 435-458.

Gaisler, J., G. Madkour & Pelikan, J. 1972. On the bats (Chiroptera) of Egypt. *Přírodovědné Práce ústavú Ceskoslovenské Akademie Věd v Brné,* new series, **6** (8): 1-40.

Hayman, R. W. & Hill, J. Edwards 1971. *The mammals of Africa. An identification manual. Part 2. Order Chiroptera.* Smithsonian Institution Press, Washington D C.

Hill, J. Eric & Carter, T. D. 1941. The mammals of Angola, Africa. *Bulletin of the American Museum of Natural History,* **78**: 1-211.

Kingdon, J. 1974. *East African mammals. An atlas of evolution in Africa. IIA (Insectivora and bats).* Academic Press, London & New York.

Kock, D. 1969. Die Fledermaus-Fauna des Sudan (Mammalia, Chiroptera). *Abhandlungen der Senckenbergischen Naturforschenden Gesellschaft,* **521**: 1-238.

Koopman, K. F. 1975. Bats of the Sudan. *Bulletin of the American Museum of Natural History,* **154**: 355-443.

Kulzer, Von E. 1962. Fledermäuse aus Tanganyika. *Zeitschrift fur Säugetierkunde,* **27**: 164-181.

Largen, M. J., Kock, D. & Yalden, D. W. 1974. Catalogue of the mammals of Ethiopia. 1. Chiroptera. *Monitore Zoologico Italiano,* (new series) supplement **5**: 221-298.

Roberts, A. 1951. *Mammals of South Africa.* "The mammals of South Africa Book Fund".

Rosevear, D. R. 1965. *The bats of West Africa.* British Museum (Natural History), London.

Asia

Bobrinskii, N. A., Kuznetzov, B. A. & Kuzyakin, A. P. 1965. *Opredelitel' Mlekopitayushchikh SSSR* [The key to the mammals of the USSR]. 2nd. ed. Izdatel'stvo "Prosveshchenie", Moscow.

Brosset, A. 1962. The bats of central and western India. *Journal of the Bombay Natural History Society,* **59**: 1-57, 583-624, 707-746.

De Blase, A. F. 1980. The bats of Iran: systematics, distribution, ecology. *Fieldiana, Zoology,* Pub. **1307** (new series, No. 4): i-xvii + 1-424.

Flint, V. E., Chugunov, Y. D. & Smirin, V. M. 1965. *Mlekopitayushchie SSSR* (Ed.) Formozov, A. N. [Mammals of the USSR]. Izdatel'stvo "Misl'", Moscow.

Harrison, D. L. 1964. *The mammals of Arabia. I. Introduction, Insectivora, Chiroptera, Primates.* Ernest Benn, Ltd., London & Tonbridge.

Imaizumi, Y. 1960. *Coloured illustrations of the mammals of Japan.* Hoikusha, Osaka. (Letterpress in Japanese).

Lekagul, B. & McNeely, J. A. 1977. *Mammals of Thailand*. Association for the Conservation of Wildlife, Bangkok.

Medway, Lord 1978, 1983. *The wild mammals of Malaya (Peninsular Malaysia) and Singapore*. (2nd. ed.: 1st. ed. published 1969 as *The wild mammals of Malaya and offshore islands including Singapore*). Oxford University Press, Oxford, etc.

Roberts, T. J. 1977. *The mammals of Pakistan*. Ernest Benn, Ltd., London & Tonbridge.

Indo-Australia

Goodwin, R. E. 1979. The bats of Timor: systematics and ecology. *Bulletin of the American Museum of Natural History*, **163**: 73-122.

Hall, L. S. & Richards, G. C. 1978. *Bats of eastern Australia*. Queensland Museum Booklet No. 12.

Hill, J. Edwards 1983. Bats (Mammalia: Chiroptera) from Indo-Australia. *Bulletin of the British Museum Natural History* (Zoology), **45**: 103-208.

Koopman, K. F. 1979. Zoogeography of mammals from islands off the northeastern coast of New Guinea. *American Museum Novitates*, No. **2690**: 1-17.

———— 1982. Results of the Archbold Expeditions No. 109. Bats from eastern Papua and the east Papuan islands. *American Museum Novitates*, No. **2747**: 1-34.

Laurie, E. M. O. & Hill, J. Edwards 1954. *Checklist of land mammals of New Guinea, Celebes, and adjacent islands, 1758-1952*. British Museum (Natural History), London.

Medway, Lord 1977. Mammals of Borneo. Field keys and an annotated checklist. *Monographs Malaysian Branch Royal Asiatic Society*, No. **7**: i-xii + 1-172. (2nd. ed.: 1st. ed. published 1965, *Journal Malay Branch Royal Asiatic Society*, **36**, (3) (1963): i-xiv + 1-193).

Phillips, C. J. 1968. Systematics of Megachiropteran bats in the Solomon Islands. *University of Kansas Publications, Museum of Natural History*, **16**: 777-837.

Smith, J. D. & Hood, C. S. 1981. Preliminary notes on bats from the Bismarck Archipelago (Mammalia: Chiroptera). *Science in New Guinea*, **8**: 81-121.

Strahan, R. (Ed.). 1983. *Complete book of Australian mammals*. Angus & Robertson Publishers, Sydney.

Taylor, E. H. 1934. Philippine land mammals. *Monograph of the Philippine Bureau of Science*, Manila, **30**: 1-548.

Van Peenen, P. F. D. 1968. A guide to the fruit bats of South Vietnam. *The Formosan Science*, **22** (2): 95-107.

CHAPTER 1

Baker, R. J. 1970. Karyotypic trends in bats. *In* Wimsatt, W. A. (Ed.). *Biology of bats*, **1**: 65-96. Academic Press, New York, etc.

———— 1979. Karyology. *In* Baker, R. J. *et al.*, op. cit. Part III. No. **16**: 107-155.

————, Jones, J. K., Jr. & Carter, D. C. (Eds.). 1976, 1977, 1979. Biology of bats of the New World family Phyllostomatidae. *Special Publications of the Museum Texas Tech University*. Texas Tech Press, Lubbock.

————, Honeycutt, R. L., Arnold, M. L., Sarish, V. M. & Genoways, H. H. 1981. Electrophoretic and immunological studies on the relationship of the Brachyphyllinae and the Glossophaginae. *Journal of Mammalogy*, **62**: 665-672.

Corbet, G. B. & Hill, J. Edwards 1980. *A world list of mammalian species*. British Museum (Natural History) / Cornell University Press, London / Ithaca.

Gotch, A. F. 1979. *Mammals—their Latin names explained. A guide to animal classification*. Blanford Press, Poole, England.

Griffiths, T. A. 1982. Systematics of the New World nectar-feeding bats (Mammalia, Phyllostomidae), based on the morphology of the hyoid and lingual regions. *American Museum Novitates*, No. **2742**: 1-45.

Honacki, J. H., Kinman, K. E. & Koeppl, J. W. (Eds.). 1982. *Mammal species of the world: a taxonomic and geographical reference*. Allen Press / Association of Systematic Collections, Lawrence, Kansas.

Jones, J. K., Jr. & Genoways, H. H. 1970. Chiropteran systematics. *In* Slaughter, B. H. & Walton, D. W. (Eds.). *About bats. A chiropteran biology symposium*, 3-21. Southern Methodist University Press, Dallas.

Mayr, E., Linsley, E. G. & Usinger, R. L. 1953. *Methods and principles of systematic zoology*. McGraw-Hill Book Company, Inc., New York, etc.

Phillips, C. G., Grimes, G. W. & Forman, G. L. 1976. Oral biology. *In* Baker, R. J. *et al.*, op. cit. Part II. No. **13**: 121-246.

Smith, J. D. 1972. Systematics of the chiropteran family Mormoopidae. *Miscellaneous Publications of the Museum of Natural History, University of Kansas*, No. **56**: 1-132.

Straney, D. O., Smith, M. H., Greenbaum, I. F. & Baker, R. J. 1979. Biochemical genetics. *In* Baker, R. J. *et al.*, op. cit. Part III. No. **16**: 157-176.

Wiley, E. O. 1981. *Phylogenetics: the theory and practice of phylogenetic systematics*. John Wiley and Sons, New York, etc.

CHAPTER 2

Altenbach, J. S. 1979. *Locomotor morphology of the vampire bat, Desmodus rotundus.* Special Publication No. 6, American Society of Mammalogists.

Baker, R. J., Jones, J. K., Jr. & Carter, D. C. (Eds.). 1976, 1977, 1979. Biology of bats of the New World family Phyllostomatidae. *Special Publications of the Museum, Texas Tech University.* Texas Tech Press, Lubbock.

Benedict, F. A. 1957. Hair structure as a generic character in bats. *University of California Publications in Zoology,* **59**: 285-548.

Dulic, B. 1978. Morphology of the hair of *Pipistrellus savii* Bonaparte, 1837. *In* Olembo, R. J. *et al.,* op. cit. 51-61.

Ellins, S. R. & Masterson, F. A. 1971. Brightness discrimination thresholds in the bat, *Eptesicus fuscus. Bulletin of the Ecological Society of America,* **52** (4): 41-42.

Findley, J. S. & Wilson, D. E. 1982. Ecological significance of chiropteran morphology. *In* Kunz, T. H. (Ed.). *Ecology of bats,* 243-260. Plenum Press, New York & London.

Forman, G. L. 1972. Comparative morphological and histochemical studies of stomachs of selected American bats. *University of Kansas Science Bulletin,* **49**: 591-729.

———— 1973. Studies of gastric morphology in North American Chiroptera (Emballonuridae, Noctilionidae, and Phyllostomatidae). *Journal of Mammalogy,* **54**: 909-923.

————, Phillips, C. J. & Rouk, C. S. 1979. Alimentary tract. *In* Baker, R. J. *et al.,* op. cit. Part III. No. **16**: 205-227.

Gaisler, G. 1971. Vergleichende Studie über das Haarkleid der Fledertiere (Chiroptera). *Přírodovědné Práce ústavů Ceskoslovenske Academie Věd v Brné,* **5** (8): 1-44.

Geluso, K. N. 1980. Renal form and function in bats: an ecophysiological appraisal. *In* Wilson, D. E. & Gardner, A. L., op. cit. 15-21.

Hackethal, H. 1981. Die Bedeutung Hirnmorphologischer Merkmale für die Taxonomie der Placentalen Säuger. *Mitteilungen aus dem Zoologische Museum in Berlin,* **57** (2): 233-340.

Henson, O. W., Jr. 1970. The central nervous system. *In* Wimsatt, W. A., op. cit. **2**: 57-152.

Hope, G. M. & Bhatnagar, K. P. 1980. Comparative electroretinography in phyllostomid and vespertilionid bats. *In* Wilson, D. E. & Gardner, A. L., op. cit. 78-89.

Kallen, F. C. 1977. The cardiovascular system of bats: structure and function. *In* Wimsatt, W. A., op. cit. **3**: 289- 483.

Kovtun, M. F. 1978. *Apparat Lokomotsii Ruku-krylykh* [Apparatus for locomotion in bats]. Institut Zoologii Akademiya Nauk Ukrainskoi SSR. Naukova Dumka, Kiev.

McDaniel, V. R. 1976. Brain anatomy. *In* Baker, R. J. *et al.,* op. cit. Part I. No. **10**: 147-200.

Olembo, R. J., Castelino, J. B. & Mutere, F. A. (Eds.). 1978. *Proceedings of the Fourth International Bat Research Conference.* Kenya Literature Bureau, Nairobi.

Quay, W. B. 1970. Integument and derivatives. *In* Wimsatt, W. A., op. cit. **2**: 1-56.

———— 1970. Peripheral nervous system. *In* Wimsatt, W. A., op. cit. **2**: 153-179.

Riedesel, M. L. 1977. Blood physiology. *In* Wimsatt, W. A., op. cit. **3**: 485-517.

Rosenbaum, R. M. 1970. Urinary system. *In* Wimsatt, W. A., op. cit. **1**: 331-387.

Schaffer, J. 1905. Anatomisch-histologische Untersuchungen über den Bau der Zehen bei Fledermäusen und einiger kletternden Säugetieren. *Zeitschrift für Wissenschliche Zoologie,* **83**: 231-284.

Schliemann, H. 1975. Über die Entstehung von Haftorganen dei Chiropteren. *Mitteilungen Hamburgischen Zoologischen Museum und Institut,* **72**: 249-259.

———— & Hoeber, M. 1978. The structure and function of the pads on the thumb and foot of *Tylonycteris. In* Olembo, R. J. *et al.,* op. cit. 39-50.

Slaughter, B. H. 1970. Evolutionary trends of chiropteran dentitions. *In* Slaughter, B. H. & Walton, D. W., op. cit. 51-83.

———— & Walton, D. W. (Eds.). 1970. *About bats. A chiropteran biology symposium.* Southern Methodist University Press, Dallas.

Storch, G. 1968. Funktionsmorphologische Untersuchungen an der Kaumuskulatur und an korrelierten Schädelstrukturen der Chiropteren. *Abhandlungen der Senckenbergischen Naturforschenden Gesellschaft,* **517**: 1-92.

Studier, E. H. 1972. Some physical properties of the wing membrane of bats. *Journal of Mammalogy,* **53**: 623-625.

Suthers, R. A. 1970. Vision, olfaction, taste. *In* Wimsatt, W. A., op. cit. **2**: 265-309.

Vaughan, T. A. 1970. The skeletal system. *In* Wimsatt, W. A., op. cit. **1**: 97-138.

———— 1970. The muscular system. *In* Wimsatt, W. A., op. cit. **1**: 139-194.

Walton, D. W. & Walton, G. M. 1970. Post-cranial osteology of bats. *In* Slaughter, B. H. & Walton, D. W., op. cit. 93-126.

Wilson, D. E. & Gardner, A. L. (Eds.). 1980. *Proceedings of the Fifth International Bat Research Conference.* Texas Tech Press, Lubbock.

Wimsatt, W. A. (Ed.). 1970, 1977. *Biology of bats.* Academic Press, New York, etc.

——— 1970. Locomotor adaptation in the disc-winged bat, *Thyroptera tricolor. Revista de Biologia Tropical,* **18**: 73-88.

CHAPTER 3

Baker, R. J. 1970. The role of karyotypes in phylogenetic studies of bats. *In* Slaughter, B. H. & Waiton, D. W., op. cit. 303-312.

Bhatnagar, K. P. 1980. The chiropteran vomeronasal organ: its relevance to the phylogeny of bats. *In* Wilson, D. E. & Gardner, A. L., op. cit. 289-315.

Haiduk, M. W., Robbins, L. W., Robbins, R. L. & Schlitter, D. A. 1980. Karyotypic studies of seven species of African megachiropterans (Mammalia: Pteropodidae). *Annals of the Carnegie Museum of Natural History,* **49**: 181-191.

Hecht, M. K., Goody, P. C. & Hecht, D. M. (Eds.). 1977. *Major patterns of vertebrate evolution.* NATO Advanced Study Institute Series, Series A, Life Science, **14**. Plenum Press, New York.

Hood, C. S. & Smith, J. D. 1982. Cladistic analysis of female reproductive histomorphology in phyllostomatoid bats. *Systematic Zoology,* **31**: 241-251.

Jepsen, G. L. 1970. Bat origins and evolution. *In* Wimsatt, W. A. (Ed.). *Biology of bats.* **1**: 1-64. Academic Press, New York, etc.

Jones, J. K., Jr. & Genoways, H. H. 1970. Chiropteran systematics. *In* Slaughter, B. H. & Walton, D. W., op. cit. 3-21.

Koopman, K. F. & MacIntyre, G. T. 1980. Phylogenetic analysis of chiropteran dentition. *In* Wilson, D. E. & Gardner, A. L., op. cit. 279-288.

Luckett, W. P. 1980. The use of fetal membrane data in assessing chiropteran phylogeny. *In* Wilson, D. E. & Gardner, A. L., op. cit. 245-265.

Marshall, A. G. 1983. Bats, flowers and fruit: evolutionary relationships in the Old World. *Biological Journal of the Linnean Society,* **20**: 115-135.

Novacek, M. J. 1980. Phylogenetic analysis of the chiropteran auditory region. *In* Wilson, D. E. & Gardner, A. L., op. cit. 317-330.

Pirlot, P. 1977. Wing design and the origin of bats. *In* Hecht, M. K. *et al.,* op. cit. 375-410.

Simmons, J. A. 1980. Phylogenetic adaptations and the evolution of echolocation in bats. *In* Wilson, D. E. & Gardner, A. L., op. cit. 267-298.

Slaughter, B. H. 1970. Evolutionary trends of chiropteran dentitions. *In* Slaughter, B. H. & Walton, D. W., op. cit. 51-83.

——— **& Walton, D. W.** (Eds.). 1970. *About bats. A chiropteran biology symposium.* Southern Methodist University Press, Dallas.

Smith, J. D. 1976. Chiropteran evolution. *In* Baker, R. J., Jones, J. K., Jr. & Carter, D. C. (Eds.). Biology of bats of the New World family Phyllostomatidae. Part I. *Special Publications of the Museum, Texas Tech University,* No. **10**: 49-69. Texas Tech Press, Lubbock.

——— 1977. Comments on flight and the evolution of bats. *In* Hecht, M. K. *et al.,* op. cit. 427-437.

——— 1980. Chiropteran phylogenetics: introduction. *In* Wilson, D. E. & Gardner, A. L., op. cit. 233-244.

——— **& Madkour, G.** 1980. Penial morphology and the question of chiropteran phylogeny. *In* Wilson, D. E. & Gardner, A. L., op. cit. 347-365.

Suthers, R. A. & Braford, M. R., Jr. 1980. Visual systems and the evolutionary relationships of the Chiroptera. *In* Wilson, D. E. & Gardner, A. L., op. cit. 331-346.

Van Valen, L. 1979. The evolution of bats. *Evolutionary Theory,* **4**: 103-121.

Walton, D. W. 1969. Evolution of the chiropteran scapula. *Texas Journal of Science,* **21**: 85-90.

Wilson, D. E. & Gardner, A. L. (Eds.). 1980. *Proceedings of the Fifth International Bat Research Conference.* Texas Tech Press, Lubbock.

CHAPTER 4

Armstrong, R. B., Ianuzzo, C. D. & Kunz, T. H. 1977. Histochemical and biochemical properties of flight muscle fibers in the Little Brown bat, *Myotis lucifugus. Journal of Comparative Physiology B,* **119**: 141-154.

Dwyer, P. D. 1965. Flight patterns of some eastern Australian bats. *Victorian Naturalist,* **82**: 37-41.

Farney, J. & Fleharty, E. D. 1969. Aspect ratio, loading, wing span, and membrane areas of bats. *Journal of Mammalogy,* **50**: 362-367.

Findley, J. S., Studier, E. H. & Wilson, D. E. 1972. Morphologic properties of bat wings. *Journal of Mammalogy,* **53**: 429-444.

Hermanson, J. W. & Altenbach, J. S. 1983. The functional anatomy of the shoulder of the Pallid bat, *Antrozous pallidus. Journal of Mammalogy,* **64**: 62-75.

Norberg, U. M. 1970. Functional osteology and myology of the wing of *Plecotus auritus* Linnaeus (Chiroptera). *Arkiv för Zoologi* (Serie 2), **22**: 483-543.

————— 1972a. Functional osteology and myology of the wing of the Dog-faced bat *Rousettus aegyptiacus* (E. Geoffroy) (Mammalia, Chiroptera). *Zeitschrift für Morphologie der Tiere*, **73**: 1-44.

————— 1972b. Bat wing structures important for aerodynamics and rigidity (Mammalia, Chiroptera). *Zeitschrift für Morphologie der Tiere*, **73**: 45-61.

————— 1976. Some advanced flight manoeuvres of bats. *Journal of Experimental Biology*, **64**: 489-495.

Pennycuick, C. J. 1973. Wing profile shape in a fruit-bat gliding in a wind tunnel determined by photogrammetry. *Periodicum Biologorum*, **75**: 77-82.

Smith, J. D. & Starrett, A. 1979. Morphometric analysis of chiropteran wings. *In* Baker, R. J., Jones, J. K., Jr. & Carter, D. C. (Eds.). Biology of bats of the New World family Phyllostomatidae. Part III. *Special Publications of the Museum, Texas Tech University*, No. **16**: 229-316. Texas Tech Press, Lubbock.

Strickler, T. L. 1980. Downstroke muscle histochemistry in two bats. *In* Wilson, D. E. & Gardner, A. L., op. cit. 61-68.

Thomas, S. P. 1975. Metabolism during flight in two species of bats, *Phyllostomus hastatus* and *Pteropus gouldii*. *Journal of Experimental Biology*, **63**: 273-293.

————— 1980. The physiology and energetics of bat flight. *In* Wilson, D. E. & Gardner, A. L., op. cit. 393-402.

————— **& Suthers, R. A.** 1972. The physiology and energetics of bat flight. *Journal of Experimental Biology*, **57**: 317- 355.

Vaughan, T. A. 1970. Flight patterns and aerodynamics. *In* Wimsatt, W. A. (Ed.). *Biology of bats*. **1**: 195-216. Academic Press, New York, etc.

————— 1970. Adaptations for flight in bats. *In* Slaughter, B. H. & Walton, D. W. (Eds.). *About bats. A chiropteran biology symposium*, 127-143. Southern Methodist University Press, Dallas.

————— **& Bateman, M. M.** 1980. The molossid wing: some adaptations for rapid flight. *In* Wilson, D. E. & Gardner, A. L., op. cit. 69-78.

Wilson, D. E. & Gardner, A. L. (Eds.). 1980. *Proceedings of the Fifth International Bat Research Conference*. Texas Tech Press, Lubbock.

CHAPTER 5

Anthony, E. L. P. & Kunz, T. H. 1977. Feeding strategies of the Little Brown bat, *Myotis lucifugus*, in southern New Hampshire. *Ecology*, **58**: 775-786.

Baker, R. J., Jones, J. K., Jr. & Carter, D. C. (Eds.). 1976, 1977, 1979. Biology of bats of the New World family Phyllostomatidae. *Special Publications of the Museum Texas Tech University*. Texas Tech Press, Lubbock.

Buchler, E. R. 1975. Food transit time in *Myotis lucifugus* (Chiroptera: Vespertilionidae). *Journal of Mammalogy*, **56**: 252-255.

Burns, J. M. 1979. General physiology. *In* Baker, R. J. et al., op. cit. Part III. No. **16**: 403-408.

Coutts, R. A., Fenton, M. B. & Glenn, E. 1973. Food intake by captive *Myotis lucifugus* and *Eptesicus fuscus* (Chiroptera: Vespertilionidae). *Journal of Mammalogy*, **54**: 985-990.

Eisenberg, J. F. & Wilson, D. E. 1978. Relative brain size and feeding strategies in the Chiroptera. *Evolution*, **32**: 740-751.

Fenton, M. B. 1974. Feeding ecology of insectivorous bats. *Bios*, **45**: 3-15.

————— 1982. Echolocation, insect hearing, and feeding ecology of insectivorous bats. *In* Kunz, T. H., op. cit. 261-285.

————— **& Fleming, T. H.** 1976. Ecological interactions between bats and nocturnal birds. *Biotropica*, **8**: 108-110.

Fleming, T. H. 1982. Foraging strategies of plant-visiting bats. *In* Kunz, T. H., op. cit. 287-325.

Forman, G. L. 1972. Comparative morphological and histochemical studies of stomachs of selected American bats. *University of Kansas Science Bulletin*, **49**: 591-729.

Freeman, P. W. 1979. Specialized insectivory: beetle-eating and moth-eating molossid bats. *Journal of Mammalogy*, **60**: 467-479.

————— 1981. Correspondence of food habits and morphology of insectivorous bats. *Journal of Mammalogy*, **62**: 166-173.

Gardner, A. L. 1976. Feeding habits. *In* Baker, R. J. et al., op. cit. Part II. No. **13**: 293-350.

Gillette, D. D. 1975. Evolution of feeding strategies in bats. *Tebiwa*, **18**: 39-48.

Glass, B. P. 1970. Feeding mechanisms of bats. *In* Slaughter, B. H. & Walton, D. W. (Eds.). *About bats. A chiropteran biology symposium*, 84-92. Southern Methodist University Press, Dallas.

Greenhall, A. M. 1972. The biting and feeding habits of the vampire bat, *Desmodus rotundus*. *Journal of Zoology*, London, **168**: 451-461.

Howell, D. J. 1974. Bats and pollen: physiological aspects of the syndrome of chiropterophily. *Comparative Biochemistry and Physiology*, **48**: 263-276.

Kunz, T. H. (Ed.). 1982. *Ecology of bats*. Plenum Press, New York & London.

Luckens, M. M., Van Eps, J. & Davis, W. H. 1971. Transit time through the digestive tract of the bat *Eptesicus fuscus. Experimental Medicine and Surgery,* **29**: 25-28.

McCann, C. 1931. On the fertilization of the flowers of the Sausage tree (*Kigelia pinnata,* DC.) by bats. *Journal of the Bombay Natural History Society,* **35**: 467-471.

McNab, B. K. 1971. The structure of tropical bat faunas. *Ecology,* **52**: 352-358.

———— 1982. Evolutionary alternatives in the physiological ecology of bats. *In* Kunz, T. H., op. cit. 151-200.

Marshall, A. G. 1983. Bats, flowers and fruit: evolutionary relationships in the Old World. *Biological Journal of the Linnean Society,* **20**: 115–135.

———— & McWilliam, A. N. 1982. Ecological observations on epomophorine fruit-bats (Megachiroptera) in West African savanna woodland. *Journal of Zoology,* London, **198**: 53-67.

O'Farrell, M. J., Studier, E. H. & Ewing, M. G. 1971. Energy utilization and water requirements of captive *Myotis thysanodes* and *Myotis lucifugus. Comparative Biochemistry and Physiology,* **39A**: 549-552.

Okon, E. E. 1978. Nutrition in bats. *In* Olembo, R. J., Castelino, J. B. & Mutere, F. A. (Eds.). 1978. *Proceedings of the Fourth International Bat Research Conference,* 297–308. Kenya Literature Bureau, Nairobi.

Porsch, O. 1931. *Crescentia*—eine Fledermausblume. *Österreichische Botanische Zeitschrift,* **80**: 31-44.

Tuttle, M. D. & Ryan, M. J. 1981. Bat predation and evolution of frog vocalizations in the Neotropics. *Science,* **214**: 677-678.

———— 1982. The amazing frog-eating bat. *National Geographic,* **161** (1): 78-91.

Vaughan, T. A. 1976. Nocturnal behavior of the African false vampire bat (*Cardioderma cor*). *Journal of Mammalogy,* **57**: 227-248.

———— 1977. Foraging behavior of the giant leaf-nosed bat (*Hipposideros commersoni*). *Journal of East African Wildlife,* **15**: 237-249.

Wilson, D. E. 1973. Bat faunas: a trophic comparison. *Systematic Zoology,* **22**: 14-29.

CHAPTER 6

Bartholomew, G. A., Dawson, W. R. & Lasiewski, R. C. 1970. Thermoregulation and heterothermy in some of the smaller flying foxes (Megachiroptera) of New Guinea. *Zeitschrift für Vergleichende Physiologie,* **70**: 196-209.

Davis, W. H. 1970. Hibernation: ecology and physiological ecology. *In* Wimsatt, W. A., op. cit. **1**: 265-300.

Ewing, W. G., Studier, E. H. & O'Farrell, M. J. 1970. Autumn fat deposition and gross body composition in three species of *Myotis. Comparative Biochemistry and Physiology,* **36**: 119-129.

Henshaw, R. E. 1970. Thermoregulation in bats. *In* Slaughter, B. H. & Walton, D. W. (Eds.). *About bats. A chiropteran biology symposium,* 188-222. Southern Methodist University Press, Dallas.

Kunz, T. H. 1980. Daily energy budgets of free-living bats. *In* Wilson, D. E. & Gardner, A. L., op. cit. 369-392.

Lyman, C. P. 1970. Thermoregulation and metabolism in bats. *In* Wimsatt, W. A., op. cit. **1**: 301-330.

McManus, J. J. 1976. Thermoregulation. *In* Baker, R. J., Jones, J. K., Jr. & Carter, D. C. (Eds.). Biology of bats of the New World family Phyllostomatidae. Part I. *Special Publications of the Museum Texas Tech University.* No. **13**: 281-292. Texas Tech Press, Lubbock.

McNab, B. K. 1969. The economics of temperature regulation in Neotropical bats. *Comparative Biochemistry and Physiology,* **31**: 227-268.

O'Farrell, M. J. & Studier, E. H. 1970. Fall metabolism in relation to ambient temperatures in three species of *Myotis. Comparative Biochemistry and Physiology,* **35**: 697-703.

Studier, E. H. & O'Farrell, M. J. 1980. Physiological ecology of *Myotis. In* Wilson, D. E. & Gardner, A. L., op. cit. 415- 424.

———— & Wilson, D. E. 1970. Thermoregulation in some Neotropical bats. *Comparative Biochemistry and Physiology,* **34**: 251-262.

Wilson, D. E. & Gardner, A. L. (Eds.). 1980. *Proceedings of the Fifth International Bat Research Conference.* Texas Tech Press, Lubbock.

Wimsatt, W. A. (Ed.). 1970, 1977. *Biology of bats.* Academic Press, New York, etc.

CHAPTER 7

Baker, R. J., Jones, J. K., Jr. & Carter, D. C. (Eds.). 1976, 1977, 1979. Biology of bats of the New World family Phyllostomatidae. *Special Publications of the Museum Texas Tech University.* Texas Tech Press, Lubbock.

Bleier, W. J. 1979. Embryology. *In* Baker, R. J. *et al.,* op. cit. Part III. No. **16**: 379-386.

Bogan, M. A. 1972. Observations on parturition and development in the hoary bat, *Lasiurus cinereus. Journal of Mammalogy,* **53**: 598-604.

Bradbury, J. W. 1977. Lek mating behavior in the Hammer-headed bat. *Zeitschrift für Tierpsychologie,* **45**: 225-255.

Carter, D. C. 1970. Chiropteran reproduction. *In* Slaughter, B. H. & Walton, D. W. (Eds.). *About bats. A chiropteran biology symposium*, 233-266. Southern Methodist University Press, Dallas.

Fenton, M. B. 1969. The carrying of young by females of three species of bats. *Canadian Journal of Zoology*, **47**: 158-159.

Forman, G. L. & Genoways, H. H. 1979. Sperm morphology. *In* Baker, R. J. *et al.*, op. cit. Part III. No. **16**: 177-204.

Gustafson, A. W. 1979. Male reproductive patterns in hibernating bats. *Journal of Reproduction and Fertility*, **56**: 317-331.

Hood, C. S. & Smith, J. D. 1982. Cladistic analysis of female reproductive histomorphology in phyllostomatoid bats. *Systematic Zoology*, **31**: 241-251.

Jeness, R. & Studier, E. H. 1976. Lactation and milk. *In* Baker, R. J. *et al.*, op. cit. Part II. No. **10**: 201-218.

Kitchener, D. J. 1975. Reproduction in female Gould's Wattled bat, *Chalinolobus gouldii* (Gray) (Verspertilionidae) in western Australia. *Australian Journal of Zoology*, **23**: 29-42.

——— **& Halse, S. A.** 1978. Reproduction in female *Eptesicus regulus* (Thomas) (Vespertilionidae), in western Australia. *Australian Journal of Zoology*, **26**: 257-267.

Kleiman, D. G. & Davis, T. M. 1979. Ontogeny and maternal care. *In* Baker, R. J. *et al.*, op. cit. Part III. No. **16**: 387-402.

Kunz, T. H. 1974. Reproduction, growth, and mortality of the vespertilionid bat, *Eptesicus fuscus*, in Kansas. *Journal of Mammalogy*, **55**: 1-13.

——— 1982. (Ed.). *Ecology of bats*. Plenum Press, New York & London.

Laval, R. K. & Laval, M. L. 1977. Reproduction and behavior of the African Banana bat, *Pipistrellus nanus. Journal of Mammalogy*, **58**: 403-410.

Merwe, M. van der. 1978. Postnatal development and mother-infant relationships in the Natal clinging bat *Miniopterus schreibersii natalensis* (A. Smith, 1834). *In* Olembo, R. J., Castelino, J. B. & Mutere, F. A. (Eds.). 1978. *Proceedings of the Fourth International Bat Research Conference*. 73-83. Kenya Literature Bureau, Nairobi.

——— 1980. Delayed implantation in the Natal clinging bat *Miniopterus schreibersii natalensis* (A. Smith, 1843). *In* Wilson, D. E. & Gardner, A. L. (Eds.). 1980. *Proceedings of the Fifth International Bat Research Conference*. 113-123. Texas Tech Press, Lubbock.

O'Farrell, M. J. & Studier, E. H. 1973. Reproduction, growth, and development in *Myotis thysanodes* and *M. lucifugus* (Chiroptera: Vespertilionidae). *Ecology*, **54**: 18-30.

Orr, R. T. 1970. Development: prenatal and postnatal. *In* Wimsatt, W. A. (Ed.). *Biology of bats*, **1**: 217-231. Academic Press, New York, etc.

Racey, P. A. 1982. Ecology of bat reproduction. *In* Kunz, T. H. op. cit. 57-104.

Richardson, E. G. 1977. The biology and evolution of the reproductive cycle of *Miniopterus schreibersii* and *M. australis* (Chiroptera: Vespertilionidae). *Journal of Zoology*, London, **183**: 353-375.

Tuttle, M. D. & Stevenson, D. 1982. Growth and survival of bats. *In* Kunz, T. H., op. cit. 105-150.

Wilson, D. E. 1973. Reproduction in Neotropical bats. *Periodicum Biologorum*, **75**: 215-217.

——— 1979. Reproductive patterns. *In* Baker, R. J. *et al.*, op. cit. Part III. No. **16**: 317-378.

Wimsatt, W. A. & Enders, A. C. 1980. Structure and morphogenesis of the uterus, placenta, and paraplacental organs of the Neotropical Disc-winged bat *Thyroptera tricolor* Spix (Microchiroptera: Thyropteridae). *American Journal of Anatomy*, **159**: 209-243.

CHAPTER 8

Airapet'yants, E. Sh. & Konstantinov, A. I. 1970. *Ekholokatsiya v prirode* [Echolocation in animals]. Akademiya Nauk SSSR, Lenigrad. (In translation, Mills, H. (Ed.), Kaner, N. (Tr.), Israel Program for Scientific Translations, Ltd, Jerusalem, 1973).

Busnel, R-G. & Fish, J. F. 1979. (Eds.). *Animal sonar systems*. NATO Advanced Studies Institute Series, Series A, Life Sciences, **28**. Plenum Press, New York & London.

Fenton, M. B. 1982. Echolocation, insect hearing, and feeding ecology of insectivorous bats. *In* Kunz, T. H. op. cit. 261-285.

——— **& Roeder, K. D.** 1974. The microtymbals of some Arctiidae. *Journal of the Lepidopterists Society*, **28**: 205-211.

——— **& Bell, G. P.** 1981. Recognition of species of insectivorous bats by their echolocation calls. *Journal of Mammalogy*, **62**: 233-243.

——— **& Fullard, J. H.** 1981. Moth hearing and the feeding strategies of bats. *American Scientist*, **69**: 266-275.

Gould, E. 1970. Echolocation and communication in bats. *In* Slaughter, B. H. & Walton, D. W. (Eds.). *About bats. A chiropteran biology symposium*, 144-161. Southern Methodist University Press, Dallas.

———— 1976. Echolocation and communication. *In* Baker, R. J., Jones, J. K., Jr. & Carter, D. C. (Eds.). Biology of bats of the New World family Phyllostomatidae. Part II. *Special Publications of the Museum Texas Tech University*, No. **13**: 247-279, 11 figs. Texas Tech Press, Lubbock.

Griffin, D. R. 1958. *Listening in the dark.* Yale University Press, New Haven, Connecticut.

Gustafson, Y. & Schnitzler, H-U. 1979. Echolocation and obstacle avoidance in the hipposiderid bat *Asellia tridens. Journal of Comparative Physiology*, A, **131**: 161-167.

Halls, J. A. T. 1978. Radar studies of bat sonar. *In* Olembo, R. J. *et al.,* op. cit. 137-143.

Henson, O. W. Jr. 1970a. The central nervous system. *In* Wimsatt, W. A., op. cit. **2**: 57–152.

———— 1970b. The ear and audition. *In* Wimsatt, W. A., op. cit. **2**: 181-263.

Jens, P. H-S., McCarty, J. K. & Lee, Y. H. 1980. Avoidance of obstacles by little brown bats, *Myotis lucifugus. In* Wilson, D. E. & Gardner, A. L., op. cit. 23-27.

Konstantinov, A. I., Makarov, A. K. & Sokolov, B. V. 1978. Doppler-pulse sonar system in *Rhinolophus ferrumequinum. In* Olembo, R. J. *et al.,* op. cit. 156-163.

Matsumara, S. 1981. Mother-infant communication in a horseshoe bat (*Rhinolophus ferrumequinum nippon*): vocal communication in three-week-old infants. *Journal of Mammalogy*, **62**: 20-28.

Novick, A. 1977. Acoustic orientation. *In* Wimsatt, W. A., op. cit. **3**: 73-287.

Olembo, R. J., Castelino, J. B. & Mutere, F. A. (Eds.). 1978. *Proceedings of the Fourth International Bat Research Conference.* Kenya Literature Bureau, Nairobi.

Pye, A. 1978. Aspects of cochlear structure and function in bats. *In* Olembo, R. J. *et al.,* op. cit. 73-83.

———— 1980. The structure of the cochlea in some New World bats. *In* Wilson, D. E. & Gardner, A. L., op. cit. 39-49.

Pye, J. D. 1978. Some preliminary observations on flexible echolocation systems. *In* Olembo, R. J. *et al.,* op. cit. 127-136.

———— 1980. A review of bat-detector techniques. *In* Wilson, D. E. & Gardner, A. L., op. cit. 15-21.

Roeder, K. D. & Treat, A. E. 1962. The detection and evasion of bats by moths. *Smithsonian Report*, (1961), 455-464.

Sales, G. & Pye, [J.] D. 1974. *Ultrasonic communication by animals.* Chapman & Hall, London.

Simmons, J. A. & O'Farrell, M. J. 1977. Echolocation by the Long-eared bat, *Plecotus phyllotis. Journal of Comparative Physiology*, A, **122**: 201-214.

———— & Stein, R. A. 1980. Acoustic imaging in bat sonar: echolocation signals and the evolution of echolocation. *Journal of Comparative Physiology*, A, **135**: 61-84.

————, Howell, D. J. & Suga, N. 1975. Information content of bat sonar echoes. *American Scientist*, **63**: 204-215.

————, Fenton, M. B. & O'Farrell, M. J. 1979. Echolocation and pursuit of prey by bats. *Science*, **203**: 16-21.

————, Lavender, W. A. & Lavender, B. A. 1978. Adaptations of echolocation to environmental noise by the bat *Eptesicus fuscus. In* Olembo, R. J. *et al.,* op. cit. 97-104.

————, Lavender, W. A., Lavender, B. A., Childs, J. E., Hulebak, K., Rigden, M. R., Sherman, J. & Woolman, B. 1978. Echolocation by Free-tailed bats (*Tadarida*). *Journal of Comparative Physiology* A, **125**: 291-299.

Wickler, W. & Seibt, U. 1974. Doppelklick-Orientierungslaute bei einem Epaulletten-Flughund. *Naturwissenschaften*, **61**: 367.

Wilson, D. E. & Gardner, A. L. (Eds.). 1980. *Proceedings of the Fifth International Bat Research Conference.* Texas Tech Press, Lubbock.

Wimsatt, W. A. (Ed.). 1970, 1977. *Biology of bats.* Academic Press, New York, etc.

CHAPTER 9

Ayensu, E. S. Plant and bat interactions in West Africa. *Annals of the Missouri Botanical Garden*, **61**: 702-727.

Baker, R. J., Jones, J. K., Jr. & Carter, D. C. (Eds.). 1976, 1977, 1979. Biology of bats of the New World family Phyllostomatidae. *Special Publications of the Museum Texas Tech University.* Texas Tech Press, Lubbock.

Bradbury, J. W. 1977. Social organisation and communication. *In* Wimsatt, W. A., op. cit. **3**: 1-72.

Buchler, E. R. & Childs, S. B. 1982. Use of post-sunset glow as an orientation cue by the Big Brown bat (*Eptesicus fuscus*). *Journal of Mammalogy*, **63**: 243-247.

Dalquest, W. W. & Walton, D. W. 1970. Diurnal retreats of bats. *In* Slaughter, B. H. & Walton, D. W., op. cit. 162-187.

Davis, R. & Cockrum, E. L. 1962. Repeated homing exhibited by a female Pallid bat. *Science*, **137**: 341-342.

Erkert, H. G. 1982. Ecological aspects of bat activity rhythms. *In* Kunz, T. H., op. cit. 201-242.

Erkert, H. G., Kracht, S. & Haussler, U. 1980. Characteristics of circadian activity systems in Neotropical bats. *In* Wilson, D. E. & Gardner, A. L., op. cit. 95-103.

Fenton, M. B. & Kunz, T. H. 1976. Movement and behavior. *In* Baker, R. J. *et al.*, op. cit. Part II. No. **13**: 351-364.

———, Jacobson, S. L. & Stone, R. N. 1973. An automatic ultrasonic sensing system for monitoring the activity of some bats. *Canadian Journal of Zoology*, **51**: 291-299.

Findley, J. S. & Jones, C. 1964. Seasonal distribution of the Hoary bat. *Journal of Mammalogy*, **45**: 461-470.

——— & Wilson, D. E. 1974. Observations on the Neotropical Disk-winged bat, *Thyroptera tricolor* Spix. *Journal of Mammalogy*, **55**: 562-571.

Foster, M. S. & Timm, R. M. 1976. Tent-making by *Artibeus jamaicensis* (Chiroptera: Phyllostomatidae) with comments on plants used by bats for tents. *Biotropica*, **8**: 265-269.

Gaisler, J. 1979. Ecology of bats. *In* Stoddart, D. M. (Ed.). *Ecology of small mammals*. Chapman & Hall, London.

Gillette, D. & Kimbrough, J. D. 1970. Chiropteran mortality. *In* Slaughter, B. H. & Walton, D. W., op. cit. 262-283.

Griffin, D. R. 1970. Migration and homing of bats. *In* Wimsatt, W. A., op. cit. **1**: 233-264.

Heithaus, E. R. 1982. Coevolution between bats and plants. *In* Kunz, T. H., op. cit. 327-367.

Hooper, J. H. D. & Hooper, W. M. 1956. Habits and movements of cave-dwelling bats in Devonshire. *Proceedings of the Zoological Society of London*, **127**: 1-26.

Humphrey, S. R. & Bonacorso, F. J. 1979. Population and community ecology. *In* Baker, R. J. *et al.*, op. cit. Part III. No. **16**: 409-441.

——— & Cope, J. B. 1976. *Population ecology of the little brown bat, Myotis lucifugus, in Indiana and north-central Kentucky*. Special Publication No. 6 of the American Society of Mammalogists.

Jones, C. 1972. Comparative ecology of three pteropid bats in Rio Muni, West Africa. *Journal of Zoology*, London, **167**: 353-370.

Kunz, T. H. 1982. Roosting ecology. *In* Kunz, T. H., op. cit. 1-55.

——— (Ed.). 1982. *Ecology of bats*. Plenum Press, New York & London.

Laval, R. K. & Fitch, H. S. 1977. Structure, movement and reproduction in three Costa Rican bat communities. *Occasional Papers of the Museum of Natural History, University of Kansas*, **69**: 1-28.

Marshall, A. G. 1983. Bats, flowers and fruit: evolutionary relationships in the Old World. *Biological Journal of the Linnean Society*, **20**: 115-135.

——— & McWilliam, A. N. 1982. Ecological observations on epomophorine fruit-bats (Megachiroptera) in West African savanna woodland. *Journal of Zoology*, London, **198**: 53-67.

Medway, Lord & Marshall, A. G. 1970. Roost site selection among flat-headed bats (*Tylonycteris* ssp.). *Journal of Zoology*, **161**: 237-245.

Mutere, F. A. 1980. *Eidolon helvum* revisited. *In* Wilson, D. E. & Gardner, A. L., op. cit. 145-150.

Nelson, J. E. 1965. Movements of Australian flying foxes (Pteropodidae: Megachiroptera). *Australian Journal of Zoology*, **13**: 53-73.

Slaughter, B. H. & Walton, D. W. (Eds.). 1970. *About bats. A chiropteran biology symposium*. Southern Methodist University Press, Dallas.

Tuttle, M. D. 1976. Population ecology of the Gray bat (*Myotis grisescens*): philopatry, timing and patterns of movement, weight loss during migration, and seasonal adaptive strategies. *Occasional Papers of the Museum of Natural History, University of Kansas*, **54**: 1-38.

——— & Stevensen, D. 1982. Growth and survival of bats. *In* Kunz, T. H., op. cit. 105-150.

Vazquez-Y, C., Orozco, A., Francois, G. & Trejo, L. 1975. Observations on seed dispersal by bats in a tropical humid region in Veracruz, Mexico. *Biotropica*, **7**: 73-76.

Williams, T. C. & Williams, J. M. 1970. Radio tracking of homing and feeding flights of a neotropical bat *Phyllostomus hastatus*. *Animal Behaviour*, **18**: 302-309.

Wilson, D. E. 1971. Ecology of *Myotis nigricans* (Mammalia: Chiroptera) on Barro Colorado Island, Panama Canal Zone. *Journal of Zoology*, **163**: 1-13.

——— & Gardner, A. L. (Eds.). 1980. *Proceedings of the Fifth International Bat Research Conference*. Texas Tech Press, Lubbock.

Wimsatt, W. A. (Ed.). 1970, 1977. *Biology of bats*. Academic Press, New York, etc.

CHAPTER 10

Baker, R. J., Jones, J. K., Jr. & Carter, D. C. (Eds.). 1976, 1977, 1979. Biology of bats of the New World family Phyllostomatidae. *Special Publications of the Museum Texas Tech University*. Texas Tech Press, Lubbock.

Clark, D. R. 1981. *Bats and environmental contaminants: a review*. Special Scientific Report—Wildlife No. 235. United States Department of the Interior, Fish and Wildlife Service.

Constantine, D. G. 1970. Bats in relation to health, welfare and economy of man. *In* Wimsatt, W. A., op. cit. 2: 319-449.

Greenhall, A. M. 1976. Care in captivity. *In* Baker, R. J. *et al.*, op. cit. Part I. No. 10: 89-131.

———— 1982. *House bat management.* Resource Publication No. 143. United States Department of the Interior, Fish and Wildlife Service.

———— & Paradiso, J. L. 1968. *Bats and bat banding.* Resource Publication No. 72. United States Department of the Interior, Fish and Wildlife Service.

Jones, C. 1976. Economics and conservation. *In* Baker, R. J. *et al.*, op. cit. Part I. No. 10: 133-145.

Marshall, A. G. 1982. Ecology of insects ectoparasitic on bats. *In* Kunz, T. H. *Ecology of bats*, 369-401. Plenum Press, New York & London.

———— 1983. Bats, flowers and fruit: evolutionary relationships in the Old World. *Biological Journal of the Linnean Society*, 20: 115-135.

Mooney, J. 1900. Myths of the Cherokee. *19th Annual Report of the Bureau of American Ethnology*, 3-548.

Morgan, H. T. 1942. *Chinese symbols and superstitions.* P. P. & Ione Perkins, South Pasadena.

Parrinder, G. *Witchcraft: European and African.* Barnes & Noble, Inc., New York.

Rasweiler, J. J., IV. 1977. The care and management of bats as laboratory animals. *In* Wimsatt, W. A., op. cit. 3: 519-617.

Roth, W. E. 1915. An inquiry into the animism and folk-lore of the Guiana Indians. *30th Annual Report of the U S Bureau of Ethnology*, 103-386.

———— 1924. An introductory study of the arts, crafts, and customs of the Guiana Indians. *38th Annual Report of the United States Bureau of Ethnology*, 25-745.

Slaughter, B. H. & Walton, D. W. (Eds.). 1970. *About bats. A chiropteran biology symposium.* Southern Methodist University Press, Dallas.

Stebbings, R. E. 1980. An outline global strategy for the conservation of bats. *In* Wilson, D. E. & Gardner, A. L. (Eds.). *Proceedings of the Fifth International Bat Research Conference*, 173-178. Texas Tech Press, Lubbock.

———— & Jefferies, D. J. 1982. *Focus on bats: their conservation and the law.* Nature Conservancy Council, London.

Sulkin, S. E. & Allen, R. 1970. Bats: carriers of human disease-producing agents. *In* Slaughter, B. H. & Walton, D. W., op. cit. 284-302.

Tuttle, M. D. & Kern, S. J. 1981. Bats and public health. *Contributions in Biology and Geology, Milwaukee Public Museum*, No. 48: 1-11.

Ubelaker, J. E. 1970. Some observations on ecto- and endoparasites of Chiroptera. *In* Slaughter, B. H. & Walton, D. W., op. cit. 247-261.

————, Specian, R. D. & Duszynski, D. W. 1977. Endoparasites. *In* Baker, R. J. *et al.*, op. cit. Part II. No. 13: 7-56.

Uchikawa, K. & Harada, M. 1981. Evaluation of bat-infecting Myobiidae (Acarina, Trombidiformes) as indicators in taxonomy and phylogeny of host bats (Chiroptera). *Zoological Magazine, Tokyo*, 90: 351-361.

Webb, J. P. & Loomis, R. B. 1977. Ectoparasites. *In* Baker, R. J. *et al.*, op. cit. Part II. No. 13: 57-119.

Wimsatt, W. A. (Ed.). 1970, 1977. *Biology of bats.* Academic Press, New York, etc.

CHAPTER 11

Andersen, K. 1912. *Catalogue of the Chiroptera in the collection of the British Museum. 1. Megachiroptera.* 2nd. ed. London: British Museum (Natural History).

Baker, R. J. & Genoways, H. H. 1978. Zoogeography of Antillean bats. *Special Publication Academy of Natural Sciences of Philadelphia*, 13: 53-97.

Baker, R. J., Jones, J. K., Jr. & Carter, D. C. (Eds.). 1976, 1977, 1979. Biology of bats of the New World family Phyllostomatidae. *Special Publications of the Museum Texas Tech University.* Texas Tech Press, Lubbock.

Corbet, G. B. & Hill, J. Edwards 1980. *A world list of mammalian species.* British Museum (Natural History) / Cornell University Press, London / Ithaca.

Daniel, M. J. 1979. The New Zealand short-tailed bat, *Mystacina tuberculata*; a review of present knowledge. *New Zealand Journal of Zoology*, 6: 357-370.

Freeman, P. W. 1981. A multivariate study of the family Molossidae (Mammalia, Chiroptera); morphology, ecology, evolution. *Fieldiana, Zoology*, Pub. No. 1316 (New Series No. 7): i-vii, 1-173.

Griffiths, T. A. 1982. Systematics of the New World nectar-feeding bats (Mammalia, Phyllostomidae), based on the morphology of the hyoid and lingual regions. *American Museum Novitates*, No. 2742: 1-45.

Handley, C. O. 1980. Inconsistencies in formation of family- group and subfamily group names in Chiroptera. *In* Wilson, D. E. & Gardner, A. L. (Eds.). *Proceedings of the Fifth International Bat Research Conference*, 9-13. Texas Tech Press, Lubbock.

Hall, L. S. 1981. The biogeography of Australian bats. *In* Keast, A. (Ed.). *Ecological biogeography of Australia*, 1557-1583. Dr. Junk bv Publishers, The Hague, etc. (Monographiae Biologicae, 41, 3).

Hill, J. Edwards 1963. A revision of the genus *Hipposideros. Bulletin of the British Museum (Natural History) (Zoology)*, 11: 1-129.

———— 1974. A new family, genus and species of bat (Mammalia: Chiroptera) from Thailand. *Bulletin of the British Museum (Natural History)*, Zoology **27**: 301-336.

———— 1977. A review of the Rhinopomatidae (Mammalia: Chiroptera). *Bulletin of the British Museum (Natural History)*, Zoology **32**: 29-43.

Honacki, J. H., Kinman, K. E. & Koeppl, J. W. (Eds.). 1982. *Mammal species of the world: a taxonomic and geographical reference.* Allen Press / Association of Systematic Collections, Lawrence, Kansas.

Jones, J. K., Jr. & Carter, D. C. 1976. Annotated checklist, with keys to subfamilies and genera. *In* Baker, R. J. *et al.*, op. cit. Part I. No. **10**: 7-38.

Koopman, K. F. 1970. Zoogeography of bats. *In* Slaughter, B. H. & Walton, D. W., op. cit. 29-44.

———— 1976. Zoogeography. *In* Baker, R. J. *et al.*, op. cit. Part I. No. **10**: 39-47.

———— 1981. The distribution patterns of New World nectar-feeding bats. *Annals of the Missouri Botanical Garden*, **68**: 352-369.

———— & **Cockrum, E. L.** 1975. Bats. *In* Anderson, S. & Jones, J. K., Jr. (Eds.). *Recent mammals of the world. A synopsis of families.* Ronald Press Company, New York.

———— & **Jones, J. K., Jr.** 1970. Classification of bats. *In* Slaughter, B. H. & Walton, D. W., op. cit. 22-28.

Miller, G. S., Jr. 1907. The families and genera of bats. *Bulletin of the U S National Museum*, **57**: i-xvii, 1-282.

Slaughter, B. H. & Walton, D. W. (Eds.). 1970. *About bats. A chiropteran biology symposium.* Southern Methodist University Press, Dallas.

Smith, J. D. 1972. Systematics of the chiropteran family Mormoopidae. *Miscellaneous Publications of the Museum of Natural History, University of Kansas*, No. **56**: 1-132.

———— & **Storch, G.** 1981. New Middle Eocene bats from "Grube Messel" near Darmstadt, W-Germany (Mammalia: Chiroptera). *Senckenbergiana Biologica*, **61**: 153–167.

Walker, A. 1969. True affinities of *Propotto leakeyi* Simpson 1967. *Nature, London*, **223**: 647-648.

Wheeler, M. E. 1979. A bibliography of the fruit bat genus *Pteropus. Technical Publication Division of Aquatic and Wildlife Resources, Department of Agriculture, Territory of Guam*, No. **4**: i-vi, 1-30.

General index

Index of vernacular names

Index of scientific names